Uncle John's GREAT BIG BATHROOM READER®

The Bathroom Readers' Institute
An Imprint of

UNCLE JOHN'S GREAT BIG BATHROOM READER®
UK Edition
is a compilation of significant new material created for this book along with material edited for the UK market from the following previously published *Bathroom Reader* titles:
Uncle John's Great Big Bathroom Reader® (ISBN: 1-879682-69-9) and *Uncle John's Absolutely Absorbing Bathroom Reader*® (ISBN: 1-879682-73-7).

ISBN: 1-59223-168-3

For information, write
The Bathroom Readers' Institute
5880 Oberlin Drive, San Diego, CA 92121
unclejohn@advmkt.com

Cover design by Michael Brunsfeld (brunsfeldo@comcast.net)
Printed in Wales by Creative Print & Design Group
First printing: October 2003

10 9 8 7 6 5 4 3 2 1 03 04 05 06

Project Team: Portable Press

Allen Orso, Publisher
JoAnn Padgett, Project Manager
Ian Fitzgerald, UK Project Editor and Writer
Lucian Randall, UK Researcher and Writer
Mana Monzavi, Art Contributor
Cindy Tillinghast, Proofreader
Amy Shapiro and Amanda Wilson, Production

CONTRIBUTORS

Susan Elkin
Ian Fitzgerald
Diane Forest
Heather Holliday
Diane Lane
Christopher Lord
Simon Majumdar
Lucian Randall
Leslie Ridgeway
Sue Steiner
Johanna Stewart

THANK YOU!

The Bathroom Readers' Hysterical Society sincerely thanks the people whose advice and assistance made this book possible.

Jeff Altemus
Jonah Bornstein
Derek Brown
Michael Brunsfeld
Jeff Cheek
Nancy Chew
Bill Crawford
John Darling
William Davis
John Dollison
Laurel Graziano
Nick Holt
Sharilyn Hovind
Gordon Javna
John Javna
Erin Keenan
Mike Kidd
Lonnie Kirk
Jay Newman
Cathy Parson
Bass Pike
Gareth Powell
Bennie Slomski
Dee Smith
Rich Stim
Tessa Vanderkop
Dale Vidmar

Hi Mom!

CONTENTS

**Extra-long articles suitable for an extended sitting session are marked with an asterisk.*

LAW & ORDER

LIFE IS STRANGE

MASTERPIECES

MILITARY MADNESS

MOUTHING OFF

MUSIC TO MY EARS

MYSTERIES & CONSPIRACIES

MYTH & LEGEND

NAME GAME

POP-POURRI

POP SCIENCE

INTRODUCTION

Greetings. Uncle John's Bathroom Reader may be new to the United Kingdom, but it's a fixture in bathrooms in the United States and Canada, and it's rapidly becoming one in Australia. It's hard to believe that it's been 16 years and almost 5 million books since we published our very first title. The Bathroom Readers' Institute is flushed with pride to introduce our books to new readers in the United Kindom.

So you're probably asking yourself, just what is a Bathroom Reader? It's an educational compendium of information and facts on a plethora of topics, all written in a light, airy style, full of irony, wit, and interesting observations, and put together in a format that doesn't start at the beginning or end at the end. Pick it up, turn to any page, and just start reading. That's where the journey—and the addiction—begins.

So open this book and learn about

- Odd Jobs From Manure Sniffer to Worm Collector
- The Birth of the Compact Disc
- Great Pretenders to the English Throne
- The Man Who Built Great Britain
- A Dancing Marquess
- The Union Jack – Our Flag of Convenience

We invite all of our readers to add to our repository of quality lavatory literature. If you have bits of weird trivia, strange but true history, or ideas to share with the BRI, please contact us through our website at www.bathroomreader.com (for inquiries about this book in particular, e-mail us at unclejohn@advmkt.com).

Thanks so much for your support. We are looking forward to becoming a permanent fixture in your bathroom.

Go with the flow!

Uncle Al
Publisher, Portable Press

OUR FLAG OF CONVENIENCE

The Union Jack is one of the most recognizable symbols of Britain. But it's only been our flag for 200 years. Here's why.

The Union flag, or Union Jack as we all call it, has appeared just about everywhere, whether it's fluttering from a flagpole atop Windsor Castle, or stretched to bursting point across Spice Girl Geri Halliwell's ample bosom. But our national flag is a fairly new invention. And if you thought it was red, white and blue because someone liked the colours, think again.

CROSS REFERENCES

England's flag has always been a red cross of St. George on a white background. This derived from the legend that when George slew the dragon, he used the beast's blood to draw a cross on his white shield. In 1603, James VI of Scotland became James I of England. To symbolize the union of the two kingdoms, the cross of St. Andrew was added to the flag. This was a white diagonal cross on a blue background, in honour of the fact that St. Andrew was crucified on an X-shaped cross.

When Ireland was dragged into the Union in 1801, the cross of St. Patrick (a diagonal red cross on a white background), came too. This cross wasn't really a national symbol at all: it was part of the coat of arms of a noble Anglo-Irish family, the Fitzgeralds.

FLAGGING SUPPORT

This new flag caused a real stink. The Scots and Irish complained that their crosses lay beneath the English one, the Welsh were upset at not being included at all, and even the English joined in, saying that their simple red-on-white flag had been ruined. But in the end everyone accepted the new flag – grudgingly.

And why is it called a Union Jack? Well, the jack is the end of the ship over which its flag is flown, so a Union flag flown over a jack became known as a Union Jack. The name caught on and was used informally for years, until in 1903 parliament passed a law saying it was officially OK to call our flag a Union Jack.

The first person to swim across the Channel was Briton Captain Matthew Webb in 1875.

THE SKIFFLE KING

Without Lonnie Donegan the 'British invasion' of rock 'n' roll might never have happened. Donegan was the creator of skiffle, a mix of American blues, jazz, gospel and folk music that caught the imagination of young British musicians like John Lennon, Paul McCartney, Pete Townshend and Elton John. Donegan racked up three number ones and numerous top 10 hits in the UK and U.S. in the 1950s and 1960s.

It took a British musician to meld uniquely American styles of music – jazz, folk, blues and gospel – into a brand new sound that swept a nation and changed the direction of music forever. Lonnie Donegan reportedly just wanted to play banjo in a jazz band. He wound up creating influential music that reverberates even in today's songs. He became one of the most respected and loved musicians in the UK with tunes that climbed up the music charts in leaps and bounds.

He was an enthusiastic performer, infusing his songs with such joy that young people were inspired to pick up guitars, banjos, basses and drums and form their own skiffle bands. Donegan reportedly picked up the word 'skiffle', an American slang term meaning 'party', from a record album. The party was still going on in 2002, when Donegan died of a heart attack in the middle of a tour, aged 71.

MUSICAL ROYALTY IS BORN

Lonnie Donegan was born Anthony James Donegan in April 1931, in Glasgow. His father was an amateur concert violinist. The boy's parents divorced when he was very young and he moved to London's East End with his mother when he was two.

The reports of how Donegan got his stage name conflict. According to one source, an over-excited master of ceremonies mixed Donegan's name up with that of blues guitarist and banjoist Lonnie Johnson, but most reports claim that Donegan took Lonnie Johnson's first name as a tribute to the musician, whom he greatly admired.

Q: What food are you most likely to be allergic to?

ALL THAT JAZZ

Donegan bought his first guitar at 14 and was inspired by the American blues and jazz he heard on the BBC. In an interview with writer Lee Raymond, he said his interest took off when he was 16 and saw a jazz band perform.

> 'I'd never heard jazz out loud – it was so dynamic!' he said. 'That's really, I suppose, what gave me the impetus. These days, for instance, if you had not heard rock 'n' roll and you walked in and heard Chuck Berry, you'd go: "Wow! What the blazes is this!"'

Donegan assembled his own band, the Tony Donegan Jazz Band, and wound up playing in London jazz clubs. One of the most exciting performances of his life was when his band was asked to open for Lonnie Johnson, his hero. He also began playing in other bands, most notably with singer/trombonist Chris Barber, with whom he began recording.

THE KING THROWS A ROCK

Jazz was exciting, but it wasn't the only music that interested Donegan. He got the chance to perform blues and folk tunes in Chris Barber's band, but it was a recording of Leadbelly's 'Rock Island Line' by Donegan in 1956 that set the UK – and the world – aflame.

The song rocketed up the British and American music charts and sold three million copies. Other popular tunes include 'Does Your Chewing Gum Lose its Flavour on the Bedpost Overnight?', 'Cumberland Gap', 'My Old Man's a Dustman' and 'Puttin' on the Style', a song he learned when he first started to play the guitar.

Donegan, who had left Barber's band, was quickly sent to America to perform his hit single, and wound up on the *Perry Como Show*, alongside other guests including Ronald Reagan and a budding comedian named Woody Allen.

INFLUENCING A GENERATION

'Rock Island Line' is credited by many as the song that inspired young British musicians like John Lennon and George Harrison, who formed their own skiffle group called The Quarrymen. They later joined with another skiffle musician, Paul McCartney, and

A: Nuts.

along the way, The Beatles were born. McCartney is said to have remarked:

> When we were kids in Liverpool, the man who really started the craze for guitars was Lonnie Donegan. We studied his records avidly. We all bought guitars to be in a skiffle group. He was the man.

Guitarist Pete Townshend started a skiffle group with singer Roger Daltrey called The Detours, which later became The Who, and singer Van Morrison played in an Irish skiffle band called The Sputniks. Elton John recalled: 'He was the first person I ever saw on British television who played something different. It was fantastic to see someone change music that much.'

Across the pond, Elvis Presley recorded one of Donegan's songs, 'I'm Never Gonna Fall in Love Again', as did Tom Jones.

THE MUSICIANS REMEMBER

When the British rock industry took off Donegan's music became less popular, but he continued to perform and tour all over the world on the cabaret circuit. He also appeared as the lead in the musical *Mr. Cinders* in London's West End in the 1980s, and in the early 1990s, he was still busy performing in his band.

The musicians Donegan influenced never forgot him. Paul McCartney organized a 1978 tribute album to the master called *Puttin' on the Style*, featuring other admirers such as Elton John, Ringo Starr, blues guitarist Albert Lee and Queen guitarist Brian May. Donegan also entered into a close relationship with Van Morrison, who collaborated with him on 1998's *Muleskinner's Blues*. Morrison also recorded *The Skiffle Sessions – Live in Belfast*, in 1998, a tribute that also featured Chris Barber.

THE END AT THE BEGINNING

Donegan was made an OBE in 2000. That year he was honoured by Martin Guitars, which created two 'Signature Editions' in Donegan's name. When Donegan died in November 2002, he was halfway through a tour of British theatres. The Skiffle King's last show was in Nottingham, the first city he performed in when he became a star in 1957.

FOREIGN FUNDS

As many countries change over to the Euro, Uncle John thought it was important to explain why different kinds of money are called what they are. Why is a franc called a franc, for example? We put together a list of various currencies and how they got their names.

DOLLAR. (American). Silver coins from the Joachimsthaler valley in Germany were in use around Europe before America was founded. The name went from 'Joachimsthalergroschen' to 'thaler', then 'dollar', and was used to refer to any large silver coin. Early American colonists adopted the term.

LIRA. (Italy). From the Latin word libra, or 'pound'.

DRACHMA. (Greece) Means 'handful'.

RUPEE. (India) Comes from the Sanskrit word '*rupa*', which means 'beauty' or 'shape'.

KORUNA. (Czech Republic) Means 'crown'.

GUILDER. (Netherlands) From the same root as 'gilded', the guilder was originally a gold coin. It was first introduced to the Low Countries from Florence in the 13th century.

ROUBLE. (Russia) Means 'cut-off', a term that dates back to the days when portions of silver bars were literally 'cut off' from the ingots and used as coins. The rouble was first issued as a silver piece in 1704.

PESO. (Mexico) Means 'weight'. It was introduced by Spain in 1497, then adopted by Mexico and other Latin American countries in the late 19th century.

PESETA. (Spain) Means 'little peso', and was created in the 18th century as a 'companion' coin to the Spanish peso (no longer in circulation).

FRANC. (France) First issued in 1360, as a gold coin. Gets its name from its original Latin inscription, Francorum Rex, which means 'King of the Franks', the title given to kings of France in the 1300s.

RIYAL. (Saudi Arabia) Borrows its name from the Spanish real, meaning 'royal'.

ESCUDO. (Portugal) Means 'shield', referring to the coat of arms on the original coin.

YEN. (Japan) Borrowed from the Chinese yuan, which means 'round', and describes the coin.

What a party: in 2002, Prince Charles spent £843,000 entertaining 11,000 official guests.

OOPS!

Everyone's amused by tales of outrageous blunders – probably because it's comforting to know that someone's screwing up even worse than we are. So go ahead and feel superior for a few minutes.

HAPPY BIRTHDAY!

'Matt Brooks of Cheshire, England, a furnaceman, thought he was 63 years old in 1981. When he applied for early retirement, he learned that he was really 79 and should have retired 14 years earlier'.

– *Encyclopedia Brown's Book of Facts*

BLIND JUSTICE

'Judge Claudia Jordan caused panic in her court in Denver when she passed a note to her clerk that read: "Blind on the right side. May be falling. Please call someone". The clerk rang for help. Informed that paramedics were on the way, the judge pointed to the sagging Venetian blinds on the right side of the room. "I wanted someone from maintenance", she said'.

– *The Fortean Times*

HIGH WIRE ACT

'During a parade through Ventura, California, a drum major twirled his baton and threw it high into the air. It hit a power cable and melted. It also blacked out ten blocks, put a radio station off the air and started a grass fire'.

– *The World's Greatest Mistakes*

AMEN

'Warren Austin, U.S. ambassador to the United Nations in 1948, expressed the wish that Arabs and Jews would settle their differences "like good Christians"'.

– *Not A Good Word About Anybody*

FLOUR POWER

'After great expense and preparation, British climber Alan Hinkes attempted to scale the 7925-metre high Nanga Parbot mountain in Pakistan. He got about halfway up and was eating a Pakistani bread called chapati, which is topped with flour, when the wind blew the flour in his face, causing him to sneeze. It resulted in a pulled back muscle that made further climbing impossible'.

– ***News of the Weird*, 28 November, 1998**

THAT'S B-U-R-T, RIGHT?

'Scrawling his way into immortality in the concrete in front of Mann's (formerly Grauman's) Chinese Theatre in Hollywood, Burt Reynolds misspelled his own name'.

– ***Hollywood Confidential***

LETTER BOMB

'The Caldor department store chain apologized this week after 11 million copies of an advertising circular showed two smiling boys playing Scrabble around a board with the word 'rape' spelled out. Caldor said it does not know who did it or how it got past the proofreaders. "Obviously, it's a mistake", said Caldor spokeswoman Jennifer Belodeau'.

– ***The Progressive*, February 1999**

FORGET ABOUT THAT RAISE

'A trader cost his employers an estimated $16 million when he pressed the wrong key on his computer during training, launching the largest single trade in German futures.

The Daily Telegraph did not name the trader of the firm, but described him as a junior trader working out of London for a German finance house.

Apparently, while training on what he thought was software simulating financial transactions, he posted an offering of 130,000 German bond futures contracts, worth $19 billion. But he had pressed the wrong button, entering the system for actual dealing'.

– ***Medford Mail Tribune*, 20 November, 1998**

* * *

TOMBSTONE HUMOUR

(In England):
Edgar Oscar Earl
Beneath this grassy mound now rests
One Edgar Oscar Earl
Who to another hunter looked
Exactly like a squirrel

A: Nine.

LET ME WRITE SIGN – I GOOD SPEAK ENGLISH

When signs in a foreign country are in English, any combination of words is possible. Here are some real-life examples.

At a Tokyo bar: 'Special cocktails for the ladies with nuts'.

At a Budapest zoo: 'Please do not feed the animals. If you have any suitable food, give it to the guard on duty'.

At a Budapest hotel: 'All rooms not denounced by twelve o'clock will be paid for twicely'.

In a Hong Kong supermarket: 'For your convenience, we recommend courteous, efficient self-service'.

At a Norwegian cocktail lounge: 'Ladies are requested not to have children in the bar'.

In a tailor shop in Rhodes: 'Order your summer suit. Because is big rush we will execute customers in strict order'.

A laundry in Rome: 'Ladies, leave your clothes here and spend the afternoon having a good time'.

In a Czech tourist agency: 'Take one of our horse-driven city tours – we guarantee no miscarriages'.

On a Viennese restaurant menu: 'Fried milk, children sandwiches, roast cattle and boiled sheep'.

In a Swiss mountain inn: 'Special today – no ice cream'.

A doctor's office in Rome: 'Specialist in women and other diseases'.

In a Moscow hotel room: 'If this is your first visit to the USSR, you are welcome to it'.

At a Vienna hotel: 'In case of fire, do your utmost to alarm the hotel porter'.

At a Hong Kong dentist: 'Teeth extracted by the latest Methodists'.

At a Swedish furrier: 'Fur coats made for ladies from their own skin'.

POOR CHATTERTON

Young, gifted and dead at 17. Meet Thomas Chatterton: an icon for sensitive, misunderstood teenagers everywhere.

Thomas Chatterton was one of the strangest of England's poets. In 1770, starving and despised, he killed himself in a London garret, aged only 17. But his works, composed from the age of 12, were praised by Wordsworth, Keats, Coleridge, Melville and Sir Walter Scott, and the sad story of his life and death have made him a symbol of tormented youth and genius.

IMITATION, IMITATION, IMITATION

The son of a poor schoolmaster, Chatterton was a charity boy at a Bristol school. He was apprenticed at 14 as a 'scrivener', or copier of legal documents, to a local lawyer. Having begun to write medieval-style poems at school, he decided to use his copying skills to fake some medieval documents. He then announced that he'd found a chest of 15th century legal papers, prose fragments and poetry in a Bristol church.

At 12, Chatterton had invented a 15th century poet called Thomas Rowley (or Rowleie), supposed author of the famous 'Rowley poems'. These were published after Chatterton's death, and it was 100 years before they were proved to be fakes. Chatterton wanted to establish Rowley as a major English poet, with himself as his discoverer. He produced letters and documents from Rowley, and started sending them to famous national figures.

A WAY WITH WORDS

Chatterton wrote in the modern English of his time but using a style of spelling that imitated the language of three centuries earlier. For example:

Harke! the dethe-owle loude dothe synge	Hark! the death-owl loud does sing
To the nyghte-mares as heie go	To the nightmares as they go
Mie love is dedde	My love is dead
Gon to hys deathe-bedde	Gone to his death bed

POETRY AND COMMOTION

In 1769, aged 16, he approached Horace Walpole, one of the most famous literary figures of the day, with a short treatise on painting by Rowley. Walpole, the inventor of the gothic novel, was enthusiastic. But when he found out Chatterton's age, and then discovered that the Rowley text was forged, he cut off all contact.

Already a gloomy and temperamental youth, this threw Chatterton further into despair. His employer, the Bristol lawyer, found a will Chatterton had written, saying he planned to kill himself, and fired him. Chatterton set off for London to seek his fortune.

POETIC INJUSTICE

Between May and August 1770, Chatterton lived in London, starving and alone. He managed to publish some short pieces, including one Rowley poem, in *Town and Country* magazine, but had no friends or protectors. Eventually he gave up the struggle, tore up most of his work, and killed himself by taking arsenic. Ironically, it was this that guaranteed him the fame he couldn't find in life. Even more so, just days later the head of an Oxford college, who had decided to befriend Chatterton, arrived to 'save' the struggling young poet from his poverty; and to add further insult to injury, at the same time a sum of money also arrived from another benefactor. But, of course, it was all too late – by then Chatterton had been buried in an unmarked pauper's grave.

A REPUTATION RESCUED

In 1871 the academic W. W. Skeat published an edition of the Rowley poems. After carefully examining the verses Skeat decided that they hadn't been written in the 15th century, and that Rowley had never even existed. Chatterton was revealed as the true author of the poems. This discovery, and the tragic story of Chatterton's life and death, suddenly made him famous. The romantic poets of the 19th century found an irresistible symbol in him. William Wordsworth called him 'the marvellous boy, the sleepless soul, that perished in his pride'. Henry Wallis' 1856 painting of Chatterton on his death-bed only furthered the myth, especially as there are no documents or any pictures from his real life to show us what he was really like. In death at least, Chatterton finally achieved the fame and recognition he always craved.

BIZARRE HEADLINES

These are 100 per cent honest-to-goodness headlines. Can you figure out what they were trying to say?

British Left Waffles on Falkland Islands

Shot Off Woman's Leg Helps Nicklaus to 66

Plane Too Close to Ground, Crash Probe Told

Juvenile Court To Try Shooting Defendant

Stolen Painting Found by Tree

BOMB HIT BY LIBRARY

After Detour to California Shuttle Returns to Earth

Boy Declared Dead, Revives as Family Protests

Dead Coyote Found in Bronx Launches Search for Its Mate

CHILDBIRTH IS BIG STEP TO PARENTHOOD

42 Per cent of All Murdered Women Are Killed by the Same Man

National Hunting Group Targeting Women

Fire Officials Grilled Over Kerosene Heaters

POLICE CAN'T STOP GAMBLING

Ability to Swim May Save Children from Drowning

LOW WAGES SAID KEY TO POVERTY

Youth Hit by Car Riding Bicycle

Hostage-Taker Kills Self; Police Shoot Each Other

TESTICLE CARGO SEIZED

Check With Doctors Before Getting Sick

Police Kill Youth in Effort to Stop His Suicide Attempt

INTERN GETS TASTE OF GOVERNMENT

Convicted S&L Chief Donated to University

Study: Dead Patients Usually Not Saved

PARKING LOT FLOODS WHEN MAN BURSTS

U.S. Ships Head to Somalia

U.S. Advice: Keep Drinking Water from Sewage

SUICIDES ASKED TO RECONSIDER

Cold Wave Linked to Temperatures

Gators to Face Seminoles With Peters Out

New Autos to Hit 5 Million

THE SCREAM HEARD 'ROUND GREAT BRITAIN

Screaming Lord Sutch: the man, the myth, the raving loony.

David 'Screaming Lord' Sutch never really hit the big time, but he always managed to make an impression. Of course, that's not hard to do when you're wearing a leopard-print top hat and, er, screaming.

SHOCK ROCKER

David Sutch was born on 10 November, 1940, in North London. His mother, a fan of Charles Dickens, named him in honour of David Copperfield, and David eventually turned to rock'n'roll in the hope of duplicating his namesake's rags-to-riches life.

He got his start in 1958 playing music at the 2 I's Coffee Bar, at that time the main venue of Britan's growing rock 'n' roll and skiffle scene. A natural showman, he attracted attention with his crazed looks (long hair, white make-up, and a top hat and cape), his growling voice and his music, a mish-mash of horror movie, over-the-top theatricality and pop.

Throughout the 1960s and early 1970s, Sutch formed multiple bands, which featured at various times some of the greatest up-and-comers of the era. Sutch's sidemen included The Who drummer Keith Moon, Deep Purple guitarist Ritchie Blackmore, Yardbirds guitarist Jeff Beck, Led Zeppelin guitarist Jimmy Page, and legendary session keyboardist Nicky Hopkins.

His songs covered subjects like love ('She's Fallen in Love With the Monster Man'), family ('Dracula's Daughter'), history ('Jack the Ripper') – and even fashion ('Monster in Black Tights'), but he never scored a hit single. And although Sutch continued to earn a living through performing, he eventually decided to direct his energies in a very different direction—politics!

The world's highest public telephone booth is on the Siachen Glacier, in India.

SCREAMING INTO POLITICS

In 1963 the Profumo sex scandal left an empty seat in Parliament, and Sutch decided to throw his top hat into the ring. His first platform – under the banner of the National Teenage Party – was to lower the voting age to 18, and commercialize radio and television. Although he lost, those policies (as well as later proposals to allow pubs to open all day Sunday and to provide passports for pets) were eventually enacted as law. Other ideas – such as filling the Thames with crocodiles and abolishing January and February to shorten winter – collapsed under their own daftness.

Sutch founded the Official Monster Raving Loony Party that year, coining the slogan 'Vote for insanity – you know it makes sense'. His biographer Peter Chippindale (*Life As Sutch*) said the slogan 'may have appeared that of a harmless clown who had found a convenient vehicle for self-promotion, but underneath he had a burning motive too; a huge and enduring contempt for his political opponents'.

RADIO, RADIO

Sutch's campaign pledge to commercialize radio wasn't the first time he'd tried to modernize the British media. In the early 1960s Great Britain was a swinging centre of musical talent and innovation, yet British radio only ever featured orchestral music. Kids had to tune in to Radio Luxembourg to hear The Beatles, Gerry and the Pacemakers, and American rock 'n' roll.

In early 1964 Radio Caroline, the first offshore 'pirate' radio station, was founded and on its heels came Radio Sutch. The station, which broadcast out of an old anti-aircraft tower, stayed on air only a few hours at a time because it was run on car batteries.

SUTCH A FITTING FAREWELL

Sutch ran unsuccessfully for Parliament 39 times, and continued to play up to 250 gigs each year. His colourful life ended in 1999, when the 59-year-old Sutch hanged himself in his London home.

His death prompted tributes from many in political circles, including one from a spokesman for Tony Blair: 'Our elections will never be quite the same without him'. And Sutch's own Official Monster Raving Loony Party remembered him not with a minute of silence, but with a minute of yelling and screaming.

A railway of the dead ran from Waterloo station to a Woking cemetery from 1854 to 1941.

CLASSIC (B)AD CAMPAIGNS

Companies are always trying to come up with new ways to make their products look attractive. These efforts are notable for achieving the opposite result.

CASHING IN YOUR CHIPS

Brilliant Marketing Idea: In 1998 the Bangkok subsidiary of the American ad agency Leo Burnett came up with a novel way to sell Thailand's 'X' brand crisps: show that they're so much fun, even 'the sourest man in history' can't help turning into a fun guy once he eats them.

Oops: The historical figure they used was Adolf Hitler. In the commercial, Hitler eats some crisps, then strips off his Nazi uniform and dances merrily as a Nazi swastika morphs into the brand's 'X' logo. The ad generated so many complaints – especially from the Israeli Embassy in Bangkok – that they had to pull it and issue apologies. 'The campaign was never intended to cause ill feelings', an agency spokesperson told reporters.

MYSTERY OF THE EAST

Brilliant Marketing Idea: In England, Smirnoff Vodka's ad agency created a campaign using the slogan 'I thought the Kama Sutra was an Indian restaurant…until I discovered Smirnoff'.

Oops: They were forced to cancel it, a company spokesperson admitted, 'when we conducted a survey and discovered that 60 per cent of people did think it was an Indian restaurant'.

HIGH FLYER

Brilliant Marketing Idea: In 1967 Pacific Airlines, a commuter airline on America's West Coast, hired award-winning adman/comedian Stan Freberg to design an unorthodox new campaign. As Bruce Nash and Allan Zullo write in *The Misfortune 500*, Freberg 'suggested PAL poke fun at the one thing airlines never mention – fear of flying'.

Oops: Pacific Airlines, at Freberg's direction, placed full-paged ads in newspapers that read:

The navel divides the body of a newborn baby into two equal parts.

> Hey there! You with the sweat in your palms. It's about time an airline faced up to something: Most people are scared witless of flying. Deep down inside, every time that big plane lifts off that runway, you wonder if this is it, right? You want to know something, fella? So does the pilot deep down inside.

Freberg also arranged for flight attendants to hand out survival kits containing rabbits' feet and the book *The Power of Positive Thinking*, and instructed that when the plane touched down on the runway, flight attendants were supposed to exclaim, 'We made it! How about that!' The airline went under two months after the campaign started.

AH-NOLD GO BOOM!

Brilliant Marketing Idea: In 1993, Arnold Schwarzenegger was America's No.1 box-office attraction. Columbia Pictures decided to promote his latest movie, *The Last Action Hero*, with a 23-metre tall balloon of Schwarzenegger's character in New York's Times Square. Instead of holding a gun, like he does in the movie, Arnold had a fistful of dynamite in his hand. 'We thought a gun was too violent an image', a Columbia spokesperson explained.
Oops: After months of planning, Columbia Pictures finally launched the balloon. Unfortunately, it was just days after the terrorist bombing of the World Trade Center. The studio tried replacing the dynamite with a police badge, but ended up just taking the balloon down. *The Last Action Hero* was one of the biggest flops of the decade.

LOVELY RING, MRS....UH...

Brilliant Marketing Idea: Executives in the jewellery department of Neiman-Marcus, an upmarket U.S. department store, thought it would be good business to send a personal note of thanks to each of their biggest customers.
Oops: According to *The Business Disaster Book of Days:* 'Most of the notes were addressed to the men, the people who had paid for the expensive baubles. But most of the envelopes were opened by women. Unfortunately for Neiman-Marcus, many of these women—wives of the purchasers, mostly—had not been the recipients of the costly purchases'.

STRAIGHT FROM MICK'S LIPS

Mick Jagger is like the Energizer Bunny — still going . . . and going . . . and going.

'People have this obsession: They want you to be like you were in 1969. They want you to, because otherwise their youth goes with you.'

'You get to the point where you have to change everything – change your looks, change your money, change your se, change your women – because of the business.'

'I'd rather be dead than singing "Satisfaction" when I'm 45.'

'Fame is like ice cream. It's only bad if you eat too much.'

'Of course we're doing this for the money . . . We've always done it for the money.'

'The best rock 'n' roll music encapsulates a certain high energy – an angriness – whether on record or onstage. That is, rock 'n' roll is only rock 'n' roll if it's not safe.'

'People ask me, "Why do you wear makeup? Why don't you just come off the street?" The whole ideas is you don't come off the street. You put on different clothes, you do your hair and you acquire this personality that has to go out and perform. When you get off the stage, that mask is dropped.'

'When I'm 33, I'll quit. That's the time when a man has to do something else. I can't say what it will definitely be. It's still in the back of my head – but it won't be in show business. I don't want to be a rock star all my life. I couldn't bear to end up as Elvis Presley and sing in Las Vegas with all those housewives and old ladies coming in with their handbags. It's really sick.'

'Sometimes an orgasm is better than being onstage. Sometimes being onstage is better than an orgasm.'

If the average male never shaved, his beard would be 4 metres long on the day he died.

VEGETABLE TRIVIA

Did you eat your vegetables today? Bathroom Reader Institute (BRI) member Jeff Cheek, a former CIA man (no kidding) loves to write about food. He sent us this potpourri of vegetable facts.

MAIZE. The most versatile of all food plants, it can be eaten at every stage of development. You can find it in more than 3,000 grocery items. It's especially popular in America. According to *The Great Food Almanac*, 'the average American eats the equivalent of three pounds of maize each day in the form of meat, poultry, and dairy products'.

GARLIC. One of the first foods ever cultivated. First written reference: 5,000 years ago, in Sanskrit. At banquets, ancient Greeks served each guest a bowl of parsley, believing it would mask 'garlic breath'. A vestige of this custom survives. Many restaurants still drop a sprig of parsley on every plate.

LETTUCE. The name comes from the Latin lactuca (milk) because of the white liquid that oozes from broken stalks. The Romans prized it so highly that any slave caught eating lettuce was given 30 lashes.

AUBERGINE. Originated in China, where it was grown as a decoration. The Chinese called aubergines 'mad apples', believing they caused insanity. It was accepted as a food only after it was brought to the Mediterranean.

LEEKS. These members of the onion family originated in Egypt, then spread to Rome. (Emperor Nero drank two pints of leek soup every day, thinking it improved his singing voice.) The Romans introduced the leek to Wales and it became the Welsh national symbol in 640, when Saxons invaded from England. With no uniforms, it was hard to tell friend from foe in the battle, so each Welsh soldier pinned a leek on his cap to identify himself. They won, and every 1 March, St. David's Day, the Welsh break out the leeks to commemorate the victory.

RADISHES. Since they're ready to harvest after only 42 days, the Greeks named them Raphanos, meaning 'easy to grow'. The Romans changed this to Radix, meaning 'root'.

Experts tell us that the human body has about 96,500 km of blood vessels.

IT WASN'T 2000 FOR EVERYONE

Would the new millennium mean the end of the world? ... the beginning of the New Age? ... We all had an opinion, but for much of the world the question was irrelevant—because, according to their calendars, it wasn't a new millennium ...

...It was 5760
Who Says? The Hebrew (Jewish) calendar. Their year 2000 occurred in 1760 B.C.
Origin: It's a lunar calendar that dates to 3760 B.C. – according to Jewish tradition, the date the world began.

...It was 4698
Who Says? The Chinese calendar. Their year 2000 occurred in 698 B.C.
Origin: A lunar calendar dating from 2600 B.C., when the Emperor Huang Ti introduced the first cycle of the zodiac. It begins at the second new moon after the winter solstice.

...It was 1921
Who Says? The Reformed Indian Calendar. Their year 2000 will arrive in 2079 A.D.
Origin: India gained independence from England in 1947. In 1957, it officially adopted this calendar, based on the beginning of the Saka Era (a Hindu time cycle).

...It was 1421
Who Says? The Muslim calendar. Their 2000 will arrive in 2579 A.D.
Origin: A lunar calendar that dates back to 622 A.D., the year Muhammad and his followers migrated from Mecca to Medina to escape persecution.

...It was 1378
Who Says? The Persian calendar. Their year 2000 arrives in 2622 A.D.
Origin: This solar calendar was created by the poet and mathematician Omar Khayyám. Iranians and many Central Asians celebrate their new year every spring equinox.

...It was 2543
Who Says? The Theraveda Buddhist calendar. Their year 2000 occurred in 1457 A.D.
Origin: Dates from 544 B.C., the commonly accepted date of Buddha's death (he was 80). Theraveda Buddhists celebrate the new year in mid-April.

Odds of being injured by a toilet seat in your lifetime: 1 in 6,500.

CHINESE DECEIVER

Sir Edmund Backhouse was an upper-class English rogue who might have passed his life in obscure debauchery in some corner of the British Empire, if not for one thing. He was a genius at languages.

Moving to China in 1899 aged 25, Sir Edmund Backhouse was soon able to speak, read and write the fiendishly difficult language of the court at Peking well enough to deal with government officials and translate legal documents. This suddenly made him an important man, since before World War I hardly any Chinese could speak English, and few foreigners could manage anything but the most rudimentary Chinese. Backhouse established a brilliant career as a businessman, translator, historian, author, diplomat and spy. It wasn't until 50 years later that people gradually began to realize his greatest gift of all had been for fraud.

CON ARTISTE

There are so many areas in which Backhouse managed to fool people that it must have been some kind of obsession for him. He did make some money out of his swindles but, like the man who sold the Brooklyn Bridge to passers by, it was a kind of personal artwork, too. In many cases his deceptions went unchallenged during his lifetime, so nobody but him ever appreciated them.

IN THE MONEY

Backhouse used his talent for languages, and his excellent contacts in the imperial court and the foreign business community, to set up huge deals for foreigners keen to operate in China. He persuaded the American Bank Note Company that China was going to switch over to using modern paper money, and the suits at the bank were naturally excited – 650 million bills were to be printed. Backhouse produced letters, contracts and other official documents, all translated from Chinese by him, and signed by the highest officials of the country – and every single one was a fake. The Chinese government knew nothing about any of it.

Which part of a map is the IDEO locator? The part that says 'YOU ARE HERE'.

How did he get away with it? He reasoned that if some big deal was supposed to be a secret in the first place, it didn't matter if the whole thing collapsed – the victims would never want to admit they had been fooled and would prefer to keep the whole thing quiet.

A LOAD OF JUNKS

Backhouse moved onward and upward. He persuaded John Brown and Co. of London that the Chinese Imperial Navy, made up at that time of wooden junks with silk sails, needed modernizing, and that the court had decided to buy some modern iron steamships – six coastal defence vessels of 10,400 tonnes, in fact. There was the same routine with secret meetings, documents, letters and contracts, and Backhouse kept the imaginary negotiations going for six years, from 1910 to 1916, before they suddenly evaporated.

He also set up a huge secret arms deal for the British government, which needed guns for World War I. Saying he had discovered that Chinese generals had built up secret stockpiles of modern weapons, he played the same old game; negotiating in secret, translating letters and contracts, and so on.

MAKING UP HISTORY

Backhouse's secret business dealings attracted the attention of the British Secret Service, who used him to spy both on the Chinese and on his European and American clients. Who knows what elaborate fantasies he was able to get them to swallow? Since the British were deeply involved in China at this time, Backhouse may very well have affected the course of history through his espionage work. Maybe one day somebody will be able to go back and unravel it all. For now, it's mainly as a historian and writer that we can see the results of his efforts.

At the beginning of the 20th century China was pretty much a mystery to the West, and Backhouse would supply some of the first popular books explaining life there. He 'discovered' a lengthy diary kept by a famous Chinese politician, Ching-shan, which was so convincing that he was offered a chair in Chinese at King's College London.

Spencer Perceval has the honour of being the only assassinated Prime Minister, in 1812.

AN EMPRESS IN NEW CLOTHES

There were other books (written with a collaborator, J.O.P. Bland, who had no idea that Backhouse was making it all up), but the most influential work was *China Under The Empress Dowager* from 1910, which explained what to many was the greatest mystery of all: what went on in the Forbidden City, where no foreigners were allowed, and where the Dowager Empress lived her hidden life.

Backhouse described the old woman as a fearsome and all-powerful manipulator who eliminated her rivals by poison or by having them thrown down wells, and who imprisoned her own son, the Emperor, so he didn't get in her way either. He spiced up the story with sex scandals and all kinds of juicy palace gossip – and foreigners fell for it. The Dowager Empress became a symbol of everything that was wrong with China.

It's only now being appreciated how complete Backhouse's deception was. The lurid life of the Forbidden City that he described was pure invention, but since no foreigners were ever allowed inside, nobody ever found out. The Chinese didn't read Backhouse's books, so they didn't understand what he was doing to their reputation overseas, any more than they knew about the arms deals or currency schemes he was floating in their name.

SUNSET IN THE EAST

Sir Edmund enjoyed a long and successful career, eventually vanishing into Chinese life full time, leaving a number of people who had trusted him scratching their heads and wondering what had happened. Pearl S. Buck and other writers picked up his tale of what went on in the Forbidden City and extended it for Western readers, and while Backhouse himself was mostly forgotten, his invented picture of life at the imperial court is still the basis of the West's idea of the old Chinese Empire today.

How did he do it? It was a combination of convincing people with elaborate detail and simply thinking big. Even today, Oxford University's Bodleian Library is still waiting for books Backhouse sold them – some 58,000 volumes in total!

10 Downing Street's last private resident left in 1735. His name was Mr. Chicken.

TWICE A HERO

Eric Liddell was famous as an Olympic champion who took a moral stand, but his greatest victories were the ones yet to come.

Lots of people know the story of Eric Liddell from the 1981 hit movie, *Chariots of Fire*. Liddell was a softly-spoken, deeply religious 22-year-old science student with a bouncy step and Scotland's fastest running times.

He was called a traitor and worse when he refused to run in the trials for the 100-metre sprint (his best event) at the 1924 Olympics, because they were held on a Sunday. Instead he entered the 400 metres and, to everyone's surprise, won it and set a new world record.

NO MORE MEDALLING

Liddell's stunning Olympic victory was the ideal set up for future races and a big career in coaching. But Liddell was more interested in returning to China, where he was born and where his parents were missionaries. (Liddell was already a popular speaker at Christian groups, despite his inherent shyness.) A year after his Olympic triumph, he boarded the Trans-Siberian railway to China, to join his family in the northern coastal city of Tientsin.

CHIPPED CHINA

China in those days was in chaos; after 100 years of corrupt rule and colonial exploitation, various political groups were struggling for control. And when the Chinese people weren't dealing with riots, political battles and warlord incursions, they had famine and other natural disasters to contend with.

Despite all the kerfuffle, Liddell's first few years in China were relatively happy and calm. He taught English and science and ran a sports programme at a mission school. He also married the daughter of Canadian missionaries and had two children.

Then, in 1937, the Japanese invaded, and China's situation got decidedly worse. Liddell was asked to serve further inland, where Communist guerrillas were fighting the Japanese. At first he refused, feeling he should stay with his family. But a year later, he decided it was his duty to go.

Best-selling posthumous hit of all-time: '(Just Like) Starting Over', by John Lennon.

BICYCLES OF FIRE

Technically, Liddell was the business manager of a hospital run by his brother, Rob. But he had also been ordained as a minister. So along with his administrative duties, he travelled through rural areas, acting as a pastor and bringing people back to the hospital for medical attention. Mounted on a bicycle, sometimes accompanied by Rob, Liddell would dash across Japanese lines, then zigzag across the plains, dodging bombs and bullets.

Liddell constantly had to convince troops from both sides that no, he really wasn't a spy, and really it would be better not to shoot him. At one point, Eric and Rob were carried off by guerrillas. Their Chinese companion was sure he would never see them again. As luck would have it, though, the guerrilla captain turned out to be a former student of Eric's.

THE DOUGH IN THE BREAD

Although he exuded integrity, Liddell was not above pulling off a scam in the right cause. One of his most nerve-wracking jobs was to smuggle in money from Tientsin to pay for staff and supplies at the hospital and inland missions, usually in a hollowed-out loaf of bread stuffed in his knapsack.

When Japanese soldiers started to search him, he would whip out his wallet and start showing them pictures of his children. 'Most of the soldiers were just farm kids conscripted into the army, and they were desperately homesick,' recalled Liddell's wife, Florence. 'They'd get out pictures of their families, too, and Eric would have them crying in no time. Then they'd pat him on the back and send him off.'

CRAMPED CAMP

In 1941, as occupied China grew more dangerous for foreigners, Florence took the children home to Canada. Eric stayed behind. Later that year, when war between Japan and the Allies became official, life for the remaining missionaries became even more difficult.

In March 1943, all the British and North Americans in Tientsin (including Liddell) were rounded up by the Japanese and sent to a prison camp at Weihsien.The prisoners there did not endure the beatings and torture common at other Japanese prisons, at least. They were allowed to run the camp their own way, as long as no one tried to escape. The internees divided up the chores – cooking, washing up, cleaning, and gathering coal dust to make fuel. Everyone did three hours' work a day. There were regular classes for the children and adults, church services, even concerts and plays.

Still, life was far from comfortable. More than 1,500 people – including missionaries, businessmen, secretaries, and prostitutes (most of them suffering from malnutrition) – were crammed into a space the size of three football fields, with no plumbing.

A MAN WITH A (NEW) MISSION

In this setting, Eric Liddell's quiet virtues shone. He helped to run the camp, smoothed over problems with the guards and always had a joke to tell or a sympathetic ear to offer. He visited the sick (including those with contagious illnesses), helped the outcasts, and counselled people who were ready to end it all. Perhaps most heroic of all, he never complained.

Then he broke the rule that had made him famous: no sports on Sunday. Liddell helped run a sports programme for the children in the camp and one Sunday, some of the teenagers decided to have a game of hockey. There was no referee to keep their perpetually frayed tempers in check, and the game turned into a fight. The next Sunday, Liddell showed up with his whistle, and the Sunday games became a fixture of camp life.

HEAVEN CAN'T WAIT

One night, back in Canada, Florence Liddell suddenly woke up. Eric was in the room, telling her that everything was all right. In the morning she realized she must have been dreaming.

A few weeks later, she found out that Eric had died of a brain tumour, right around that time. It happened on 21 February, 1945, less than six months before the end of internment. He was just 43.

* * *

The executive producer on the film *Chariots of Fire*, which details Eric Liddell's success at the Paris Olympics, was the late Dodi Fayed.

Every year there is a Yorkshire pudding throwing competition in Ramsbottom, Lancs.

IT'S A WEIRD, WEIRD WORLD

Proof that truth really is stranger than fiction.

A STRANGE BE-LEAF

'A Swiss woman has left over a half-million dollars to a houseplant. The millionairess, from Geneva, once described her newly rich jade plant as her "best and only friend". She is believed to have conversed with the plant for the last five years'.

– *The Edge*, 19 April, 1999

LOOK AT THOSE MELONS!

'Britain's biggest supermarket chain has asked growers to supply smaller melons after research showed women shoppers subconsciously compared them to the size of their breasts.

'*The Daily Telegraph* said buyers working for Tesco were told by researchers that a current preference for smaller busts was the reason why traditional big, fleshy melons were remaining unsold.

'"We were surprised", said a Tesco spokesman. "But it's certainly produced results. Since we introduced smaller melons two months ago we have sold more than a million"'.

– *Reuters*, 3 May, 1999

A SILLY SUPERSTITION?

'Gerald Steindam, 24, of Miami, Florida, vowed never to fly Eastern Airlines' flight 401 (New York–Miami) after luckily missing a flight 401 in 1972 that went down in the Everglades.

'In 1980 he overcame his superstitious fear and took the flight. The plane was hijacked and flown to Cuba'.

– Encyclopedia Brown's Book of Strange Facts

A REAL CONDOM-NATION

'Police in Sri Lanka recently arrested a man after finding a condom in his wallet. "Why would anyone want to carry a condom in his wallet, unless of course he was up to some mischief", a police officer was quoted as saying. The man was released after questioning'.

– *San Francisco Chronicle*, 1993

The tomato comes in over 4,000 varieties.

Q & A: ASK THE EXPERTS

Everyone's got a question or two they'd like answered – basic stuff, like 'Why is the sky blue'? Here are a few of those questions, with answers from books by some top trivia experts.

KNUCKLE UNDER

Q: Why do our knuckles crack?

A: 'The bones in our fingers are separated by small pads of cartilage, and in between are small pockets of a thick liquid. When you bend your fingers, the bones pull away from the pads of cartilage and a vacuum forms. As the bending continues...the vacuum bubble bursts, making the cracking sound you hear. The process is very similar to what happens when you pull a rubber suction cup off a smooth surface'. (From *Ever Wonder Why?*, by Douglas B. Smith)

SEEING THINGS

Q: What are those little squiggles you see floating on your eyes when you look at the sky?

A: 'They're called "floaters". To some people they look like spots; to others, like tiny threads. They're not on your eyes, though; they're in your eyes. That's why blinking doesn't make them go away. Floaters are all that's left of the hyaloid artery. The hyaloid artery carried blood to your eye and helped it grow...when you were still inside your mother's womb.

'When your eyes were finished growing, the hyaloid artery withered and broke into pieces. But since these pieces were sealed up inside your eye, they had no place to go. You'll see them floating around the rest of your life'. (From *Know It All!*, by Ed Zotti)

STOP, POP AND ROLL

Q: How does quicksand work?

A: 'Not by pulling you down. Quicksand is nearly always found above a spring, which creates a supersaturated condition that makes the sand frictionless and unable to support weight. In addition, quicksand is airless, which creates suction as you struggle to get free. The most effective way to escape quicksand is to position yourself on top of it and "roll" out'. (From *The Book of Answers*, by Barbara Berliner)

LONG-DISTANCE RUNAROUND

Q: Why does the alphabet on a phone start on the No.2 button rather than on the No.1?

A: Back when dial phones were used, a pulse or clicking sound was made whenever you dialled. The pulses corresponded to the number dialled, so 'when you dialled the number 1, it sent out one click...2, sent two clicks, and so on. Sometimes a random clicking caused equipment to think someone was dialling a number beginning with 1, when they actually weren't. Thus a rule was made: No phone number can start with 1. This rule is still observed, though solely for the sake of tradition'. (From *Why Things Are, Volume II: The Big Picture*, by Joel Achenbach)

I CAN SEE CLEARLY NOW

Q: How does an X-ray photograph your bones but not your flesh?

A: 'An X-ray camera fires electrons at a plate covered with silver halide crystals, which are sensitive to light. Your leg is put in the way of the penetrating stream of particles. When an electron reaches the plate unimpeded, it turns a halide crystal black. The crystals that receive no electrons fall away when the plate is developed and leave that area white under the light. X-ray particles are so highly energized that most of them pass right through flesh. Bones, on the other hand, are very densely packed and contain large amounts of calcium. They stop the X-rays by absorbing them – the crack in your tibia shows up black on the plate because that's where bone isn't'. (From *How Do They Do That?*, by Caroline Sutton)

* * *

SLIPPERY WHEN WET

Ice isn't slippery. What makes people and things slip on ice is water. A thin layer of ice melts when pressure is applied to it and it is this wet layer on top of the ice that is slippery.

The worldwide code word to warn of terrorist threats is BIKINI.

WEIRD THEME RESTAURANTS

For a while, it looked as though restaurants modelled after the Hard Rock Cafe were going to sweep the world. Guess which of the following is Uncle John's personal favourite.

THE ROADKILL CAFE, Greenville, Maine
Theme: Animals squashed on the highway
Details: The menu features only 'critters that don't move fast enough' to get out of the way of traffic. Sample items: 'The Chicken That Didn't Make It Across the Road', and 'Bye Bye Bambi Burgers'. It's actually just a little black humour, but the staff gets into the act: 'A cook named Freddy is fond of yelling "down boy, down boy" as he pounds on chicken breasts before grilling them. When he's done, he might throw handfuls of feathers out the door'.

THE OUTHOUSE, Winnipeg, Manitoba
Theme: Bathrooms
Details: The entire restaurant was decorated to look like a public restroom – 'toilet bowls alternate with tables in the main dining room. And their logo, a toilet seat, was on all the menus'. Shortly after the Grand Opening in the mid-1970s, health officials shut it down. The reason: 'Not enough working bathrooms'.

ALCATRAZ BC, Tokyo
Theme: Maximum-security prison
Details: 'Diners are handcuffed, eat in cells, and must beg permission from the guards to be allowed out to visit the restroom'.

CRASH CAFE, Baltimore
Theme: Disasters and human carnage (just what we like to contemplate over dinner)
Details: The smoking fuselage of what appears to be a crashed DC3 juts from the exterior of the flagship restaurant. 'The roof is askew, windows are cracked and the outer wall is shattered in spots. In the drive, a car looks as if it has just smashed into a fire

hydrant, which is spewing water'. Inside, diners are 'entertained' by film clips of train wrecks and collapsing bridges and buildings. 'Some may say that it teeters on the verge of unacceptable', says founder Patrick Turner, 'but that is precisely its strength. Crash Cafe seduces us to look closer, to indulge our undeniable fascination with the destructive, erotic nature of crashing'.

DIVE!, Los Angeles and Las Vegas
Theme: Submarines
Details: 'A submarine-shaped restaurant that specialized in gourmet submarine sandwiches'. Partners included Hollywood moguls Steven Spielberg and Jeffrey Katzenberg. It had 'millions of dollars in special effects', including 'computer-controlled flashing light, steam blasts, deep-sea scenes on video screens, and a surging water wall to recreate the experience of "an actual submarine dive"'. Singer and synth boffin Thomas Dolby provided interactive sound effects that were a little too real: 'Apparently, the virtual aquatic experience was so convincing that it prompted an upsurge in customers visiting the toilet'. The L.A. restaurant closed in 1999.

HOUSE OF MAO, Singapore
Theme: Chairman Mao Zedong – who ruled China from 1949 until his death in 1976 – as a pop icon
Details: 'Scores of Mao pictures, poems and sculptures peer down from the walls. The staff wear uniforms similar to those of China's People's Liberation Army (though waitresses are miniskirted)'. 'Chairman Mao was one of the most feared individuals in the world', the founder says, 'but when you come to the restaurant, you see the human side of him, swimming, playing poker'. On the menu: Mao burgers, Mao pizza, Mao fajitas, and Mao pasta. 'Mao would probably turn in his grave', one Singapore journalist wrote following the restaurant's grand opening.

* * *

Truth or Urban Legend?

On an American one-dollar bill, there's supposedly an owl in the upper left-hand corner of the '1' encased in the 'shield' and a spider hidden in the front upper right-hand corner.

Unless specially marked, all swans in open water belong to the Queen.

STRANGE LAWSUITS

These days, it seems that people will sue each other over practically anything. Here are a few real-life examples of unusual legal battles.

THE PLAINTIFF: A Chinese restaurant in Stansted, Essex
THE DEFENDANT: Kevin Clifford, a customer
THE CASE: In 1996 Clifford walked into the restaurant and ordered a large meal. While he was waiting for it, he explained later, the smells from the kitchen made him so hungry that he lost control. He began ripping the leaves off potted plants, eating them. 'By the time his order was ready', according to one report, 'he had eaten the leaves off every plant in the place'. The restaurant owner sued him for the cost of the plants.
THE VERDICT: Guilty. Clifford's unusual salad cost him £400.

THE PLAINTIFF: Donald Drusky
THE DEFENDANT: 'God, the sovereign ruler of the universe'
THE CASE: In 1999 the 63-year-old Drusky took legal action against God for 'taking no corrective action' against an ex-employer who'd fired him 30 years before. His demands: God must grant him guitar-playing skills and resurrect either his pet pigeon or his mother.
THE VERDICT: Drusky claimed that since God didn't show up in court, he won by default. The judge declared the suit 'frivolous'.

THE PLAINTIFF: Nellie Mitchell, a 98-year-old Arkansas woman
THE DEFENDANT: Globe International, publishers of the American supermarket tabloid *The Sun*
THE CASE: In 1990 *The Sun* ran a 'report' about a 101-year-old newspaper delivery girl in Australia 'who'd quit her route because she'd become pregnant by a millionaire customer'. They picked a photo of Mitchell to illustrate it. Why? They assumed she was dead. She wasn't, and sued for invasion of privacy.
THE VERDICT: The jury awarded her £800,000 (later reduced

to £500,000). A judge compared her experience to being 'dragged slowly through a pile of untreated sewage'.

THE PLAINTIFF: Dave Feuerstein
THE DEFENDANT: Tesco supermarkets
THE CASE: Enthusiastic about Tesco's low prices during a special promotion, Feuerstein kept going back to buy more. In three days, he redeemed over 300 coupons – then claimed he'd hurt his back carrying all the cheap merchandise, and sued. 'Offers like this are too good to refuse', he told a reporter. 'Tesco should have been more considerate and made it impossible to do what I did. If Tesco hadn't had this offer, I wouldn't have hurt my back'.
THE VERDICT: Unknown.

THE PLAINTIFF: Kenneth Bruckner of Gering, Nebraska
THE DEFENDANT: Presbyterian/St. Luke's Medical Center in Denver
THE CASE: In the spring of 1993, Bruckner sued the hospital, claiming the 'highly toxic' cleanser they used to disinfect toilet seats had caused him 'permanent burns, neurological injuries, and urologic and sexual dysfunction'. Said Bruckner's attorney: 'What's the world coming to if it's not safe to sit on the toilet and read the paper'?
THE VERDICT: Unknown – but you know how we'd rule.

THE PLAINTIFFS: Two college students
THE DEFENDANT: Pace University, Long Island, New York
THE CASE: The students took an introductory computer-programming course at Pace. One day the teacher required them, as homework, to calculate the cost of an aluminum atom. The answer is $6.22054463335 x 10^{-26} – less than a trillionth of a American dime. Outraged that such a high level of work was required in an introductory course, the pair sued.
THE VERDICT: Believe it or not, the judge found their instructor guilty of 'educational malpractice'.

At more than 2,000 metres, Southend-on-Sea pier is the world's longest.

THIS BECKS FOR YOU

A mega-rich, perfectly coiffed, trend-setting superstar. Friend to the stars and one half of Britain's most (sort of) glamorous couple. But did you know that David Beckham also played football. But never mind about that. The boy done so good that he became his own brand. Wanna piece?

It wasn't long into David Beckham's career with Manchester United that people simply forgot he played football. By the time Labour won their second term in government in 2001, you could be forgiven for thinking that the Prime Minister was the Rt. Hon. D. Beckham M.P. Two years later, a study by Warwick University claimed that he was probably the 'most influential' figure in the UK for everyone aged between 5 and sixty.

WORKING-CLASS HERO

The clues to his iconic status, if there are any, are certainly not to be found in his upbringing. David Robert Joseph Beckham was born 2 May, 1975 in Leytonstone, East London. He showed early talent as a footballer and was snapped up as a kid by Manchester United. By the time he left that club in 2003, few argued that he was not only a world-class footballer, but an icon for all sport in the UK. It still didn't explain why even those who had never watched a football game in their life knew him and loved him.

PERFECT PITCH

Perhaps he scored so well with the public because of his reputation for being a nice, ordinary family man in an age when footballers were seen as drunken, violent, sex-crazed yobs (which they are). Being married to Victoria Adams, the Poshest of the Spice Girls, helped raise his profile, as did his chiselled, blond good looks. Their 1999 wedding was the event of the year. Her dress cost £60,000 and the reception itself came in at £500,000 – well, 437 staff and matching his'n'hers thrones don't come cheap. The couple were as much ridiculed as they were admired, both for those expensive tastes and their supposed lack of brain power.

In medieval Japan, dentists extracted teeth with their hands.

I SAY, I SAY

The Beckham joke quickly supplanted Essex girl gags as a mainstay of pub humour ('What's the difference between Airfix and David Beckham? One is a glueless kit and the other's... a clueless git'). But he never seemed to be riled by the sniping. It was said that he wore Posh Spice's knickers, and he was photographed in a sarong. His daring outfits were topped off by an increasingly wild selection of haircuts. The man's got style!

Openly admitting to being in touch with his feminine side, a rare thing for a footballer, he appeared delighted to learn he was a gay icon. 'The face of an angel', sighed gay style magazine *Attitude*, 'and the bum of a Greek god'. At the same time, *Hello!* magazine proclaimed that the Beckhams were ideal representatives of family values. *Hello!* was right in that everyone could see the parents were devoted to their divine offspring: Romeo, born on 1 September, 2002, a brother for the Beckhams' other son, Brooklyn.

GOODBYE THE REDS

Beckham's world became a more troubled one in 2002. His boss at United, Sir Alex Ferguson, was said to be fed up with his star player's increasing fame and dropped him from key matches. At the same time, the Beckhams were caught up in a bizarre kidnap plot against them involving Albanian gangsters. Not surprisingly, it was later revealed to be a fabrication. By the end of 2002 Beckham was the world's most searched-for sportsman on the Internet, inspiring fanatical devotion across Europe and into China, Japan and south-east Asia. Where will it all end? Watch this space...

Here are some interesting facts and figures about our Dave:

• A 2003 study found a third of Britons wanted David Beckham's picture to replace Charles Dickens on the £10 note.

• One survey showed that eight out of 10 Japanese would buy products if he endorsed them

• Despite his world fame, Beckham has yet to crack the USA: in May 2003 *USA Today* called him 'The most famous man Americans don't know'.

Your brain uses 40 per cent of the oxygen that enters your bloodstream.

THE BOLEYN BROOD

Tudor party girl Mary Boleyn laid the royal groundwork. Did she get jealous when Henry VIII dumped her for her sister Anne? Yes and no.

Mary Carey, née Boleyn, was a buxom teenage wife and member of the court when she caught the roving eye of the ageing and increasingly fat King Henry VIII in 1522.

Young as she was, Mary's reputation was already colourful. At the age of 15 she had been mistress to King Francis I of France and to plenty of his *bon amis* – she'd been passed around the French court like *fromage* at a cocktail party. Francis called her his 'English mare' because he had 'ridden' her so often. Years later, hiding his bluntness behind a veil of pretty Italian, he called her '*una grandissima ribalda, et infame supra tutte*' ('a great whore, and infamous above all others').

HENRY'S HAPPY LITTLE FAMILY

Henry VIII, meanwhile, had masses of mistresses under his belt, so to speak. He and his wife, Catherine, had been trying for a male heir for 15 long years. The only live child they had produced was a daughter who eventually became the hated and neurotic 'Bloody' Mary, a devoutly Catholic queen who tortured and killed thousands of her protesting Protestant subjects. Hence her other claim to fame; the vodka and tomato juice cocktail named for her.

A FLING WITH THE KING

Back to Mary Carey. She wasn't just another popsy. She'd been born into the Boleyn family, a bunch of scheming, ambitious manipulators who craved wealth and power.

For four years, Mary jumped into Henry's bed whenever he summoned. By 1526 his interest in her had begun to wane – at about the same time he started to take notice of her older sister, Anne, which made for a tricky situation. However, as sisters the girls were loyal to each other, and plotted to do what was best for the family. Being the favourite in the king's bed is pretty significant, but is a position only one person could hold at a time. Anne strung the king along for nearly six years until he was so besotted with her that he divorced Catherine, parted company with the

Pope, and made Anne his queen in 1536. Anne and Mary's brother George was also up to his neck (from which his head would soon be separated) in intrigue. He was a hanger-on at court (widely thought to prefer men to women) who wasn't above encouraging his sisters to catch the king's eye if there was something in it for him or the family.

PUTTING ON HEIRS

During Mary's four years as Henry's paramour, she bore two children: Henry and Catherine. Their family name was Carey but they couldn't have been fathered by Mary's husband, William Carey, because the rules were that while she was 'dating' the king, she was forbidden to have sex with her husband. (Poor William died in 1528, just when he might have got his wife back. All the perks he'd been given to keep him quiet reverted to the king.)

NO MALE DELIVERY

Anne didn't do male heirs any better than wife number one, and Mary's royal bastards made her seethe with envy. Anne may have given birth to our greatest queen, Elizabeth I, but at the time that wasn't good enough. The sisters quarrelled bitterly and as Anne became more desperate, Henry became more disenchanted.

GAME, SET, MATCH TO MARY

So which Boleyn sister had the last laugh? Anne may have made it to the top spot as queen, but she eventually lost her head on trumped-up charges, one of which was adultery with none other than brother George, beheaded two days before her. Mary settled down peacefully in the country with a new husband, started another family, and lived until 1543.

Mary's children by Henry VIII didn't do too badly either. Catherine Carey was appointed Maid of Honour to Anne of Cleves (Henry VIII's fourth wife) and later married Sir Francis Knollys, an ancestor of our present queen. Her brother Henry was never officially acknowledged as a royal family member, but actions speak louder than words. His half-sister (and first cousin) Elizabeth I made him a viscount and paid for his funeral and a splendid tomb in Westminster Abbey. She couldn't have made it much more obvious that he was a 'sort of' brother, could she?

The Archers is the world's longest-running radio serial. It started on the BBC in January

MR TOAD'S WILD RIDE, PART I

The Wind in the Willows is one of the best-loved books in the English language, and a milestone in children's literature. But it took some very unusual circumstances to get it written and published. And then it took the intervention of the president of the United States to make it a success. Here's the story.

BACKGROUND

By the 1890s, Kenneth Grahame was already a celebrated author. His two books, *The Golden Age* and *Dream Days* – tales of childhood written for adults – had established him as an authority on children's literature. Editors were constantly asking him to review new books and to edit collections of poems and stories.

But Grahame didn't want to write for a living. He was solidly middle-class, and the English middle-class ideal at the time was to be a 'gentleman author' – someone who wrote part-time, for love, not money. In his professional life, Grahame was a successful banker – in 1898 he landed the prestigious job of Secretary of the Bank of England.

Wedded Miss

In 1899 Grahame married Elspeth Thompson. It was an unmitigated disaster. Elspeth wound up writing despondent letters and poems to her friends; Grahame developed a severe case of writer's block. He became so distracted that, less than a decade later, he was asked to retire from the bank.

The only good thing to come from the marriage was their son, Alastair. But he had problems, too – he was born 'blind in one eye and squinting out of the other'. His parents called him Mouse.

MAN OF LETTERS

Writing was difficult for Grahame, but he could still tell stories. Every evening he invented one for Mouse, letting the little boy choose the subject.

One night, Mouse asked his father to make up something

about a rat, a mole, and a giraffe. (The giraffe was soon replaced with Toad – a loose caricature of Alastair.) The trio's ongoing experiences became such a favourite that in 1907, when Mouse was supposed to leave on a holiday with his governess, he refused to go – he didn't want to miss his father's bedtime stories.

Grahame promised to write down a new adventure every day and send it to his son – luckily, he kept his word. According to Elspeth, the child's governess was so impressed by the unusual stories that she saved the 15 letters and brought them back to her. These later became the basis for *The Wind in the Willows*.

A SAMPLE LETTER

(Ed. note: Toad was sent to prison for stealing a newfangled motorcar [it was 1907, remember] but escaped dressed as a washerwoman. Now, as he nears home, he looks up and sees the same car he stole headed toward him, and assumes it's pursuing him.)

16 Durham Villas
Campden Hill, W.

7th August, 1907

Dear Mouse:

When the Toad saw that his enemies were close upon him…he sank down in a shabby miserable heap in the road, murmuring to himself…'It's all over now! Prison again! Dry bread and water again!…O what a fool I have been! What did I want to go strutting around the country for, singing conceited songs?…O unhappy toad! O miserable animal!' And his head sank down in the dust.

The terrible motor-car drew nearer and nearer…Then it stopped. Some gentlemen got out. They walked round the trembling heap of misery lying in the road, & one of them said – 'O dear! Here is a poor washerwoman who has fainted in the road…Let us lift her into the motor-car and take her to the nearest village.

…When the Toad heard them talk that way, & knew he was not recognized, his courage began to revive, & he opened one of his eyes. Then one of the gentlemen said: 'See, she is feeling better already! The

Polari: the secret language used by gays before homosexuality was legalised. Bona! (Good.)

fresh air is doing her good! How do you feel now, washerwoman?'

The toad answered in a feeble voice, 'Thank you kindly, Sir, I'm feeling rather better. I think if I might sit on the front seat, beside the chauffeur, where I could get more air, I should soon be quite right again'.

'That's a very sensible woman', said the gentleman. So they helped him into the front seat....The Toad began to sit up & look about & presently he said to the chauffeur, 'Please Mr. Chauffeur, I wish you would let me try to drive the car for a little; it looks so easy; I'm sure I could do it quite well!'

The chauffeur laughed, heartily. But one of the gentlemen said, 'Bravo, washerwoman! I like your spirit! Let her try. She won't do any harm'.

So the chauffeur gave up his seat to the toad, & he took the steering wheel in his hands, and set the car going, & off they went, very slowly and carefully at first, for the toad was prudent. The gentlemen clapped their hands & cried, 'Bravo, washerwoman! How well she does it! Fancy a washerwoman driving a motor-car! Bravo!'

Then the Toad went a little faster. The gentlemen applauded....The Toad began to lose his head. He went faster and faster still. The gentlemen called out warningly, 'Be careful, washerwoman!' Then the Toad lost his head entirely. He stood up in his seat and shouted 'Ho, ho! Who are you calling washerwoman! I am the Toad! The famous Mr. Toad! The motor-car driver, the toad who always escapes, who baffles his enemies, who dodges policemen, who breaks out of prison, the always victorious, the triumphant Toad!...'

Grahame had already written much of the story, but he had no intention of turning it into a commercial work. Nothing could have been further from his mind.

For Part II of Mr. Toad's Wild Ride, *turn to page 195*.

Queen termites can lay an egg every second, or 86,000 eggs a day.

THE NOSE KNOWS

Smell is an amazing and complex function carried out in a tiny chamber, half the size of an egg, situated just behind your nose. With it, we are able to smell thousands of different odours.

THE SCIENCE OF SMELL

How do we smell things? The mystery is still unfolding, but it starts with 'odour molecules'. Scientists tell us the air is filled with them. They enter your nasal cavity every time you breathe, 23,000 times a day.

- Just behind your nose, these molecules are absorbed by mucous-covered tissue.
- This tissue is covered with 'receptor' cells. (Some scientists say you have millions of them.) Each one is mounted on a microscopic hair.
- The receptor cells stick out and wave in the air currents we inhale. Forty of them must detect odour molecules before a smell is registered.
- When a new smell is detected, the tiny olfactory bulb, located just above the nasal cavity, flashes data directly to the most ancient and mysterious part of your brain – the limbic system – which 'handles feelings, lust, instincts, and invention'. The limbic system reacts immediately, without intervention of reason or language, and may provoke powerful emotions, images, or nostalgia.

THE DARK AGES OF SMELLING

A keen sense of smell is now accepted as part of the good life – coffees, wines, cheeses and gourmet foods would all be lost on us if we lacked our immense range of smell. However, this faculty wasn't always appreciated.

- The ancient philosopher Plato looked down on smell as a lowly instinct that might lead to gluttony and lust, while vision and hearing opened one to geometry and music and were therefore 'closer to the soul'.
- During the 18th and 19th centuries, it was commonly believed that many diseases were caused by smells. Odours from corpses, faeces, urine, swamps and cracks in the Earth were called 'miasmas' and were thought to have the power to kill. To ward off these

The earliest-known English patent went to John of Utynam in 1449 for making stained glass.

smells, people carried and inhaled 'antimephitics', such as garlic, amber, sulphur and incense. When exposed to miasmic odours, people did not swallow their saliva, but spat it out. The Viennese physician Semmelweis was ostracized by colleagues when he declared that washing one's hands, not breathing antimephitics, would stop most disease from spreading.

• According to some sources, the stethoscope was invented not to hear the heartbeat better, but to give doctors some distance from a patient's bodily odours.

TASTE AND SMELL

• We taste only four things: sweet, sour, salt and bitter. It's the smells that make things really taste. For example, wine's smell, not its taste, is what makes it delicious. With a head cold, drinking wine is an entirely different experience.

• Scientists have categorized smells into seven groups: minty like peppermint, floral like roses, ethereal like pears, musky like – well – musk, resinous like camphor, foul like rotten eggs, and acrid like vinegar.

• Talking with your mouth full expels taste molecules and diminishes the taste of food.

SMELL FACTS

• Women have a keener sense of smell than men.

• By simply smelling a piece of clothing, most people can tell if it was worn by a woman or man.

• Each of us has an odour that is, like our fingerprints, unique. One result, researchers say: Much of the thrill of kissing comes from smelling the unique odours of another's face.

• Smells stimulate learning. Students given olfactory stimulation along with a word list retain much more information and remember it longer.

• Many smells are heavier than air and can be detected only at ground level.

• We smell best if we take several short sniffs, rather than one long one.

There were 31 Carry On movies in total. Bernard Bresslaw appeared in 14 of them.

SHELL-SHOCKED

'Humpty Dumpty' must be one of the best-loved of all nursery rhymes, sung by children the world over. But few people know the true origins of the tale about the downfall of the talking egg.

There are many different theories about the rhyme's origins. Some believe Humpty was the name given to a huge cannon; others that it referred to Richard III (who supposedly had the Princes in the Tower, his nephews, murdered).

HARD-BOILED ROUNDHEADS

The best explanation comes from the period of the English Civil War (1642–1649) when Charles I besieged the Parliamentarian stronghold of Knaresborough in Yorkshire. The Royalist army had laid siege to the town for nearly three months, but could not breach the Roundhead army's defences. Charles ordered a great siege engine to be built to help his men storm the battlements.

Watching this terrible weapon of war being built, the children of the town became very afraid and the adults came up with the name 'Humpty Dumpty' as a way to ridicule the engine and stop the children becoming too alarmed.

The resourceful defenders of the town decided to dig under the ground, to weaken the area where Humpty would sit, and they also soaked the ground around the battlements at night.

EGG ON ROYALIST FACES

When the time came for the big attack, Humpty was wheeled into place against the battlements ('sat on the wall') but because of its weight and the weakened ground, the earth beneath it collapsed and it fell over ('had a great fall'). Despite the troops' best efforts to pull it out of the quagmire, it was too damaged to repair. ('All the king's horses and all the king's men couldn't put Humpty together again.') At this point Charles abandoned the siege, and a war that had been going in his favour began to turn against him. The rest, as they say, is history.

JUST PLANE WEIRD

If you bought this book in an airport, you might want to skip this chapter until your flight is over and you're safely back on the ground.

NOTHING TO SNOOZE AT

In May 1995, the pilot of Delta Airlines Flight 198, approaching Palm Beach International Airport, USA, was unable to make contact with the control tower. The pilot landed the plane without any assistance, then alerted the Federal Aviation Administration. According to news reports, 'Palm Beach sheriffs deputies entered the control tower and found the lone air traffic controller shoeless and apparently just waking up'. The deputies also found a pistol, ammunition and a gun-cleaning kit nearby (it's against federal law to have a gun in a control tower), and speculate he was cleaning the gun and fell asleep. FAA officials launched an investigation. 'Meanwhile', the Associated Press reported, he 'remains on the job'.

UNLUCKY BREAK

In June 1999, a plane approaching Benbecula Airport in Western Scotland was forced to circle for half an hour while the air traffic controller stopped working to eat lunch. According to wire service reports, 'Officials at the airport said there was just one controller at Benbecula, and she had to take a break at the time she did because national air traffic rules forbid any controller from working more than two hours without one....There was an uproar in the terminal building as families watched the plane from Glasgow linger in a holding pattern, "tantalizingly within view"'.

UNLUCKIER BREAK

In 1999 the air traffic controller at Bournemouth Airport stepped away from his post for a few minutes to get some coffee – but was gone a lot longer than he'd planned. Greg Fanos, 39, fell down a flight of stairs and broke his ankle. 'Crawling back to the tower was only two or three yards', Fanos says, 'but it took forever'. By the time he made it back to his desk and called an ambulance, several planes, unable to reach the tower on the radio, had gone into a holding pattern over the airport. Two other planes landed safely without assistance.

CLOSE ENCOUNTER

In April 1998, an air traffic supervisor at New York's LaGuardia Airport spilled some coffee in the control tower. One of the controllers turned from his position to help clean it up, and the momentary distraction caused what may be the closest near-miss in U.S. aviation history. A landing U.S. Airways plane came within 6 metres of colliding with an Air Canada plane that was taking off from an adjoining runway. According to news reports, 'experts were unable to immediately cite another incident in which two airborne passenger jets came so close without colliding'. When the National Transportation Safety Board investigated the incident and began taking statements from people in the control tower, 'neither the supervisor nor the controller mentioned the spilled coffee in their statements'.

RATS!

In August 1999, a woman on an Air New Zealand flight from Los Angeles to Auckland felt something on her leg. She lifted her blanket and saw a rat sitting on her knee. The rat had been spotted earlier, but according to an airline spokesperson, 'attempts by the crew to catch it failed'. According to wire service reports, 'Quarantine officials met the plane when it landed in Auckland and conducted a search of the plane including passengers' hand baggage. The rat wasn't found, so the plane was quarantined and fumigated'.

SUFFICIENT GROUNDS

In 1999 guards manning security checkpoint at more than 300 U.S. airports began ordering travellers carrying cups of coffee to sip their coffee to prove it really was coffee. 'That's policy', says security spokesman Jeff Sledge. 'It's so we'd be able to make sure that what's supposed to be in the cup is in the cup – not a weapon of some sort'. The policy was reportedly put into place following a U.S. Federal Aviation Authority (FAA) test in which an FAA employee made it past security with a 'simulated device in a coffee cup'. But the FAA denies that it's behind the 'clearing of liquids', or 'sip test'. 'It's not an FAA requirement at all', a spokesperson told the *Wall Street Journal*. If the airlines are doing it, she said, 'they're doing it on their own'.

In the old days, freckles were called 'moth-patches' and were considered an affliction.

HIS NAME IS MY NAME, TOO!

Remember the tune that goes, 'John Jacob Jingleheimer Smith, his name is my name too...'? If you do, you probably won't be able to get it out of your head for the rest of the day. Sorry. Anyway, we've come across some stories about people with the same names as other folks (and one Supreme Being). Here they are.

NOT THE DICTTATTOR

'Adolf Hittler is alive and well. But probably not the guy you're thinking about. Unlike the Nazi leader, this gentleman spells his last name with two Ts, disdains fascism, and never aspired to take over the world. He's a 61-year-old retired school bus driver from Landeck, Austria, and he doesn't like to be teased. "My whole life this has been a problem", he says. "Just try checking into a hotel with my name....But it is in part my choice. I decided not to change my name. I thought it would be an insult to my parents".

'Hittler's problem is rare. Only about 2 per cent of German men before World War II were named Adolf, and during his reign, Hitler forbade Germans to name children after him'.

– *The Wolf Files,* 1 October, 1998

GOD AMONG MEN

'A man who legally changed his name to Ubiquitous Perpetuity God began serving a nine-month sentence for indecent exposure in Marin County, California on Wednesday. God, 68, has been convicted 18 times for similar offenses since 1968. His latest arrest came in October, when he exposed himself to a woman waiting in line at a coffee shop. He did it so that women "could have some type of awareness of God", according to police reports....God will be released to a residential mental health facility, if one agrees to admit him'.

– *Ashland, Oregon, Daily Tidings,* 1996

FRANK STATEMENT

'Say hello to Frank J. Manibusan and his brother, Frank, both of

Alameda, California. And their brother, Frank. And their other brother, Frank. And his brother, Frank, and one other brother: Frank. Then, of course, there are children: Frank, Frank, Frank, Frank, Frank, and Frank. Frankly speaking, there are 12 Franks in all, at the moment – 13 if you count the patriarch, 58-year-old Francisco. …The sons and grandsons all have middle initials: J., J., J., J., J., J., J., J., J., J., J., and J.

'Of course, the advantages definitely outweigh the detriments, they explain. Can't do jury duty? Not to worry. Which Frank are the authorities going to chastise? And if one brother is out of cash, who cares? He need only tear out a cheque from the wallet of one of his siblings. "We don't leave no cheques lying around", explained Frank Joe, No. 2 son, while his brothers and father nodded in agreement'.

– *San Jose Mercury News*

A FAN AMONG FANS

'A fanatical British pop fan has changed his name to include the titles of his favourite group's records. And for good measure, Anthony Hicks, 23, added the names of the original line-up of the group, Level 42.

'Hicks this week signed legal papers changing his name to: "Ant Level Forty Two The Pursuit Of Accidents The Early Tapes Standing In The Light True Colors A Physical Presence World Machine Running In The Family Platinum Edition Staring At The Sun Level Best Guaranteed The Remixes Forever Now Influences Changes Mark King Mike Landup Phil Gould Boon Gould Wally Badarou Lindup-Badarou".

'"If they release any album or single, I will alter my name to have the new title incorporated into it", Hicks told reporters'.

– *Reuters*, 30 July, 1994

SPLIT DECISION

'When Denise Mason of Glasgow, Scotland, gave birth to a son six weeks ago, picking a name created a stir. Clark Kearny, the child's father and a big fan of... Glasgow Rangers... wanted to name the boy after his favourite [player] but couldn't make a decision. So, he didn't. The lad is named Cairo Lionel Sergio Lorenzo Colin Giovanni Barry Ian Jorge Gabriel Stephane Rod Mason Kearney – after 11 Rangers'.

– *USA Today*, 3 February, 1999

THE SHAPE OF THE EARTH

What shape is the Earth? You'd say round, right? But scientists, being scientists, will tell you something different. In science-speak, the Earth is in fact an 'oblate spheroid'.

YOU ARE HERE

In the age of space travel, we all know the world is 'round'. But ancient civilizations had no way to measure the size or shape of the Earth. So they came up with their own imaginative explanations. For example:

• In the Cherokee nation, people believed that mud rose from under the waters and formed an island with four corners – the Earth. The sun went underneath the island at night, and rose again the next day.
• Ancient Babylonians thought the Earth was inside a hollow mountain, floating on a sea. Everything – the sun, moon, sky, stars, water – was inside this mountain.
• Ancient Egyptians believed the whole Earth was part of their god, Keb. The stars were the jewels of a goddess in the sky and their god of air held her aloft.
• Ancient Hindus thought the Earth was in an upside-down bowl, being carried by elephants. The elephants stood on the back of a turtle that was standing on top of a snake. What the snake stood on, they hadn't quite worked out.
• Polynesian creation stories set the Earth in a basket with a lid. A hole cut in the top by a god lets in light. The woven grass at night lets light peek through in the form of stars.

THE GREEKS KNEW

Many people believe that Columbus was the first to realize that the world is round. Actually, the round-Earth concept has been with us since ancient Greece.

The very early Greeks thought Earth was a flat disc floating on water. But in about 540 B.C., the renowned mathematician

Except by Madonna's house. She won the right to keep ramblers off her Wiltshire estate.

Pythagoras proposed the theory that the world was a sphere. The concept had many supporters, including Aristotle.

ALL'S WELL

In about 250 B.C., Eratosthenes, librarian at the Library of Alexandria, even came up with a calculation of the Earth's spherical size.

He'd heard that in midsummer in the town of Syene, Egypt, the noonday sun shone directly into a deep well. He measured and discovered that in Alexandria, 787 kilometres north, the angle of the sun was about 7.2 degrees on the same date. With these measurements, he computed the circumference of the Earth. Amazingly enough, considering how he came up with the numbers and how little he had to prove them, Eratosthenes' estimates were very close.

Another scholar, Posidonius (135–51 B.C.), did something similar over a century later, using the bright star Canopus. He measured the angles of the star from the horizon in two locations to get a fairly accurate estimate of the Earth's circumference.

IN FOURTEEN HUNDRED AND NINETY-TWO...

Fifteen hundred years later, Christopher Columbus came along, trying to make his now-famous voyage to Asia by going west. The decision over whether to fund his trip came down to analyzing the accumulation of estimates that had been gathered over the centuries.

Based on Eratosthenes' numbers, King Ferdinand of Spain believed that Columbus' fleet could never make it all the way to Asia: it was simply too far. He didn't see any reason to supply ships and crews only to have them die halfway from their goal.

Columbus decided that if Eratosthenes' numbers didn't add up, he would find some that did. He found another estimate by Ptolemy dating from about 150 A.D. It incorrectly stated that the Earth was about half its true size. Based on these figures Queen Isabella, Ferdinand's wife, agreed to support the voyage.

Luckily for Columbus, America got in his way, or he never would have reached India or anywhere else. Crossing both the Atlantic and the Pacific combined would have been an impossible feat with the ships and supplies he had.

FLAT AND FAT

It wasn't until 1958 that the *Vanguard I* satellite took the first photographs of Earth from space and scientists were able to determine the planet's exact shape. The photographs proved the world is round – right?

Well, not exactly. Scientists reported that the Earth is an oblate spheroid – i.e., it's not quite round.

Since the Earth spins, it gets a slight bulge near the equator. Near yes, but not (as you might suspect) exactly on the equator. Because of this bulge, the Earth is flattened very slightly on either end. Its circumference at the equator is 39,843 km , and the circumference around the poles is 43 km less than that: 39,800 km. Not a big deal, really – if the world were the size of a football, it would be more perfectly round than a real football is. But still, after guessing for so long, scientists can't resist the opportunity to get it exactly right.

* * *

THE WORLD IS PEAR-SHAPED

Ironically, toward the end of his life, Columbus came to believe the Earth was shaped like a pear. He developed this theory during his third voyage to the New World. When he was sailing west near the equator, he noticed that the North Star made a wider circle around the Pole than it did when he was sailing in more temperate latitudes.

From this he deduced that he had been sailing gradually uphill and therefore closer to the sun, which explained why the weather was getting warmer. 'I have come to the conclusion', he wrote in a letter to Queen Isabella, '…that the Earth is not round, but of the form of a pear.…Where the stalk grows being the highest and nearest the sky'.

Columbus believed that if he sailed far enough, he would eventually reach the Garden of Eden, which was located in the pear's stalk. *(Ripley's Believe It or Not!)*

Victorians were expected to mourn for a minimum period—a spouse was worth two years.

THE EARTH IS FLAT!

For centuries, scientists have been able to prove that the Earth is round, but that hasn't stopped people from developing their own unique – and entertaining – theories about its shape.

THE EARTH IS FLAT
Who Says So: The International Flat Earth Research Society
What They Believe: The world is a big flat disc, with the North Pole at the centre. What is mistakenly believed to be the South Pole is actually a 46-metre high mass of ice that forms a big square around the Earth-disc (the way an album cover makes a square around a record). People who think they're sailing around the world are actually sailing in a circle on the surface of the disc. Flat-Earthers believe the Bible must be interpreted literally. Passages like Revelation 7:1 and 20:8, which refer to 'the four corners of the earth', are all the proof they need.
History: In 1849 an English 'itinerant lecturer' named Samuel Birley Rowbotham resurrected the flat-Earth theory (which had been widely discredited by the eighth century). The flat-Earth movement grew sporadically over the next 70 years, finally peaking in the 1920s when Wilbur Glen Voliva organized a flat-Earth religious community with several thousand followers in Zion, Illinois. Voliva owned one of the country's first 100,000-watt radio stations, and used it to preach the flat-Earth gospel to folks in the American Midwest. Today the movement lives on in Charles Johnson's Flat Earth Society, which published *Flat Earth News* – until Johnson's house burned down in 1995, incinerating the 3,500-person mailing list. No word on what he's doing now.

THE EARTH IS HOLLOW
Who Said So: Captain John Cleves Symmes, a hero of the U.S.–BritishWar of 1812.
What He Believed: The Earth has four layers, like a big onion. Each is a 'warm and rich land, stocked with vegetables and animals, if not men…'. What we perceive as the surface of the Earth is actually the fifth and outer layer. And the North and South poles aren't just poles, they're also holes leading to the four interior worlds.

Less is more: 95 per cent of the creatures on Earth are smaller than a chicken egg.

History: In 1823 Symmes managed to get a bill introduced in the U.S. Congress to finance a steamship voyage to the 'North Hole' and to the inner worlds beyond. When the bill received only 25 votes, Johnson talked President Adams' secretaries of the Navy and the Treasury into outfitting three ships for a voyage to the middle of the Earth. But before it got underway, Andrew Jackson became president and scuttled the trip. Symmes died in 1829, unfulfilled, but his theory remained popular with unconventional thinkers until 1909, when Robert Peary set foot on the North Pole (or at least came close) – and found no hole.

Even after 1909, the hollow-Earth theory had its admirers – including Adolf Hitler. Today, a few diehard hollow-Earthers believe that Hitler survived World War II, escaped to an interior world under the South Pole, and may still be hiding there, mingling with 'a race of advanced hollow-Earth beings who are responsible for the UFO sightings throughout history'.

THE EARTH IS SHAPED LIKE THE INSIDE OF AN EGG

Who Said So: Cyrus Reed Teed, in the late 1860s.

What He Believed: Instead of living on the outside of a solid round ball, we're on the inside surface of a hollow one. The rest of the universe – sun, stars, etc. – is where the yolk would be.

Background: For years, Teed grappled with the notion of an infinite universe...but just couldn't accept it. Then one night in 1869, he had a dream in which a beautiful woman explained everything:

> The entire cosmos...is like an egg. We live on the inner surface of the shell, and inside the hollow are the sun, moon, stars, planets, and comets. What is outside? Absolutely nothing! The inside is all there is. You can't see across it because the atmosphere is too dense. The shell is 100 miles thick...

The woman in Teed's dream also said he would be the new Messiah, and he took it to heart. In the 1890s, he bought land outside Fort Meyers, Florida, and founded a community called The New Jerusalem that he preached would one day be the capital of the world. He expected 8 million residents, but only got 200. In 1908 Teed died from injuries suffered during a run-in with the local marshal; his dwindling community held on until the late 1940s, when the last of his followers disbanded following a property dispute.

Salisbury Catherdral's 123 metres makes it even taller than St. Paul's, a mere 108 metres.

THE WHO?

Ever wonder how rock bands get their names? So did we. After some digging around, we found these 'origin' stories.

THE GIN BLOSSOMS. A gin blossom is slang for the capillaries in your nose and face that burst because of excessive drinking.

PROCUL HARUM. Named after a friend's cat. It's Latin for 'Beyond All Things'.

THE BOOMTOWN RATS. Named after a gang in Woody Guthrie's autobiography, *Bound for Glory*.

GENERATION X. Named after a book that singer Billy Idol found in his mother's bookcase. It was a mid-1960s sociological essay by Charles Hamblett and Jane Deverson that featured interviews with British teenagers in rival gangs of Mods and Rockers.

10,000 MANIACS. Came from the cult horror film *2,000 Maniacs*. One of the band members misunderstood the film's name.

FOO FIGHTERS. World War II fighter pilot slang for UFOs.

RAGE AGAINST THE MACHINE. Name refers to a (hoped-for) reaction of ordinary people against corporations, governments and other invasive institutions that control our society.

HOT TUNA. Originally Hot S**t. The band's record label made them change the second word to Tuna.

DIRE STRAITS. Suggested by a friend who was concerned about the state of the band's finances.

MOTHERS OF INVENTION. Frank Zappa's group was originally just The Mothers. But their record company was concerned it would be interpreted as an Oedipal reference and insisted they change it. The band chose the name from the old saying 'necessity is the mother of invention'.

The first open-heart surgery was performed in 1893.

PEARL JAM. Singer Eddie Vedder suggested the name in honour of his Aunt Pearl's homemade jam, supposedly a natural aphrodisiac containing peyote. 'Pearl Jam' is also slang for semen.

BEASTIE BOYS. Beastie supposedly stands for Boys Entering Anarchistic States Towards Inner Excellence.

SQUIRREL NUT ZIPPERS. From a brand of old-time peanut-flavored candy containing caramel and nuts.

BLIND MELON. According to bassist Brad Smith, the name was slang for unemployed hippies in his Mississippi town. Also sounds suspiciously like an anagram of blues singer Blind Lemon.

BLUE ÖYSTER CULT. An anagram of 'Cully Stout Beer'. It was chosen by a band member one night as he was mindlessly doodling while at a bar with the band's manager.

DEVO. An abbreviation of de-evolution, something that the members of the group believe is happening to the human race.

R.E.M. An acronym for rapid eye movement. R.E.M. sleep is the state of sleep in which dreams occur.

MATCHBOX 20. Took its name from the combination of a softball jersey bearing the number 20 and a patch that read 'matchbox'. The name is meaningless. 'The two parts aren't even related', singer Rob Thomas has said.

311. The police code for indecent exposure in California.

ZZ TOP. Said to be have been inspired by a poster of Texas bluesman Z. Z. Hill, and rolling-paper brands 'Zig Zag' and 'Top'.

COUNTING CROWS. A reference to an old British poem that said life is as meaningless as counting crows.

L7. Fifties slang for someone who is 'square', or uncool.

THE WHO. According to legend, the group, first called The High Numbers, was looking for a new name. Every time someone came up with an idea, they jokingly asked, 'The who'? Finally, a friend said 'Why not just call yourselves "The Who"'?

The parliamentary record is named after Thomas Hansard. He began printing debates in 1809.

THE LAST LAUGH: EPITAPHS

Some unusual epitaphs and tombstone rhymes, sent in by our crew of wandering BRI tombstone-ologists.

Botany cemetery, Sydney, NSW
When William Jackson was killed by a drunken David Hennesy riding his horse into a group of pedestrians, his family made sure the circumstances were not forgotten.
Sacred to the memory of
William Jackson
Who was carelessly rode over
And killed returning
from the races
May 21 1831
Aged 21 years
O Hennesy you did kill
And would not pay my doctor's bill
Your drunkenness
has caused my fall
But you must come
when GOD doth call

MAN'S BEST FRIEND
Bendigo, Victoria
Mr W. Webb
Erected in grateful remembrance of my faithful dog Fido, who died on March 28, 1904. A patient partner during ten years of life's journey, who has eaten the same bread with me and was to me a friend. The more I know of men, the more I admire dogs.

In St David's Park, Hobart, Tasmania:
Stranger take heed as you pass by;
As you are now so once was I,
As I am now so you will be
Prepare yourself to follow me.

In Massachusetts:
Matthew Mudd
Here lies Matthew Mudd,
Death did him no hurt;
When alive he was only Mudd,
But now he's only dirt.

In England:
Sir John Strange
Here lies an honest lawyer,
And that is Strange.

In Scotland:
Stranger, tread this ground with gravity:
Dentist Brown is filling
His last cavity.

In England:
My wife is dead
And here she lies:
Nobody laughs
And nobody cries:
Where she is gone to
And how she fares
Nobody knows
And nobody cares.

In New York:
He angled in the
babbling brook
With all his angler's skill.
He lied about the fish he took
And here he's lying still.

In Ireland:
Tears cannot
Restore her:
Therefore I weep.

In England:
Beneath this stone
Lie Humphrey and Joan,
Who rest together in peace,
Living indeed,
They disagreed,
But now all quarrels cease.

In Belgrave:
John Racket
Here lies John Racket
In his wooden jacket:
Kept neither horses nor mules
Lived a hog
Died a dog
And left all his money to fools.

In Massachusetts:
Here lies Ann Mann.
She lived an old maid
But died an old Mann.

In England:
Mrs Nott
Nott born, Nott dead
...Here lies a woman
Who was,
And who was Nott.

In England:
Dr. I. Lettsom
When people's ill, they comes to I,
I physics, bleeds, and sweats'em;
Sometimes they live,
sometimes they die;
What's that to I?
I. Lettsom.

A: Someone who blushes easily.

TRICK SHOTS: FAMOUS FAKED PHOTOS

If there's a lesson to be learned from these historic hoaxes, it's that people believe what they want to believe. In the face of overwhelming logic – or even solid contrary evidence – people have clung to the notion that the real truth was revealed in these photographs.

FAIRY TALE

Famous Photo: English fairies

Trick Shot: In 1917 Sir Arthur Conan Doyle, 'an ardent believer in the occult', announced that, just as he'd always believed, sprites, gnomes and other types of fairies really did exist. His proof: photographs of fairies taken by 16-year-old Elsie Wright and her 10-year-old cousin Frances Griffiths. 'The pictures showed the girls by a wooded stream, with winged sprites and gnomes who danced and pranced and tooted on pipes', Michael Farquhar wrote in the *Washington Post*. 'Several of the photography experts who examined the pictures declared them free of superimposition or retouching', and the photos, backed by Conan Doyle's testament to their authenticity, launched a national fairy craze.

The Real Picture: In 1983, the girls, by then old women, admitted that they had posed with paper cutouts supported by hatpins.

SECOND TIME AROUND

Famous Photo: American troops raising the flag on Iwo Jima

Trick Shot: The bloody battle of Iwo Jima (an island 1040 km from Tokyo) took place on 23 February, 1945. The Japanese were nearly wiped out, and the Americans lost over one-third of their troops. When the U.S. Marines finally took Iwo Jima's highest point, Mt. Suribachi, they raised an American flag at the summit. AP photographer Joe Rosenthal was on hand to catch it on film; his dramatic picture is one of the most famous images of the 20th century. It won the Pulitzer Prize, was commemorated with a postage stamp, and was the inspiration for the Marines Memorial in Arlington National Cemetery in Virginia.

The Real Picture: Rosenthal's photograph was so good that *Life* magazine editor Daniel Longwell wondered if it was too good. He asked a *Life* correspondent on Iwo Jima to investigate. Stephen Bates writes in *If No News, Send Rumors:*

> The correspondent reported, that as Longwell suspected, the photo had been staged. The marines had raised a small flag for a photographer from *Leatherneck*, the Marine Corps magazine. Rosenthal had arrived four hours later. At his request, the marines had reenacted the event with a larger flag.

Longwell refused to use a staged photograph in *Life*, but other publications did run it, and it caught on with the public. 'The country believed in that picture', Longwell recounted later, 'and I just had to pipe down'.

UN-LOCH-ING THE TRUTH

Famous Photo: Loch Ness monster
Trick Shot: On 19 April, 1934, Robert Wilson and a companion were walking along the shore of Loch Ness when the friend suddenly shouted, 'My God, it's the monster!' Wilson grabbed his camera and snapped a quick photograph of what appears to be 'a sea beast with a humpback and a long neck' – the legendary Loch Ness monster, an elusive creature with sightings dating as far back as 565 A.D. The *Daily Mail* ran the photograph, and news of the find spread round the world. Based largely on the strength of Wilson's photograph, it remains one of the most widely believed monster legends to this day. Nearly one million tourists visit Loch Ness each year, hoping to spot 'Nessie' and pumping £20 million into the local economy while they're there.
The Real Picture: In 1995 a friend of Wilson's named Christian Spurling made a deathbed confession that the photograph was a hoax and the 'monster' was actually 'a toy submarine fitted with a fake sea-serpent head' that Spurling had made himself. 'Wilson', the Associated Press reported in 1995, 'was part of a hoax hatched by his friend Marmaduke Wetherell, a film maker and self-styled big game hunter hired by London's *Daily Mail* newspaper in 1933 to look for Nessie'.
Note: Hard-core believers are unimpressed by the revelation. 'Eyewitness accounts still suggest that there is something powerful in the loch', says Adrian Shine, founder of a group called The Loch Ness Project.

Poll results: 57 per cent of women would rather go on a shopping spree than have sex.

WEIRD TOYS

Looking for a gift for a special young friend or relative? Want to surprise them with something out of the ordinary? Well, if you don't mind being thrown out of the house, you might want to pick up one of these 100 per cent real (we guarantee it) playthings.

The Tamahonam. Sold in Hong Kong, the Tamahonam is a Tamagotchi toy with Mafia connections. Instead of feeding Tamahonam like you would other virtual pets, you 'care' for Tamahonam by plying him with cigarettes and booze; instead of playing with him, you give him a knife 'to let him wage turf battles'.

Feral Cheryl. 'A doll that has unshaved legs, dreadlocks, tattoos, pubic hair, and pierced nipples'. Made in Australia.

The Grossinator. Made by SRM, the company that brought you the Insultinator. 'A minicomputer with a sound chip and programmable buttons with phrases you can mix and match'. This one says things like, 'I'm going to make a horrible, gross fart' and 'How about a foul, smelly barf'?

Brian Jones Pool Toy. 'An inflatable, life-size pool toy of Brian Jones, deceased member of the Rolling Stones, that floats face-down in the water, simulating the guitarist's death by drowning in his pool'.

Gooey Looey. Exciting action! 'Children use their fingers to relieve Louie's congested proboscis before the top of his head flies off'.

Savage Mondo Blitzers. 'A line of 48 characters named Bad Fart, Snot Shot, Projectile Vomit, Puke Shooters, Loaded Diaper, Eye Pus, and the like'.

Letter Bomb. The manufacturer urges kids to 'have fun and become a terrorist'. Looks like an airmail envelope – 'kids write the target's name on it, clap on it heavily, and then give it to the victim within seven seconds so it "explodes" in his hand'. Sold in the Philippines.

Who said the US can't play football? In the 1950 World Cup they beat England 1-0.

THE OSSIAN FRAUD

No-one reads the work of the ancient Celtic poet Ossian now, and with good reason – he never existed. But in the mid-1700s he was all the rage amongst a deluded public.

Johann Wolfgang von Goethe, Germany's greatest writer, said that he was as good as Shakespeare; Napoleon carried a volume of his poetry with him on military campaigns for inspiration; and Mendelssohn, Schubert and Brahms all composed music inspired by his work. So who was Ossian? And why is he all-but-forgotten today?

INVENTING OSSIAN

The short answer is because he never really existed. Ossian the poet was a product of the fevered imagination of James Macpherson, an 18th-century Scottish schoolmaster who dreamt of literary glory. In Celtic folklore there was a character called Ossian, who was the son of legendary Irish folk hero Finn Mac Cumhaill (pronounced 'Finn Mc Cool'), but he was certainly not the author of a series of poems published under his name in the 1760s.

MYTH-MAKING AND POETIC LICENCE

In mid 18th-century Britain there was a fad for all things Scottish, after the failed exploits of Bonnie Prince Charlie and his fight against the English in the 1740s. James Macpherson, an ambitious young Scot in his mid-twenties, decided he was the man to give the public what they wanted. Myths, legends and old poetry were especially popular, but when Macpherson found that there was not a lot of material available, he decided to write some of it himself.

In 1760, he published *Fragments of Ancient Poetry Collected in the Highlands of Scotland*, a selection of Gaelic poems that he claimed to have collected and translated on his travels through the Highlands.

AN EPIC SUCCESS

This book was a smash hit, and Macpherson realized he was on to a winner. The following year, 1761, he published *Fingal*, which

The Marquess of Bath (b. 1938) has shared his Longleat stately home with over 70 'wifelets'.

was, according to Macpherson, a newly-discovered unknown epic poem, written by the legendary figure, Ossian.

With this book, Macpherson became one of the most famous literary figures in Europe. The poem was translated into all the major European languages and praise was heaped upon it – and on Macpherson for his great feat of literary detection and translation.

HOW VERY ROMANTIC

Of course, it was all a big fraud. Macpherson had written the poem himself, but no-one seemed to notice as it's popularity grew and grew. The poem's fantasy world of heroes and gods, and swords and sorcerers, helped to kick-start the Romantic and Gothic movements in art and literature. Even today its influence is still obvious, from *Lord of the Rings* to *Buffy the Vampire Slayer*.

A POEM TOO FAR

Flushed with success, Macpherson tried his luck one more time – and came a cropper. In 1763 he published *Temora*, another 'lost' epic by Ossian. Literary experts questioned whether it was really possible to find two lost masterpieces from the third century A.D. More questions were asked when readers noticed similarities between parts of *Temora* and the Bible and Milton's *Paradise Lost*. Samuel Johnson, the grand old man of British letters, declared straight out that it was all a fraud perpetrated by Macpherson.

MAKING A FIGHT OF IT

Displaying a huge amount of brass neck, Macpherson replied that he had never been so insulted in his life. As 'proof' of the authenticity of *Temora* he published sections of it in what he claimed was the original Gaelic. It was an impressive stunt (even if later analysis showed that it wasn't very good Gaelic). Johnson remained unconvinced, but others rallied to Macpherson's defence. At one point, fed up with Johnson's constant criticisms, Macpherson challenged his literary rival to a duel (luckily, it never took place).

THAT'S NOT VERY ORIGINAL

Carrying on as if nothing was wrong, Macpherson published *The Works of Ossian* in 1765, with his own misleading footnotes. By this time, Ossian was established as an important poet, but the rumours about Macpherson's relationship to him never went away,

The world's largest cut diamond is the second Star of Africa, part of the Crown Jewels.

especially as Macpherson never got round to presenting the Gaelic originals of the poems he claimed to possess – despite the more than generous offer of £1,000 by one rich Highlander to see the 1,400 year-old manuscripts. Macpherson managed to stall those who wanted to see the originals for 36 years, right up to his death in 1796. It is not hard to see why – his whole reputation as a literary figure rested on his deception not being uncovered. In later years Macpherson also became an MP, yet more reason for not wanting to risk public humiliation.

OSSIAN UNCOVERED

It was only in the late 19th century that the Ossian issue was settled once and for all. A commission set up to investigate the poems declared that they were indeed fakes. Parts of them, they decided, were based on genuine Gaelic songs and poems, but the vast majority of the works were fabricated by Macpherson. Almost overnight, the poems were dropped from the literary canon. Today, they are practically forgotten. It is as if they never existed.

ART MEETS ARTIFICE

The most bizarre aspect of the whole Ossian saga is that if Macpherson had come clean, the Ossian poems would probably still be read today. Macpherson really did have talent as a writer – how else could he have fooled so many people for so long? If he had simply published the poems under his own name as re-creations of a vanished past things may have worked out better. After all, it is pretty much what Sir Walter Scott did in the series of historical novels, such as *Ivanhoe*, that he churned out in the early 19th century.

It is even safe to say that the Ossian poems, in the 100 or so years that they were read, were some of the most influential pieces of literature of modern times. They were much copied, and everybody who was anybody in literary circles (apart from Dr. Johnson, of course) loved them and was influenced by their breathless, heroic evocations of a bygone age. Bearing in mind the huge influence they had on the Romantic movement and figures such as Goethe, Schubert and Brahms, it is safe to say that if Macpherson had never put pen to paper the history of Western culture would be very different. Not a bad way for a common-or-garden fraudster to be remembered!

Roll over, Rover: 63 per cent of pet owners sleep with their pets.

THE IRON DUKE'S THING FOR RUBBER

No, the Duke of Wellington wasn't a Victorian rubber fetishist. He just found it easier to be brave if his feet weren't wet.

Arthur Wellesley was born in 1769 in wet and windy Ireland. He always claimed that he couldn't think straight unless his feet were dry and they often weren't, given the climate and the fashionable but leaky footwear our 18th and 19th century ancestors wore. Dainty shoes were fine for ladies who rarely ventured outdoors, or for men who only sat on horses or inside carriages. But rugged types like Wellesley wanted something more robust covering their feet when they were out in the field.

THE 18:15 TO WATERLOO

And Wellesley did spend an awful lot of time out-of doors: after the French Revolution of 1789 Britain was almost continuously at war with France until 1815. And Wellesley, as one of Britain's top military men, spent most of those years literally up to his knees in mud fighting the enemy.

In 1814 Wellesley was created the first Duke of Wellington, and the following year led the British troops to victory against Napoleon at Waterloo, that tiny dot on the map a few miles south of the Belgian capital, Brussels.

BOOTY CALL

As your classic huntin', shootin' and fishin' type – never mind being a career soldier – Wellington knew that dry feet were essential to any sort of outdoor activity. He also knew that rubber, as long as it's properly sealed, doesn't leak. Which led him to his brilliant idea – why not wear boots made of rubber? He ordered a pair to be made, and that's why rubber boots have been known since then as Wellington's or 'wellies'.

WELLINGTON PILES ON THE AGONY

Poor old Napoleon didn't stand a chance. Historians tell us he was distinctly under the weather on 18 June, the day of the battle of Waterloo. Napoleon is supposed to have suffered from

Belgians once tried to deliver the post using cats. (It didn't work.)

piles. So sitting astride a horse would have made it hard for him to concentrate on the job in hand. Wellington, his feet securely dry and cosy in the famous boots, even after hours of overnight rain, was by far the best prepared of the two great military minds.

HE DIED WITH HIS BOOTS ON – NOT!

After Waterloo, Wellington went on to have a long and distinguished political career. He was prime minister twice, and to the end of his days was revered as a national hero for his exploits against the revolting French.

In old age 'The Iron Duke' spent much of his time at Walmer Castle on the Kent coast. He had the use of the place as Lord Warden of the Cinque Ports – one of the many honours showered upon him in his dotage. He died at Walmer in 1852.

Today the castle is open to the public. The room in which old Arthur breathed his last is maintained in ghoulish authenticity: see the bed he slept in and the chair he died in. And, of course, a pair of those boots is on prominent display.

ONE OF BRITAIN'S BEST

Wellington was given a state funeral with lots of pomp and circumstance, an honour rarely accorded to non-royals. The carriage that bore his coffin is on display at St. Paul's Cathedral.
Today, a statue of Wellington dominates Waterloo Place, a relatively quiet corner of central London between Trafalgar Square and Buckingham Palace.

WELLIE-MANIA

The boots weren't the only thing named after Wellington. They named the capital of New Zealand after him in 1840, for example. There are more than a few pubs up and down the land called 'The Duke of Wellington', too. You may even find yourself walking up a Wellington Street or Wellington Road to get to one.

And how many people get a tree named after them? Wellington did. *Wellingtonia* is a member of the sequoia family, a type of redwood tree commonly found in parks and large gardens around the country.

Last but not least, you have Beef Wellington – that oh-so-English dish of beef on a bed of liver paté wrapped inside a pastry crust. Funnily enough, it *wasn't* named after the duke. Because of the way it looks when it's cooked, it was named after the boot!

Copy this out one hundred times: King's School in Canterbury dates back to around 600 AD.

THE LOST PRINCE

In 1998 an old photograph found during a house clearance uncovered a forgotten member of the royal family – Prince John, who died in 1919 while still in his early teens. Here is his story.

It is unthinkable that a member of the royal family could live and die out of the public eye, but that is what happened to the youngest child of King George V and Queen Mary. Prince John was born in 1905. Two of his brothers became kings, Edward VIII and George V1, while his other two brothers, the Duke of Kent and the Duke of Gloucester, were well-known society figures of their day. So why was Prince John kept out of the limelight?

A PROBLEM CHILD

The answer is that he was 'not quite right'. From the age of five he developed epilepsy. He was also mentally retarded. At this time, both conditions were poorly understood and were seen as shameful. When the prince's problems became evident, he was removed from public life. The press, in those days a lot more respectful toward royalty, asked no questions when the prince disappeared.

HIDDEN FROM THE WORLD

Although Prince John was a happy and carefree boy his condition meant that he could never have a public life. Added to his epilepsy and retardation, from the age of 10 he began growing much too quickly, soon becoming enormously outsized. He was sent to live on a secluded farm near the royal palace of Sandringham, where he was looked after by his beloved nurse, Mrs. Bill.

GONE BUT NOT FORGOTTEN

It was here that the prince's short life came to an end in 1919. Following a severe epileptic fit, the prince died suddenly in the early hours of 18 January. He was buried in private at Sandringham. He was 13 years old. The prince was soon forgotten, until in early 1998 pictures of the prince and letters written by him were discovered in an attic in Kent. The memorabilia belonged to Winifred Thomas, who died in 1980 aged 75. She was a childhood friend of the prince and had kept his letters and photos – ensuring that his memory lived on, even from beyond the grave.

UNCLE JOHN'S LISTS

Here at Uncle John's we love lists so much that we've compiled a list of our favourite lists!

TITLES OF 4 HOLLYWOOD FILMS RE-DUBBED IN HONG KONG:

1. *Fargo:* 'Mysterious Murder in Snowy Cream'.
2. *The English Patient:* 'Don't Ask Me Who I Am'.
3. *Boogie Nights:* 'His Powerful Device Makes Him Famous'.
4. *Nixon:* 'The Big Liar'.

4 NAMES FOR THINGS YOU DIDN'T KNOW HAD NAMES

1. Aglet: 'The covering on the end of a shoelace'.
2. Phosphenes: 'The lights you see when you close your eyes hard'.
3. Kick or Punt: 'The indentation at the bottom of wine bottles'.
4. Harp: 'The metal hoop that supports a lampshade'.

2 PRESIDENTIAL SUPERSTITIONS

1. Franklin Roosevelt (1933–1945) refused to sit at a table set for 13 guests.
2. Woodrow Wilson (1913–1921) Believed 13 was his lucky number. He once ordered a ship to slow down so he would arrive in Europe on the 13th instead of the 12th.

9 BEANS THAT CAUSE THE MOST WIND

1. Soybeans
2. Pink beans
3. Black beans
4. Pinto beans
5. California small white beans
6. Great northern beans
7. Lima beans
8. Garbanzos
9. Blackeyes

– *U.S. Department of Agriculture*

3 MOST INFLUENTIAL PETS OF THE MILLENNIUM

1. Lassie
2. Snoopy
3. Arnold the Pig (from U.S. TV's *Green Acres)*

– *The American Pet Product Manufacturers Association*

5 THINGS YOU SHOULDN'T SAY WHEN A COP PULLS YOU OVER

1. 'Aren't you the guy from the Village People'?
2. 'That's great. The last guy only gave me a warning also'.
3. 'You're not gonna check the boot, are you'?
4. 'Hey, you must've been

22 million viewers saw the final episode of Only Fools and Horses in 1997, a UK record.

doing 100 just to keep up with me'.
5. 'I thought you had to be in good physical condition to be a cop'.

3 REAL EXCUSES USED IN COURT

1. 'I was thrown from the car as it left the road. I was later found in a ditch by some stray cows'.
2. 'The indirect cause of the accident was a little guy in a small car with a big mouth'.
3. 'To avoid hitting the bumper of the car in front, I struck the pedestrian'.

TOP 5 U.S. BILLBOARD SONGS ON APRIL 5, 1964

1. 'Can't Buy Me Love' (The Beatles)
2. 'Twist and Shout' (The Beatles)
3. 'She Loves Me' (The Beatles)
4. 'I Want to Hold Your Hand' (The Beatles)
5. 'Please Please Me' (The Beatles)

3 CELEBRITIES WHO SAY THEY'VE SEEN A UFO:

1. Muhammad Ali
2. Jimmy Carter
3. William Shatner

7 WEIRD PLACE NAMES

1. Peculiar, Missouri
2. Smut Eye, Alabama
3. Loudville, Massachusetts
4. Disco, Illinois
5. Yeehaw Junction, Florida
6. Slaughter Beach, Delaware
7. Humptulips, Washington

3 MEN KNOWN BY THEIR MIDDLE NAMES

1. James Paul McCartney
2. William Clark Gable
3. Ruiz Fidel Castro

5 MOST-HATED HOUSEHOLD CHORES

1. Washing dishes
2. Bathroom cleaning
3. Ironing
4. Vacuuming
5. Washing windows

– *Gallup Poll*

4 WORDS NOBODY USES ANYMORE

1. Podge ('To walk slowly and heavily'.)
2. Roinous ('Mean and nasty'.)
3. Battologist ('Someone who pointlessly repeats themselves'.)
4. Battologist ('Someone who pointlessly repeats themselves'.)

3 MOST PRIZED AUTOGRAPHS

1. Shakespeare (six are known to exist)
2. Christopher Columbus (eight exist)
3. Julius Caesar (None are known to exist)

JUST THE FAX, PLEASE

Here are a few things to think about the next time you find yourself standing at a fax machine.

ONE WORLD

Fax machines are so common today that it's easy to forget how rare they once were. In 1977 fax machines cost more than £14,000 each – and transmitted one blurry, hard-to-read page every six minutes.

By 1989, fax machines began changing not just the way the world did business, but perhaps even the course of history. For example:

• When Lithuania seceded from the USSR, the secessionist government bypassed Soviet censors and communicated directly with the outside world using fax machines.

• Pro-democracy demonstrators on China's Tiananmen Square used fax machines to communicate with supporters within the country and around the world.

• When Nelson Mandela, still a political prisoner in South Africa, began negotiating the terms of his release from prison, the end of apartheid, and South Africa's transition to a full democracy, he did it using a fax machine.

The fax machine revolution 'makes totalitarianism impossible', says Max Kampelman, the head of Freedom House, a human rights organization. 'Totalitarianism requires the total control of information. That isn't possible anymore'.

FAX HISTORY

The fax machine isn't a new idea. Believe it or not, the first one – called a pantelegraph because it was supposed to transmit messages over telegraph lines – was patented in 1843, 33 years before Alexander Graham Bell patented the telephone. It was created by Alexander Bain, a Scottish clockmaker who envisioned using pendulums at each end of the telegraph to transmit messages, (we won't get into exactly how it worked – it's too confusing).

Unfortunately, Bain never figured out how to synchronize the pendulums, and he eventually gave up.

However, in 1864 a Catholic priest named Giovanni Caselli and his partner, Gustav Froment, finally got all the bugs out of Bain's invention. Their version not only worked, it sent messages written on ordinary paper, and could send several of them simultaneously over a single wire.

The duo demonstrated their machine to Emperor Napoleon III of France – and he loved it. Under his direction, the French legislature passed a law establishing the world's first fax service between Paris and Lyons – a distance of more than 200 miles. It was inaugurated on 16 May, 1865, and by 1868 it was capable of sending more than 110 telegrams an hour. But it never really had a chance to catch on with the public. The system was disrupted by war and the siege of Paris in 1870, and was never resumed.

PHOTO AGE

Over the next four or five decades, scientists worked at perfecting the technique of sending not only messages, but pictures. In 1902 a German physicist named Arthur Korn figured out how to send photo-quality images using special wires. And in 1913 Edouard Belin invented what he called a 'Belinograph' (Belino for short), a portable machine, smaller than a typewriter, that could transmit photographic images over standard telephone lines.

This invention revolutionized news reporting. For the first time in history, a newspaper could send someone to any corner of the globe (or at least any corner that had telephones) and, with the portable Belino machine, get photographic images in a matter of minutes – not weeks or months as had been the case before. Invented just in time for the outbreak of World War I, the Belino had an immediate impact on wartime news coverage. By the early 1920s, it was even possible to send 'wirephotos' using radio waves, eliminating the need for telephones.

MODERN FAXES

For the next 50 years, these early machines were used almost exclusively to send news pictures around the world and to transmit weather maps by radio to ships at sea. The system was too expensive and too slow to be of much interest to other types of businesses. Besides, AT&T had a monopoly on telephone service in the United States – and because they didn't manufacture fax machines, they fought to prevent customers from using telephone lines for anything other than voice. However, by the late 1960s the courts had abolished most of AT&T's restrictions, opening the way for big companies like Xerox, IBM and others to create the technology that resulted in the modern fax.

MADE IN JAPAN

• Still, fax machines might never have come into widespread use were it not for the fact that the Japanese language uses thousands of characters (too many to fit on a typewriter keyboard). Typing and telexing is thus much more difficult in Japanese than it is in English.

• Japanese businessmen needed a way to send handwritten communications quickly and accurately over the telephone, so companies like Matsushita, Ricoh, Canon and NEC spent tens of millions of pounds working out how to make fax machines cheaper, faster and easier to use. They succeeded.

• Sales of fax machines boomed in Japan in the early 1980s, and by the late 1980s the fever had spread to the rest of the world. The steady decline of the price of the machines fuelled the boom: by 1983 fax machines in the U.S. that had cost $21,000 in 1977 were selling for $2,600; by 1988 the price slipped under $1,000 for the first time, enabling millions of small businesses to afford them. By the mid-1990s, the price as low as $130 and most companies – even small ones – couldn't afford not to have a fax machine. Of course, now everyone needs computers and e-mail – but, that's another story.

* * *

FAX LINGO

Fax Potato: Someone who faxes materials from one floor of a building to another, because they're too lazy to use the lift.

IN THE NAVY

Britannia may no longer rule the waves, but did you know that many of the sayings we still use every day actually originated in the lingo of Admiral Nelson's navy?

In the 18th and 19th centuries the navy was a harsh employer. For example, boys as young as 10 were used to carry cannonballs from the ship's armoury to the gun placements. The poor lads were known as 'powder monkeys' and the wood and metal stand they placed the cannonballs on was called the 'brass monkey'. In extreme cold weather, the wood and metal of its rails expanded, causing the balls to roll off on to the deck. Hence the term: 'It's cold enough to freeze the balls off a brass monkey.'

SWINGING THE LEAD

This phrase is still frequently used to imply someone who's lazy or workshy. It comes from the method that ships used to measure their speed through the water. A long piece of hemp rope was tied with knots at equal distances along its length and a lead weight was tied to the end to help it sink. The rope was then thrown out to sea and pulled in after a set time; the amount of knots that disappeared underwater showed the speed at which the ship was travelling. 'Knots' remain the official measure of speed for all sailing vessels.

An unfortunate deckhand (usually someone on a punishment) performed this backbreaking task, and had to swing the leaded rope around his head to create enough momentum to get it over the wake of the ship. If he wanted to avoid the really hard work of dragging the sodden rope back in, he'd keep swinging the rope around his head, until a whip from the Bosun's cat-o'-nine-tails made him stop 'swinging the lead'.

A CAT WITH TOO MANY TAILS

The British Navy was the most highly disciplined navy in the world and punishment for even minor crimes was swift and brutal. The most feared punishment of all was a series of lashes from the cat-o'-nine-tails, a whip made from nine lengths of leather with knots along each length. The damaged wreaked on the back of the unhappy recipient often led to death. But this not-so-charming instrument of torture is also the source of many phrases we use today. For example:

'To let the cat out of the bag': the whip had to be kept moist in a wet leather carrying bag.

'No room to swing a cat': punishment often took place in a small area of the deck, making the man doing the lashing complain he didn't have enough space to do it properly.

'A cat has nine lives': a well-trained whip man could make each of the nine tails of the cat land separately, causing increased damage to the recipient's back.

'You scratch my back and I'll scratch yours': it was such a punishment-based society on board ship, the person being whipped knew that one day he might be the one dishing out flogging to the man now punishing him. He wanted to encourage his tormentor to go lightly on him.

* * *

THINGS ONLY A SAILOR WOULD KNOW

RUN THE GAUNTLET: An old naval punishment for men convicted of theft was to make the offender walk between two rows of men each equipped with rope ends with which to strike him. The offender could not pass through too quickly because the Master-At-Arms held a sword against his chest to slow the miscreant down.

SON OF A GUN: Wives of Royal Navy crewmen were allowed to accompany their men on some long voyages. If any of the women became pregnant while at sea, the safest place for them to give birth was in a shelter behind the canons on the gun decks. If a male child was born, he was called a Son of a Gun. The term was also used to imply that the identity of the father might be in question. Today the term is not used to cast aspersions on a person's parentage and is generally used to mean a 'good fellow'.

No wonder they're gone: in ancient Egypt, pillows were made of stones.

RANDOM ORIGINS

We ask – and answer – the question: where did this stuff come from?

GOLD RECORDS

In 1941 RCA Victor released Glenn Miller's 'Chattanooga Choo Choo' after he performed it in the movie *Sun Valley Serenade*. It was a huge hit: 1.2 million records were sold in less than three months. So RCA came up with a great publicity gimmick to promote it: they sprayed one of the 'master records' with gold paint and on 10 February, 1942, presented it to Miller during a radio broadcast in honour of his selling a million copies.

Eventually the Record Industry Association of America (RIAA) copied the idea and started honouring million-selling records with an official Gold Record Award.

Nobody knows for sure what the first million-selling record was. One likely candidate: 'Ragging the Baby to Sleep', recorded by Al Jolson on 17 April, 1912. *(Yankee Ingenuity)*

CIRCUS TIGHTS

'Tights are believed to have been introduced in 1828 by Nelson Hower, a bareback rider in the Buckley and Wicks Show, as the result of a mishap. The performers wore short jackets, knee breeches, and stockings, but Hower's costume failed to arrive and he appeared for the show in his long knit underwear'. *(The People's Almanac)*

KITTY LITTER

In January 1948, in Cassopolis, Michigan, a woman named Kay Draper ran into trouble: the sandpile she used to fill her cat's litter box was frozen solid. She tried ashes, but wound up with paw prints all over the house. Sawdust didn't work, either.

As it happened, her neighbours, the Lowes, sold a product called Fuller's Earth, a kiln-dried clay that was used to soak up oil and grease spills in factories. Ed Lowe, their 27-year-old son, had been looking for a new market for the stuff – he'd tried unsuccessfully to sell it to local farmers as nesting material for chickens. On

Oldest form of surgery on Earth: trepanning – drilling holes into the skull.

the spur of the moment, he convinced Draper that this stuff would make great cat litter. He really had no idea if it would – but it did! He sensed the sales potential, put some Fuller's Earth in paper bags and labelled it 'Kitty Litter' with a grease pen. Then he drove around, trying to sell it. (Actually, he gave it away at first to get people to try it.) Once people tried it, they invariably came back for more.

'The success of kitty litter enabled pet owners to keep cats inside their homes with little muss or fuss (let's not discuss smell). As a result, an entire industry consisting of cat foods, toys, grooming products, and the like was launched'.
(Useless Information Web site)

RUGBY

William Webb Ellis was playing football at the Rugby School in Warwickshire in 1823. His team was losing so badly that he grabbed the ball and started running toward the opposing goal, his team-mates and opponents staring on in amazement. When he got close he drop-kicked the ball into the goal. The goal didn't count, of course, and the captain of Ellis's team was so embarrassed that after apologizing to the referee, he suspended Ellis from the team.

The tale of 'that play at Rugby' circulated for years afterward, and in 1839 Arthur Pell, the star striker of the Cambridge football team, drew up some rules for a new game – named after the Rugby School – that legalized holding, throwing, and running with the ball. The new sport was also the direct forerunner of American football. (Fenton & Fowler's *Best, Worst and Most Unusual)*

AEROSOL CANS

In 1943 the U.S. Agriculture Department came up with an aerosol insect spray. It used liquid gas inside steel tins to help World War II soldiers fight malaria-causing insects (malaria was taking a heavy toll on the troops). By 1947, civilians could buy insect sprays, too, but they were heavy 'grenadelike' things. Two years later, America's Robert H. Abplanalp developed a special 'seven-part leak-proof' valve that allowed him to use lightweight aluminium instead of heavy steel, creating the modern spray can.

Jack and Chloe are the most popular children's names in the U.K.

HOW TO MAKE A MONSTER, PART I

Godzilla is one of the most popular movie monsters in film history. Now here's the story behind Japan's largest export.

NUCLEAR AGE

On 1 March, 1954, at the Bikini atoll in the South Pacific, the United States tested the world's first hydrogen bomb. It was 1,000 times more powerful than the A-bombs that had been dropped on Hiroshima nine years earlier.

American ships were warned to stay out of the test area – but because the project was top-secret, the U.S. government provided little advance warning to other countries. U.S. officials were certain that the resulting nuclear fallout would land in an empty expanse of the Pacific Ocean and no one would be in jeopardy. Unfortunately, they were wrong. The fallout didn't travel in the direction they expected, and a small Japanese fishing boat named the *Daigo Fukuryo Maru* ('Lucky Dragon') was in the area where the nuclear cloud came to earth. Within hours of the blast, the boat's entire crew became violently ill from radiation poisoning.

On 23 September, 1954, after more than six months of agony, the ship's radioman, Aikichi Huboyama, died.

The fate of the crew of the *Daigo Fukuryo Maru* made international news. In Japan, headlines like 'The Second Atomic Bombing of Mankind' compared the incident to the bombing of Hiroshima and Nagasaki in 1945.

ART IMITATES LIFE

While all of this was going on, Japanese movie producer Tomoyuki Tanaka arrived in Indonesia to oversee a film called *Beyond the Glory*. It was scheduled to be the main release for Japan's Toho Studios the next year but it never got off the ground; the Indonesian government refused to issue work visas to the film's two stars.

Suddenly, Tanaka found himself with time, money and actors – but no film to make. In addition, Toho Studios had a big hole in their release schedule. The producer had to come up with a new movie concept – *fast*.

On his flight back to Tokyo, Tanaka stared out the window at the ocean below, desperately trying to think of something. His mind wandered to the H-Bomb tests in the South Pacific and the crew of the *Daigo Fukuryo Maru* – and then it hit him: he would combine an American-style monster movie with a serious message about the threat of radiation and nuclear weapons tests.

PROJECT G

Commercially, it made sense. For obvious reasons, the Japanese public was very concerned about nuclear testing. And in cinemas, monster movies were hot. The 1933 classic, *King Kong*, had been re-released in 1952 and made more than £1.5 million in international ticket sales – four times what it had earned the first time around. *Time* magazine even named the giant ape 'Monster of the Year'. Its huge success inspired a 'monster-on-the-loose' film craze.

One of the first to cash in on the fad was *The Beast from 20,000 Fathoms*, which featured a dinosaur attacking New York City after nuclear tests awakened it from a million-year sleep. The film cost $400,000 to make and was a critical flop – but with $5 million in box office receipts in the U.S., it was one of the top-grossing movies of the year.

Tanaka got approval from his studio to do a Japanese version. He hired a prominent Japanese science fiction writer to prepare a knock-off screenplay tentatively titled *Big Monster from 200,000 Miles Beneath the Sea*, but he still wasn't sure what kind of monster to use, or what to call it. So to start out, the film was referred to simply as 'Project G' (for Giant).

A PAIR OF EXPERTS

Meanwhile, he began assembling a crew. For director, Tanaka picked Ishiro Honda, a documentary filmmaker who had been Akira Kurosawa's assistant on *The Seven Samurai* (considered the best Japanese film ever made by most critics). Like many of the Toho Studios crew, Honda was a veteran of the Imperial Army. He had visited Hiroshima several months after the atomic bomb was dropped. 'When I returned from the war and passed through Hiroshima', he told an interviewer years later, 'there was a heavy atmosphere – a fear that the Earth was already coming to an end.

At age 43 in 1997, Tony Blair was the youngest Prime Minister since 1812.

That became my basis. Believe it or not, we naively hoped that Godzilla's death in the film was going to coincide with the end of nuclear testing'.

Special effects were handled by Eiji Tsuburaya. During the war, he had made unusual propaganda films for the Imperial Army – he recreated battles in miniature, so Japanese movie audiences could follow the progress of the war. His work was so skilful that when the American occupation forces got hold of his reenactment of the bombing of Pearl Harbor, they were convinced they were watching actual combat footage. Since childhood, Eiji had dreamed of making monster movies with his miniature sets. Now he would have his opportunity.

FAT CHANCE

As it turned out, finding a name for the monster was easy. 'At the time there was a big – I mean huge – fellow working in Toho's publicity department', director Ishiro Honda recalled. 'Employees would argue, "that guy is as big as a gorilla". "No, he's almost as big as a *kujira* (whale)". Over time, the two mixed and he was nicknamed Gojira (pronounced GO-dzee-la). So when we were stuck for a name, Tanaka said, "Hey, you know that guy over in publicity…?"'

The name *Gojira* would turn out to be a great choice, but in the beginning it was very confusing. 'Very few people, even the cast, knew what Gojira would be', says actor Yoshio Tsuchiya. 'Since the name was derived from *kujira* (whale) and gorilla, I imagined some kind of giant aquatic gorilla'.

GETTING STARTED

Since the scenes using human actors were filmed separately from the special-effects monster footage, Honda didn't have to wait for Tanaka to work out the monster details before beginning to film.

And he didn't: 'Honda would direct me to act surprised that Gojira was coming', recalled actor Yu Fujiki, who played a sailor in the film. 'But since I didn't know what Gojira would look like, it was kind of weird. So I asked Honda what Gojira would be like, and he said, "I don't know, but anyway, the monster is coming!"'.

For Part II of *How to Make a Monster*, turn to page 139.

The Gold rush of 2075? Scientists think there's gold on Mars, Venus, and Mercury.

DUMB CROOKS

With crooks like these, we hardly need the police.
Here's proof that crime doesn't pay.

GIVE ME ALL YOUR COUPONS

OSWEGO, New York – 'His name may be Jesse James, but that's where any similarity ends. Jesse Clyde James IV was arrested last week after he used his shopper's bonus card to get a discount...just before allegedly robbing a grocery store.

'Police said James asked a market clerk if three pies would be cheaper if he used his card. The clerk scanned the card. Then James and two accomplices pulled out a pellet gun and demanded money, police said. They made off with $600. James was arrested soon after'.

– Medford, Oregon, *Mail Tribune*, 8 June, 1999

MUG SHOT

'There are dumb criminals, and then there's the fellow who was found guilty of stealing Matthew Holden's car in London. In the glove compartment, the thief found a camera, which his girlfriend used to photograph him posing with the car in front of his own house. The vehicle was later recovered – with the camera and film still inside. Holden had it developed and brought the prints to the cops on the case...who recognized the crook, and arrested him'.

– *Christian Science Monitor*, 26 July, 1999

CAUGHT WITH HIS PANTS DOWN

'Knife-wielding James Boulder was caught in September 1993 when his [trousers] fell down as he fled from a store in New Jersey that he'd just robbed. He then tripped over a fire hydrant and knocked himself out'.

– The *Fortean Times* Book *lnept Crime*

DUMB AND UNLUCKY

CARDIFF, Wales – 'Mark Cason, 29, decided to rob a local post office. He purchased gloves and a mask but forgot to put them on....

'Mark took more than [£10,000], but his arms were so full he could not open the post office door to leave. So he asked two children to hold the door for him. They did, and jotted down his car licence number as he pulled into traffic.

'Mark promptly got stuck in a traffic jam, so he ran to a train station, where he caught a train to a nearby town. He checked into a hotel using a fake name and said to the clerk, 'If the police ask for me, I'm not here'. He asked if he could put 'a large amount of money' in the hotel safe.

'When police arrived, Mark told them his occupation was "armed robber". He was sentenced to five years in prison'.

– *The Portland Oregonian*

NO ANCHOVIES, PLEASE

'Christopher Kennedy, 36, and Johnny Poston, 26, allegedly ordered a couple of pizzas using their real names, phone number and home address. When the delivery man had trouble finding their house, he called and arranged to meet the two men nearby.

'"The delivery person got out carrying the pizzas and they put a gun to his face", Lt. Julius Lee said. "So the delivery person threw the pizzas at them, got back in his car and drove off". He called the police, who had no problem finding the correct house. The pair was charged with armed robbery'.

– *Dumb Crooks Web site*

WOULD YOU LIKE FRIES WITH THAT GUN?

YPSILANTI, Michigan – 'The *Ann Arbor News* reported that a man failed to rob a Burger King because the clerk told him he couldn't open the cash register without a food order. So the man ordered onion rings, but the clerk informed him that they weren't available for breakfast. The frustrated robber left'.

– *A Treasury of Police Humour*

RIGHTEOUSLY INDIGNANT

'A robbery suspect in a Los Angeles police lineup apparently just couldn't control himself. When detectives asked each man in the lineup to repeat the words, "Give me all your money or I'll shoot", the man shouted *"That's not what I said!"*'.

– *The Edge*, 12 April, 1999

Real Tennis was the first racket game. Falkland Palace (1541) in Fife is the oldest court in use.

THE MIND EXPANDER

Aldous Huxley (1894-1963). With a name like that, he was never going to be an accountant or a train driver. It's the sort of name you'd give to a wizard or a philosopher – and that's kind-of-sort-of what this English man of letters was.

Huxley was born in July 1894 into a wealthy and brilliant family of eminent scientists and intellectuals. His grandfather Thomas Henry Huxley was a colleague and contemporary of Darwin, and one of his greatest champions. Given his highly evolved pedigree, it is no surprise that Aldous attended Eton and then sailed through his English degree at Oxford.

BLIND AMBITION

But it wasn't all plain sailing for the young Huxley. His beloved mother died of cancer when he was 14, one of his brothers committed suicide, and he lost several college friends during World War I. Not only that, while he was still at school Huxley developed a serious eye infection that left him blind for more than two years. He didn't let blindness defeat him, though; he taught himself Braille in just three weeks and even learned to play the piano. (He would play the 'right hand' notes of a song written in Braille while reading them with his left hand, and vice versa, until he had the piece off by heart.)

Huxley eventually regained partial vision, although not enough to study medicine as he'd originally intended. Years later he improved his eyesight by diligently doing a series of exercises called the Bates Method. Likewise, he corrected a pronounced slouch (he was very tall and thin) by practising back exercises now well-known as the Alexander Technique.

AMONG THE VERY BRIGHT YOUNG THINGS

At Oxford, Huxley's contemporaries included soon-to-be-famous literary stars like D.H. Lawrence and Virginia Woolf. After graduating, he held a series of odd jobs in farming, office work and teaching (which he hated). Huxley then sat down to write some plays. They brought in some money, so he decided to be a writer.

In the post-war years of the 1920s, wealthy and upper-class

Ben Nevis is one of the cloudiest places in the UK. It averages 736 hours of sunshine yearly.

'Bright Young Things' enjoyed a life of luxurious decadence. Huxley, having learned the hard way the importance of humanity over pleasure and materialism, ruthlessly mocked their shallow self-indulgence in his early satirical writings, such as *Antic Hay*.

BEAT ROOTS

During his prodigious career Huxley wrote almost 50 books including *Brave New World*, his best-known work. This chilling, futuristic classic portrays Huxley's increasing concern that modern society, with its constant stream of new gadgets, was turning people into mindless robots. (Huxley's early predictions, which included genetic engineering and environmental pollution, turned out to be amazingly accurate.) With the publication of more novels and articles (not least *Doors of Perception*), Huxley came to be considered a sage and an advocate for the loosening up of social values. In his own, oh-so-English, way he was an influence on the leading figures of the 1950s 'Beat Generation', such as Jack Kerouac. Huxley's books repeatedly explored the complexity of human nature – that the 'ideal' human should combine emotions with rational thought in a healthy manner.

MAKING MOVIES

In 1937 Huxley settled in Hollywood with his first wife, Maria. To supplement his income he took a day job as a screenwriter, and wrote intelligent, witty scripts for movies such as *Jane Eyre*, *Pride and Prejudice* and a biopic about Madame Curie. If he was around today, it's unlikely he would have been asked to lend his pen to *Showgirls* or *Top Gun*. Whilst in Hollywood, Huxley's glamorous new movie star chums included Greta Garbo. But he wasn't just living the high life: during the run-up to World War II, Huxley involved himself in the pacifist movement, inspired by his hero, Mahatma Gandhi.

CONSTANTLY CRAVING INSIGHT

One abiding feature of Huxley's life was his never-ending quest for knowledge. During his time in the U.S., Huxley, his wife and his friend and fellow writer Gerald Heard would take frequent car tours around the country. Huxley would stash a set of the *Encyclopaedia Britannica* in the back of the car, reading it inces-

Side by side, 2,000 cells of the human body would cover about three square centimetres.

santly as they drove. In fact, his literally encyclopedic knowledge was a source of amusement among his friends. The philosopher Bertrand Russell joked of Huxley: 'You could always tell by his conversation which volume of the *Encylopaedia Britannica* he'd been reading. One day it wold be Alps, Andes and Apennines, and the next it would be Himalayas and Hippocratic Oath'.

But it seems the more Huxley learned, the more it made him question things. The horrors of two world wars made him question the very meaning of existence itself, and he later developed the idea that brainpower alone wouldn't help him to develop the deeper understanding of life he craved. Instead, under the influence of Gerald Heard, Huxley began to study Eastern religions such as Buddhism and Hinduism. This led him to embrace mysticism, which he claimed could bring about peace and cure the world's ills. As he usually did with any newly absorbed knowledge, Huxley added these fresh ideas to his writings.

TURN HIM ON, BUT DISCREETLY

Eventually, Huxley's quest for mystic knowledge led him to try radical solutions. In 1953, he visited Dr. Humphrey Osmond, an English psychiatrist who was experimenting with mescaline as a method of treating his patients. Mescaline is a chemical extracted from the peyote cactus that causes hallucinations. Huxley began using mescaline, saying the trips it caused helped him to explore knowledge beyond the limits of human perception. Even though he invented the word 'psychedelic' to refer to an opening of the mind, Huxley didn't intend to become a founding father of the 1960s 'tune in, turn on, drop out' generation, with its routine use of hallucinogenic drugs. Rather, he thought experimenting with drugs like LSD, which was legal at the time, should be done only by professionals for research purposes.

In the years before his death from cancer in 1963, Huxley received an abundance of literary awards. But far greater than these plaudits is his legacy of insightful, influential writing and ideas that continue to inspire knowledge-seekers to this day.

* * *

'Single-mindedness is all very well in cows or baboons; in an animal claiming to belong to the same species as Shakespeare it is simply disgraceful.'

– Huxley

Aristotle called the wind 'the dry sighs of the breathing Earth'.

'SPEAK FOR YOURSELF, JOHN!'

Ever let someone speak for you? Sometimes it works, sometimes it doesn't. The other day Uncle John was in the – ahem – reading room with nothing but a book of poetry. He opened it to Longfellow's 'The Courtship of Myles Standish', and emerged wondering out loud how often 'that sort of thing' happened. We took the hint and began looking for examples. Here's what we found.

MARRIAGE PROPOSAL
Who Said It: John Alden
Speaking For: Myles Standish
What Happened: As military leader of the pilgrims, Capt. Myles Standish was fearless. With ladies, however, he was the opposite. Standish was so afraid of expressing his love to Priscilla Mullens that he asked his young friend Alden to do it for him. The only problem: Alden was also in love with Mullens. Nonetheless, he went off to proclaim Standish's love to the woman, keeping his own a secret.

As it happened, Mullens harboured her own secret feelings for Alden. When Alden delivered Standish's proposal instead, legend has it she replied, 'Why don't you speak for yourself, John?'
Note: Mullens married Alden. Standish supposedly went into the woods for a few days and sulked. He eventually got over it.

HISTORIC SPEECH
Who Said It: Norman Shelley
Speaking For: Winston Churchill
What Happened: A week after the demoralizing defeat of British and French troops by Germany at Dunkirk in 1940, Prime Minister Winston Churchill made one of the most stirring radio addresses in history. Speaking to the nation, he declared, in no uncertain terms, that his countrymen would not fold.

> We shall fight on the beaches, we shall fight on the landing grounds, we shall fight in the fields and in the streets, we shall fight in the hills; we shall never surrender.

Historians say that this specific speech provided the morale boost that helped Britain summon the strength to continue the war effort – and ultimately win.

But Churchill didn't make the speech. He was 'too busy to appear on the radio', so he asked Shelley to fill in – an actor who had perfected the Churchillian delivery to such a degree that few people could pick which voice was Shelley's and which was Churchill's.

PRESIDENTIAL QUOTE

Who Said It: Larry Speakes
Speaking For: President Ronald Reagan
What Happened: In 1985 President Reagan and Soviet premier Mikhail Gorbachev met for a summit in Reykjavik, Iceland. Afterward, Speakes told the press that Reagan had declared to the Russian: 'There is much that divides us, but I believe the world breathes easier because we are talking together'.

In truth, Reagan hadn't said it – or anything Speakes considered worth quoting that day. So the press secretary made it up. No one at the White House objected at the time. But when Speakes later admitted it in his 1988 book *Speaking Out*, all hell broke loose. The press was 'outraged', and Reagan (who had to have at least implicitly condoned it at the time) strongly condemned the quotes as 'fiction'. Speakes paid for it: he was pressured to resign his job as senior public relations officer at Merrill Lynch, which had hired him after he left the White House. Speakes later apologized publicly for his 'mistake'.

PHILOSOPHICAL RAMBLINGS

Who Said It: Yoda
Speaking For: Obi-Wan-Kenobi (Alec Guinness)
What Happened: On the set of *The Empire Strikes Back*, Alec Guinness had an easy way of avoiding dialogue he didn't feel comfortable saying. Yoda was in nearly all of his scenes, so 'if he didn't want to deliver one of his philosophical speeches', Dale Pollock writes in his book *Skywalking*, 'he'd say to the director, "Why doesn't the little green thing do this one?"' And Lucas would accommodate him.

Dolly the sheep was cloned from a mammary cell. She was named after Ms. Parton.

WIGS IN THE DOCK

Silence in court! Stop that sniggering! No, it's not a dead ferret on the judge's head! Of all the odd rituals in English law is anything odder than making judges and barristers wear wigs in court?

Surely that's not the judge's real hair, making him look like a superannuated sheep. Of course not, it's a wig – and a ruddy stupid one at that. No court is complete without a full complement of be-wigged advocates, swapping legal arguments whilst dressed as Regency pantomine villains. But why? Well, it turns out the history of legal wigs is long and as dignified as it's possible for anything made out of horsehair to be.

LOOK SMART

The courtroom falls silent as the judge rises to pass sentence. But first he zips up his tracksuit top and adjusts his backwards-facing baseball cap to a jauntier angle and... It's not a very likely scenario, is it? The legal system needs to look as authoritative as it sounds, and it's hard to picture that courtroom scene without a stern-faced judge in formal attire topped off by a wig.

HAIR TODAY

The wig, that most solemn piece of head furniture, dates back to ancient times. Some have been found buried with the remains of Egyptian mummies. By contrast, its legal role came relatively recently, in 1680. There had long been some kind of official headgear used in court until then – in early Tudor times it was the flat, black cap. In 17th century fashion, wigs or periwigs (the word comes from the French *perruque*) were a part of everyday culture and a natural badge of authority for the legal authorities. Their formal black dress worn in court dated from a little later, 1714, originally donned as a sign of mourning for Queen Anne.

WIGGED OUT

Times change and those white wigs the judges still wear would look distinctly odd in any other workplace – even bishops no longer sport wigs and they can hardly be accused of living on the edge of fashion. Only judges and barristers are be-wigged in the 21st century. As a sign of modernity, wigs are not worn during cases involving children.

It's not even as if wearing a wig is comfortable. True, they can cover a multitude of sins for some of the more follically-challenged members of the legal community, but that's not a great excuse for continuing to wear them in this day and age. It seems that the reason judges and barristers still wear them is that great old British stand-by: tradition.

HAIR TODAY

All the finest wigs are made by hand and start at around £300-£350 for the basic barrister style (which can last for an entire career), worn on the back of the head with a ponytail hanging down. The best part of £1,500 goes on those full shoulder-length ones used for ceremonial purposes (from which we get the term 'big wig' for someone who fancies themselves as a major player). Modern wigs are made of horsehair, although they were originally made from human hair.

The owner will keep a wig in good shape by taking it to a professional cleaner, although there is a bonus to be had in them looking a little shabby, as it conveys a sense of age and, hopefully, wisdom. For junior barristers, that authority is much needed and for the same reason it's a source of annoyance for solicitors that they are not allowed to wear wigs in court (apart from solicitor Q.C.s). Judges have another use for the wig – as a disguise, figuring that, once they've taken it off after work, it's far less likely they might be recognized on the street and have an awkward discussion with someone they once put away for a long stretch.

TO WIG OR NOT TO WIG

These days, experts are divided over whether to keep wigs in court. Scottish lawyers came out broadly for wigs when surveyed in late 2002. The next year, another survey found that only 30 per cent of the public favoured wig wearing, in line with what senior legal types think (the junior members are still quite taken with the idea). It remains to be seen whether or not this outmoded yet oddly timeless accessory will survive another 300 years.

Southport has a lawnmower museum with more than 200 machines on display.

A BRIEF HISTORY OF BUGS BUNNY

Who's your favourite cartoon character? Ear's ours.

IMPRESSIVE STATS

Bugs Bunny is the world's most popular rabbit:

• Since 1939, he has starred in more than 175 films.

• He's been nominated for three Oscars, and won one – in 1958, for *Knighty Knight, Bugs* (with Yosemite Sam).

• Every year from 1945 to 1961, he was voted 'top animated character' by U.S. cinema owners (when they still showed cartoons in theatres).

• In 1985 he became only the second cartoon character to be given a star on the Hollywood Walk of Fame (Mickey Mouse was the first).

• For almost 30 years, starting in 1960, he had one of the top-rated shows on U.S. Saturday-morning TV.

• In 1976, when researchers polled Americans on their favourite characters, real and imaginary, Bugs came in second – behind Abraham Lincoln.

THE INSPIRATIONS

Bugs was born in the 1930s, but cartoon historians say his ancestry goes further back. A few direct descendents:

• Zomo. You may not have heard of this African folk-rabbit, but he's world-famous. Joe Adamson writes in *Bugs Bunny: Fifty Years and Only One Grey Hare:*

> Like jazz and rock 'n' roll, Bugs has at least some of his roots in black culture. Zomo is the trickster rabbit from Central and Eastern Africa who gained audience sympathy by being smaller than his oppressors and turning the tables on them through cleverness – thousands of years before Eastman invented film. A con artist, a masquerader, ruthless and suave, in control of the situation. Specialized in impersonating women.

• Br'er Rabbit. Slaves brought Zomo to America and in the New World, he became Br'er Rabbit, whose stories were retold by Joel

Chandler Harris in *Tales of Uncle Remus* (1880). Typical plot: Br'er Fox catches Br'er Rabbit, who begs not to be thrown in the briar-patch (which is exactly where he wants to go). Br'er Fox falls for it, tosses him in, and the rabbit laughs all the way home. Occasionally, you'll see Bugs pull the same trick.

Closer to home, a few comedic geniuses helped mould Bugs:
• Charlie Chaplin. 'It was Chaplin who established that "gestures and actions expressing attitude" give a screen character life', Adamson writes. The Looney Tunes directors, all fans of Chaplin, even stole many of his gags. For example:

> The abrupt and shocking kiss Charlie plants (on) someone who's getting too close for comfort in *The Floorwalker* went on to become one of Bugs' favourite ways to upset his adversaries. (And) the walking broomstick in *Bewitched Bunny* does Chaplin's trademark turn, with one foot in the air, at every corner.

There are literally dozens of other Chaplin rip-offs. Bugs also lifted bits from silent comedians Harold Lloyd and Buster Keaton.
• Groucho Marx. 'Bugs uses his carrot as a prop, just as Groucho used his cigar', points out Stefan Kanfer in *Serious Business*. 'Eventually Bugs even stole Marx's response to an insult: "Of course you know, this means war!"'

TIMELINE
1937: Warner Bros. animation director Tex Avery makes *Porky's Duck Hunt*. Porky Pig hunted a screwball duck named Daffy – 'who didn't get scared and run away when somebody pointed a gun at him, but leapt and hopped all over the place like a maniac'. 'When it hit the theatres', recalls another director, 'it was like an explosion'.
1938: Warner Bros. director Ben 'Bugs' Hardaway remakes the cartoon with a rabbit instead of a duck, as *Porky's Hare Hunt*. Says one of Bugs's creators: 'That rabbit was just Daffy Duck in a rabbit suit'.
1939: Bugs Hardaway decides to remake *Porky's Hare Hunt* with a new rabbit (as *Hare-um Scare-um*). Cartoonist Charlie Thorson comes up with a grey and white rabbit with large buck teeth. He labels his sketches 'Bugs Bunny'.
1940: Director Tex Avery becomes the real father of Bugs Bunny

Lubberwort is another word for junk food.

with *A Wild Hare*. Bugs is changed from a Daffyesque lunatic to a streetsmart wiseass. 'We decided he was going to be a smart-aleck rabbit, but casual about it', Avery recalled. 'His opening line was "What's up, Doc?" It floored 'em!...Here's a guy with a gun in his face!...They expected the rabbit to scream, or anything but make a casual remark....It got such a laugh that we said, "Let's use that every chance we get". It became a series of "What's Up, Docs?" That set his entire character. He was always in command, in the face of all types of dangers'.

• Bugs also gets his voice in *A Wild Hare*. Mel Blanc, who did most Looney Tunes voices, had been having a hard time finding one for the rabbit – until Bugs Hardaway showed him the latest sketch for *A Wild Hare*. Blanc wrote:

> He'd obviously had some work done. His posture had improved, he'd shed some weight, and his protruding front teeth weren't as pronounced. The most significant change, however, was in his facial expression. No longer just goofy, he was a sly looking rascal.

'A tough little stinker, ain't he'? Hardaway commented – and the light went on in Blanc's brain.

> A tough little stinker....In my mind I heard a Brooklyn accent....To anyone living west of the Hudson River at that time, Brooklynites were associated with con artists and crooks....Consequently, the new, improved Bugs Bunny wouldn't say jerk, he'd say joik.

• The rabbit is now so popular that he needs a name. According to some sources, he is about to be dubbed 'Happy Rabbit'. Tex Avery wants 'Jack E. Rabbit'. But when Thorson's year-old drawing labelled 'Bugs Bunny' is found, producer Leon Schlessinger chooses that. Avery hates it. 'That's sissy', he complains. 'Mine's a rabbit. A tall, lanky, mean rabbit. He isn't a fuzzy little bunny!' But the name sticks.

1941: Bugs Bunny becomes competitive. Four extremely talented directors – Avery, Friz Freleng, Bob Clampett, and Chuck Jones – try to top each other by adding new gags and extra aspects to Bugs' personality. It's the key to the character's success – he's constantly growing. 'As each director added new levels to this character', Adamson explains, 'it was picked up by the others and became a part of the mix'.

Snow skiing rule of thumb: most men fall on their faces, most women on their behinds.

1943: Animator Robert McKimson (later a director himself), working for Bob Clampett, refines Bugs's features into what they are today. 'We made him cuter, brought his head and cheeks out a little more and gave him just a little nose', McKimson says. He looks more 'elfin' and less 'ratlike' now.
1945: During World War II, Bugs has become a 'sort of national mascot'. Critic Richard Schickel writes: 'In the war years, when he flourished most gloriously, Bugs Bunny embodied the cocky humour of a nation that had survived its economic crisis (in surprisingly good shape), and was facing a terrible war with grace, gallantry, humour and solidarity that was equally surprising'. By the end of the war, Bugs isn't just a cartoon character, but an American icon.

BUGS FACTS

Saved by a Hare. The inspiration for the original rabbit came from Walt Disney. In 1935 Disney put out a cartoon featuring a character called Max Hare. Hardaway's rabbit looks suspiciously like Max.

Trademarks. Where did Bugs's carrot-crunching and 'What's up, Doc?' come from? No one's sure, but experts have suggested they might have been inspired by a couple of popular films:

• In Frank Capra's 1934 Oscar-winning comedy, *It Happened One Night*, Clark Gable nervously munches on carrots.

• In the classic 1939 screwball comedy *My Man Godfrey*, William Powell uses the line 'What's up, Duke?' repeatedly.

On the other hand, Tex Avery had a habit of calling everyone Doc – so he may have inspired the phrase. (Mel Blanc also claims in his autobiography that he ad-libbed the line, but he seems to take credit for everything – so we don't believe him.)

Tough Act. Blanc, Bugs' voice, says that recording the 'What's up, Doc?' line turned out to be the most physically challenging part of doing the voice:

> 'What's up, Doc?' was incomplete without the sound of the rabbit nibbling on the carrot, which presented problems. First of all, I don't especially like carrots, at least not raw. And second, I found it impossible to chew, swallow, and be ready to say my next line. We tried substituting other vegetables, including apples and celery, but with unsatisfactory results. The

The village of Edensor was moved in the 1830s as it spoiled the view from Chatsworth House.

> solution was to stop recording so that I could spit out the carrot into the wastebasket and then proceed with the script. In the course of a recording session I usually went through enough carrots to fill several wastebaskets. Bugs Bunny did for carrots what Popeye the Sailor did for spinach. How many…children were coerced into eating their carrots by mothers cooing… 'but Bugs Bunny eats his carrots'. If only they had known.

Eat Your Veggies. Actually, there were pressures to switch from carrots. 'The Utah Celery Company of Salt Lake City offered to keep all the studio's staffers well supplied with their product if Bugs would only switch from carrots to celery', Adamson reports. '(And) later, the Broccoli Institute of America strongly urged The Bunny to sample their product once in a while….Mel Blanc would have been happy to switch…but carrots were Bugs's trademark'.

Surprise Hit. To his creators, Bugs Bunny was just another character that would probably run in a few cartoons and fade unnoticed into obscurity. 'We didn't feel that we had anything', Avery recounted years later, 'until we got it on the screen and it got a few laughs. After we ran it and previewed it and so forth, Warner's liked it, the exhibitors liked it, and so of course (the producer) ran down and said, "Boy, give us as many of those as you can!" Which we did'.

Bugs Bunny became so popular with the public that he got laughs even when he didn't deserve them. 'He could do no wrong', remembers dialogue writer Michael Maltese. 'We had quite a few lousy Bugs Bunnies. We'd say, "Well we haven't got time. Let's do it". And we'd do it, and the audience would laugh. They loved that rabbit'.

* * *

LOONEY TRIVIA

• The name 'Looney Tunes' is a takeoff on Walt Disney's popular 1930s cartoon series, 'Silly Symphonies'.

• The real name of the Looney Tunes theme song is 'The Merry-Go-Round Broke Down'. It's a pop tune from the 1930s.

• The first Looney Tune, *Sinking in the Bathtub*, appeared in 1930. It featured a character called Bosko.

Average surface temperature of Venus: 864°F, the hottest of any planet in the solar system.

LIFE AFTER DEATH

What do Sherlock Holmes, Davy Crockett, and Superman have in common? They were all popular characters whose creators killed them off – and then had to bring them back from the dead.

SHERLOCK HOLMES

Born: 1887 – Died: 1893
Resurrected: 1903

Background: Sherlock Holmes first appeared in 1887 but didn't become famous until 1891, when the story 'A Scandal in Bohemia' was published in London's *Strand* magazine. Overnight, Holmes and his creator, Arthur Conan Doyle, became national celebrities, and the public wanted more.

Over the next two years, Doyle turned out an average of one new story per month. But the more popular Holmes became, the less Doyle liked him. Doyle considered his historical novels to be his real work and felt that Holmes kept people from appreciating them. By 1893, Doyle loathed the detective.

Untimely Death: In 1893, at the end of *Strand's* 24th Holmes story, Doyle placed Holmes on top of Switzerland's Reichenbach Falls, grappling with his arch-enemy, Professor Moriarty. Then he had both characters plunge to their deaths.

The author gleefully wrote to his mother: 'The gentleman vanishes, never to return!' But others weren't so happy. Twenty thousand *Strand* readers (an enormous number for the time) cancelled their subscriptions; businessmen in London wore black bands to mourn Holmes' death; Doyle was inundated with letters. But he was unmoved, and snapped: 'Holmes is at the bottom of Reichenbach Falls, and there he stays'.

Resurrection: What could change Doyle's mind? Money. In 1903 *McClure's* (a U.S. magazine) offered him the astronomical sum of $5,000 dollars per story if he would resurrect the character – and *Strand* offered more than half that for the British publication rights. Doyle decided to 'accept as much money as slightly deranged editors were willing to pay'. Soon after, excited readers learned that Holmes hadn't died after all; he had merely gone into hiding – and was now ready to come back.

The publisher couldn't print copies of the new Holmes stories fast enough. People waited in huge queues and mobbed bookstalls to get them. Doyle continued writing about Sherlock Holmes until 1927, then retired the detective for good.

DAVY CROCKETT

Born: 15 December, 1954 – Died: 23 February, 1955
Resurrected: 16 November, 1955

Background: Walt Disney's first TV programme, *Disneyland*, began in October 1954. A few months later, it featured TV's first miniseries – a three-part adventure about a real-life Tennessee politician and frontiersman named Davy Crockett. The Disney version was mostly fiction, but America took it to heart. One critic recalls, 'Disney's Crockett instantly became the most popular hero television had ever seen. Just about every boy in the country owned a coonskin cap like Davy's'. Coonskin caps sold so quickly that raccoons actually became hard to find – forcing hat makers to use foxes and rabbits instead. All Crockett items – colouring books, play sets, bubblegum cards, etc. – sold like wildfire. It was TV's first huge, merchandising fad, and it was making Disney a fortune.

Untimely Death: There was just one problem – when the three episodes had been filmed months earlier, no one at Disney had a clue the public would respond so enthusiastically. So they followed Crockett's standard biography, and killed him off at the end of the third episode (while defending the Alamo). Uncle Walt couldn't believe the blunder. 'We had one of the biggest hits in television history', he moaned, 'and there we were with a dead hero'.

Resurrection: 'This was the first time that a major hero had died in a television series', writes Jeff Rovin in The Great TV Heroes, 'and many youngsters went into mourning for the noble warrior.

More important, however, is the way in which television and the profit incentive were able to conquer death! Disney was not so foolish as to let a financial giant stay long expired'.

The company went to work on new episodes, which they set before the Alamo. But it took too long to produce them. 'We tried to come back with two more called *The Legend of Davy Crockett*',

Walt Disney told a reporter, 'but by that time the fever had run its course'. The King of the Wild Frontier returned on 16 November, 1955, in *Davy Crockett's Keelboat Race* and 14 December, 1955, in *Davy Crockett and the River Pirates*.

'Those two never did catch on the way the original three did', Disney sighed. After that, Crockett stayed dead.

SUPERMAN

Born: 1938 – Died: 18 November, 1992
Resurrected: 1993

Background: DC Comics' Superman was the nation's first superhero. He was introduced in 1938, took the nation by storm, and over the next three decades, became the most successful comic book character in history.

Untimely Death: By the 1990s, comics had changed. They featured complex heroes who were tormented by angst and who killed their foes in vengeful bloodbaths. Comic fans delighted in 'the smart-aleck snarl of Wolverine', and 'the devilish depravity of Spawn'. But Superman never killed his enemies; he preferred to turn them over to the proper authorities. Fans found his patriotism and politeness – boring. Superman's comic sales 'plummeted faster than a speeding bullet', so DC Comics made plans to kill him.

The impending death was nationwide news in the U.S. Social commentators lamented a society that could no longer find interest in a 'decent' hero. Comic stores played up the hype, flying flags with the Superman 'S' dripping blood, displaying Superman art, and having the 'Death' issue delivered in hearses. Sales of Superman skyrocketed, but after a few issues that explored the world without Superman, DC stopped publishing the title.

Resurrection: But not for long. It turned out that Superman's death was a publicity stunt. Four months later, he was back. It turned out his dead body had been taken to a space-age 'regeneration centre' and brought back to life. Buyers of the 'Death' issue who thought they were getting a collector's item were outraged, and loyal fans resented DC's tricking them. But the publicity increased sales, at least temporarily – leading DC's executive editor Mike Carlin to proclaim death 'good for Superman'.

SPECIAL UNDERWEAR

At the BRI, we don't believe in keeping underwear innovations under cover. Here are three to take us into the future.

SAFETY FIRST

'A Vermont inventor has figured out a way to prevent senior citizens from breaking bones when they take a spill: underwear air bags. Carl Clark, who also devised the first air bags for Lockheed Martin in the 1960s, says his emergency underwear has a sensor that automatically inflates two cushions around the wearer's hips when it detects the person starting to fall'.

– Los Angeles Times

LARGER THAN LIEE

'A Tokyo man made international news recently when his inflatable underpants accidentally went off in the subway. He had invented the special underwear to allay his phobia of drowning. The good news is, they worked, inflating to 30 times their normal size. They had to be stabbed with a pencil to stop them from crushing other passengers'.

– The Edge

THE ARMAGEDDON BRA

Nostradamus' prophecies are popular in Japan; millions there believed his prophecy that a terrible calamity would strike in July 1999 – a war that would kill a third of the world's population. One company decided to take advantage of this, as *The Times* reported:

'Now the lingerie firm, Triumph International Japan, is cashing in on the nation's doomsday boom with a hi-tech "Armageddon Bra" that alerts its wearer to incoming missiles.

'Presented at a fashion show yesterday, the "Armageddon Bra" includes a sensor on the shoulder strap, and a control box to warn of objects falling from the skies.

'Ideally the Armageddon Bra should be worn without outer garments to work efficiently'.

– The Times

Pharmacist rule of thumb: if it's a drug, it has a side effect.

MY BODY LIES OVER THE OCEAN: PART I

This section was inspired by a magazine article about the fact that Albert Einstein's brain was removed when he died. We at the BRI wondered if other famous people 'lost' a body part or two when they died. We did a little research – and were surprised by what we found.

GALILEO'S MIDDLE FINGER

Where It's Located: Museum of the History of Science, Florence, Italy

How It Got There: In 1737, when Galileo's body was being moved from a storage closet to its final resting place in a mausoleum in the church of Santa Croce, a nobleman named Anton Francesco Gori cut off three fingers from Galileo's right hand for a souvenir. The middle finger was eventually acquired by the Museum of the History of Science; the other two surviving fingers 'are in a private collection'.

NAPOLEON'S 'NOBLE ORGAN'

Where It's Located: Columbia University's College of Physicians and Surgeons

How It Got There: In 1828 Abbé Ange Paul Vignali, the priest who administered last rites to Napoleon in 1821, was murdered. Among the many Napoleonic souvenirs found in Abbé Vignali's personal effects was the most personal effect of all – a tiny, 'unpleasant looking piece of desiccated tissue' alleged to be Napoleon's private part – which was supposedly removed from the deposed emperor's corpse following his autopsy.

The artifact remained in the Vignali family until 1916, when it was sold to a London dealer of rare books. In 1924 it was sold to Dr. Abraham Rosenbach, who placed the withered item 'inside a glass casket, in a tasteful case of blue morocco leather and velvet bearing Napoleon's crest', where it was displayed to friends, family, and just about anyone else who asked to see it. 'Few so intimate portions of a man's anatomy', Rosenbach's biographer writes, 'have ever been displayed to so many'.

Extra! Extra! The UK has 1,286 local newspapers, including 642 weekly free titles.

In November 1944, the 'shriveled short arm', – which by now was said to look like 'a maltreated strip of buckskin shoelace, or a shriveled eel' – was sold to a Philadelphia autograph dealer named Bruce Gimelson. He tried to auction it at Christie's, but withdrew it when it 'failed to attract a $40,000 minimum bid'. Seven years later, he sold it to a urologist named John K. Lattimer for a mere $3,000. Dr. Lattimer owns it to this day, and it's only one of the many odd but historically significant items in his collection. As Harvey Rachlin reports in *Lucy's Bones, Sacred Stones, and Einstein's Brain*, Dr. Lattimer also owns 'Hermann Goering's suicide capsule container, a lock of Hitler's hair, and the nooses used to hang two of the conspirators for the murder of President Lincoln, Mary Surratt and Lewis Powell'.

EINSTEIN'S BRAIN

Where It's Located: Lawrence, Kansas

How it Got There: When Einstein died in April 1955, he left a request that his friend and colleague Dr. Harry Zimmerman examine his brain. So Dr. Thomas Harvey, the pathologist who performed the autopsy on Einstein, removed the brain and had it cut into 200 pieces, some of which he gave to Zimmerman. The rest (representing about 75 per cent of Einstein's brain) he took home and stored in formaldehyde-filled jars that he kept under his sink for nearly 40 years – occasionally doling out specimens to brain researchers upon request. (One such researcher keeps his section in his refrigerator, in a jar marked 'Big Al's Brain'.)

The last time he was heard of, Harvey, who'd lost his medical licence and was working in a plastics factory, was looking for a research lab or some other institution to take possession of Einstein's brain and preserve it for posterity.

PHAR LAP'S HEART

Where It's Located: National Museum, Canberra

How It Got There: Phar Lap was one of the greatest racehorses of all time. He was born in New Zealand in 1926 and sold for the bargain price of 160 guineas. He was sent to Australia and soon became a racing legend by winning 37 out of his 51 starts including the 1930 Melbourne Cup. In 1932, he was shipped over to America to race in the prestigious Caliente Handicap, America's richest horse race but died in mysterious circumstances on 4 April 1932. When an autopsy was performed on Phar Lap, it was found that the great gelding's heart weighed 6.4 kilograms compared to the average 4 kilograms. His heart today is housed in Australia's National Museum, Canberra.

OTHER CELEBRITY BODY PARTS

• Walt Whitman's brain. The American poet's organ was donated to the Wistar Institute at the University of Pennsylvania, where it 'was dropped on the floor by a lab technician and was discarded long ago'. The Wistar Institute is no longer accepting new brains.
• Lord Byron's lungs. 'Kept in a jar, somewhere in Greece'.

More on page 143.

* * *

OOPS!

'British education officials were red-faced Friday after having to scrap 48,000 literacy posters sent to teachers with two glaring spelling mistakes. It shouldn't have happened. The Department of Education failed to notice that "vocabulary" was misspelled 'vocabluary' and that pupils were being urged to learn about writing 'though' their own work instead of 'through' it. The posters have been reprinted and sent to schools with letters blaming the blunder on (the proofreaders)'.

– *Reuters*

'Wine merchant William Sokolin had paid $300,000 for a 1787 bottle of Châteaux Margaux once owned by Thomas Jefferson. He presented it before a group of 300 wine collectors at Manhattan's Four Seasons restaurant in 1989, hoping that one of them might offer $519,000 for it. Before bidders could get out their checkbooks, he dropped the bottle and broke it'.

– *Oops!*, by Smith and Decter

Sleeping around: Louis XIV owned 413 beds.

AMAZING LUCK

Sometimes we're blessed with it, sometimes we're cursed with it – dumb luck. Here are some examples of people who've lucked out – for better and for worse.

CELLULAR MEMORY

'In the Dent de Crolles region in France, shepherd Christian Raymond, 23, was rescued from a cliff from which he had been hanging by his fingers. He had called the emergency rescue operator on his cell phone earlier in the day and managed to make another call from the cliff by pressing 'redial' with his nose against the phone, which had fallen down the mountain with him but had landed right beside him'.

– *The Edge*, 25 March, 1999

TRAIN KEPT A-ROLLIN'

'Participants in this tale of survival still can't believe it really happened. Thrown through the steel roof of his car in a head-on collision, a Denver man landed 30 metres away – on railroad tracks, directly in the path of a speeding train. Too late to brake before passing over the body, the engineer stopped as fast as he could and rushed back to the spot, certain he had killed the man. What he found was a guy limping, shaken, but very much alive. His only injury was the broken leg he suffered in the car collision'.

– *Oops*

LUCK BE A LADY

'A mistake on a national Pick 7 ticket was worth $1.6 million to a bettor who selected the wrong number on Breeders' Cup Day.

'The 51-year-old engineer who bought the winning ticket said he punched 11 instead of 1 for his selection in the seventh race.

'"I liked the one and 11 horses in the sixth race, and I liked the No. 1 in the seventh", the bettor said. "But when I punched out my ticket for the seventh, I hit one and 11 – the same numbers I had in the sixth – by mistake".

'The 11 turned out to be Arcangues, the unknown French horse who won the Classic at odds of 133 to 1. It was the largest in Breeders' Cup history'.

In India, playing cards are round.

'He had three other tickets with six winners, too, and collected a total of $1,152,317 after taxes'.

– ***San Francisco Chronicle,* 11 November, 1993**

BLESS THE TORPEDOES!

'A charmed life. That describes the experience of seaman Roy Dikkers during World War II. Sealed in a compartment when a German torpedo struck his tanker, he was freed by a second torpedo explosion. Racing on deck he found the sea around the floundering vessel ablaze with oil fires. He never had to make the fateful decision whether to stay with the sinking ship or risk the fiery sea. A third torpedo blew him far from the scene, beyond the oil slick. Landing near a floating raft, he crawled aboard and was found by a Norwegian freighter three days later'.

– ***Oops***

MY FORTUNE FOR A KISS

'Hauled before a Melbourne court in 1907 for hugging and kissing spinster Hazel Moore when she entered his shop, young Michael O'Connor defended himself by claiming it had been a lovely spring day and he was in high spirits. O'Connor had to serve a few months for breach of peace. So imagine his amazement ten years later when an attorney representing Miss Moore's estate gave him her bequest of £20,000! She left the fortune in memory of the only kiss she had received from a man in her adult life'.

– ***Oops***

AMAZING LOTTERY WINNERS

- 'Randy Halvorson was one of 14 employees to share a $3.4 million jackpot in 1988. The Iowa resident then won $7.2 million with his brother in 1990'.
- 'In Wisconsin, Donald Smith of Amherst has won the state's SuperCash game three times: on 25 May, 1993,17 June, 1994, and 30 July, 1995. He won $250,000 each time. The odds of winning the SuperCash game just once are nearly one in a million'.
- 'Joseph P. Crowley won $3 million in the Ohio lottery in 1987. Six years later, he retired to Boca Raton, Florida, and played the Florida Lotto on Christmas Day of 1993. He won $20 million'.

– ***The Good Luck Book***

If you tried to count off a billion seconds, it would take you 31.7 years.

ANIMAL MYTHS

Here are a few examples of things that some people believe about animals – but just aren't true.

Myth: Bats are blind.
Fact: Bats aren't blind. But they evolved as nocturnal hunters, and can see better in half-light than in daylight.

Myth: Monkeys remove fleas in each other's fur during grooming.
Fact: Monkeys don't have fleas. They're removing dead skin – which they eat.

Myth: Male seahorses can become pregnant and give birth.
Fact: What actually happens is that female seahorse expels eggs into the male's brood pouch, where they are fertilized. And while the male does carry the gestating embryos until they are born 10 days later, he doesn't feed them through a placenta or similar organ (as had previously been thought). Instead, the embryos feed off nourishment in the egg itself – food provided by the female. Basically, the male acts as an incubator.

Myth: Porcupines can shoot their quills when provoked.
Fact: A frightened porcupine tends to run from danger. If a hunter catches it, though, a porcupine will tighten its skin to make the quills stand up – ready to lodge in anything that touches them.

Myth: Whales spout water.
Fact: Whales actually exhale air through their blowholes. This creates a mist or fog that looks like a water spout.

Myth: Moths eat clothes.
Fact: Not exactly. Moths lay their eggs on your clothes, which eventually develop into larvae. It's the larvae that eat tiny parts of your clothes; adult moths do not eat cloth.

Myth: Bumblebee flight violates the laws of aerodynamics.
Fact: Nothing that flies violates the laws of aerodynamics.

There are 115,000 post boxes in the UK. They were first painted red in 1874.

SCOTLAND'S WORST POET

Devotees and fan clubs worldwide celebrate William McGonagall as Scotland's – and perhaps the world's – worst poet. Just how bad does a poet have to be to inspire such devotion?

McGonagall was born in Edinburgh in 1825 but grew up in Dundee, where his father had moved for work. Following in his father's footsteps, McGonagall worked as a hand-loom weaver until mechanization made his job obsolete. In 1877, at the age of 52, he suddenly became convinced that he was a poetic genius. He was inspired to compose a short tribute to a priest he admired. After a weekly paper published the stanzas, his new career – which lasted for the next 25 years – was launched.

DINNER AND A SHOW

McGonagall made a living, just barely, by giving poetry readings and by selling poems on the street. Crowds attended readings just to heckle him. Convinced of his talent, he chose to interpret the laughing, jeering and chucking of food as unwavering admiration.

TRILOGY OF TERROR

In total, McGonagall published over 200 poems, of which his best remembered are a trilogy commemorating the Tay Bridge. The first of these, 'The Railway Bridge of the Silvery Tay', includes this stanza, which is rather morbid for a poem celebrating the completion of a new bridge:

> Beautiful Railway Bridge of the Silv'ry Tay!
> I hope that God will protect all passengers
> By night and by day,
> And that no accident will befall them while crossing
> The Bridge of the Silvery Tay,
> For that would be most awful to be seen,
> Near by Dundee and the Magdalen Green.

There are 373,000 km of road in the UK, from motorways to country lanes.

Unfortunately, McGonagall's hopeless verse was prophetic. Two years later, an accident did happen. The bridge collapsed during a storm, inspiring McGonagall's most famous verse, 'The Tay Bridge Disaster'. The first verse has since been inscribed on a walkway close to the bridge:

Beautiful Railway Bridge of the Silv'ry Tay
Alas! I am very sorry to say
That ninety lives have been taken away
On the last Sabbath day of 1879.
Which will be remember'd for a very long time.

The bridge was rebuilt in 1881, and naturally McGonagall was on the scene, praising the new bridge's 'strong brick piers and buttresses in so grand array', and generally overusing any words he could think of that rhymed with 'Tay'.

THE GRAND DELUSION

Often the butt of practical jokes, McGonagall once received a letter from an Irish 'playwright' who invited him for a lunch date. He was greeted by a group of gentlemen and the phoney writer, who offered McGonagall a large salary for a poetry reading tour around Britain. The promises, of course, were never met and McGonagall realized that he had been duped.

Despite such events, McGonagall remained convinced of his poetic brilliance. In 1878 he even walked to Balmoral Castle, a distance of about 80 km, determined to read Queen Victoria his poetry. (He dreamed of being named Poet Laureate.) At the door he was turned away and told that if he ever came back he would be arrested.

In 1894, McGonagall received a letter from 'King Theebaw of Burmah and the Andaman Islands', who also declared himself a poet. In it, the King (or, more accurately, the group of prankster students pretending to be the king) gave McGonagall the title of Sir William Topaz McGonagall, Knight of the White Elephant of Burmah. Oblivious to the possibility that this was yet another practical joke, McGonagall proudly assumed the title (and his new middle name) until the end of his days.

TWO-FINGERED SALUTE

We've all given someone the 'two-fingered salute' at some point. Many people believe this very British gesture dates back to the 15th century.

During the Hundred Years War, Henry V was en route to Calais in France to meet reinforcements. His army decimated by disease and hunger, he had a mere 6,000 or so weary troops left. But his enemy Charles d'Albret, Constable of France, still had 25,000 well-rested, well-armed troops at his command. The scene was set for the Battle of Agincourt.

VIVE L'ARROGANCE

The French were hugely dismissive of the English, because the French forces consisted of men from noble families and their retainers, while the English army was a ragtag bunch of lesser nobility and rough peasant stock. The French were also contemptuous of the English archers (mainly, in fact, from Wales), even though they were considered to be the best in the world and their arrows could pierce armour at many paces. So sure of victory were the French that they issued a warning – once they had defeated the English, they would cut off the first and middle fingers of any archer left alive, so he would never be able to draw a bow again.

FRENCH TOASTED

History reports the disaster that befell the French from the very beginning of the encounter. Their horses, laden down with knights in heavy armour, became bogged down in mud in front of the English lines, where they were torn to shreds by the arrows of the archers. The battle was over in a matter of hours, with horrendous losses to the French.

The French had no choice but to surrender. Later that day, when their surviving troops and leaders were paraded in front of their victors, the English archers raced to the front and waved their two fingers in front of the faces of the shamed French, in a final act of triumphant defiance. Five hundred years later, we still use this gesture to succinctly demonstrate our contempt.

Researchers say 1 in 4 people admit to nosing about in their host's medicine cabinet.

HOW EN-LIGHTNING

Zap! BRI member Kurt Stark requested these facts about lightning.

Every second, there are 100 to 125 flashes of lightning somewhere on Earth.

A lightning bolt can be anywhere between 61 metres and 32 km long, but the average length, cloud-to-ground, is 3.2 to 16 km.

Lightning speeds toward the Earth at an average of 322,000 kilometres per hour.

The average flash of lightning contains 125 million volts of electricity – enough to light a 100-watt bulb for more than three months.

The chances of being hit by lightning in your lifetime are about 1 in 600,000. Still, anywhere from 500 to 1,000 people are struck by lightning every year in the U.S.

The temperature of a lightning stroke can reach 50,000°F – hotter than the sun's surface.

Lightning bolts actually flicker – a flash is a series of strokes that follow the exact same path as the first one. The record number of strokes ever recorded in a single flash is 47.

When you see a lightning flash, count the seconds until you hear the bang of thunder. Divide by five – sound travels about 1.6 km every five seconds – and this will give you an approximation of the storm's distance from you.

About one-quarter of all lightning strikes occur in open fields; 30 per cent happen in July; 22 per cent in August.

You can get struck by lightning while you're on the phone. It happens to about 2.5 per cent of all lightning-strike victims.

Trees are lightning bolts' favourite targets – lightning is the largest cause of forest fires in the western U.S.

Estimated diameter of a lightning channel: 1.5 to 2.5 centimetres.

A charge of 100 million to 1 billion volts of electricity needs to be generated in a cloud to start a cloud-to-ground lightning strike.

For the last decade, an average of 20 million cloud-to-ground flashes have been counted over the continental U.S. each year.

Top speed of a chicken at full gallop: 14 kmh.

WE AIN'T LION: THE MODERN ZOO IS BORN

It wasn't that long ago that seeing an elephant at London Zoo was about as shocking to the average person as meeting a Martian would be today. Here's the story of how zoos got their start.

OLD-TIME MENAGERIES

People have 'collected' exotic animals for more than 5,000 years. Priests in ancient Egypt raised lions, tigers, and other sacred animals in and around temples, and as early as 1100 B.C., China's Zhou Dynasty established what was called the 'Garden of Intelligence', a 900-acre preserve filled with deer, antelope, birds, fish, and other animals that were studied as well as hunted.

Exotic animals were also popular in ancient Rome, where they were collected by wealthy families and used in gladiator games. Sometimes the lions, tigers, bulls, bears and other creatures fought each other to a bloody death for public amusement; other times they were pitted against Christians, heretics, or condemned criminals (or, if none were available, ordinary criminals). Sometimes the Romans even filled their coliseums with water, so gladiators in boats could hunt water animals like hippos and crocodiles.

These games were so popular – and killed so many animals – that by the time they finally came to an end in the 6th century A.D., numerous species in the Roman empire, including the elephants of North Africa, the hippopotami of Nubia, the lions of Mesopotamia and the tigers of Hycrania, had all been driven to extinction.

THE DARK AGES

When Rome fell in the 5th century A.D., interest in animals declined, and it wasn't until the 13th century that nobles and other wealthy Europeans began collecting animals on a large scale again. They even exchanged them like trading cards.

King Frederick II of Sicily was a typical collector of the era: his menagerie included hyenas, elephants, camels, lions, monkeys, cheetahs and a giraffe – and when he got tired of the giraffe, he swapped it with the sultan of Egypt for a polar bear.

THE LONDON ZOO

In 1235 King Henry III moved his grandfather's animal collection to the Tower of London. The collection included camels, lions, leopards and lynx – and King Louis IX of France contributed an elephant – the first one ever seen in Great Britain. The animals were put on display for the royal family and its guests, but were also occasionally pitted against one another – tigers vs. lions, bears vs. dogs – to entertain royal visitors. However, the novelty eventually wore off, and the animals became neglected.

Then, in 1445, Margaret of Anjou, wife of Henry VI, received a lion as a wedding gift – which inspired her to have the entire Royal Menagerie – what was left of it – restored. But when the royal family moved out of the Tower in the early 1700s, they left their animals behind. That created a problem: if the royal family wasn't going to support the menagerie, who was? Finally, someone came up with the idea of opening the collection to the public, and charging them admission. Price: three half-pence, or if you preferred, a dog or cat to feed to the lions.

CHANGING TIMES

As the British Empire expanded to the far corners of the globe in the early 1800s, interest in exotic animals grew beyond mere curiosity. In 1826 the explorer Sir Stamford Raffles founded the London Zoological Society, which took its name from the ancient Greek word *zoion*, which means 'living being'.

Two years later, the Society moved the royal family's animal collection from the Tower of London to a new site in Regent's Park. It was a big hit with members of the royal family, many of whom contributed animals.

But unlike the Tower of London, the Zoological Park was closed to the public – the animals were 'objects of scientific research', Raffles explained, 'not of vulgar admiration'. Only members of the Zoological society and their guests were allowed to visit. (A written voucher would allow a non-member to enter, and

At the moment of conception, you spent about half an hour as a single cell.

these became very common and were even traded in pubs.)

The public was officially excluded from the 'zoo', as it had become known, until 1846, by which time the novelty had worn off and attendance had fallen dramatically. So the Zoological Society opened its doors to anyone with a penny, and hundreds of thousands of new visitors streamed into the park. 'For the city dweller', Linda Koebler writes in *Zoo*, '(it) provided a place of greenery that was a relief from the ugly, dirty cities of this period'.

The term 'zoo' entered mainstream culture a year after the London Zoological Garden opened to the public, thanks to the popularity of one particular song: 'Walking in the Zoo is an Okay Thing to Do'.

ZOOS IN EUROPE

In the early 1800s, having a public zoo became a status symbol for any European city that considered itself modern and sophisticated. If they still had royal collections of animals available, they quickly converted them to zoological parks. If they didn't, they created new zoos. Zoos in Dublin, Berlin, Frankfurt, Antwerp and Rotterdam were among the best known.

Le Zoo

In France, however, the development of public zoos was slowed by the Revolution of 1789. Common people saw private collections of captive animals as a way for the rich to flaunt their wealth. According to one account, when a mob of revolutionaries arrived at the Ménagerie du Parc to free the animals, 'The crowd wanted the animals set free so that others could catch them and eat them, outraged that these animals grew fat while the people starved. But once the zoo director explained that some of the creatures would eat the crowd rather than vice versa, the du Parc revolutionaries decided to liberate only the more edible captives'.

Cat got your tongue? Did someone call you a cheetah?
Don't monkey around, turn to page 203
for more wild facts about zoos.

ODD JOBS

Looking for an exciting new job? Here's a list of the most unusual-sounding occupations we could find.

Killer Bee Hunter. Your mission: Track down Africanized 'killer' bees, which are migrating north from Central America, and destroy them before they can take up residence in North America.

Chicken Shooter. Fire dead chickens out of a cannon at aircraft to see what kind of damage occurs.

Mother Repairer. It's not what you think. It actually entails repairing metal phonograph record 'mothers' (the master from which records are pressed) by removing dirt and nickel particles from the grooves.

Anthem Man. A unique profession: King Alfonso of Spain was tone deaf so he employed one man whose job was to alert him when the Spanish national anthem was playing (so he would know when to salute).

Worm Collector. Get ready to crawl through grass at night with a torch, to catch the best worms for fishing. Tip: Grab them in the middle to avoid bruising.

Weed Farmer. If you like gardening, here's a change of pace: grow weeds then sell them to chemical companies for herbicide research.

Pig Manure Sniffer. Workers try to recognize chemical markers in manure so researchers can determine which foods make pig manure so foul smelling. Women only, because estrogen increases sensitivity to smell.

Sewage Diver. Put on a diving suit and plunge into a sewage-containment vat. Sound tempting?

Animal Chauffeur. We've only heard of one – a chap named Stephen May. His 'limousine' is equipped with, among other things: a blanketed floor, 20-cm colour television, stereo speakers, and silk flowers.

Flush Tester. A gold star from Uncle John to the gallant professionals who test toilet-bowl standards by trying to flush rags down various toilets.

Armpit Sniffer. Enough said.

FRANKLY, MR SHANKLY

Bill Shankly (1913-1981) the hard-boiled Scottish manager of Liverpool in the club's 1960s and 1970s heyday was as famous for his tough turn of phrase as he was for his managerial skills. Here's a selection of some of his best lines.

'Football's not a matter of life and death... it's much more important than that'

'Brian Clough's worse than the rain in Manchester. At least God stops that occasionally'.

'You son, could start a riot in a graveyard' (To Liverpool hardman defender Tommy Smith).

'If he isn't named footballer of the year, football should be stopped and the men who picked any other player should be sent to the Kremlin' (On Tommy Smith).

'Take that poof bandage off. And what do you mean it's your knee? It's *Liverpool's* knee!' (To an injured Tommy Smith).

'The trouble with referees is that they know the rules, but they do not know the game'.

'If you are first you are first. If you are second you are nothing'.

'Don't worry Alan. At least you'll be able to play close to a great team!' (To Alan Ball after he signed for Everton).

'I know this is a sad occasion but I think that Dixie would be amazed to know that even in death he could draw a bigger crowd than Everton can on a Saturday afternoon' (Address given at the funeral of Everton legend Dixie Dean).

'Sickness would not have kept me away from this one. If I'd been dead, I would have had them bring the casket to the ground, prop it up in the stands and cut a hole in the lid' (After beating Everton in the F.A, Cup semi-final, 1971).

'Of course I didn't take my wife to see Rochdale as an anniversary present. It was her birthday. Would I have got married in the football season? Anyway, it was Rochdale reserves'.

Scout who had a young player rejected by Shankly: 'But he has football in his blood'. Shankly: 'You may be right, but it hasn't reached his legs yet'.

'At a football club there's a holy trinity – the players, the manager and the supporters. Directors don't come into it. They are only there to sign the cheques'.

Radio Merseyside interviewer: 'Mr. Shankly, why is it that your team's unbeaten run has suddenly ended?' Shankly: 'Why don't you go and jump in the lake!'

'If a player isn't interfering with play, what's he doing on the pitch?' (On the offside rule).

'Jock, do you want your share of the gate receipts now or shall we just return the empties?' (To Jock Stein after a raucous Celtic v Liverpool cup tie).

'There are only two teams in Liverpool. Liverpool and Liverpool reserves.'

'Just tell them I completely disagree with everything they say' (To an interpreter about excited Italian journalists).

'The problem with you son, is that your brains are all in your head' (To a young Liverpool trainee).

'If you're not sure what to do with the ball, just pop it in the net and we'll discuss your options afterwards' (To Ian St John).

An anemophobic person is someone who's afraid of high winds.

THE LAW IS A ASS

The Law is something we should all treat with respect and deference. But when you look at some of these truly stupid regulations, that's something that's easier said than done.

Around the world there are some unbelievably silly laws. For example, it is illegal to wear a fake moustache in church on a Sunday in Louisiana. Presumably, this means it's O.K. to wear one every other day? But when it comes to dumb, pointless laws, we in this sceptred isle more than hold our end up. Many have their origins in days of yore, and we just never got around to repealing them. So, did you know...

* *It is illegal to impersonate a Chelsea Pensioner.* This law is not to be confused with the Chelsea Football Team, whose players have been impersonating footballers for years.

* *It is illegal for a woman to eat chocolates on public transport.* Oh well, perhaps if they repeal that law, they can replace it with one making it illegal to chow down on fast food on the bus!

* *It is illegal for a Member of Parliament to enter the House of Commons wearing a suit of armour.* But who on earth would want to attack a politician? Form an orderly queue now.

* *It is illegal to hang a mattress out of a window.* Especially if someone's still lying on it, you would imagine.

* *It is illegal to commit suicide.* The maximum penalty for this offence is death. So, does that make execution following a failed suicide attempt a fate worse than death?

* *All London taxi's should carry a bail of hay in the boot.* In case passengers get peckish when they're stuck in traffic?

* *In York, it is still perfectly legal to shoot a Scotsman so long as you do it on a Sunday and you use a bow and arrow.* So they're not all stupid laws, after all!

AESOP: FACT OR FABLE?

Chances are, you've heard of Aesop's fables – people have been repeating them for thousands of years. But did you know there was a real person named Aesop?

BACKGROUND

If you were asked to name the most influential writers in Western history, you might include Aristotle, or Shakespeare, or even Delia Smith. But you probably wouldn't even think of Aesop.

Yet his works have been around for over 2,000 years, and he's had an impact on everything from ancient Greek philosophy to 20th-century American culture. Adages such as 'Don't cry over spilled milk' and expressions like 'sour grapes', for example, come directly from his fables.

On the other hand, Aesop wasn't technically a writer. Nothing was written down during his lifetime; it was oral tradition that kept both his legend and his fables alive. Still, scholars are reasonably certain he existed – and that he was a revered storyteller. 'The best evidence we have of Aesop's life comes from remarks about him in early ancient sources like Herodotus, Aristotle, Aristophanes and Plato', writes Leo Groarke Wilfrid of Laurier University. In fact, Socrates, considered the greatest philosopher of ancient Greece, 'is said to have passed the time awaiting execution by putting Aesop's fables into verse'.

A BRIEF BIOGRAPHY

Scholars have established a few facts about Aesop's life:

- He was born a Greek slave in the sixth century B.C.
- He had a natural gift for fables and became famous in ancient Greece because of it. Eventually his 'learning and wit' earned him his freedom.
- As a freed man he travelled widely until Croesus, the rich and powerful king of ancient Lydia, invited him to become an ambassador. Aesop accepted and was sent to various republics in Greece,

trying to establish peace 'by telling his wise fables'.

• Aesop's last diplomatic mission was to Delphi. Croesus gave him gold to distribute to the citizens. However, Aesop was so offended by the Delphians' greed that he sent the cash back to Croesus. Proving his point, the Delphians became so enraged that they accused Aesop of 'impiety' – a major crime – and executed him as a public criminal. According to legend, they pushed him off a cliff.

• Following the execution of Aesop, a myth grew up around the incident. It was said that a series of calamities befell the citizens of Delphi. The disasters got worse and worse until, finally, the people confessed their crime and made reparations. After that, 'the blood of Aesop' became a common reference to the fact that evil deeds will not go unpunished.

HOW THE FABLES CAME TO US

After his death, Aesop became a sort of mythical figure (like Mother Goose) to whom fables were automatically attributed, no matter who invented them. For a thousand years after his death, he was more famous than ever. But with the coming of the Dark Ages, he was forgotten.

Then, 600 years later, in the 1300s, a Turkish monk named Planudes assembled a collection of about 150 of Aesop's fables. When Italian scholars of the mid-1400s became interested in antiquity, Planudes' book was one of the first works they translated and printed, along with works by Homer and Aristotle.

Aesop's tales spread from Italy to Germany, where his popularity grew. The 'great fathers of the Reformation' used his fables to inveigh against the Catholic Church; Martin Luther himself translated 20 of Aesop's fables and said that next to the Bible, he valued *Aesop's Fables* above all other books.

Finally, in 1610, a Swiss scholar named Isaac Nicholas Nevelet printed a version of Aesop's fables called *Mythologica Aesopica*. It was popular all over Europe and made Aesop a permanent part of Western civilization. 'No book', wrote the compiler of a 19th-century collection, 'with the exception of the Holy Scriptures, has had a wider circulation than *Aesop's Fables*. They have been translated into the greater number of the languages both of Europe and of the East, and have been read, and will be read, for generations by the inhabitants of all countries'.

AESOP'S FABLES

Aesop's fables (see page 111) have been told and retold for thousands of years. Here are some of our favourites.

THE FOX & THE CRANE

A fox once invited a crane to dinner and served soup in a very shallow dish. He thought it was funny that the crane, with his long beak, couldn't drink any of the soup.

Then he said, 'My dear crane, I'm so sorry to see that you're not eating anything. Didn't you like the soup'?

'Oh, everything is just fine', the crane answered. 'And now you must do me the honour of paying me a visit'.

When the fox came to the crane's house and sat down to dinner, a very tall jar was placed in front of him. It was so tall and narrow that the fox couldn't get his snout into it.

'I'm so glad to be able to return your courtesy', said the crane as he reached his long beak into the jar. 'I hope you enjoy your dinner every bit as much as I did mine when I visited you'.

Moral: *What goes around, comes around. You get what you deserve.*

THE FIR TREE & THE BRAMBLE

A fir tree boasted to a bramble, 'You're useful for nothing at all; while I am used for roofs and houses and all kinds of things'. The bramble answered: 'You poor creature, if you would only call to mind the axes and saws which are about to cut you down, you would wish you'd grown up a bramble, not a fir tree'.

Moral: *Better to suffer poverty without care, than have riches with a worried life.*

BELLING THE CAT

Long ago, a group of mice had a general council to consider what measures they could take to outwit their common enemy, the cat. Some said this, and some said that; but at last a young mouse got up and said he had a proposal to make, which he thought would meet the case. 'You will all agree', said he, 'that our chief danger consists in the sly and treacherous manner in which the enemy approaches us. Now, if we could receive some signal of her approach, we could easily escape from her. I venture, therefore, to propose that a small bell be procured, and attached by a ribbon round the neck of the cat. By this means we should always know when she was about, and could easily retire while she was in the neighbourhood'.

This proposal met with general applause, until an old mouse got up and said: 'That is all very well, but who is to bell the cat'? The mice looked at one another and nobody spoke. Then the old mouse said: 'It is easy to propose impossible remedies'.

Moral: *Talk is cheap.*

THE BUFFOON & THE COUNTRYMAN

At a country fair there was a Buffoon who made all the people laugh by imitating the cries of various animals. He finished off by squeaking so like a pig that the spectators thought that he had a porker concealed about him. But a Countryman who stood by said: 'Call that a pig's squeak! Nothing like it. You give me till tomorrow and I will show you what it's like'. The audience laughed, but next day, sure enough, the Countryman appeared on the stage, and putting his head down squealed so hideously that the spectators hissed and threw stones at him to make him stop. 'You fools!' he cried, 'see what you have been hissing', and held up a little pig whose ear he had been pinching to make him utter the squeals.

Moral: *Men often applaud an imitation and hiss the real thing.*

THE DOG'S REFLECTION

Once there was a dog who was given a fine, meaty bone. With the bone firmly between his teeth, the dog trotted homeward, thinking of what a fine meal he was going to enjoy.

On the way, he had to cross a narrow bridge over a brook. As he looked over the side of the bridge, he caught sight of his own reflection in the water. Thinking it was another dog carrying a bone between his teeth, the foolish animal made up his mind that he would have that bone, too.

He leaned over and snapped at the dog beneath him. As he did, the bone fell into the water and was lost.

Moral: *Be careful that you don't lose what you have by trying to get more.*

See page 198 for more of Aesop's Fables.

WILLIAM'S WORLD

The poet and painter William Blake (1757–1827) was a peculiarly British genius. A true visionary, his work is complex but also enduringly popular – even if we don't always understand it.

Just about everyone recognizes at least a few lines written by William Blake, whether it's 'Tyger, Tyger, burning bright/in the forest of the night' or the inspiring, uplifting words of 'Jerusalem'. But have you ever noticed that at first sight his writing doesn't actually seem to make much sense? Is he being deliberately obscure, or is there more to William Blake's poems than meets the eye?

DIVINE INSPIRATION

'Jerusalem', for example, seems to be about a visit to England by Jesus Christ. His long historical poems, 'America' and 'The French Revolution', don't seem to be about these places or events at all. Instead, they are filled with exotic imagery, detailing the exploits of characters such as Los and Urizel – mythological beings that Blake invented. As far as his contemporaries were concerned, there was a simple explanation for the poet's wild flights of fancy. 'Poor Blake' they would say, tapping their heads. But Blake wasn't mad – he was possessed! From an early age Blake claimed he could see angels and even talk to them. It was a belief he carried through his life and into his work. The ideas and images he expressed in his poems were, he claimed, partially dictated to him by his heavenly visitors. His work was, literally, the word of God.

OH BROTHER!

Blake was a bright boy, but being from a poor London family never had the chance to go to school. Instead, he was apprenticed at age 14 to an engraver. As he grew, Blake began to develop his own natural gifts in drawing, painting and poetry. He used his engraving skills to develop a new method of printing which allowed him to illustrate and publish his own poems. In characteristic fashion, he claimed that he developed his new engraving method following a vision in which his dead brother came to him and explained what he needed to do.

In the 2001 Census, 390,000 people in the UK said they followed the Jedi religion.

GUESS WHO'S COMING TO DINNER

Part of the reason people thought Blake was slightly barking was because he was so up front about his halluncinations. He would tell people that, as he walked the streets of the capital, he would see angels and spirits and devils. He would talk to God. He claimed to have dined with the Biblical prophets Ezekiel and Isaiah. Outwardly, he lived a quiet life in south London, but in his own mind he claimed to live in a universe of infinite spaces and golden visions. It's quite possible that William Blake was the world's first hippy.

A MESSAGE IN HIS MADNESS

Blake saw himself as nothing less than a prophet for his time. Because his poems, paintings and engravings were divinely inspired, if you didn't understand them it was because you didn't have enough faith or God-given insight. But there was another reason for the obscurity of Blake's poems – they were deeply subversive. Although he was a Christian, Blake's brand of belief was very different from that of his contemporaries. He despised the organized religion of his day, feeling that it stifled man's true nature. Unsurprisingly, he didn't want to shout this part of his beliefs from the rooftops, so he wrapped it up in complex language that only like-minded souls would be able to fully appreciate.

REBEL WITH A CAUSE

Typically, Blake's genius was not recognized in his day. He was just a bit too odd for the times he lived in. As a result, his life was spent on the edge of poverty, picking up a few painting commissions here and there, but mostly just scraping by. Yet in many ways Blake blazed a trail for the Romantic poets, writers and artists of the early 1800s who came after him. His message of faith, passion, love and inspiration struck a chord with writers such as Byron and Shelley, who, like Blake, rebelled against the conformity of the 'Age of Reason' in which they lived.

For Blake, emotion and passion were much more important than reason and intellect, and that is what made him so popular to generations of readers after his death: it is not so much *what* Blake believed but *how* Blake believed that made him such a powerful writer and artist, and a truly inspirational figure.

The Queen's train cost £872,000 to run in 2002. That's £45,894.72 for each of its 19 trips.

'RUMOURS OF MY DEATH...'

While he was visiting England in 1897, Mark Twain received an inquiry from the U.S. about a report that he had died. 'Rumours of my death', he cabled back, 'are greatly exaggerated'. He's not the only celebrity whose death has been erroneously reported. Here are three of our favourite 'false death' stories, and their impact.

A PRIZE MISTAKE

Who 'Died': Alfred Nobel, Swedish inventor of dynamite, blasting caps, smokeless gunpowder, and hundreds of other explosion-related items

Cause of 'Death': Mistaken identity. On 13 April, 1888, Nobel awoke in Paris, opened a newspaper, and was astonished to read his own obituary. But it was actually his brother Ludwig who'd died; the newspaper had messed up.

What Happened: As a result of this mistake, Nobel was given a rare gift – a chance to see how he would be remembered – and he didn't like what he saw. As David Zacks writes in *An Underground Education:*

> Alfred was shocked to see himself portrayed as the Merchant of Death, the man responsible for escalating the arms race....(Even though) he had made high-powered explosives much easier to use and was proud of how this power had been unleashed to mine precious minerals and to build roads, railways, and canals.

The obituary painted him as a 'bellicose monster' whose discoveries 'had boosted the bloody art of war from bullets and bayonets to long-range explosives in less than 24 years'.

Determined to change his image and redeem the family name, Nobel hatched a shrewd plan. He used his wealth to create prizes in several areas – including peace. (Sort of like 'the Exxon award for environmental safety...(or) the John F. Kennedy award for marital fidelity', Zacks says). It was successful spin control. Today, the Nobel Prizes are the most prestigious in the world – and few of us connect their creator to 'the art of killing'.

When it was introduced in 1848, the modern golf ball was called a 'gutta-percha' ball.

JUST A RUMOUR

Who 'Died': American Vice President Thomas Jefferson
Cause of 'Death': Dirty politics. America's first really nasty presidential campaign was underway in 1800 when, on June 30, the *Baltimore American* reported that Jefferson (running against incumbent president John Adams) had died suddenly at his Virginia home. The story was confirmed the next day by the *Philadelphia True American*.
What Happened: According to Bruce Felton and Mark Fowler in their book *The Best, Worst and Most Unusual:*

> Reports of the death of the vice president elicited no statements of sympathy, no words of grief from President Adams, vice presidential candidate Charles Cotesworth Pinckney, or any other prominent Federalist politician, which is a measure of the bitterness of the campaign. On the other hand, Jefferson's friends spent 4 July in sombre mourning. News travelled slowly in that era, and reports of Jefferson's death did not reach some outlying areas until the middle of July. And the truth followed about one week behind.

What happened? The *Gazette of the United States* explained: 'An old Negro slave called Thomas Jefferson, being dead at Monticello (Jefferson's estate), gave rise to the report of the demise of the Vice-President – the slave having borne the name of his master'.

But the whole episode 'was no innocent misunderstanding', write Felton and Fowler. 'The rumours and reports were cleverly calculated to underscore Jefferson's slave-owning status, and the gossip about his affairs with black women. Had the timing been better, it might have influenced the election'.

WRITTEN IN THE STARS

Who 'Died': John Partridge, best-known English astrologer of the early 1700s and publisher of the annual astrology almanac *Merlinus Liberatus*
Cause of 'Death': A practical joke. Satirist Jonathan Swift, author of *Gulliver's Travels*, hated astrologers (he thought astrology was nonsense) but loved April Fools' Day jokes. In 1708 he pulled one on Partridge. Taking the pen name Isaac Bickerstaff and posing as a 'true astrologer' who wanted to expose the 'gross…

Big Ben isn't a clock – it's the name of the bell. The building it's in is St Stephen's Tower.

nonsense, lies and folly' put out by 'false astrologers' like Partridge, Swift published a penny pamphlet of bogus prophesies, titled *Predictions for the Year 1708*. He wrote:

> (My first prediction) relates to Partridge the almanac-maker; I have consulted the star of his nativity by my own rules, and find he will infallibly die upon the 29th of March next, about eleven at night, of a raging fever.

What Happened: On 30 March, Swift – using a different pen name this time – published a second pamphlet: *The Accomplishment of the First of* Mr. *Bickerstaff's Predictions*. It supplied a graphic description of Partridge's supposed final moments, including a scene in which the anguished, repentant astrologer admitted in a deathbed confession that he was a fake. 'All pretences of foretelling by astrology are deceits', Partidge supposedly said, 'and none but the poor ignorant vulgar give it any credit'. One historian comments:

> Swift's plan succeeded beyond his wildest expectations. His own penny pamphlet sold in multitudes and pirate publishers were soon offering halfpenny reprints, replies, and imitations....What had begun as a simple practical joke grew into a full-blown fantasy until more people knew of Partridge's death than had ever heard of him alive.

In the next issue of his almanac, Partridge protested that he wasn't really dead, and attacked Bickerstaff as an 'impudent, lying fellow'. Swift anonymously shot back with another pamphlet, *Vindication of Isaac Bickerstaff*, in which he provided several 'proofs' that Partridge really was dead. He even accused Partridge of being an impostor of himself.

Result: People really came to believe that Partridge was dead and that the person claiming to be him – Partridge – was an interloper trying to take over the business. Because of this, sales of Partridge's almanacs plummeted, forcing him out of business. He never found out who was behind the hoax.

OOPS!

More tales of outrageous blunders to let us know that someone's screwing up even worse than we are. So go ahead and feel superior for a few minutes.

JUST DO IT

TICONDEROGA, New York – 'A company is trying to erase an embarrassing mistake it made on pencils bearing an anti-drug message. The pencils carry the slogan: "Too Cool To Do Drugs".

'But a sharp-eyed fourth-grader in northern New York noticed when the pencils are sharpened, the message turns into "Cool To Do Drugs" then simply "Do Drugs".

'"We're actually a little embarrassed that we didn't notice that sooner", spokeswoman Darlene Clair told today's *Press-Republican* of Plattsburgh'.

– Associated Press, 11 December, 1998

WELL, NEVER MIND THEN

'We shall never know the identity of the man who in 1976 made the most unsuccessful hijack attempt ever. On a flight across America, he rose from his seat, drew a gun and took the stewardess hostage.

'"Take me to Detroit", he said.

'"We're already going to Detroit", she replied.

'"Oh...good", he said, and sat down again'.

– *Book of Heroic Failures*

STAMPS OF APPROVAL

WASHINGTON – 'The Grand Canyon has been misplaced by the post office.

'A newly printed batch of 100 million 6-cent international stamps carry a picture of the canyon and, on the bottom of each stamp, the words 'Grand Canyon, Colorado'.

'The Grand Canyon is actually located in the state of Arizona'.

– Associated Press, 17 May, 1999

Humber Estuary's bridge, built in 1980, is the UK's longest at 1,410 metres.

BEASTLY MISTAKE

'After Cody Johnston, 22, of Bozeman, Montana, was fined $195 for a traffic violation, a court computer error turned it into a conviction for deviate sexual conduct. That's the way it appeared in a crime report in the *High Country Independent Press*, where Johnston's parents read it. When he told them it wasn't true, his wife and his sister accused him of being in denial and urged him to seek counselling. Even though the *Independent Press* printed a correction, Johnston filed a libel suit against the paper and the court system, noting, "I've heard every sheep joke you can imagine"'.

– *Weird News*

IF YOU DON'T COUGH, YOU MIGHT GET OFF

CARDIFF – 'When a juror coughed, defendant Alan Rashid had a right to feel sick'

'The cough came just as the jury foreman announced a verdict of "not guilty" in Rashid's trial on a charge of threatening homicide'.

'The cough coincided with "not", Judge Michael Gibbon only heard "guilty" and Rashid was sentenced to two years in prison.

'As the jury left the court Thursday, one inquisitive member of the panel asked an usher why Rashid was going to jail after being found innocent. So the jurors were herded back into court.

'Rashid was brought back to court, the jury confirmed its "not guilty" verdict and Gibbon told the defendant he was free to go.

'"I am very relieved, as you would imagine", Rashid said'.

– Associated Press, 16 April, 1999

HAPPINESS IS A WARM GUN

'Madison, Wisconsin, police chief Richard Williams turned on his oven to roast some turkey but forgot that was one of his favourite hiding places for his gun. "Shortly thereafter: boom!" police spokesperson Jeanna Kerr said, adding that Williams was given a one-day, unpaid suspension for violating his department's firearms policy'.

– *News of the Weird,* November 1998

CREME dé la CRUD

Most celebrities are famous because they're good at what they do – but a rare few are remembered as the absolute worst. We at the BRI salute them.

THE CHERRY SISTERS, *world's worst variety act*
Background: In the mid-1890s, Broadway impresario Oscar Hammerstein promoted a number of spectacular stage shows, only to see them lose money due to lack of public interest. So he decided to change gears. 'I've been putting on the best talent and it hasn't gone over', he groused to reporters. 'Now I'm trying the worst'. He was referring to the Cherry Sisters.
Career Notes:
The four Cherry Sisters were from Cedar Rapids, Iowa. Tall, thin Addie, Effie and Lizzie were the singers in the group; short fat Jessie 'kept time', thumping intermittently on a bass drum.

• The sisters started by touring vaudeville houses in the Midwest and were so awful – even to small-town audiences starved for entertainment – that wire screens had to be erected across the front of the stages where they performed, to protect them from rotten vegetables and other rubbish that audiences routinely threw at them.

• Hammerstein signed them to a $1,000-a-week contract to play at his Olympia Theatre. Their debut on 16 November, 1896, marked a turning point in their career: instead of being pelted with rotten vegetables, they were met with a shower of bad reviews. In an article titled 'Four Freaks From Iowa', a *New York Times* reviewer described the sisters as 'genuine products of the barnyard', and speculated that their performance might be due to poor diet. 'It is sincerely hoped', he wrote, 'that nothing like them will ever be seen again'.

• Just as motorists slow down to look at traffic accidents, more and more people went to see the Cherry Sisters perform. Their reputation for being the world's worst variety act grew, and soon they were playing to sold-out crowds. Hammerstein made a small fortune off the act, and the Cherry Sisters became 'the best-known, if not the best-loved stage performers in America'.

Q: What is a gnomon?

FLORENCE FOSTER JENKINS, *world's worst opera singer*
Background: There may have been worse opera singers, but none who achieved fame for it. 'She clucked and squawked, trumpeted and quavered', said one observer. Another noted that she was 'undaunted by…the composer's intent'. And in *The Book of Heroic Failures*, Howard Pyle writes: 'No one, before or since, has succeeded in liberating themselves quite so completely from the shackles of musical notation'.
Career Notes:
• Singing opera was Jenkins' lifelong dream. But she was unable to pursue it until 1909, at age 40, when her father died and left her a fortune. Since no one in their right mind would finance Jenkins' recitals, she paid for them herself, and developed an enthusiastic following.
• 'Different audiences reacted in various ways', writes Carl Sifakis in *Great American Eccentrics*. 'Some roared with laughter until tears rolled down their cheeks; others sat in utter silence, according her unique voice an attention befitting the world's greatest singers'.
• Critics were at a loss as to how to describe her. Some called her 'The First Lady of the Sliding Scale'. When she released a record, *Newsweek* commented: 'In high notes, Mrs. Jenkins sounds as if she was afflicted with a low, nagging backache'.
• Jenkins' trademark was outrageous costumes. Pyle writes: 'One minute she would appear sporting an immense pair of wings to render 'Ave Maria'. The next she would emerge [as] a senorita, with a rose between her teeth and a basket full of flowers'. She often threw roses into the audience – then sent her accompanist to gather them up so she could throw them out again. Once she became so excited that she threw the basket, too.
• On 25 October, 1944, the beloved 75-year-old diva rented out Carnegie hall – and performed to a sold-out crowd. 'So great was the demand for tickets', writes Sifakis, 'that they were scalped (touted) at the then-outrageous price of $20 apiece. More than 2,000 lovers of music had to be turned away'. La Jenkins took it in her stride, as she had over her 30-year career. 'Some may say I couldn't sing', she quipped, 'but no one can say that I didn't sing'. A month later, she died.

BRI'S WIND HALL OF FAME

It used to be that no one talked about farts – now, it's no big deal. You can't get away from it. Which is fine by us. Here is the very first section honouring people and institutions that have made an art out of passing wind. (By the way – if this is your favourite part of the book, we recommend a tome called Who Cut the Cheese?, *by Jim Dawson.)*

Honorary: Caryn Johnson, a.k.a. Whoopi Goldberg
Notable Achievement: First Hollywood star named after frequent farting
True Story: In her autobiography, Goldberg says she came up with the stage name Whoopi because she 'frequently passed gas and sounded like a walking whoopee cushion'.

Honorary: Taoism
Notable Achievement: Most interesting philosophy about farts
True Story: A 1996 BBC programme about the first Chinese emperor, reported that 'Chinese Taoists believe everyone is allotted a certain amount of air at birth which it is important to conserve. Belching and farting are considered to shorten one's life. Taoists therefore carefully control their diet, avoiding foods which lead to flatulence'.

Honorary: King Ahmose of Egypt
Notable Achievement: Most effective use of a fart as a political statement
True Story: In 568 B.C., King Apries of Egypt sent a trusted general named Amasis to put down a mutiny among his troops. But when Amasis got there, the troops offered to make him their leader instead – and he accepted.

King Apries couldn't believe it. He sent a respected adviser named Patarbemis to bring Amasis back. Amasis responded to the king's entreaties by raising himself from his saddle and farting. Then he told Patarbemis to 'carry that back to Apries'. Unfortunately, the king was so enraged by the message that he had

Patarbemis' nose and ears hacked off. Committing such a barbarous act against such a respectable man was the last straw for many Egyptians – they turned pro-Amasis. With their support, Amasis' troops attacked and defeated Apries' army.
Note: Amasis became King Ahmose and reigned for 44 years, from 569 to 525 B.C., which modern historians call one of Egypt's most prosperous periods.

Honorary: Richard Magpiong, a career criminal
Notable Achievement: The ultimate self-incriminating fart
True Story: In 1995 the residents of a home on Fire Island (near New York City) were awakened by a noise. They got up and looked around, but couldn't find anyone. They were about to go back to bed when, according to the *New York Daily News*, 'they heard the sound of a muffled fart'. Magpiong was discovered hiding in a closet and was held until the police arrived.

Honorary: Edward De Vere, the seventh earl of Oxford and a courtier in Queen Elizabeth's court
Notable Achievement: Craziest overreaction to a fart
True Story: De Vere accidentally farted while bowing to the queen. He was so embarrassed that he left England and did not return for seven years. When he got back, the queen pooh-poohed the whole affair. 'My Lord', she reportedly said, welcoming him back, 'I had forgot the Fart'.

Honorary: Spike Jones and His City Slickers
Notable Achievement: Bestselling fart record
True Story: According to *Who Cut the Cheese?*: 'During World War II, Bluebird Records released a disc called "Der Fuehrer's Face" by Spike Jones and His City Slickers (an orchestra noted for parodying pop tunes), only a few months after the U.S. joined the war. Jones's band, armed with rubber razzers to create flabby farting noises, (created) a zany gas attack on Adolf Hitler: "And we'll Heil! (fart!) Heil! (fart!) right in der Fuehrer's face!" It sold a million and a half copies in the U.S. and Great Britain'.

MYTH-CONCEPTIONS

Common knowledge is frequently wrong. Here are a few examples of things that people believe – but that just aren't true.

Myth: The captain of a ship at sea can perform weddings.
Fact: Nautical law – and the laws of most nations of the world – actually prohibits ships' commanders from joining couples in marriage.

Myth: Your hair and nails continue to grow after you die.
Fact: They don't. Your tissue recedes from your hair and nails, making them appear longer.

Myth: Bananas spoil faster when you put them in a refrigerator.
Fact: This belief comes from an old ad jingle. The purpose of the jingle was to tell people to keep bananas out of the refrigerator – but only until they had ripened. Once ripened, bananas will last longer in the refrigerator.

Myth: You should never wake a sleepwalker.
Fact: There's no reason not to wake a sleepwalker. This superstition comes from the old belief that a sleepwalker's spirit leaves the body and might not make it back if the person is wakened.

Myth: Anyone can make a citizen's arrest.
Fact: According to law enforcement officials, the concept of a citizen's arrest is pure fiction.

Myth: Shaving your hair makes it grow faster and thicker.
Fact: The rate of your hair's growth is determined by hereditary factors. Shaving will have no effect on the rate of its growth.

Myth: During a flight, you'll sometimes hit an 'air pocket'.
Fact: What's often called an 'air pocket' is actually a downdraft.

Myth: It's darkest just before the dawn.
Fact: Actually, it's darkest at about 2 a.m.

The islands of Antigua and Barbuda issued Elle Macpherson postage stamps in 1999.

FAKED PHOTOS

A few more historic photographs that people chose to believe, even though they were pretty obvious forgeries.

FICTIONAL NEWS

Famous Footage: The 'California Election Report'

Trick Shot: In 1934 Upton Sinclair, legendary muckraker and author of *The Jungle*, an exposé of Chicago's meatpacking industry, ran for governor of California. Sinclair's candidacy marked one of the best chances a socialist had ever had of winning a political office in the U.S. That's when newsreels like the 'California Election Report' appeared. It featured interviews in a railyard with one hobo after another, each saying that 'he rode the rails to the Golden State just as soon as he heard that the new governor would be handing out free lunches'.

The Real Picture: The newsreels were pure Hollywood, put together by director Irving Thalberg with the support of Samuel Goldwyn. Both considered Sinclair 'a dangerous red who wanted to rob the rich to support the poor'. The hobos were just actors (Thalberg and his crew wanted real hobos, but couldn't find any in the L.A. railroad yard), and the 'railyard' was a set on the MGM back lot. Other newsreels were just as fake.

Development: In the days before television, newsreels were a primary source of news for the public, and this negative coverage – shown repeatedly in California theatres – helped ensure Sinclair's defeat.

ON TOP OF THE WORLD

Famous Photos: Frederick Cook at the North Pole

Trick Shots: On 6 September, 1909, an exhausted Robert Peary wired from Labrador, 'Stars and Stripes nailed to the Pole – Peary'. Peary, 53, had apparently realized a goal he'd set 23 years earlier – to be the first person to reach the North Pole. But it turned out that he was too late: on September 1, explorer Frederick Cook had wired from the Shetland Islands that he'd made it to the North Pole the year before. Cook's proof: photographs of him and his Eskimo companions at the Pole. Cook's photographs, which were published all over the world, marked the completion of one

of the last great exploratory challenges on earth – or did they?
The Real Picture: As it turned out, it was another of Cook's 'accomplishments' that got him into trouble. Cook had previously claimed he'd been to the summit of Mount McKinley. 'On the day Cook received the keys to New York City for his North Pole trek', write the editors of *Reader's Digest* in *Strange Stories of America's Past,* 'the man who'd supposedly climbed McKinley with him admitted they'd never really been near the 6,193 metre peak'. The Explorer's Club investigated and found that the McKinley 'summit' picture had been taken from a 1,615 metre ridge.
Development: The scandal brought Cook's North Pole claims into question but, amazingly, he so charmed the public that many people sided with him over Peary. His spurious North Pole pictures weren't totally discredited until 1918, two years before Peary's death. (Dr. Cook later served four years in Leavenworth prison for promoting shares in a company owning oil he 'discovered' in Wyoming.)

WHO'S WHO IN THE REVOLUTION?
Famous Photos: Spanish Loyalists committing atrocities in the Spanish Civil War (1936–1939)
Trick Shot: In 1936, 'when the Spanish Civil War broke out, U.S. newspaper baron William Randolph Hearst jumped into the fray. He ran photos showing atrocities – being committed by the pro-democracy Loyalists against Fascist followers of Francisco Franco'.
The Real Picture: The Spanish picture was actually Franco's men committing atrocities against the Loyalists.
Development: The controversy helped turn public opinion against the Loyalists and hastened the start of World War II. Without more support from the U.S. and other powers, the Loyalists faltered and the Nazi-supported fascists were able to defeat their enemies – providing momentum for Hitler and Mussolini.

* * *

FAKED INITIALS

B. of B. K. were the mysterious initials the Tichborne Claimant Arthur Orton applied to himself in his diary. The initials were supposed to denote 'Baronet of British Kingdom.'

UNFINISHED MASTERPIECE: LEONARDO'S HORSE

Here's an unfinished masterpiece from one of the Renaissance's greatest geniuses.

THE HORSE STATUE. *Created by Leonardo da Vinci. Would have been the largest equestrian monument on earth if it had been built. Leonardo considered it a crowning achievement.*

Background: In the 1480s, Milan's Duke of Sforza commissioned Leonardo to build a huge statue of a horse to honour his father, Francesco Sforza. Da Vinci worked on it for nearly 17 years, studying horses and making a series of models, including a full-sized clay model that was 7.3 metres tall. Next he made moulds, into which more than 50 tonnes of molten bronze would be poured to create the final horse. Then a war broke out.

Unfinished Masterpiece: On 10 September, 1499, before da Vinci could cast the horse, the French captured Milan. Some soldiers camped nearby – and a company of them used the clay model for target practice, riddling it with holes. Afterwards, the model was totally destroyed by exposure to the weather. When Leonardo died 20 years later, he was 'still mourning the loss of his great horse'.

Update: In 1977 an American named Charles Dent happened to pick up a copy of *National Geographic* magazine, which contained an article on Leonardo and his horse. Dent was an Italian Renaissance buff and decided that completing Leonardo's horse would be a fitting way to honour the greatest mind of the period. Leonardo had left no detailed drawings or other notes that indicated what the final horse was supposed to look like; all that survived were preliminary sketches. No matter – Dent decided to wing it, and on 10 September, 1999, exactly 500 years to the day that Da Vinci was forced to abandon his dream, his horse (or at least an approximation) was unveiled in Milan. It was intended, Dent explained, as a gift 'to all the Italian people from the American people'. But, ironically, few Italians attended the unveiling – mostly Americans showed up (not Dent, though, he'd died a few years earlier).

DRAT, SHE'S DEAD!

You don't always get a Hollywood ending when you're making a Hollywood film. Sometimes the star dies or becomes incapacitated during filming. It happened in these movies. Here's how they handled it.

SARATOGA (1937), *starring Jean Harlow and Clark Gable*
The Situation: The 26-year-old Harlow, 'Hollywood's original platinum blonde', died of kidney failure when the film was only about half complete. MGM wanted to abandon production and scrap what they had, but Harlow's fans protested. So the studio 'and a very reluctant Gable' continued filming.
Body Double: Harlow's scenes were filmed with her stand-in, Mary Dees, who was 'carefully lit and photographed in long shots, over the shoulder, from behind, looking through binoculars, or under wide-brimmed hats'. Ironically, the film was the most successful of Harlow's career – and also the most critically acclaimed (although the *New York Times* complained that in the film, 'Harlow was patently not her tempestuous self'.)

THE CROW (1994), *starring Brandon Lee – son of martial-arts legend Bruce Lee*
The Situation: A horrible accident occurred just three days before filming was due to be completed. In the story, Lee's character is shot and killed. In real life, that's what happened to Lee. The tip of one of the blanks loaded in a .44-calibre handgun hit Lee, 27, in the stomach when the gun was fired during a scene. He died shortly after. Police said it was an accident.

Producer Ed Pressman says: 'We weren't so sure if we wanted to finish it. But Brandon's mother and his girlfriend, whom he planned to marry just after it was finished, wanted it finished and released. So we finished it'.
Body Double: The producers altered some of the existing footage digitally and made plans to film new footage using stuntmen who would be wearing special face masks made from a plaster cast of Lee's face. But, perhaps understandably, the stuntmen refused to wear the masks, on the grounds that they were in bad taste. 'No one felt good about wearing the masks', says make-up artist Lance Anderson. 'The director finally got around that problem by filming long shots instead'.

Hop to it: in the 13th century, Europeans baptized children with beer.

YOU CAN'T CHEAT AN HONEST MAN (1938), *starring W. C. Fields*

The Situation: Fields was one of Hollywood's legendary drunks. Most of the time that didn't interfere with his films, but *You Can't Cheat an Honest Man* was different – Fields, who was supposed to both write the film and star in it, was too drunk to do either.

Body Double: Director George Marshall compensated by hiring a writing 'assistant' named Everett Freeman for Fields, and by casting other stars like Edgar Bergen and Charlie McCarthy in the film to take up some of Fields' screen time. He also hired a double for Fields and filmed him in long shots. That turned out to be a particularly smart move: one afternoon, in the middle of production, Fields shuffled off the set into his limousine (which had a well-stocked bar in the back) and never returned.

Marshall still didn't have all the footage of Fields that he needed to finish the film – so he improvized. He combined what he had with shots of Fields' double and put Edgar Bergan and Charlie McCarthy onscreen even longer.

Despite its flaws – or more likely because of them – the movie was a hit and to this day is considered a W. C. Fields classic. 'All the critics', says Everett Freman, 'referred to the movie's daring innovations, its departure from formula, and its innovative use of the camera – especially on the long shots intercutting to the close-ups'.

THE THREE STOOGES (1955)

The Situation: Shemp Howard replaced his brother Curly in the Stooges in 1949 and co-starred with them for six years. In 1955, while working on several Stooges films, he had a heart attack and died.

Body Double: Moe and Larry considered appearing as a duo, but Columbia Pictures wouldn't hear of it. They also wouldn't scrap the unfinished Shemp episodes. Instead, they hired Joe Palma as a double. His face was never seen – his back was always to the camera.

The four episodes: *Hot Stuff*, *Rumpus in the Harem*, *Scheming Schemers*, and *Commotion on the Ocean*. Check them out sometime.

TO SLEEP – OR NOT TO SLEEP?

Here are some random facts about sleeping that you may not know. Complied for us by the BRI's own John Darling, who has never met Peter Pan and would like us to stop asking if he has, already. (He probably hasn't had enough sleep.)

THE NEED FOR SLEEP

Newborn babies sleep about 16 hours a day – adults average half that. Teens, especially girls, are gluttons for sleep (10 hours average), but it's not because they're lazy, as many parents think. U.S. researchers found it was tied to the complex inner labours of puberty. This hunch is underlined by teen girls' need for extra Z's during their periods.

• We sleep best at certain times and if we stray from our required sleep needs, there's no telling what will happen. The nuclear disasters at both Chernobyl and Three Mile Island, as well as the *Exxon Valdez* wreck and *Challenger* shuttle explosion, have been linked to lack of sleep or altered sleep cycles among key people at key moments.

• 'Jet lag' shifts our sleep cycle, often creating confusion, mental dullness and a desire to sleep at odd times. The Army was disappointed to find that troops flown overseas often require a week to overcome their disorientation. This phenomenon is the bane of passenger jet crews. In one instance, for example, all three members of a jetliner crew fell asleep as they reached the end of their overnight New York-to-Los Angeles flight. While air traffic controllers radioed them frantically, the jet flew 100 miles out over the ocean. Finally, one of the crew woke up and saw the sea in every direction. They had just enough fuel to make it back to the Los Angeles airport.

TO NAP OR NOT TO NAP?

• According to Stanley Coren, in his book *Sleep Thieves*, science has identified the two big peaks in our need for sleep – at 3 a.m. and 3 p.m. The first is dead in the centre of our sleep cycle, but the second is smack in the middle of our workday. Should we be napping in mid-afternoon? At present, only 38 per cent of us do.

• Who's getting the most sleep? Surveys find:

– In the U.S., Westerners and Southerners sleep longer than Easterners and Midwesterners.

– Women sleep more than men.

– Poor people sleep more than the rich.

– People who work evening or night shifts get far less sleep – about 5.6 hours – than day workers. No matter how hard they try, researchers say, people who sleep out of their normal cycle never fully adjust.

DOES LESS SLEEP = SUCCESS?

• A short sleep cycle is not inherently bad. Some people seek it out and sing its praises. Multi-millionaire magnate Donald Trump boasts of needing only three to four hours a night. Former Prime Minister Margaret Thatcher managed on four or five hours.

• This raises the question: is there a link between sleep and success? U.S. researcher Ernest Hartmann found that people who sleep less than 5.5 hours tend to be extroverted, ambitious and efficient, while people who sleep more than 9 hours tend to be anxious, insecure, introverted and indecisive. Other researchers think this is nonsense, noting that short-sleepers tend to be fast-paced, Type-A personalities (thus prone to heart disease), while long-sleepers include society's creative, alternate type thinkers and artists.

• Researchers hoped a survey of the CEO's and chairs of the Fortune 500 companies would settle the question of whether 'the early bird really does get the worm'. Apparently, it does. They found that 46 per cent of the leaders they surveyed slept an hour less than the national average of 7.5 hours. Fifteen per cent slept 5–6 hours and 2 per cent slept 4–5 hours.

THE TRICK OF GETTING MORE SLEEP

Most of us, however, aren't looking for ways to sleep less – our focus is on how to get more. Here are some tips from the experts:

• Go to bed about the same time each night.
• Avoid nightcaps, except warm milk.
• Avoid illuminated clocks (they're a reminder you can't sleep).
• Exercise before going to bed.
• A dark and slightly cool bedroom is best (about 18° C).

How did 'venereal disease' get its name? From Venus, the Roman goddess of love.

STRANGE LAWSUITS

These days, it seems that people will sue each other over practically anything. Here are a few real-life examples of unusual legal battles.

THE PLAINTIFF: Wendy Potasnik, a nine-year-old from Carmel, Indiana
THE DEFENDANT: The Cracker Jack Division of Borden, Inc.
THE CASE: In 1982, Wendy and her sister Robin each bought a box of Cracker Jacks. Robin got a prize in her box, but Wendy didn't...which made her 'really mad'.

'They advertise a free toy in each box', she told a reporter. 'I feel that since I bought their product because of their claim, they broke a contract with me'. So she sued, asking the court to make Borden 'pay court costs and furnish a toy'.
THE VERDICT: Wendy dropped the suit after Borden apologized and sent her a coupon for a free box of Cracker Jacks...even though the company refused to pay the $19 that Potasnik had spent on court costs.

THE PLAINTIFF: Alan Wald
THE DEFENDANT: The Moonraker Restaurant in Pacifica, California
THE CASE: In 1993, Wald went to the Moonraker for an all-you-can-eat buffet. He'd already eaten between 40 (Wald's count) and 75 (the restaurant's count) oysters – and was still at it – when the restaurant cut him off. Apparently, other customers were complaining that there were no oysters left. The restaurant offered to refund Wald's $40 to get him to go, but Wald insisted he was within his rights – he hadn't had all he could eat yet. He demanded $400 for 'humiliation and embarrassment'.
THE VERDICT: Wald was awarded $100 by the judge – but the restaurant was the real winner. 'It was great publicity', said the owner. 'We're going to get a shovelful of oysters and present them to (Wald) at his table. He can come back anytime'.

THE PLAINTIFF: The Swedish government
THE DEFENDANT: Elisabeth Hallin, mother of a five-year-old

Coconut shells can absorb more impact than most crash helmets.

boy named Brfxxccxxmnpcccclllmmnprxvclmnckssqlbb11116 (which she pronounces 'Albin')
THE CASE: For five years, the Hallins, who say they believe in the surrealist doctrine of 'pataphysics', refused to give their son a name. Then Swedish tax officials informed them it was a legal requirement. They chose Brfxxccxxmnpcccclllmmnprxvclmnckssqlbb11116 – which was immediately rejected by the authorities. The couple insisted that the 'typographically expressionistic' name was merely 'an artistic creation', consistent with their pataphysical beliefs.
THE VERDICT: The government disagreed. The Hallins were fined 5000 kronor (about £450) and ordered to come up with a different name.

THE PLAINTIFF: Lorene Bynum
THE DEFENDANTS: St. Mary's Hospital in Little Rock, Arkansas
THE CASE: In 1992, Bynum visited her husband, a patient at the hospital. She wanted to use the bathroom, but the toilet seat was dirty – and there wasn't enough toilet paper to spread out on it. So she took off her shoes and tried to go to the toilet standing on the toilet seat. Unfortunately the seat was loose. Bynum fell, spraining her lower back. She sued the hospital for negligence.
THE VERDICT: A jury awarded Bynum $13,000. But the Arkansas Supreme Court overturned the verdict. 'The injuries resulted from her act of standing on the (toilet) seat, which was neither designed nor intended to be used in that way', they explained.

THE PLAINTIFF: Victoria Baldwin
THE DEFENDANT: Synergy, a hair salon in Sydney, Australia
THE CASE: In July 1996, Baldwin had her hair cut at the salon. The result was so bad, she complained, that it made her 'look like Hillary Clinton'. She sued for damages, plus reimbursement for money spent on hats to cover her head until the hair grew back.
THE VERDICT: Baldwin won £450, plus £140 for the hats.

When you pop a champagne cork, it can travel as fast as 160 kmh.

THE ULTIMATE TASTE TEST

According to Dr. Alan Hirsch's Smell & Taste Treatment and Research Foundation, the fruits and vegetables you prefer tell a lot about your personality. Want proof? Take this test that Dr. Hirsch has put together – no cheating! – then let us know if you think we should print more.

1. Which groups of fruits do you prefer?
a) Oranges, Bananas and Grapes
b) Aubergine, Corn and Tomatoes
Analysis: If you prefer the first group, this indicates a strong-minded, ambitious, aggressive, dominant individual, who is a natural leader. If you prefer the second group, this indicates an introspective, self-searching person who is sensitive to the needs of others. You tend not to be impulsive in your decision-making processes, but rather weigh all the alternatives in question before making your decision.

2. Of these pairs of fruits, which do you prefer? (Must choose one of each pair.)
a) Applesauce or Fresh Apples
b) Pineapple Chunks or Pineapple Glaze
c) Creamed Corn or Corn on the Cob
Analysis: If at least two of the above are the first choice, then you are a passive, easy-going, agreeable sort, who tries to solve problems without raising a commotion. If at least two of the above are the second choice, you tend to be an aggressive 'go-getter' who will not take 'No' for an answer. You work hard and play hard.

3. Do you like spicy pickles?
Analysis: If YES, you tend to be pessimistic. If NO, you tend to be optimistic.

4. Do you like:
a) Bananas; **b)** Boiled fish; **c)** Fruit; **d)** Honey;
e) Tapioca; **f)** Celery; **g)** Nuts; **h)** Hot Curry

How do you know when you're playing with an Italian deck of cards? No queens.

Analysis: If five or more is YES you are a natural optimist and view life through rose-coloured glasses. You are a pleasant work colleague and would make a good friend. If five or more is NO, you tend to be pessimistic. Before being involved in social intercourse, you tend to be careful, doubting others' intentions.

5. Which do you prefer?
a) Green Olives or Black Olives
b) Pecans or Almonds
c) Pickles or Cucumbers
Analysis: If two or more are the first choice, you tend to be assertive in your relationships and enthusiastic in all endeavours. Although anxious at times, you are a decisive, resilient person, prone to action. If two or more are the second choice, you tend to take responsibility for your actions. You are self-confident and a natural leader.

6. Which do you prefer?
a) Lemons or Oranges
b) Potatoes or Yams
c) Grapefruit or Tangerines
Analysis: If two or more are the first choice, you tend to be reserved, quiet, and contemplative. You usually are not impulsive. You tend towards introspection. If two or more is the second choice, you tend to be an out-going, gregarious person who enjoys a sound relationship. Many consider you to have a good sense of humour. You would make a good disc jockey, used car salesman, or politician.

* * *

RANDOM ANIMAL FACT

A female lobster, called a hen or chicken, can lay as many as 100,000 eggs at one time. Most end up as 'food for other marine life'.

BEEN NOWHERE, DONE NOTHING

BRI member Debbie Thornton sent in this list of real-life bumper stickers. Have you seen the one that says...

SUBURBIA: *Where They Tear Down the Trees and Name Streets After Them*

I Have No Idea What I'm Doing Out of Bed

Been Nowhere, Done Nothing

Support Bacteria: It's the Only Culture Some People Have

I Used to Be Indecisive; Now I'm Not Sure

No Sense Being Pessimistic – It Wouldn't Work Anyway

The More You Complain, the Longer God Lets You Live

Forget About World Peace – Visualize Using Your Turn Signal!

Warning: *Dates in Calendar Are Closer Than They Appear*

Consciousness: That Annoying Time Between Naps

Age Is a Very High Price to Pay for Maturity

I Doubt, Therefore I Might Be

The Older You Get, the Better You Realize You Were

Dyslexics Have More Fnu

Men Are from Earth. Women Are from Earth. Deal With It.

The Gene Pool Could Use a Little Chlorine

So You're a Feminist – Isn't That Cute!

Time Is What Keeps Things from Happening All at Once

Your Kid May Be an Honour Student but You're Still an Idiot

We Have Enough Youth, How About a Fountain of 'Smart'?

HOW TO MAKE A MONSTER, PART II

Here's the second instalment of our history of Uncle John's favourite movie monster – Gojira, the original Japanese name for Godzilla. (Part I starts on page 73.)

DESIGNING A MONSTER

It took the model department three tries to come up with the right design for Gojira. The first model had fishlike scales for skin and a line of pointy spikes running down its back. Producer Tomoyuki Tanaka liked the spikes, but thought the head was too big and the scales too 'fishy'. Next they created a 'warty' Gojira with a smaller head and large rounded bumps on the skin. Tanaka didn't like this treatment either, so they came up with 'alligator' Gojira, this time with much smaller, linear bumps arranged in rows like bumps on an alligator's back. Alligator Gojira got the nod.

SUITS ME FINE

Now Tanaka had a name and a look for his monster – but what kind of special effects would he use? Stop-motion animation, (e.g. claymation) used tiny, moveable clay models, and was filmed frame by frame. It produced excellent results – King Kong was filmed with stop-motion animation – but was time consuming and expensive. Plus, it limited the amount of detail that could be shown – a big problem, since so much of the script involved the monster knocking down buildings. (It's almost impossible to make a building collapse realistically when filming frame by frame.)

The alternative: use a man in a monster suit. That could be filmed at a larger scale, making higher levels of detail possible. And because the footage would be filmed in 'real time' instead of frame by frame, it could be finished in a few weeks instead of several months. The problem with such a low-tech technique was that if the filmmakers weren't careful, the man in the monster suit would end up looking like – a man in a monster suit.

In the end, it was scheduling that decided the issue – a

monster suit was quicker, and Toho studios had only a year to produce the film, so Gojira became a man in a costume.

The special-effects crew built a full-sized Gojira model, which they used to create plaster moulds for the monster suit. Then they poured latex rubber into the moulds to make Gojira's skin. The skin was then attached to a cloth 'inner skin', made of cloth stuffed with polystyrene foam and bamboo to provide the monster's bulk. The fully assembled suit weighed more than 100 kilos.

The actor entered the costume via a zipper that ran along the dorsal fin; he was (barely) able to see out of the costume through four tiny holes in Gojira's neck. The monster's head was then mounted on a brace that rested on the actor's head; an offscreen technician used a radio-controlled mechanism to open and close the mouth.

SWEATY WORK

Gojira's action sequences were filmed at a high speed so that when it was slowed down for viewing, the buildings crumbled more realistically. But this meant that the set had to be lit twice as bright as when filming at normal speed, and the hot lights caused temperatures inside the suit to climb as high as 49° C (120°F), with the only ventilation provided by the eyeholes in Gojira's neck.

Under these conditions it was nearly impossible to film for more than a few minutes at a time. Typically, the actor inside the suit would spend 7 to 10 minutes rehearsing a scene in costume with the studio lights turned off. Then the lights came on and the scene was filmed for about 3 minutes, which was all the actor could take before he risked passing out from heat exhaustion and suffocation. Collapsing mid-scene was not unusual, and two actors who alternated as Gojira sweated so profusely that the crew drained as much as half a pint of sweat from the suit at the end of the day.

The on-screen result of filming in such difficult conditions was a slow, lumbering creature who shuffled and lurched across the tiny cityscapes – but that was just the look that Tanaka wanted: in the 1950s, paleontologists incorrectly assumed that most dinosaurs were huge, slow-witted, slow-moving creatures, and Tanaka's quest for dinosaur accuracy dovetailed nicely with the limitations imposed by the heavy suit and hot studio lights.

TINY TOWN

Entire city blocks of downtown Tokyo were reconstructed in elaborate detail for the film. For the scene in which Gojira destroys Tokyo's famous Ginza district, special effects man Eiji Tsuburaya's technicians reproduced a three-square-block section of the district in miniature, complete with interior floors and walls to make sure the buildings would crumble realistically when Gojira smashes them. Tsuburaya also insisted that the tiny automobiles, buses, and trains be hand made from cast iron to ensure that when Gojira stepped on them, the sturdy little vehicles would crush realistically.

MAKING NOISE

Finding a suitable roar for Gojira was one of the trickier aspects of creating the monster. The film's sound-effects team tried numerous actual animal sounds: grunts, growls, roars and other noises. They played them backward, forward, individually and in groups, but nothing seemed to work. Then composer Akira Ifukube tried rubbing the strings of a bass violin with the fingers of a resin-coated rubber glove, and reverberating the sound. That did the trick.

OPENING NIGHT

Finally, after 122 days of filming, *Gojira* premiéred in Japan on 3 November, 1954. The film had cost a fortune to make – the final tally was 60 million yen (about £40 million in 1999 sterling), about 250 times the average cost of a Japanese film at that time.

But it turned out to be a good investment: *Gojira* was one of the most popular films of the year and earned a fortune for Toho.

Gojira was also a critical success. 'While American monster-on-the-loose films used radiation to get the monster up and running around', David Kalat writes in *A Critical History and Filmography of Toho's Godzilla Series*, 'Honda saw his monster as a narrative device to discuss the terror of the nuclear age'. Less than a decade after World War II, Japanese critics understood and appreciated the implicit message.

Turn to page 175 for Part III.

The fastest train in the UK is a Eurostar, which reached 208 mph in July 2003.

MODEL CITIZENS

Some thoughtful commentary from the mouths of 'babes'.

'I don't have to fake dumb. I am dumb'.

– Jerry Hall

'I don't wake up for less than $10,000 a day'.

– Linda Evangelista

'Everywhere I went, my cleavage followed. But I learned I am not my cleavage'.

– Carole Mallory

'I'm so naive about finances. Once when my mother mentioned an amount and I realized I didn't understand, she had to explain: "That's like three Mercedes". Then I understood'.

– Brooke Shields

'Blah, blah, blah. I'm so tired of talking about myself'.

– Elle Macpherson

'I don't think I was born beautiful. I just think I was born me'.

– Naomi Campbell

'I've always been a bit more maturer than what I am'.

– Samantha Fox

'Everyone should have enough money to get plastic surgery'.

– Beverly Johnson

'I believe that mink are raised for being turned into fur coats and if we didn't wear fur coats those little animals would never have been born. So is it better not to have been born or to have lived for a year or two to have been turned into a fur coat? I don't know'.

– Barbi Benton

'People think modelling's mindless, that you just stand there and pose, but it doesn't have to be that way. I like to have a lot of input. I know how to wear a dress, whether it should be shot with me standing up or sitting. And I'm not scared to say what I think'.

– Linda Evangelista

'I look at modelling as something I'm doing for black people in general'.

– Naomi Campbell

'I can do anything you want me to do so long as I don't have to speak'.

– Linda Evangelista

'I wish my butt did not go sideways, but I guess I have to face that'.

– Christie Brinkley

What do tongue prints and fingerprints have in common? No two are alike.

MY BODY LIES OVER THE OCEAN: PART II

More stories about miscellaneous body parts removed from famous people after they died.

EINSTEIN'S EYES

Where They're Located: Bank vault in New Jersey

How They Got There: It turns out Dr. Harvey wasn't the only sticky-fingered professional at Einstein's autopsy (see p. 102): at about the same time Harvey was absconding with the brain, Einstein's ophthalmologist, a doctor named Henry Abrams, was removing the eyes. He placed them in a jar and locked them away in a bank vault until 1994, when he reportedly began looking for a buyer. 'When you look into his eyes, you're looking into the beauties and mysteries of the world', he told *The Guardian*. 'They are clear as crystal; they seem to have such depth'.

JOSEPH HAYDN'S SKULL

Where It's Located: In Haydn's marble crypt in Eisenstadt, Austria, after being separated from the rest of the body for more than 145 years

How It Got There: Haydn's patron, the Prince of Esterhazy, saw to it that Haydn's body was buried intact following the composer's death in 1809. But some phrenologists (people who 'read' skulls) wanted to see if they could divine the source of the composer's genius by looking at his skull. So they dug up his body, removed the head, took it away for study – and then refused to bring it back unless the Prince of Esterhazy paid them a ransom. The prince balked at paying the blackmail, so Haydn was reburied, without his head.

The head eventually ended up in the Musikverein museum in Vienna, where it was stolen, eventually resurfacing 'in the home of an Austrian professor, who displayed it on his piano', and then returned to the museum in 1895. That year the village of Eisenstadt began lobbying for the head's return to Haydn's crypt.

They negotiated until 1935, to no avail. Then, at the end of

World War II, they tried again. Negotiations dragged on for nine years, and finally, in 1954, Haydn's head was reunited with the rest of his body.

SANTA CLAUS' FINGERS

Where They're Located: 'Now on display in the city of Antalya, Turkey'

How They Got There: Saint Nicholas, the Catholic bishop believed to be the inspiration for Santa Claus, died in the fourth century A.D. He was buried in his old church, in what is now the Turkish town of Demre, on the Mediterranean coast. But somehow, his remains ended up in a church in the Italian port of Bari (tradition has it Italian merchants from Bari stole them in 1087), and the town of Demre has been trying to get the bones back for 900 years. All they have left is 'a finger or two', on display in a nearby city.

'One reason Christians aren't keen to send the bones back', the *Wall Street Journal* reports, 'is because Turkey is now predominantly Muslim. In fact, some believe the 11th-century Christian monks in Myra allowed the Italians to remove the bones in order to save them from the advancing Turkish armies'.

Muammer Karabulut, chairman of the Santa Claus Foundation, which seeks the return of the bones, says his group's mostly Muslim membership should not be an issue. After all, he insists, 'Santa Claus is [a] universal figure'.

STONEWALL JACKSON'S ARM

Where It's Located: The Chancellorville battle site near Fredericksburg, Virginia

How it Got There: On May 2, 1863, as he was returning to camp after engineering an important victory for the Confederacy, the legendary U.S. Civil War general was accidentally shot by his own troops. Jackson was hit in the right hand and in the left wrist and shoulder, and his left arm had to be amputated above the elbow.

Jackson's chaplain, B. Tucker Lacy, had a brother who owned a house near the hospital, so he took the severed limb to his brother's for burial. Confederate troops buried the arm in a nearby field, complete with a religious ceremony and a marble tombstone. When Jackson died from complications eight days later, he was buried in Lexington, Virginia.

The record for fewest Premier League season wins goes to Swindon: 5 out of 42 in 1993–94.

According to the book *Roadside America*, 'The arm was exhumed in 1929 and reburied in a steel box on a plantation known as Ellwood. Around the field in which it now lays, there is only one gravestone: the one belonging to Jackson's arm'.

OTHER CELEBRITY BODY PARTS

• **Thomas Hardy's heart.** 'Hardy's heart was to be buried in Stinsford, England, his birthplace, after the rest of his body was cremated in Dorchester. All went according to plan until the great poet's sister's cat snatched the heart off her kitchen table and disappeared into the woods with it'.

• **Emanuel Swedenborg's skull.** The famous Swedish philosopher's skull was stolen by a retired sea captain 50 years after Swedenborg's death. It turned up in an antique shop in Wales a century later. When Swedenborg's descendents learned of the skull's existence, they went to Wales and bought it – and then auctioned it off at Sotheby's for £2,000.

• **Buddha's teeth.** Tradition has it that two or three teeth (depending on who you ask) were found in Buddha's cremated remains following his death 2,400 years ago. Today the teeth are in temples in Beijing, China; Sri Lanka; and Taipei, Taiwan.

• **Percy Bysshe Shelley's heart.** When he drowned in 1822, Shelley 'was cremated on the beach to which his body had washed. For some reason his heart would not burn and it was taken from the fire and given to his wife, Mary Wollstonecraft Shelley (author of *Frankenstein*), who carried it with her in a silken shroud everywhere she went for the rest of her life'.

• **Chang and Eng Bunker's liver.** The two brothers, born in Thailand in 1811, were attached at the chest. P. T. Barnum made them world-famous (coining the term 'Siamese twin'). One or both of their livers was apparently removed upon their death, and now sits in a jar at the Mutter Museum in Philadelphia.

* * *

Random Fact: On average, cats spend 30 per cent of their waking hours grooming themselves. They purr at 26 cycles per second, about the same frequency as an idling diesel engine.

WORD ORIGINS

Ever wonder where words come from?
Here are some interesting stories.

JACKPOT
Meaning: A huge prize
Origin: 'The term goes back to draw poker, where stakes are allowed to accumulate until a player is able to "open the pot" by demonstrating that among the cards he has drawn he has a pair of jacks or better'. (From *Dictionay of Word and Phrase Origins, Vol. II*, by William and Mary Morris)

GRENADE
Meaning: A small, hand-thrown missile containing an explosive
Origin: 'The word comes from the French pomegrenade, for pomegranate, because the military missile, which dates from the sixteenth century, both is shaped like the fruit and explodes much as the seeds burst out from it'. (From *Fighting Words*, by Christine Ammer)

AMMONIA
Meaning: A potent, pungent cleaning fluid
Origin: 'Ammonia is so called because it was first made from the dung of the worshippers' camels at the temple of Jupiter Ammon in Egypt'. (From *Remarkable Words with Astonishing Origins*, by John Train)

HEATHEN
Meaning: An ungodly person
Origin: 'Christianity began as primarily an urban religion; people in rural districts continued to worship older gods. The Latin word for countryman was paganus – whence, of course, pagan; the Germanic tongues had a similar word, something like *khaithanaz*, "dwelling in the heath" (wilderness) – whence heathen'. (From *Loose Cannons and Red Herrings*, by Robert Claiborne)

Besides human sacrifices, what did Aztecs offer the gods? Minced beef and tacos.

CALCULATE

Meaning: Add, subtract, divide, and/or multiply numbers or money

Origin: 'In Rome 2,000 years ago the merchant figured his profit and loss using what he called calculi, or "little stones" as counters. So the Latin term calculus, "pebble", not only gave us calculate but...our word calculus...one of the most complicated forms of modern mathematics'. (From *Word Origins*, by Wilfred Funk, Litt. D.)

MUSEUM

Meaning: Building or collection of art, music, scientific tools, or any specific set of objects

Origin: A shrine to the Greek Muses. 'Such a shrine was known as a mouseion...When the Museum at Alexandria was destroyed in the fourth century...the word nearly dropped out of use. Three hundred years ago, a scholar rediscovered the word'. (From *Thereby Hangs a Tale*, by Charles Earle Funk)

DOPE

Meaning: Drugs

Origin: 'This word was originally a Dutch word, doop, meaning a sauce or liquid. Its first association with narcotics came when it was used to describe the viscous glop that results from heating opium. Then, by rapid extension, it came to mean any narcotic'. (From *Dictionary of Word and Phrase Origins, Vol. III*, by William and Mary Morris)

RIVAL

Meaning: Competitor

Origin: 'A rival is etymologically "someone who uses the same stream as another". The word comes from Latin *rivalis*, meaning "of a stream". People who use or live by the same stream are neighbours and, human nature being as it is, are usually in competition with each other'. (From *Dictionary of Word Origins*, by John Ayto)

Q & A: ASK THE EXPERTS

Here are some more random questions, with answers from trivia experts.

THE COLD, WET TRUTH

Q: Why does your nose run in cold weather?

A: 'It is not necessarily because you have a cold. If very cold air is suddenly inhaled, the mucous membranes inside your nostrils first constrict, then rapidly dilate as a reflex reaction. This permits an excess of mucus to form, resulting in a runny nose or the "sniffles"'. (From *The Handy Weather Answer Book*, by Walter A. Lyons, Ph.D.)

HAPPY TRAILS

Q: Why do jets leave a trail of white behind them?

A: 'The white trail that you see is, in fact, a man-made cloud. At low altitudes, the air is able to absorb large quantities of water. But at high altitudes, water has a tendency to come out of the air, which can form a cloud. This only happens, though, if the air contains small particles – such as dust – on which the water can condense. It also helps the process if the air is agitated.

'Now enter the high-flying jet. Its exhaust fills the air with a huge supply of spent fuel particles, and at the same time it shakes or agitates the air...leaving a long, narrow cloud behind it'. (From *Ever Wonder Why?*, by Douglas B. Smith)

EURASIA, EURASIA

Q: Why are Asia and Europe considered two continents even though they appear to be one?

A: 'The ancient Greeks thought the Eurasian landmass was divided in two by the line of water running from the Aegean Sea to the far shore of the Black Sea.

'By the time they found out otherwise, Europeans were not about to surrender their continental status'. (From *Why Things Are*, by Joel Achenbach)

The London Zoo reportedly employs an 'entertainment director' for the animals.

YOU EXPECT ME TO SWALLOW THAT?

Q: How do circus sword swallowers do it?

A: Believe it or not, they really do swallow the sword. The main problem is learning how to relax the throat muscles and stop gagging. This takes weeks of practise – but it can be done.

'The sword doesn't cut the sword swallower's throat because its sides are dull. The point is usually sharp, but that's not a problem as long as the sword swallower doesn't swallow any swords long enough to poke him (or her) in the pit of the stomach'. (From *Know It All!*, by Ed Zotti)

YOU GET WHAT YOU PAY FOR

Q: If you dropped a penny from the top of the Empire State Building (or any skyscraper) and it happened to hit someone on the head, would it easily pierce their skull?

A: 'Given that the Empire State Building is 381 metres tall and ignoring such factors as wind resistance, a penny dropped from the top would hit the ground in approximately 8.8 seconds, having reached a speed of roughly 85 metres per second. This is not particularly fast. A low-powered .22 or .25 calibre bullet, to which a penny is vaguely comparable in terms of mass, typically has a muzzle velocity of 244 to 335 metres per second....

'On top of this we must consider that the penny would probably tumble while falling, and that the Empire State Building...is surrounded by strong updrafts, which would slow descent considerably. Thus, while you might conceivably inflict a fractured skull on some hapless New Yorker, the penny would certainly not "go through just like that"'. (From *The Straight Dope*, by Cecil Adams)

* * *

SMILE WHEN YOU SAY THAT

'One of Oscar Hammerstein's rarer finds was "Sober Sue", whom he introduced to audiences at New York's Victoria theatre in 1908. During intermissions, Sue would appear on stage and Hammerstein would offer $1,000 to anyone who could make her laugh. There were lots of takers, but no one succeeded. What they didn't know: she couldn't laugh – her facial muscles were paralyzed'.

(Felton & Fowler's Best, Worst, and Most Unusual)

MONKEY SEE, MONKEY DO

Do television and movies influence our actions? Of course, but unfortunately, some people take it to extremes. There's just no cure for stupidity.

MONKEY SEE: In the 1971 film *The Godfather*, Corleone family henchmen intimidate a Hollywood mogul by killing his prize race horse and sticking the horse's head in his bed.
MONKEY DO: In 1997 two New York crooks decided to use a similar method to intimidate a witness scheduled to testify against them at trial: 'On the morning the witness was scheduled to testify, they left the head of a slaughtered animal as a death threat. 'We wanted to leave a cow's head because his wife was from India, and they consider cows sacred', one said. 'But where do you find a cow's head in Brooklyn? So I went to some butcher in Flatbush and found a goat head. I figured it was close enough'. One crook was sentenced to 4 years in prison; the other got 14 to 42 years.

MONKEY SEE: In the video for Joe Diffie's song 'John Deere Green', a boy climbs a water tower and paints a green heart'.
MONKEY DO: 'This apparently gave some genius in Mississippi the bright idea of scaling his local water tower and painting "Billy Bo Bob Loves Charlene" in green paint. Perhaps tuckered out from having to write all three of his first names on the water tower, the guy then lost his balance and was seriously injured when he hit the ground'. *(Chicago Sun-Times)*

MONKEY SEE: In the 1993 film *The Program*, 'drunk college football players lie down in the middle of a busy road to prove their toughness'.
MONKEY DO: 'A scene in the movie *The Program* will be deleted after one teenager was killed and two others critically injured while apparently imitating the scene, the Walt Disney Co. said Tuesday....Sources indicated it will cost $350,000 to $400,000 to re-edit'. *(Daily Variety)*

According to sleep researchers, only about 5 per cent of people dream in colour.

MONKEY SEE: In 1997 Taco Bell introduced a new advertising campaign featuring a talking Chihuahua that has since become known as the 'Taco Bell Dog'.
MONKEY DO: Since then, sales and adoptions of Chihuahuas have gone through the roof. 'Before the Taco Bell commercials became popular, no one wanted Chihuahuas', says Marsha Teague of the Portland, Oregon, humane society. 'Now people ask specifically for the "Taco Bell Dog"'. The dogs, priced from $300 to $600, 'sell within two days, faster if their colouration resembles the actual TV star'. 'We can't even keep them in stock', a pet-shop owner says. 'Everybody always comes in and imitates the Taco Bell commercial'. *(Portland Oregonian)*

On the other hand, it isn't necessarily all bad:

MONKEY SEE: The *Nancy Drew* series is about a strong-willed, independent teenage detective who constantly finds herself in danger, then has to think her way out of it.
MONKEY DO: In the early 1990s, an eleven-year-old Michigan girl was kidnapped and thrown into the boot of a car. 'Instead of panicking', The *Christian Science Monitor* reported, 'she asked herself what Nancy Drew would do in such a situation. Then she found a toolbox, pried the trunk open, made a call from a nearby phone booth, and her assailant was arrested'.

* * *

MORE MORE MORE!

• In 1997 an employee at a Bangkok hotel was sent to prison for robbing guests' safe deposit boxes. His method: he rubbed his nose on the buttons, making them oily so he could tell which ones the guests had pushed to open the safe. His inspiration: an episode of the TV show *MacGyver*.

• In 1996, 17-year-old American Steve Barone was booked for robbing a gun store. He claimed he did it 'only because he was taken over by another personality, which was an amalgam of guys from the movies *Pulp Fiction*, *Reservoir Dogs*, and *Goodfellas*'. *(News of the Weird)*

SHADES OF GREY

The queen always takes her own tea with her when she travels. And she insists on making it herself so that she can have it exactly the way she likes it. The blend? Earl Grey, of course.

Some British prime ministers will always be remembered for their towering political achievements. Winston Churchill won us the war; Clement Attlee gave us the Welfare State. And Earl Grey...? Well, he gave us a nice cup of tea. Earl Grey tea, obviously. It's probably not how he would want to be remembered, especially as his other great achievement was in forcing through parliament one of the most important pieces of legislation ever, the Great Reform Act of 1832, but that's us Brits for you. When it comes to the crunch, *everything* stops for tea.

NICE WORK, DAD

Charles Grey, as he was in his pre-Earl days, was born in 1764 in Northumberland. He came from an old and illustrious northern family. His father had been a British general in the American War of Independence. Although his father fought well and successfully, the rest of the British army didn't. We lost that war – and America with it – but General Grey's efforts were not forgotten by the crown, and he was made an hereditary earl in 1806.

YOUNG MAN IN A HURRY

Young Charles was groomed for power from an early age. He went to Eton, of course, then Cambridge, naturally, before joining the Whig party and easing himself into the safe parliamentary seat for Northampton aged just 22 in 1786. By 1830 he had successfully climbed to the top of the greasy pole to become prime minister. In the meantime, he still found time to father 15 children.

MR POPULAR

As a Whig (the Liberal Democrats of their day, but with power) Grey was a bit of a radical. One of his main concerns was equal rights for Catholics, for example. But his really big idea was parliamentary reform. In 1832 he forced through the Great Reform Bill, an act which got rid of lots of corrupt practices in

The heaviest pumpkin ever recorded weighed 480 kilos.

elections, and which gave many more people than ever before the vote (though not women – they had to wait another 100 years). Electoral reform was a huge and controversial issue at the time, and Grey's championing of it made him immensely popular, especially amongst the middle classes.

CHINESE WHISPERS

But where does the tea come into the story? Legend has it that Grey had spent some time in China, and whilst there had rescued a prominent Chinese diplomat's son from drowning. In response, a grateful Chinese nation created a blend of tea in Grey's name. While this is a nice story, it's also a load of old twaddle. Grey never even set foot in China.

BY GEORGE, HE'S GOT IT

The real story is not quite as colourful. In the early 1830s, an upper-class British traveller in China, one Sir George Staunton, noticed that the Chinese used herbs and fruits to flavour their tea. He particularly liked one flavoured with bergamot, a pear-shaped orange named after the town of Bergamo in Italy. He brought the recipe back to England and gave it to his friend Sir Joseph Banks, the explorer and botanist who had once sailed with Captain Cook. Banks owned a tea house in the basement of his Soho Square mansion in London and there he cooked up a few bergamot-based tea recipes. The one he liked best became Earl Grey.

WHAT'S IN A NAME?

So how did the tea get its name? The truth is no-one really knows. The most likely answer is that the tea's introduction into British society coincided with Earl Grey's spell as prime minister (1830-1834). As Grey was at the time such a hero to the middle classes, and this new, bergamot-scented tea was such a hit with polite society, it seemed natural that the two should be linked together.

MAKE IT SO

Ever since, Earl Grey has become synonymous with 'posh' tea, best drunk from bone china and served with cucumber sandwiches. If we are to believe *Star Trek* scripts, it will still be drunk well into the 24th century – as any Trekkie will tell you, it's the favourite computer-generated drink of Captain Jean-Luc Picard, who can never resist a drink of 'Tea, Earl Grey, hot'.

The average cow produces 70,000 glasses of milk in her lifetime.

DANCE YOURSELF DIZZY

The weekend starts here! Get your dancing gear on: this is the story of how Britain was clubbed into submission.

Clubbing has become a painfully trendy business these days, but it wasn't always such an exclusive pastime. Our love affair with club culture started in the 1960s and has continued ever since – and, boy, has it seen some changes along the way. All in all, it's been a pretty wild ride.

HOW'S ABOUT THAT THEN

God help us all, but did you know that the British club scene was invented by Sir Jimmy Savile! Yes, that's right, in the 1960s the strangely-hairstyled, cigar-chomping, jewellery-wearing, does-a-lot-of-work-for-charidee D.J. was the first man to have the idea of a club where people danced to records rather than live bands. Many scoffed at the thought of kids frugging to the sounds of a record player, but the idea caught on. It was especially popular in France, where a Parisian bar, The Discothèque, opened. It was a place where you could request records to listen to while you drank.

I BELIEVE IN MIRROR BALLS

The first wave of what we think of as clubbing, with outrageous clothes, even more outrageous behaviour and nights of irrepressibly danceable, repetitive grooves, was the 1970s phenomenon of disco. It came from the U.S., and was very much an underground scene, the music of the excluded: blacks, latinos and gays. Over in the UK, it was more mainstream, finding popularity at first with devotees of the Northern Soul movement.

Northern Soul was a scene based around the Wigan Casino dancehall in Lancashire. In the early- and mid-1970s groovers from all over the UK would descend on the venue every weekend to dance to Motown and Stax soul classics. Although many Northern Soul fans were a bit sniffy about disco (as soul purists they saw it as a bit tacky), the new music was certainly danceable – and if there

The Mona Lisa has no eyebrows. Shaved eyebrows were the fad when she was painted.

was one thing Northern Soul fans liked to do, it was dance. However, for non-soul fans, disco, at first, was beyond the pale. 'I Will Survive'? 'Y.M.C.A.'? This wasn't rock 'n' roll they argued, but trashy, camp throwaway music. It seems that disco's enemies were missing the point – it was supposed to be trashy, camp and throwaway. Once listener's cottoned on to this, disco really got going in the UK.

SHUT UP AND DANCE

The Northern Soul crowd were serious about their music. For them, the scene was about unearthing rare soul classics that no-one else had heard, and devising killer dance moves. That was why it never went mainstream. Disco, however, was all about having fun – the bright lights, the smoke and mirrors, and the posing and pulling. Hedonism! It was a glamorous way of escaping everyday life, if only for a few hours.

As dated as it seems now, the blockbuster film *Saturday Night Fever* captured this mood perfectly. Following its release in 1977, the dancefloor's of Britain's discos were crammed with posing, preening John Travolta wannabes. White flared suits and gold chains were compulsory disco-wear for men, while women of all shapes and sizes squeezed themselves into sparkly spandex leggings and gravity-defying boob-tubes.

THE DEATH OF DISCO

By the end of the decade, disco was on its last legs. Rock fans in the U.S. launched a 'Disco Sucks' campaign that saw records being burned or crushed at torchlit rallies. Artists such as Donna Summer fought a valiant rearguard action, bringing in synthesizers and flashy production to create the harder-edged sound of electronica, but this only succeeded in forcing the music back into the gay underground and out of the popular mainstream. It looked like disco's goose was cooked.

In the UK, disco staggered on for a bit, but tottered into the ghetto of dingy clubs filled with hairy-chested middle-aged men eyeing up groups of permed and peroxided women dancing around their handbags to tired old beats. Something new was needed to shake things up. If anything, dance music needed it's equivalent of punk rock to shock it back into life.

If you weigh 55 kilos on Earth, you'll weigh about 9 kilos on the moon.

IN THE HOUSE

It wasn't until the mid-1980s that things got back on track. Word reached the UK of something new and exciting that was happening in Chigaco's gay dance scene. Pioneer D.J.s such as Frankie Knuckles were fusing classic disco sounds with electronica to create house music. Kids in the UK loved it – house music was exciting, bass-heavy and *hard*. It had none of the lily-livered soppiness that had always characterized disco. In 1980s Britain this was important. These were difficult years, especially for young people. Unemployment was rife, and the inflexible Conservative government of Margaret Thatcher stirred up huge social divisions in the country: between rich and poor, young and old, black and white. In such a harsh climate, people took their fun very seriously, and escapism became more important than ever.

Which is where drugs came in. There had always been drugs in the UK dance scene, mostly speed to help dancers keep going all night. With the house scene a new drug made its debut: ecstasy. Whether you call them Smarties, disco biscuits or just plain old E, ecstasy had a major impact on the house scene. The sense of euphoria it created in users gave the whole movement a chilled, trippy, hippy vibe. Posing and pulling gave way to spaced-out dancing and loving thy neighbour. To mark this hippy-influenced aspect, the music was dubbed 'Acid House'. The downside, however, was that ecstasy was dangerous, and a number of E-related deaths forced the police to crack down on the acid house scene. Once more, dance music was forced underground.

RAVE ON

By the mid-1980s the UK media was filled with horror stories of how house music was creating a nation of drug-crazed teenagers. The Home Office and the police cracked down on house music clubs, closing them down or raiding them in random sweeps. So what did house music's fans do? They took it on the road, and the 'rave' was born.

One important aspect to the rave scene was its look. Raves were usually hot and sweaty affairs, so loose, baggy clothing was the order of the day. Usually, some article of clothing would be emblazoned with the smiley logo, a simple happy face on a yellow circular background. For a time, smileys were everywhere: on clothing, bags, magazine covers, ads. Whoever invented the smiley, you'd think, must be rolling in it, right? Wrong. It was designed in 1963 by an American called Harvey Ball, who produced it for a local insurance company! He was paid less than $50 for his work.

Rave organizers took over abandoned warehouses for the first wave of parties. As their popularity grew, the venues got bigger. Eventually, no building could contain them, and impromptu raves were held in fields, much to the annoyance of local farmers (a class not known for their love of dance music). Special phone lines were set up to direct clubbers to the latest raves. It was all top-secret stuff and very exciting. Motorway service stations would suddenly fill up in the middle of the night with dazed and confused young clubbers, who had been sent there by a rave organizer to await the next clue to the party's secret location.

Naturally, the press had a field day with all this, running lurid tales of sexual deviancy, drug-taking and mayhem, not all of which were true. After a particularly enormous rave at Castlemorton in Worcestershire in 1992, in which 20,000 revellers took part, the government reacted with legislation that effectively killed off the scene. With a muttered 'Bummer, man', many of the rave scenes most hardcore devotees headed off to terrorize Europe.

MAD FOR IT

It's always been fashionable to think that everything cultural begins and ends in London, but just as Liverpool proved otherwise in the 1960s, Manchester took the clubbing crown in the 1980s and early 1990s. The city became 'Madchester', as hordes came from far and wide to experience some of the best nights around, based on a Northern take on funk and dance. At the centre of it all, between 1988 and 1992, was the Hacienda. Set up by Tony Wilson's Factory Records, the wild club was packed every night with clubbers dancing everywhere, even in the queues for the toilets or the cloakroom.

The club was a focal point for the talent in the city, which included the likes of the Happy Mondays and those deities of late 1980s indie-dance, the Stone Roses. By 1989, the Roses had freshened up rock'n'roll by fusing it with E-flavoured house music. If there was a music fan in the country who remained untouched by the new groove, they were definitely in the minority. The Roses' legendary Spike Island gig of 1990 caught the band at the peak of its popularity, at a time when dance music had its greatest energy.

LARGIN' IT

By the 1990s, club culture had spread everywhere. The D.J.s who'd started off in grimy clubs in the mid-1980s were now the contemporary equivalent of rock'n'roll stars, with fans, groupies and huge amounts of cash. Pete Tong, Paul Oakenfold, and above all Fatboy Slim were household names. Even Boy George, that 1980s fashion victim in every sense of the word, successfully re-invented himself as a club D.J.

Dance music had definitely gone mainstream. Its beats were used in adverts, in mobile phone ringtones and as trailer music for primetime TV programmes. Even Barbie had a D.J. doll friend, Guy Blaine. College courses in music production and D.J.-ing were set up, and students were turning in learned dissertations on the cultural significance of the club scene.

Clubland's influence spread into almost every area of fashion, design and music. Soon it wasn't enough to go to a mere club, as they were supplanted by superclubs. Ministry of Sound and Cream seemed to be taking over the world. Perhaps they got too big. One ambitious organization set up Home, the *Titanic* of superclubs, in Leicester Square in 1999. Less than two years later its doors closed forever, its licence revoked amid allegations of 'open' drug-dealing on the premises.

BIG UP, SIR JIMMY

Yet despite the setbacks, the changes in music, the drugs, the creeping commercialization and everything else that has happened to it over the years, UK club culture has shown that it can survive and adapt to any situation. If clubbing can survive its early association with Jimmy Savile, or the 2003 dance remix of Cherie Blair singing 'When I'm Sixty-Four', it can survive anything. So long as there are still people who want to boogie on a Saturday night, there will be clubs to welcome them in.

Pass the java: People who drink coffee are less likely to commit suicide than people who don't.

THE RIDDLER

What's white, and black, and read in the middle? This page of riddles. Here are some BRI favourites.

1. What unusual natural phenomenon is capable of speaking in any language?

2. A barrel of water weighs 9 kilos . What do you have to add to it to make it weigh 5 kilos)?

3. Before Mount Everest was discovered, what was the highest mountain on Earth?

4. What word starts with an 'e', ends with an 'e', and usually contains one letter?

5. Forward I am heavy, but backward I am not. What am I?

6. He has married many women, but has never been married. Who is he?

7. How many bricks does it take to complete a building made of brick?

8. How many of each animal did Moses take on the ark?

9. How many times can you subtract the number 5 from 25?

10. If you have it, you want to share it. If you share it, you don't have it. What is it?

11. In Okmulgee, Oklahoma, you cannot take a picture of a man with a wooden leg. Why not?

12. The more you have of it, the less you see. What is it?

13. The more you take, the more you leave behind. What are they?

14. The one who makes it, sells it. The one who buys it, never uses it. The one who uses it, never knows that he's using it. What is it?

15. What can go up a chimney down but can't go down a chimney up?

16. What crime is punishable if attempted, but is not punishable if committed?

17. What happened in the middle of the 20th century that will not happen again for 4,000 years?

18. What is the centre of gravity?

19. What question can you never honestly answer 'yes' to?

20. You can't keep this until you have given it.

Answers are on page 462.

One mother shark can give birth to as many as 70 baby sharks per litter.

SPECIAL UNDERWEAR

More important underwear innovations to keep abreast of.

SIX-DAY UNDERWEAR

'The Honda Motor Company's bi-annual inventiveness contest for employees has unearthed some unique innovations, but none to match 6-day underwear, the 1987 winner. According to the story in the *Wall Street Journal*, the underwear has three leg holes, which enables it to last for six days without washing. The wearer rotates it 120 degrees on each of the first three days, then turns it out and repeats the process'.

– Forgotten Fads and Fabulous Flops

THE ALARM BRA

LONDON – 'A newly developed techno-bra – the latest in personal alarm systems – is the brainchild of Royal College of Art design student Kirsty Groves. Targeted at young urban women, the bra uses miniature electronics and conductive fabric to monitor the wearer's heart rate. If it detects a sudden change in pulse – one that indicates panic – it radios a distress call to police and identifies the bra's location. And since the electronics are contained in gel-like cushions inside each cup, the bra enhances the wearer's figure. "You can also have some lift and support if you like", Groves says'.

– Wire Service Report, 1999

SWEAT PANTS

Want to give off a manly, territorial odour without having to sweat for it? Japanese scientists have a new product – sweat-laced underpants.

Apparel and cosmetics maker Kanebo Ltd. says millions of tiny capsules in the fabric contain a synthesized pheromone found in the sweat of a man's underarms. Friction breaks the capsules, releasing the pheromone; an added musk scent intensifies the effect.

'Unfortunately, the power is fleeting – Kanebo estimates the pheromones are completely dissipated after ten washings'.

– Parade Magazine, 1998

HOW SCROOGE INVENTED CHRISTMAS

Christmas was being Scrooged out of existence until a ghost story came along to make it popular all over again.

Everyone knows about Ebenezer Scrooge—that coldhearted miser who won't help his underpaid but jolly employee, Bob Cratchit, to celebrate Christmas. Fortunately, on Christmas Eve, the Ghosts of Christmas Past, Present and Future give Scrooge such a fright that he reforms and changes his money-grubbing ways. But did you know that the tale of Scrooge not only changed how we celebrate Christmas; it probably saved it from extinction, too?

On 19 December, 1843 a slim, gilt-edged book, *A Christmas Carol*, by Charles Dickens, appeared in London bookshops. In that same year, no one wished each other a Merry Christmas. They'd probably never even heard the phrase. And Christmas itself was on the wane. In the 17th century, Oliver Cromwell and his Puritans came to power and abolished the holiday. Even after the monarchy was restored, Christmas traditions never really recovered.

By winter 1843, the industrial revolution was hammering the final nails in the Christmas coffin. Many people had migrated from the countryside to cities. The old country Christmas that had been celebrated for twelve festive (and boozy!) days was already gone. Most urban employers, like old Scrooge, weren't about to give workers even one day off just to have a party with their families. The dying traditions of Christmas, it seemed, would soon be a quaint part of England's history – if they were remembered at all.

CHARLES 'SCROOGE' DICKENS

When Dickens wrote *A Christmas Carol*, he was making a plea for the renewal of the customs his own father had known – mulled wine, roasted goose and the warmth of yule logs on a snowy Christmas night. But like Scrooge, what he really hoped for was profit, namely 'a thousand clear' from his holiday tale.

Francis Lee of Manchester United scored a record 13 penalties in the 1971–72 season.

In his push to make *A Christmas Carol* a best-seller, Dickens gave readings of his little book, sometimes for charity, often for a fee. Dickens was a wonderful storyteller and his readings achieved as much for Christmas as they did for his bank balance. 'I feel,' an American factory owner said, 'that after listening to Mr. Dickens' reading of *A Christmas Carol* tonight, I should break the custom we have hitherto observed of opening the works on Christmas Day.'

NOT SO HAPPY FAMILIES

Dickens' own parents had never been as warm and loving as the Cratchits. At 12, his careless father went to debtors' prison and Dickens laboured in a rat-infested boot-blacking factory. The dark memory made the author into a passionate reformer of workhouses and child labour laws. It also helped him value family celebrations like the one he created in *A Christmas Carol*. And, of course, it made him desperate to be as rich as Scrooge.

MERRY CHRISTMAS

As *A Christmas Carol* became beloved throughout the English-speaking world, Dickens' idea of how to celebrate Christmas caught on. People couldn't spend twelve days at it, but, like Bob Cratchit, they could wish each other Merry Christmas. They could spend Christmas Eve and Christmas Day with their families. They could strive for good times and goodwill.

In 1870, so the story goes, a young Cockney girl heard that Dickens was dead. She gasped: 'Dickens dead? Then will Father Christmas die too?' The reformed Scrooge would have been happy to tell her that Father Christmas would remain alive and well.

* * *

DICKENS TRIVIA

Q: What character was inspired by Dickens' own father?
A: The character of Wilkins Micawber in *David Copperfield* (said to be Dickens' favourite work) was based on Dickens' father, a navy clerk who seldom had the wherewithal to support his large family, but who remained endlessly optimistic.

Q: What was Dickens' job at Warren's Blacking Factory?
A: He pasted labels on shoe polish bottles.

IN MY EXPERT OPINION...

Think the experts and authorities have all the answers?
Well, they do – but often the wrong ones.

'Animals, which move, have limbs and muscles; the Earth has no limbs and muscles, hence it does not move'.

– Scipio Chiaramonti, Professor of Mathematics, University of Pisa, 1633

'Nature intended women to be slaves. They are our property. What a mad idea to demand equality for women! Women are nothing but machines for producing children'.

– Napoleon Bonaparte

'I must confess that my imagination refuses to see any sort of submarine doing anything except suffocating its crew and floundering at sea'.

– H. G. Wells, 1902

'You ain't goin' nowhere, son. You ought to go back to drivin' a truck'.

– Jim Denny, Manager of the Grand Ole Opry, to Elvis Presley, 1954

'If excessive smoking actually plays a role in the production of lung cancer, it seems to be a minor one'.

– The National Cancer Institute, 1954

The horse is here to stay, but the automobile is only a novelty – a fad'.

– Marshall Ferdinand Foch, French military strategist, 1911

'With over 50 foreign cars already on sale here, the Japanese auto industry isn't likely to carve out a big slice of the U.S. market for itself'.

– Business Week, 1968

When medieval Europeans burned witches, the witches' families had to pay for the firewood.

READ ALL ABOUT IT!

Two good reasons not to believe everything you read in the newspapers.

THE STORY: In the early 1920s, the *Toronto Mail and Empire* reported that two scientists named Dr. Schmierkase and Dr. Butterbrod had discovered 'what appeared to be the fossil of the whale that had swallowed Jonah'. The whale had a muscle that functioned just like a trapdoor, which gave access to its stomach.

The next day, evangelists all over Toronto read the story from the pulpit, citing it as confirmation that the Biblical story of Jonah and the whale was true – and the day after that, a rival newspaper ran a story reporting on the evangelists' speech.

THE TRUTH: Three days after the original story ran, the *Toronto Mail and Empire* ran a second story exposing the first one as a hoax, the work of a journalist named Charles Langdon Clarke.

Clarke liked to spend his free time cooking up news items based on Biblical stories, and then attributing them to fictional newspapers like the *Babylon Gazette* or the *Jerusalem Times* for added credibility. Anyone who spoke German would have had an inkling that the story was a joke – Dr. Schmierkase and Dr. Butterbrod translates as Dr. Cheese and Dr. Butter Bread.

THE STORY: In January 1927 the *Chicago Journal* reported that a 'killer hawk' had been seen preying on pigeons in the downtown area. The next day other Chicago papers ran the story on their front pages, and continued doing so for five consecutive days, igniting considerable public hysteria in the process: a prominent banker offered a reward for the capture of the hawk dead or alive; a local gun club sent marksmen downtown to stalk the bird, with help from local Boy Scouts who joined in the hunt.

THE TRUTH: A week after the *Journal* ran the hawk story, it announced the start of a newspaper serial called 'The Pigeon and the Hawk'. The other papers, realizing they'd been tricked into publicizing a rival paper's promotion on their front pages for an entire week, never printed another word about the killer hawk.

The New Forest was created by William the Conqueror in 1079. So it's not really all that new.

THE MAN WHO BROKE INTO MECCA

This is not the story of the late Welsh actor and husband of Liz Taylor. The original Sir Richard Burton's adventures make his actor namesake look like a stay-at-home fuddy-duddy.

Much of Sir Richard Burton's 69-year life seems to have been dedicated to proving he was better than everyone else at just about everything. The thing is, he pretty much was. Burton was tall and broad-shouldered with 'questing panther eyes' (hypnotism was one of his hobbies), a wolfish grin, and an air of romantic melancholy. He was said to be the greatest swordsman of his time: he also knew 40 languages and dialects – he could learn a new language in two months – wrote 53 books, countless articles and could supposedly seduce any woman he desired at 30 paces.

AN EVENTFUL CHILDHOOD

Burton was born in 1821. His father, a retired British army officer, suffered from lung disease and perpetually moved his family across Europe in search of the perfect climate. Burton and his younger brother were constantly in trouble – fighting duels and consorting with women of dubious virtue. Eventually, their father decided both sons should be trained as clergymen.

LIFE AMONG THE GROCERS

Richard was sent off to Oxford, where his tutors and fellow students were appalled by his 'European' manners. Richard was equally appalled by their provincialism. Worse, most of his tutors knew less about what he was supposed to be learning than he did. 'I am among grocers,' he complained to his mother. He finally managed to get himself sent down from Oxford for attending horse races. To celebrate, he drove a cart and horses through the flowerbeds and then raced out of town while sounding a loud coach horn.

Most common phobia in the world: odynophobia – the fear of pain.

PUT THAT NUN DOWN!

Burton moved to India after joining the East India Company, the giant trading group which virtually ruled the sub-continent. Impressed by his ability to learn languages and blend in, his superiors made him an intelligence officer. But Burton's high jinks (once he accidentally kidnapped an elderly nun) and his endless curiosity about other cultures (especially their sexual practices) earned him an unsavoury reputation. When his boss asked him to look into rumours that British officers were frequenting male brothels, Burton did extensive research and filed a very thorough report. Even though Burton found no officers in flagrante, his enthusiasm for the assignment and rumours about the report's contents damaged his reputation.

After seven years in India, Burton realized that his unconventional approach had doomed any sort of successful military career. He was also suffering from various fevers and a chronic eye infection. He returned to England to stay with his family, and to pass the time during his convalescence he wrote five books based on his experiences in India.

HIGH INFIDELITY

Never one to keep still, Burton had an outrageous new adventure in mind: he wanted to visit the holy cities of Mecca and Medina. Other non-Muslims had been there, but as Westerners they weren't admitted to the holiest sites. Burton thought he could get an inside view if he disguised himself as a pilgrim. If discovered, there was a good chance he'd be killed.

He set off for Arabia, pretending to be a wandering mystic. He survived both the gruelling desert travel and his visits to the sacred shrines by following the proper rituals and customs to the letter. His success made him famous, and hungry for more adventure. So he set off for another forbidden Muslim site, the city of Harar in Somaliland. He set off in disguise, but since most people thought he was a Turk – a group much hated in that region – he decided to present himself instead as a British officer. Impressed by Burton's manners and knowledge of Islam, the ruler of Harar allowed him to stay for 10 days – very generous, since tradition had it that the first infidel to enter Harar would bring doom to the city. Burton became the first foreigner to leave the city alive.

Shirley Williams screen tested for the Liz Taylor role in National Velvet.

DE NILE IS NOT JUST A RIVER IN EGYPT

In 1855 Burton set out to discover the source of the Nile, a geographical mystery of the time. His first attempt was unsuccessful – Burton and his team were attacked by local warriors. One member died and Burton wound up with a spear through his cheek.

A few years later, he returned. With him came John Speke, another veteran of India and of the previous expedition. This time, despite a horrible journey and constant illness, Burton and Speke arrived at Lake Tanganyika, rumoured to be the source of the Nile. It wasn't clear if the lake was the ultimate source, and Burton was too sick to do a thorough exploration. He'd heard of another large lake and he sent Speke off to find it. Speke did and named it Lake Victoria (after the queen).

BITTERNESS AND BETRAYAL

Originally an admirer and protégé of Burton, Speke then turned against him. Speke returned to England first and took credit for finding the source of the Nile – Lake Victoria. He also revived all the old rumours about Burton from his Indian days. The Geographical Society asked Speke to head a new expedition to clarify the Nile's source, and Speke refused to take Burton with him.

THE LADY AND THE TRAMP

At this point, Burton did the one respectable thing in his life: he got married. When Isabel Arundell and Richard Burton first set eyes on each other in 1851, the 19-year-old Isabel told her sister: 'That man is going to marry me'. She was even more convinced when she found out his name – a gypsy fortune-teller had told her she would marry a man named Burton. But Isabel was beautiful, highborn and Catholic. Burton was poor, Protestant (or Muslim, Hindu, or an atheist depending on the day of the week) and had a horrible reputation. Fortunately, Isabel also had a lot of gumption, and in 1861 she defied her family's wishes and eloped with Burton.

JUST DESSERTS IN THE DESERT

Meanwhile, Speke was winning a reputation as a total bounder, treating his new collaborators as badly as he'd treated Burton. His subsequent explorations did not establish the real source of the Nile, mainly because he was a lousy explorer. Moreover, he

Four most dangerous steps on most staircases: the two at the top and the two at the bottom.

dropped hints suggesting he'd cavorted with some of his hostesses on the trip – a definite Victorian no-no. The day before Speke was scheduled to debate with Burton on the true source of the Nile at a scientific meeting, Speke died in a mysterious gun accident.

Burton's path after that led him to all manner of other interesting places. Burton was appointed to a series of diplomatic posts in Africa, Brazil and Damascus in Syria. He didn't last long in any of them, due to illness and his talent for annoying important people. (Burton loved to shock people. Among other major leg-pulls, he hinted that he had killed people, been wounded by a jealous husband and eaten a chubby cabin boy during a shipwreck.)

Though always short of cash, the Burtons lived well and kept travelling. In 1872 the government appointed Burton as Consul in Trieste, Italy, calculating correctly that he couldn't create too much trouble there. He lasted 18 years, until his death in 1890.

THE ORIGINAL SEXPERT

Even as he aged, Burton kept himself sharp. He once played – and won – four games of chess simultaneously, while blindfolded. His diplomatic postings gave him more opportunity to explore, study cultures, and write about it all: he published books on archaeology, mining, engineering, anthropology, military science, geography, mountain climbing, religion, slavery and folk tales. He also translated some of the great works of Eastern literature – among them the erotic classics *The Kama Sutra* and *The Scented Garden*. As usual, the Victorian world wasn't quite ready for Burton. (Or claimed it wasn't. Somehow these books managed to become bestsellers.) But his best-loved literary achievement was a translation of the *Arabian Nights*, which some consider the best ever.

FINAL RESTING TENT

Burton accomplished and wrote so much that Queen Victoria gave him a knighthood. But he still wasn't respectable enough to be buried in Westminster Abbey or St. Paul's Cathedral. Instead, the ever-faithful Isabel built him a tomb in Mortlake, near Richmond. It was shaped like the tent they'd shared in many of their travels. Six years later she was buried beside him.

10 per cent of London's surface area is road. In the average US city it's 25 per cent.

PAST PRESENTS

'The Twelve Days of Christmas' – a jolly Yuletide ditty that's little more than a nonsense rhyme. In fact, the song's roots reach back over 500 years to the persecution of Roman Catholics in Britain.

In the mid-16th century, when the song is thought to have originated, expressing your Catholic faith in any but the most guarded terms could earn you a place at the stake. Those who openly professed the 'true faith' were ever more inventive in their ways of expressing their beliefs and teaching the catechism to their children. This song was one way of passing the faith from generation to generation.

GIFTS THAT KEEP ON GIVING

The 'My true love' who gives the singer 12 marvellous presents meant God, not any earthly lover. And 'Me' referred to anyone baptized into and following the Catholic faith. And what about all those peculiar presents themselves? Well, this is what they really signified to in-the-know Catholics:

'Twelve drummers drumming' were the 12 points of faith in the Creed of the Apostles.
'Eleven pipers piping' were the 11 faithful apostles.
'Ten lords a-leaping' were the ten commandments.
'Nine ladies dancing' were the professed gifts of the Holy Spirit.
'Eight maids a-milking' were the eight beatitudes.
'Seven swans a-swimming' were the seven blessed sacraments.
'Six geese a-laying' were the six days in which God created Earth.
'Five gold rings' were the first five books of the Old Testament.
'Four calling birds' were the four gospels and the four evangelists who wrote them.
'Three French hens' were faith, hope and charity.
'Two turtle doves' were The Old and New Testaments.
'A partridge in a pear tree' was Jesus Christ.

So the next time you sing this 'nonsense' song with your children at Christmas, it'll probably take on a whole new meaning.

VEGETABLE NAMES

Vegetable facts from BRI member Jeff Cheek.

CABBAGE
Originated in Asia and introduced to Europe by Alexander the Great, about 325 B.C. The name comes from the Latin *caput*, meaning 'head'. It's high in vitamin C, but contains sulphurous compounds that, when cooked, give off odours similar to rotten eggs or ammonia.

SCALLIONS
These tiny green onions owe their name to the biblical city of Ashkelon. When the Romans conquered the city, they called the tiny onions they found there *caepa Ascolonia* or 'onions of Ashkelon', This became 'scallions'.

JERUSALEM ARTICHOKES
These sweet, starchy roots did not grow in Jerusalem and they are not artichokes. Native Americans used them as bread. The mix-up came when a Spanish explorer thought they were some kind of sunflower. *Girasol* (turn to the sun) is 'sunflower' in Spanish. An American heard it as 'Jerusalem'. No one knows why he also added 'artichoke'.

BROCCOLI
The word comes from the Latin *bracchium*, or 'branch'. It was developed about 2,500 years ago on the island of Cyprus and was a popular dish at ancient Roman banquets. (The Roman emperor Tiberius, who ruled from 14 to 37 A.D., once publicly scolded his son for eating all the grilled broccoli at a state banquet.) It was popularized in the U.S. by Italian immigrants.

KIWI FRUIT
Originally from China, they were imported to New Zealand in the early 1900s and renamed 'Chinese Gooseberry'. They finally made it to the U.S. in 1962, and a Los Angeles distributor named Frieda Caplan named it after the New Zealand national bird, the kiwi. It took another 18 years before the American public started buying them.

CANTALOUPE
A type of muskmelon brought to Italy from Armenia, in modern-day Turkey, in the first century A.D., and grown in the town of Cantalupo, which is where it gets its name.

STRANGE ANIMAL LAWSUITS

In the Middle Ages, it was not unusual for animals to be put on trial as if they could understand human laws. These lawsuits were serious affairs.

THE PLAINTIFFS: Vineyard growers in St.-Julien, France
THE DEFENDANTS: Weevils
THE CASE: In 1545 angry growers testified to a judge that the weevils were eating and destroying their crops. According to one source: 'Legal indictments were drawn, and the insects were actually defended in court'.
THE VERDICT: Since the weevils were obviously eating the crops, they were found guilty. In 1546 a proclamation was issued by the judge demanding that the weevils desist – and amazingly, they did. The farmers weren't bothered by weevils again until 1587. Once more, the insects were put on trial; however, the outcome is unknown.

THE PLAINTIFFS: The people of Mayenne, France
THE DEFENDANT: Mosquitoes
THE CASE: In the 1200s, a swarm of mosquitoes were indicted as a public nuisance by the people of the town. When the creatures failed to answer the summons, the court appointed a lawyer to act on their behalf.
THE VERDICT: The lawyer did such a good job pleading their case that the court took pity. The judge banished them, but gave them a patch of real estate outside town where they would be allowed to swarm in peace 'forever'.

THE PLAINTIFF: The city of Basel, Switzerland
THE DEFENDANT: A rooster
THE CASE: In 1474 the rooster was accused of being (or helping) a sorcerer. The reason, according to the prosecutor: It had laid eggs – and as everyone knows, an egg laid by a rooster is prized by sorcerers. On top of that, it was shown 'that Satan employed witches to hatch such eggs, from which proceeded

winged serpents most dangerous to mankind'.

The rooster's lawyer admitted it had laid an egg, but contended that 'no injury to man or beast had resulted'. And besides, laying an egg is an involuntary act, he said, so the law shouldn't punish it.

THE VERDICT: The judge refused to allow the lawyer's argument and declared the rooster guilty of sorcery. Both the unfortunate fowl and the egg it had allegedly laid were found guilty and burned at the stake.

THE PLAINTIFFS: Barley growers in Autun, France
THE DEFENDANTS: Rats
THE CASE: In 1510 the rodents were charged with burglary, having eaten and destroyed the barley crop. A young lawyer named Bartholomew de Chassenée was appointed to defend them. When the rats failed to appear in court, Chassenée successfully argued that since the case involved all the rats of the diocese (the area under jurisdiction of one bishop), all of them should be summoned. When the rats failed to appear again, Chassenée argued that it was because they were scared by 'evilly disposed cats which were in constant watch along the highways'. Since, by law, the rats were entitled to protection to and from court, the plaintiffs 'should be required to post a bond' that would be forfeited if the cats attacked the rats on their way to court.
THE VERDICT: Unknown, but the publicity from the case helped Chasenée to establish a reputation as a sharp lawyer. In fact, many historians now regard him as one of France's greatest ever lawyers.

THE PLAINTIFF: The Grand Vicar of Valence, France
THE DEFENDANTS: Caterpillars inhabiting his diocese
THE CASE: In 1584 the Grand Vicar excommunicated the insects for causing destruction to crops, and ordered them to appear before him. When they didn't appear, a lawyer was appointed to defend them.
THE VERDICT: The lawyer argued his case, but lost. The caterpillars were banished from the diocese. 'When the caterpillars failed to leave, the trial continued until the short-lived caterpillars died off. The Vicar was then credited with having miraculously exterminated them'.

Napoleon III enrolled as a special constable in the UK in 1848, before returning to France.

WEIRD DOLL STORIES

Maybe it's because they look human that dolls seem to inspire such bizarre behavior in people. Here are a few examples.

STAR TREK'S MR. SPOCK DOLL

In 1994, England, under the auspices of the European Union, slapped import quotas on all 'nonhuman creature' dolls manufactured in China. The quota did not apply to human dolls, which meant that Captain Kirk dolls were allowed into the country. But the quota did apply to Mr. Spock, since he is a Vulcan and therefore a nonhuman creature (even though Spock's mother was human). 'It seems very strange', said Peter Waterman, a spokesperson for the British toy industry, 'that we should have customs officials involved in a discussion of whether Mr. Spock is an alien or a human being'.

GROWING UP SKIPPER

Introduced by Mattel in the spring of 1975, Skipper – Barbie's little sister – really did grow up. When you cranked her arm, she grew 7 millimetres taller and sprouted breasts and an hourglass figure. The doll was attacked by feminists, who charged that the doll was 'a grotesque caricature of the female body', and 'caters to psychotic preoccupation with instant culture and instant sex object'. The doll sold well anyway.

EARRING MAGIC KEN

In 1993 Mattel introduced Earring Magic Ken; a version of Barbie's boyfriend that came complete with a fetching lavender mesh shirt, a lavender vest and an earring. It became an instant camp classic in the gay community – which interpreted Ken's choice of clothing and jewellery to mean that there was a very good reason why, after more than 30 years of dating, Barbie and Ken had never married.

Mattel insisted there was no hidden agenda. 'The designers were amazed when all of this surfaced', they claimed. Then they took the doll off the market.

TALKING BARBIE AND G.I. JOE DOLLS

In 1993 a group calling itself the Barbie Liberation Organization (BLO) claimed it switched the voice boxes on as many as 300 G.I. Joe and Barbie dolls in France, England and the U.S. at the peak of the Christmas shopping season, to protest against 'gender-based stereotyping in children's toys'. So when kids opened their G.I. Joes, they said things like, 'I love school. Don't you'? and 'Let's sing with the band tonight' in a female voice; Barbie said 'Dead men tell no lies', in a deep, booming male voice.

TELETUBBIES

In 1998 – shortly after U.S. televangelist Jerry Falwell attacked Tinky-Winky as a stalking-horse for gay culture – a woman who bought a Teletubby at a New York toy shop claimed that when she got the doll home, it shouted obscenities like 'bite my butt' and whispered anti-gay remarks. A spokesman for the manufacturer said that the doll, named Po, was actually bilingual – and was saying 'Faster, faster!' in Cantonese.

THE CABBAGE PATCH SNACKTIME DOLL

The 1996 Snacktime doll came with a motorized set of gears that powered its lower jaw, allowing it to chew and 'eat' plastic carrots and biscuits. That, however, was not all it liked to eat – in 1997 the Consumer Produce Safety Commission in the U.S. received more than 100 reports of children getting their fingers and hair stuck in the mechanical mouth, 'which would not stop chewing until the battery back was removed'. Mattel later admitted that it had not fully tested the product, withdrew the doll from the market, and offered to buy back dolls for $40 apiece. Only about 1,000 of the 500,000 dolls sold were returned.

FURBIES

In 1999, the National Security Agency in America issued a Furby Alert, warning that the dolls – which come with sophisticated computer chips that allow them to record and mimic human speech – might 'overhear secret information and "start talking classified"', inadvertently passing secret information on to America's enemies. Accordingly, Furbies were banned from sensitive areas in the Pentagon.

HOW TO MAKE A MONSTER, PART III

Here's the third installment of the Godzilla story. *(Part II starts on page 139.)*

COMING TO AMERICA

Gojira's box-office success in Japan caught the attention of American movie studios; in 1955 Joseph E. Levine of TransWorld Films bought the film's U.S. rights for $25,000. The spelling of the monster's name was changed to Godzilla, an approximation of how it was pronounced in Japanese (GO-dzee-la); and the title was changed to *Godzilla, King of the Monsters*.

Levine knew that if he released *Godzilla* with Japanese dialogue, it would appeal only to art-house film crowds – and he wouldn't make back his investment. A subtitled film would miss the youth audience entirely, since many kids were too young to read them. So Levine adapted the film for Americans by dubbing it into English.

MADE IN USA

It wasn't the only change Levine made: the plot was revised, scenes were rearranged or removed entirely, and brand-new scenes were filmed to insert an American character into the previously all-Japanese film. The American, played by Raymond Burr (of TV's *Ironsides* and *Perry Mason)*, is a newspaper reporter named Steve Martin who happens to be on assignment in Japan when Godzilla goes on the attack.

Burr couldn't appear on screen at the same time as the Japanese actors in the original version of the film, but numerous scenes of Japanese actors talking to one another were re-edited to make it look like they were talking to him.

FROM A TO B

The effect of Levine's changes was to turn what had been a polished, serious film for adults into a monster movie made for drive-in movie theatres and kiddie matinées. But that was precisely what he wanted: in the mid-1950s, the American film industry

When BBC2 launched in 1964, the power failed – so, there really was nothing on that night.

was in a slump. The advent of television, combined with laws that had forced the major studios to sell off their theatre chains, caused a dramatic drop in movie attendance and movie profits. Major studios became extremely cautious, making fewer A-films than they had in the 1940s.

As a result, several companies sprang up to make cheapo B-movies for drive-ins and faded downtown movie palaces. Then, along came *Gojira*. 'Though a big budget, major studio film in Japan', Stuart Galbraith writes in *Monsters are Attacking Tokyo!*, 'the Americanized Gojira was released (solely) as an exploitation feature'. Because it was intended for the B-movie market, the changes were done on the cheap, which lowered the quality of the American version of the film. The poor dubbing and cheesy dialogue made it difficult for Western filmgoers, already used to clichéd American monster movies, to take the film seriously. And they didn't.

SON(S) OF GODZILLA

Say what you will about the changes Levine made to the original *Gojira*, he knew his audience. *Godzilla, King of the Monsters*, opened in the U.S. on 26 April, 1956, and made more than $2 million at the box office, an astonishing sum for the 1950s. The American version did so well that it was exported back to *Japan* under the title *Monster King Godzilla* (Raymond Burr's dialogue was dubbed into Japanese), where it added to the profits already made by the original *Gojira*. And Burr's character was so popular with Japanese audiences that reporter characters became a staple of later *Godzilla* movies in the 1960s and 1970s.

Enthused by the success of the first *Gojira* film, Toho ordered up the first of what would become more than 20 sequels. *Gojira's Counterattack* (the U.S. version was called *Gigantis the Fire Monster)* was released in 1955. Toho made nine non-Gojira monster movies between 1955 and 1962, featuring monsters such as the Abominable Snowman, and a robot mole named Mogera. But as J. D. Lees writes in *The Official Godzilla Compendium*, the release of *King Kong vs. Godzilla* in 1962 made Godzilla a superstar. 'The pairing with the famous ape elevated Godzilla from the swelling ranks of interchangeable atomic monsters of the fifties and placed him among the classic pantheon of cinema creatures'.

GODZILLA FLICKS

• **Godzilla Raids Again (1955).** The first naff Godzilla sequel, it was released in America in 1959 as *Gigantis the Fire Monster,* to avoid any confusion with the original film. Plot: 'Yearning for a change of pace, the King of Monsters opts to destroy Osaka instead of Tokyo, but the spiny Angorous is out to dethrone our hero. Citizens flee in terror when the battle royale begins'. *Director:* Ishiro Honda *(Videohound's Golden Movie Retriever)*

• **King Kong vs. Godzilla (1963).** Developed from an idea – and what an idea – by Willis O'Brien, creator of the original *King Kong's* stop-motion animation back in the 1930s. O'Brien's story was about a fight between King Kong and 'the Ginko', a monster created by – of all people – Dr. Frankenstein's grandson. But the only studio willing to make the film was Toho – and they insisted on using Godzilla. The Japanese sensibly filmed it as a satire, with the two monsters wrestling in Tokyo (where else?) and on top of Mt. Fuji. King Kong wins. *Director:* Ishiro Honda *(A Critical History of Godzilla)*

• **Godzilla vs. Mothra (1964).** Released as *Godzilla vs. the Thing.* 'When the egg of giant monster Mothra is washed ashore by a storm, a greedy entrepreneur is quick to exploit it. Meanwhile, Godzilla reappears and goes on a rampage.... Godzilla, who seems to be really enjoying his reign of destruction, shows more personality than in previous appearances....Excellent in all departments'. *Director:* Ishiro Honda *(Cult Flicks and Trash Pics)*

• **Godzilla vs. Monster Zero (1965).** 'Novel Godzilla adventure with the big guy and Rodan in outer space. Suspicious denizens of Planet X require the help of Godzilla and Rodan to rid themselves of the menacing Ghidra, whom they refer to as Monster Zero. Will they, in return, help Earth as promised, or is this just one big, fat double cross'? *Director:* Ishiro Honda *(Videohound's Golden Movie Retriever)*

• **Godzilla vs. Sea Monster (1968).** 'This exercise in cardboard mayhem stars the saucy saurian as a crusty critter suffering a case of crabs when he's attacked by colossal crustaceans (notably Ebirah, a giant lobster) and does battle with the Red Bamboo bad-guy gang'. *Director:* Jun Fukuda *(Creature Features Movie Guide Strikes Again)*

On average, adults have 2 gallons of air in the space between their skin and their clothes.

• **Godzilla on Monster Island (1972).** 'In this harmless, toy-like movie, Godzilla talks, as he and spiny Angillus battle alien-summoned Ghidrah and new playmate Gigan, who has a buzzsaw in his belly'. *Director:* Jun Fukuda *(Leonard Maltin's Movie & Video Guide)*

• **Godzilla vs. the Smog Monster (1972).** 'A Japanese industrial city has an ecology woe; its bay of waste and rotting animal life breeds Hedorah, which shoots laser beams from its eyepods and flies at will....To the rescue comes the flat-footed Godzilla to indulge in a duel-of-the-titans'. Godzilla flies in this one, and it looks really cheap – 'the army consists of about 10 guys'. *Director:* Yoshimitsu Banno *(Creature Features Movie Guide Strikes Again)*

• **Godzilla vs. Megalon (1973).** 'The 122 metre-tall green lizard is aided by a jet-packed robot in fighting off Megalon (a giant cockroach with Zap Killer Beam), Baragon the stomper, and a race of underground Earthlings, the Seatopians'. *Director:* Jun Fukuda *(Creature Features Movie Guide Strikes Again)*

• **Godzilla vs. the Cosmic Monster (1974).** 'Japanese sci-fi sukiyaki with the King of Monsters battling a cyborg Godzilla controlled by aliens bent on conquest. A huge rodent creature said to embody Asian spirits comes to the real Godzilla's aid when the languid lizard squares off against antagonistic Angorus'. *Director:* Jun Fukuda *(Creature Features Movie Guide Strikes Again)*

• **Godzilla: 1985 (1984).** 'After 30 years, the Big G recovers from his apparent death...and returns to destroy Tokyo all over again. Disregarding the previous fourteen sequels (most of which were set in 'the future' anyway), the plot marches along much like a '70s disaster film'. *Director:* Kohji Hashimoto. *(Cult Flicks and Trash Pics)*

• **Godzilla vs. Biollante (1989).** 'Genetic scientist Surigama uses cells from Godzilla's body to create hardy new crop strains, while also splicing the cells' DNA to that of his dead daughter, using that of her favourite rose as a catalyst. His experiments result in the gigantic plant/animal monster Biollante, a nightmare of creeping vines, snapping teeth, and corrosive sap'. *Director:* Kazuki Ohmori *(Cult Flicks and Trash Pics)*

• **Godzilla (1998).** Charmless big-bucks travesty starring Matthew Broderick. Bad career move.

Injured fingernails grow faster than uninjured ones.

WORD ORIGINS

Here are some more interesting word origins.

PUNCH
Meaning: A fruity drink
Origin: 'From Sanskrit panca or Hindustani panch, which means "five", the theory being that there were five ingredients – alcohol, water, lemon, sugar and spice'. (From *The Story Behind the Word*, by Morton S. Freeman)

EAVESDROP
Meaning: Secretly listen to someone else's conversation
Origin: 'In Anglo-Saxon England, a house had very wide overhanging eaves...to allow rain to drip safely away from the house's foundation. So the eavesdrip, later the eavesdrop, provided a place where one could hide to listen clandestinely to conversation within the house'. (From *Morris Dictionary of Word and Phrase Origins*, by William and Mary Morris)

CHEAT
Meaning: A dishonest person; the act of deceiving someone for gain
Origin: Comes from escheat – a medieval legal term for 'the reversion of property to the state in the absence of legal heirs, and of the state's rights to such confiscation. The officer who looked after the king's escheats was known as the cheater....The dishonest connotations of the word evolved among thieves in the 16th century'. (From *Wicked Words*, by Hugh Rawson)

SNOB
Meaning: A snooty person; someone who puts on airs
Origin: 'It seems that Oxford (students) were required to register "according to rank". Those not of noble birth added after their names the phrase sine nobilitate which was then abbreviated to 's. nob.', thus creating...a perfect definition for the commoner who wishes to mingle with the nobles'. (From *Dictionary of Word and Phrase Origins, Vol. III*, by William and Mary Morris)

An exocannibal is a cannibal who eats only enemies. An endocannibal eats only friends.

ZANY

Meaning: Crazy

Origin: 'Dates back to the *commedia dell'arte* in Italy of the 16th century. The *zanni* (as it was spelled in Italian) was a buffoon who mimicked one of the characters, usually the clown. The English changed its spelling to zany and used it to refer to any simpleton or bumbling fool'. (From *Dictionary of Word and Phrase Origins, Vol. II*, by William and Mary Morris)

AMBITION

Meaning: Single-minded drive toward achieving a goal

Origin: '*Ambitio* is the Latin term for "running around". The term originally referred to the way politicians in ancient Rome ran around "in search of voters to persuade or buy"'. (From *Loose Cannons and Red Herrings*, by Robert Claiborne)

ALCOHOL

Meaning: An intoxicating beverage

Origin: 'The word comes from Arabic al-kuhul, a powder used as a cosmetic. Borrowed into English, alcohol came to mean any distilled substance. Alcohol of wine was thus the 'quintessence of wine'...by the middle of the 18th century alcohol was being used on its own'. (From *Dictionary of Word Origins*, by John Ayto)

DIAPER (American for 'nappy')

Meaning: A cloth used to capture a baby's waste

Origin: 'From Greek *diaspros*, meaning "pure white"....Originally, a fabric woven of silk, sewn with gold threads, and used for ecclesiastical robes'. (From *Thereby Hangs a Tale*, by Charles Earle Funk)

DOODLE

Meaning: Aimless, absent-minded scribbles on scraps of paper

Origin: 'The word doodle comes from the German word *dudeln*, meaning "to play the bagpipe". The notion seems to be that a person who spends his time playing bagpipes would be guilty of other frivolous time-wasting activities'. (From *Dictionary of Word and Phrase Origins, Vol. III*, by William and Mary Morris)

Most-used expression of any language on earth: 'OK'.

PLAYMATE IQ TEST

In 1997, two Playboy 'Playmates of the Year' – Julie Cialini (1995) and Stacy Sanches (1996) – showed up on Howard Stern's radio show. Because playmates are role models for young girls everywhere, Stern asked a few questions to test the girls' grasp of current affairs. Here's the text of the quiz.

Q: Who is President of Russia?
Julie: 'Gorbachev'.
Stacy: 'Gretzky'. (U.S. ice hockey star)
(CORRECT ANSWER: Boris Yeltsin.)

Q: What is the centre of our solar system?
Julie: 'The equator'.
Stacy: 'The moon'.
(CORRECT ANSWER: The sun.)

Q: Define the NAACP.
Julie: 'Something, something, something, for Certified Pianists'.
Stacy: 'It's some kind of police organization'.
(CORRECT ANSWER: National Association for the Advancement of Coloured People.)

Q: Who invented the lightbulb?
Julie: 'I know Edison invented the telephone, but I can't remember the lightbulb guy'.
Stacy: 'I don't know'.
(CORRECT ANSWER: Thomas Edison. Alexander Graham Bell was the telephone guy.)

Q: Who's the Speaker of the House?
Julie: 'Gore or something-or-other'.
Stacy: 'Bill Clinton'.
(CORRECT ANSWER : Newt Gingrich.)

Q: Define the meaning of the letters CIA.
Julie: 'I don't know'.
Stacy: 'Certified Investigation Association'.
(CORRECT ANSWER: Central Intelligence Agency.)

To give the playmates better odds, Stern tried a few 'industry-related' questions.

Q: What do the initials 'DK' stand for?
A: Both playmates knew it was fashion designer Donna Karan.

Q: What car company has a model known as '911'?
A: Both knew it was Porsche.

Q: Whose face is on the $100 bill?
A: Both knew it was Benjamin Franklin.

The average computer worker types 90,000 keystrokes in an eight-hour shift.

A STRAIGHT FACE

Ever wonder what the Big Guys of poker know that you don't? They swear it's all in keeping a straight face, and watching the table for the players who don't. Here are a few pointers from the experts.

IT'S ALL IN THE GAME

There are well over 400 great professional poker players in the world today. So if poker is truly a game of 'chance', then how can so many people be consistently good at winning? It's not the card itself, say the experts, as much as the flip of the card that gives away the game to people who know what to look for. Players, particularly weaker players, give away 'tells', or unconscious reflexes during the game that really good card sharps can use to get one over on their opponents.

One of the poker greats, the self-proclaimed 'Mad Poker Genius' Mike Caro, has made a living from poker and a killing from studying the psychology of the game. On his web site, Mike Caro's World, he talks at length about the various 'tells' to watch for in others, and how to avoid them yourself.

No.1: WEAK AND STRONG

The first rule of thumb in gauging your fellow players is the 'Strong When Weak' guideline.

• In general, players who have bad hands subconsciously act more aggressively; players with strong hands act indifferent and passively. Why? 'Because', Caro says, 'deception is fundamental to poker – otherwise we'd play with our hands fully exposed'.

• When a player looks down and has a lousy hand, he doesn't want to give away his emotions because then he's lost the game up front. So unconsciously, he usually acts the opposite of the way he is feeling. An experienced player knows this and watches for the cues. An even better player will play off these psychological indicators against each other.

TELL ME TRUE

'Tells' are far more prevalent in weak and mediocre players than in the pros. But watch out – really good players are good actors, and a top-of-the-line poker player knows how to fake a 'tell' to throw

There is no leading cause of death for people who live past the age of 100.

off his opponents. The situation can become so complex that it's next to impossible to tell whether a gulp (for example) was a sign of fear – or simply a great acting job. Here, according to Caro, are some of the universal poker tells to watch for.

The Heavy Heart: A sad sigh during the bet usually means a player has a good hand. Be somewhat cautious and don't call unless your hand is very good too.

Shifty Eyes: A glance away from the table once the hand has been dealt. This usually indicates a player who's holding a good hand and wants to hide his excitement.

Stare Down: A direct stare into another player's eyes after the cards have been dealt or during a bet is usually a sign of a weak hand. Staring into anyone's eyes is considered somewhat aggressive and can therefore be read that a player is bluffing.

Pokerclack: Pokerclack is a soft clucking noise that sounds morose or shameful. It's a term coined by Caro, and he describes it as the noise you'd make after saying something like, 'I'm feeling terrible today. My old dog Shep ran into the street and got run over'.

Flair: An extra flamboyance at the toss of a poker chip during a bet is almost always a sign that a player is trying to hide a bad hand. He's bluffing.

The Jitters: Shaky hands during a bet suggests excitement, nervousness, tension in the player. Even skilled players often mistake this sign and think the shaky player is bluffing and scared he's going to lose. That's almost never the case, however, according to Caro. Players who are bluffing tend to be rock-steady, not jittery. It's the player who's got a monstrously good hand who sometimes can't contain his excitement.

The Big Chill: When a player goes quiet after betting, you can almost guarantee he's got a lousy hand and he's bluffing.

The Babbling Brook: When a talkative player begins babbling somewhat incoherently or absentmindedly during or after a bet, he's usually got a lousy hand. His hand disrupted his normal conversation and he didn't want to go silent for fear he'd give himself away. But this cowboy's almost surely bluffing.

Chameleon rule of thumb: if it loses a fight, it turns grey; if it wins, it turns green.

Chip Fondling: The hands have been dealt and the player on your right is fingering his poker chips. Read it as a sign that he's raring to place his bet; he's got a great hand.

The Stiff: If you see a player suddenly go rigid and hold his breath following a bet, take it as a sign of bluffing. Call him.

TELLING TALES
It's betting time around your Friday night poker table and your friend flips his chip in the air with flair and a wink. With all of this newfound knowledge, you know you've just spotted a bluff. What should you do when you notice a 'tell'? Mike Caro says: 'Don't let your pride destroy the profit you could make from tells. Never announce that, "I knew you were bluffing", if you successfully call and win with a weak hand. Say, instead, "I don't know why I called. I almost didn't, but at the last second I decided to test you one time. I guess I got lucky". That kind of talk will encourage an opponent to try again'.

* * *

THE NAME GAME

There are hundreds – maybe thousands – of poker variations, and some of them sound downright funny when said out loud. A few of our favourite strange-sounding poker games:

Change the Nappy
Dirty Schultz
Making Babies
Three Legged Race
Howdy Doody
Grocery Store Dots
Linoleum
Navy Nurse
Screwy Louie
Cowpie Poker
Five Card Stud with a Bug
There Can Only Be Juan
Rubbish Bin
Want It? Want It? Got It!
The Good, the Bad, and the Ugly
Mexican Sweat
Pass the Rubbish

IT'S YOUR ROUND

Come the end of a Saturday night in your local, it's a safe bet that most regulars will be barely capable of coherent speech. So it may surprise you to know how many pub-based phrases there are.

There is no more important institution in the whole of British society than the good old pub. It's the hub of many of our social lives, where we meet friends, have a chat, share a joke – and get plain, old-fashioned, falling-down drunk. Here are some well-known sayings that originated in pubs

A BIT OF ORDER PLEASE, GENTLEMEN

In the last century, beer was served in two measures, Pints and Quarts. When things got a bit rowdy toward closing time, as they usually did, here was a good chance that most of the beer mugs would get smashed or damaged. So, whenever a fight broke out, the landlord would cry out 'Mind your Pints and Quarts, folks'. Which is why we still ask people to 'mind your P's and Q's'.

MAKE MINE A PINT

The pint measure comes from the attempt by government to regulate standard measurements, with the Weights and Measures Act of 1824. All beer mugs had a mark painted on them to show the measure the customer could expect. This was known as the 'paint mark'. Over time, probably with a bit of help from one too many beers, 'paint' was garbled into 'pint' and the name stuck.

THE LONG STRETCH

There is a rather grisly origin for two well known drinking phrases. In the 18th century, executions in London were carried out at Tyburn (now Marble Arch).The condemned were brought along what is now Oxford St., which in those days was little more than a country road. Prisoners would be allowed to stop off in a pub at the beginning of Oxford St., where they would be offered their last drink, or 'one for the road'. After drinking their final ever draught of the good stuff, they went outside and climbed 'back on the wagon' to be taken off to execution.

What a horrible thought. It's enough to drive you to drink!

Q: How did black sheep get their bad name?

THE BLACK SHEEP OF THE BRONTËS

Get out your handkerchiefs. The sad, sad story of the brilliant Brontë family and the brother who never quite got his act together.

The brilliant writers Charlotte and Emily Brontë had four siblings: three sisters and a brother. Two of the sisters died of consumption (tuberculosis) like their mother had, leaving sister Anne (also a writer, but not as famous) and brother Patrick Branwell (known as 'Branwell'), who dragged the good Brontë name through the dirt of mid-19th-century England.

A PICTURE OF LOVELINESS

While his sisters worked as governesses and scribbled away at their books in their spare time, Branwell tried his hand at portrait painting. His most famous work – of Charlotte, Emily and Anne – hangs in London's National Portrait Gallery and graces the cover of almost every book about the Brontës. It is the only picture of the three girls together – which is precisely why it hangs in the National Portrait Gallery, because, as a work of art, it's really not terribly good.

THE SWEET SMELL OF EXCESS

Being at best a mediocre artist, Branwell failed to make his name as a painter, so he tried his hand instead at private tutoring for the rich. He was fired after less than a year. His next job was as a railway clerk, but that didn't work out either. He missed – or may have created – a discrepancy in the accounts. So out he went on his ear again. By now he was a hard drinker. He was also taking a lot of opium. His sisters strongly disapproved of their brother's 'wildness and intemperance'.

HERE'S TO YOU, MRS. ROBINSON

Branwell's fourth and most disastrous attempt at making a living came in 1843, when Anne put in a good word for him with a family she knew named Robinson. They need a tutor for their son,

A: Their wool is harder to dye than that of white sheep.

Edmund, and Branwell thought he was just the man for the job.

Mrs. Robinson was a sexy woman, 17 years older than Branwell. On top of this, Mr. Robinson was in ill health and unable to perform his, er, conjugal duties. Branwell, on the other hand, was not only in full working order but was young, good-looking, manly, and in the house all day, every day. He claimed in letters to friends that he had a torrid affair with Mrs. R. Word leaked out – and back to Mr. Robinson – and Branwell was dismissed from the family's service and sent home in disgrace in 1845. From there, it was a short ride to the bottom.

OH BROTHER!

Meanwhile, Branwell's sisters were producing some of the most famous classics in English literature. Charlotte's *Jane Eyre*, Emily's *Wuthering Heights*, and Anne's *Agnes Grey* were all published in 1847. Anne published two other books the next year. *The Tenant of Wildfell Hall*, published in 1848, has a character, Arthur Huntingdon, who is a violent and infantile, but sexually attractive, drunkard. Sound like anyone we know?

THE LAST OF THE BRONTËS

Branwell died in September 1848 – of consumption, of course, which was worsened by years of drugs and drinking. Consumption also claimed Emily three months later and Anne the following May. Poor Charlotte had lost all three of her siblings in less than a year. Not even the public excitement about *Jane Eyre* could have compensated for that. She lasted a few more years before pregnancy complications and consumption got her, too. She died in 1855, having married her father's curate a few months earlier.

* * *

A THOUGHT FROM SISTER CHARLOTTE

'It is vain to say human beings ought to be satisfied with tranquility: they must have action; and they will make it if they cannot find it.'

Jane Eyre

YOU'RE MY INSPIRATION

It's always fascinating to find out who, or what, inspired cultural milestones like these.

STAR WARS. According to *Leonard Maltin's Movie Guide*, the 1958 Japanese film that was 'acknowledged by George Lucas as a primary inspiration for Star Wars' is *Hidden Fortress*, directed by Akira Kurosawa. The comedy-adventure 'deals with the adventures of a strong-willed princess – à la Carrie Fisher, in the space fantasy – and her wise, sword-wielding protector – Toshiro Mifune, in the role adapted for Alec Guinness', says *Video Guide*. The two other main characters, a pair of bumbling farmers, are said to have been models for C-3PO and R2-D2.

THE 'MAN WITH NO NAME'. The character in *A Fistful of Dollars* (1964), who made Clint Eastwood a movie star, was also inspired by Kurosawa. 'It is almost a scene-for-scene remake of Akira Kurosawa's *Yojimbo*, the tale of a lone samurai (played by Toshiro Mifune) who comes to a town torn by two rival gangs of fighters. He plays them against each other...and in the end finishes off pretty much the whole town and leaves with all the money. Replace a samurai with a gunslinger and replace the Japanese village with a small Western town, and you have *A Fistful of Dollars*'. (Real Video)

DOLLY PARTON. Her famous 'look' was inspired by a woman in her hometown. (No, not Toshiro Mifune.) Parton says: 'There was this (floozy) that lived in our town, I better not say her name, 'cause she's probably got kids and grandkids now. But back then, she wore these bright-coloured clothes and she had this peroxide yellow hair – yellow, not blonde – and she used to walk up and down the streets of our hometown and they always said, "Oh she's just trash, she's just a whore". But I thought she was beautiful'.

When you're looking at someone you hate, your pupils dilate, too.

IT'S A WEIRD, WEIRD WORLD

More proof that truth really is stranger than fiction.

YO QUIERO CASA SANCHEZ!

'A Mexican restaurant in San Francisco offered a lifetime of free lunches to anyone willing to get a tattoo of its logo, Jimmy the Corn Man, a sombrero-wearing mariachi boy riding a blazing corncob. Amazingly, 38 people have braved the needle for a permanent coupon at Casa Sanchez so far. "I think people have gotten much stupider tattoos for much stupider reasons", says tattoo artist Barnaby Williams, who created 30 of the "body coupons'.

– *USA Today*, 13 April, 1999

TERRORIST VOGUE

'Carlos the Jackal was one of the world's most notorious and elusive terrorists, accused of 83 deaths worldwide and more than a dozen other charges stemming from a 20-year killing spree.

'After two decades of evading the law, he was arrested in a Sudanese hospital while undergoing liposuction and a tummy tuck'.

– San Francisco Chronicle

NOSING AROUND

'Ruth Clarke, 23, of London, underwent surgery to correct a lifelong breathing problem in 1981. She was presented with a tiddlywink, which doctors had removed from her nose.

'Clarke vaguely recalled losing the disk as a tot, but she didn't dream it was right under her nose all the time'.

– Encyclopedia Brown's Book of Strange Facts

THE POSTMAN RINGS MORE THAN TWICE

'From 1974 to 1976, a young man in Taiwan wrote 700 love letters to his girlfriend, trying to talk her into marriage. He succeeded – she married the mailman who delivered the letters to her'.

– Weird News and Strange Stories

Sean Connery used to deliver milk to Fettes, the school James Bond attended.

ZZZZ-Z-Z-Z-Z-Z

According to experts we've been chatting with, horses, deer and giraffes sleep an average of only 3 hours a day – while cats get a whopping 15 hours. Humans fall between them, with an average of 7.5 hours. What happens during those 7 (or so) hours while you're sleeping? That will probably always be a big mystery, but we have more answers now than we did just half a century ago.

THE MYSTERY OF SLEEP

It wasn't until 1954 that science made a big breakthrough and recognized that R.E.M. (rapid eye movement) during sleep was caused by dreaming. Since then, the science of sleep has expanded rapidly, with over 100 distinct sleeping disorders now classified and many doctors devoting their careers exclusively to sleep problems.

Into the Waves

Scientists now recognize four stages of sleep:

Stage 1) After your muscles relax, your brain produces smaller waves of 9-12 cycles per second. You think normal, everyday thoughts. Pulse and breathing are regular.

Stage 2) Brain waves get larger with sudden bursts. Your eyes go 'off' and wouldn't register anything if they were opened. Eyes may roll slowly back and forth.

Stage 3) Brain waves get slower and bigger, about five times larger than in stage 1.

Stage 4) Profound unconsciousness, with the biggest, slowest brainwaves. It takes over an hour to reach this stage.

Most people only go to stage 4 once or twice, then come back to lighter sleep (generally stage 1), and experience R.E.M. (dream-state).

THE R.E.M. EXPERIENCE

Once you're in R.E.M.:

- The muscles of your middle ear begin vibrating (science doesn't know why).
- Brain waves resemble a waking state, but you're dreaming.

- Muscles are relaxed, but may twitch or move.
- Pulse and breathing speed up. But we breathe less oxygen and use fewer calories than in other stages of sleep.
- Blood flow and brain temperature accelerate.
- Eyes dart all over the place, 'seeing' what we're dreaming.

The first R.E.M. episode averages 10 minutes; then episodes recur on a 90- to 100-minute cycle, with the deeper sleep stages (3 or 4) getting shorter in between. During R.E.M., our bodily processes are not operated by the larger, evolved parts of our brain, but by the brain stem – the 'ancient brain' we had millions of years ago when we were arboreal (tree-dwelling) mammals.

R.E.M. FACTS

We can dream without R.E.M., but scientists have established that these dreams are simple and uneventful. R.E.M. dreaming, on the other hand, is the more exciting, dramatic kind. We do R.E.M. dreaming about two hours a night. In a lifetime, this adds up to 5 or 6 years of R.E.M. dreaming.

You may think that because your body seems to go offline, your mind does too. Not so. Your brain spends the night integrating the info and experiences you've gained during the day, and most of this happens during R.E.M. sleep. Labouratory tests showed that if mice learned complex tasks and then were deprived of their R.E.M. time, they forgot what they learned. In tests on University of Ottawa students, researchers noticed that the faster students learned things, the more R.E.M. time they required. Slower learners needed less R.E.M. time.

- Life stresses and changes also increase the need for R.E.M. Using a group of divorcing women in their early 30s as subjects, psychoanalyst Rosalind Cartwright conducted a study that showed they needed more R.E.M. time to assimilate their big changes.

- Among people over 65, those who are mentally sharper experience R.E.M. more frequently.

- Most of us don't reach R.E.M. until about an hour and a half after nodding off; people with depression, however, get to R.E.M. in about half this time. They also experience it more intensely.

- R.E.M. occupies approximately 22 per cent of sleeping time. Pleasant dreams.

Hot chocolate: in Japan, you can buy cocoa flavoured with 2 per cent chilli pepper sauce.

LOST IN TRANSLATION

Have you ever thought you were communicating brilliantly, only to find out that others thought you were a lunatic? That's an especially easy mistake to make when you're speaking a foreign language or dealing with a foreign culture. A few examples:

PRODUCT CONFUSION

• **Gerber Baby Food:** Gerber used the same packaging strategy in Africa that it used in America – a picture of the Gerber baby on the label. They apparently didn't realize that since many Africans don't read, it's standard practice to put pictures of the contents on jar labels. As you might guess, the product didn't go over well.

• **The Dairy Association:** Taking their 'Got Milk'? campaign to Mexico, this American organization translated their slogan into Spanish. Unfortunately, it came out as 'Are you lactating?'

• **Johnson Wax:** When Johnson introduced their furniture cleaner Pledge into the Netherlands, they didn't know that, in Dutch, Pledge means 'piss'.

MEDIA TRANSLATIONS

• In the late 1970s, the TV sitcom *Laverne and Shirley* was shown in Bangkok, Thailand – where women did not act like the show's main characters. Each program was preceded by a disclaimer saying: 'The two women depicted in the following episode are from an insane asylum'.

• According to one source, audiences in Lebanon were going to see *Titanic* because the title in Arabic slang translates as *Let's Have Sex.*

MIXED-UP MENUS

These items are from real menus. Bon appétit.

- Horse-rubbish sauce (Rome)
- Torture soup (Djerba)
- Crab Meat Shaag and Botty Kebab (New York)
- Terminal soup (Istanbul)
- Farte aux Fraises (Turkey)
- Frozen soap with Peccadilloes (Madrid)
- Stewed shellfish with 3 things and lucky duck (Bangkok)

SCREWED-UP SIGNS

• When English/Spanish signs were first posted at Sky Harbour International Airport in Phoenix, Arizona, they were full of mistakes. One sign, meant to remind arriving travellers to declare fruits, vegetables and meats, read '*Violadores Seran Finados*', which translates as 'Violators Will Be Deceased'.

DIPLOMATIC COCK-UPS

• A French ambassador, M. Cambon, once thanked a Chicago mayor for a tour of the city. 'Thank you', he said. 'But I am sorry so to cockroach on your time'. The mayor replied, 'But you don't mean "cockroach", Mr. Cambon; it is "encroach" you mean'. 'Oh, is it'? Cambon asked. 'I see, a difference in gender'.

• An Englishwoman at a French diplomatic party asked a Frenchman for a light. What he heard instead was, 'Are you a dung-hill'?

CAMPING INSTRUCTIONS

These regulations were posted at a camp site in Italy:

• Cars must enter or go away from the camp with motors out.

• THEN IS STRICTLY FORBIDDEN TO:

a) Reserve box parking, spaces with chairs, fences, rape or other means

b) Dainage of the plants and equipman

c) Dig simples around tents

d) Set to go into the camp, not authorized from the direction

• The above listed rules are inappellable. All of the camping personnel are authorized to send away anyone who does follow them.

IT'S JUST A TITLE, AFTER ALL

You wonder what Chinese movie audiences think they're going to see when western films are shown in China as (for example):

Kindergarten Cop: Devil King of Children
Indecent Proposal: Peach-Coloured Transaction
The Shawshank Redemption: Excitement 1995

GO, GO GOETHE

He's reluctant to admit it, but Uncle John does read things besides The History of Parking Meters *and* Famous Movie Monsters. *He even has a favourite philosopher – Johann Wolfgang von Goethe.*

'What is the best government? That which teaches us to govern ourselves'.

'Legislators and revolutionaries who promise liberty and equality at the same time are either utopian dreamers or charlatans'.

'Only law can give us freedom'.

'If a man stops to ponder over his physical or moral condition, he generally discovers that he is ill'.

'Preoccupation with immortality is for the upper classes, particularly ladies with nothing to do. An able man, who has a regular job and must toil and produce day by day, leaves the future world to itself, and is active and useful in this one'.

'Never tell people how you are: they don't want to know'.

'If youth is a fault, one soon gets rid of it'.

'Fools and wise men are equally harmless. It is the half-fools and the half-wise who are dangerous'.

'A clever man commits no minor blunders'.

'Know thyself? If I knew myself, I'd run away'.

'Whatever you can do, or dream you can, begin it. Boldness has genius, power and magic in it'.

'Only the artist sees spirits. But after he has told of their appearing to him, everybody sees them'.

'You can't understand something if you don't possess it'.

'Nothing shows a man's character more than what he laughs at'.

'Viewed from the summit of reason, all life looks like a malignant disease and the world like a madhouse'.

MR. TOAD'S WILD RIDE, PART II

Here's the second part of the story of Kenneth Grahame's classic, The Wind in the Willows – *which has been adapted by everyone from A.A. Milne, who wrote the play* Toad of Toad Hall *in 1930, to Walt Disney, who animated it in 1949.* *(Part I starts on page 36.)*

SMEDLEY'S WILES

Magazines and publishers regularly begged Kenneth Grahame for articles – or perhaps a sequel to *The Golden Age* or *Dream Days*. But Grahame had become a notorious recluse; even getting an interview with him was nearly impossible.

In 1907 an American magazine called *Everybody's* put Constance Smedley on the job. The editors told Smedley to get Grahame to write something – anything. She was clever, and wrote to the author saying she was a relative of Governess Smedley – a fictional character in *The Golden Age* and *Dream Days* – who wanted to visit. Grahame was delighted. The two became good friends – but he still wouldn't write for her. Grahame said writing 'was like physical torture', and 'he hated it'.

Smedley visited often. One evening, she overheard Grahame telling Mouse his bedtime story and, as one biographer put it, 'moved in for the kill'. She insisted that Grahame already had a story – he just needed to write it down. He even had much of the material for the book in the letters he'd written to Mouse. To his own surprise, Grahame agreed, and began expanding the letters into a book – the first professional writing he'd done in nine years.

He finished *The Wind in the Reeds* (as he called it) by Christmas 1907, 'and packed it up and sent it to the eager Constance Smedley, who dispatched it to her editors, waiting excitedly in New York'.

FALSE START

The New Yorkers were stunned. Grahame's other books had been about children – not wild animals. To Smedley's mortification, they turned the book down flat. The manuscript was sent back to Grahame, who gave it to his agent. But the agent couldn't find anyone in England who was willing to publish it, either.

The problem seemed to be that adults didn't understand *The Wind in the Willows* (now changed from 'Reeds' to avoid confusion with an upcoming book by W.B. Yeats). It was a new genre – a novel-length animal fantasy that was not an allegory and had no human protagonist. '*The Wind in the Willows* had no clear generic predecessor', explains a Grahame biographer. '[It] shifted the identification of the reader to the animals themselves...and the first adults to read the work simply couldn't adapt to the change'.

When Grahame finally did get his book published, he discovered that critics couldn't relate to his story, either. Some criticized it as a poorly thought-out allegory ('Grown up readers will find it monstrous and elusive'); others assumed that since it expressed such an 'intimate sympathy with Nature', it was meant to be natural history. One newspaper commented that *The Wind in the Willows* – a book featuring a toad driving a car – would 'win no credence from the very best authorities on biology'. Even *The Times* wrote irrelevantly: 'As a contribution to natural history the work is negligible'.

One result of the confusion was that the book sold poorly. Another: Grahame couldn't find an American publisher.

THE PRESIDENT STEPS IN

This is where President Teddy Roosevelt figures in the story. Roosevelt was a big fan of Grahame's work. Years earlier, he had met millionaire book collector Austin Purves and learned that Purves knew Grahame. He sent Purves back to England with a request for autographed copies of *The Golden Age* and *Dream Days*.

Grahame, of course, complied, and Roosevelt wrote back, saying 'No one you could have sent those books to would have appreciated them more than Mrs. Roosevelt and I'. He invited Grahame to stay at the White House if he visited Washington, but Grahame never did.

When *The Wind in the Willows* was published in England, Grahame sent Roosevelt an autographed copy. But Roosevelt chose not to read it. He had recently written an article denouncing stories that confused animals with human beings, and after seeing the reviews of *Willows*, feared it would ruin his love of Grahame's other books.

During the summer months in Reykjavik, Iceland, the sun is visible 24 hours a day.

However, Roosevelt's wife found the book at the White House and started reading it aloud to their children. Roosevelt overheard her and became fascinated with the story. He later wrote to Grahame:

> For some time I could not accept the mole, the water-rat and the badger....But after a while Mrs Roosevelt and two of the boys, Kermit and Ted, all quite independently, got hold of *The Wind in the Willows* and took such a delight in it that I began to feel that I might have to revise my judgement. Then Mrs Roosevelt read it aloud to the younger children, and I listened now and then....I have since read the book three times, and now all the characters are my dearest friends.

The Roosevelt children sent their copies of the book to England to be autographed by Grahame. Meanwhile, Grahame's agent was still trying to find an American publisher. He had just sent the manuscript to Scribner's – who informed him that they were not interested – when a note arrived at the publisher from President Roosevelt. It said: '*The Wind in the Willows* is such a beautiful thing, Scribner must publish it'.

'With an apologetic cough, Scribner did'. And never regretted it. The book sold slowly at first, but caught on and went through many printings. Its success in the U.S. made it a hit in England, too.

By 1908 Grahame (no longer with the bank) was living comfortably off the royalties from his books. *Willows* changed popular tastes and paved the way for the genre of animal fantasies, which includes everything from Mickey Mouse to *Charlotte's Web*.

NOTE: The story doesn't have a particularly happy ending, however. Like Peter, who inspired the character of Peter Pan (see page 425), Mouse committed suicide. One day while he was at college, he went for a walk and never came back. He had been hit by a train. Officials called it an accident, but the wounds showed he had been lying on the tracks when the train came.

Oxford's Brasenose College is named after a 'Brazen Nose' medieval door-knocker.

AESOP'S FABLES

Aesop's fables (see page 113) have been told and retold for thousands of years. Here are a few more we've picked to pass on.

THE FOX & THE GRAPES

A fox was walking along the road, when he spied some delicious-looking grapes growing on a high trellis. 'My, they look good!' he said. He jumped up, but couldn't reach them. He tried again and again, but to no avail. Finally he looked angrily at the grapes and said, 'Hmmm, who wants the old grapes? They're probably sour anyway'.

Moral: It's easy to despise what you can't have.

THE SICK LION

A lion, unable from old age and infirmities to provide himself with food by force, resolved to do so by trickery. He returned to his den, and lying down there, pretended to be sick, taking care that his sickness should be publicly known. The beasts expressed their sorrow, and came one by one to his den, where the Lion devoured them. After many of the beasts had thus disappeared, a Fox, presenting himself to the Lion, stood on the outside of the cave, at a respectful distance, and asked him how he was. 'I am very middling', replied the Lion, 'but why are you standing out there? Please come in and talk with me'. 'No, thank you', said the Fox. 'I notice that there are many footprints entering your cave, but I see no trace of any returning'.

Moral: The wise person learns from the misfortunes of others.

THE FOOLISH TRAVELLERS

A man and his son were walking along the road to market with their donkey. As they walked, they met a couple. 'Did you ever see anything so silly'? the man said to his wife. 'Two men walking when they have a donkey with them. What's a donkey for, after all, if not to carry a man?'

Hearing this, the man put his son on the back of the donkey and they went on their way. Soon they met two countrymen. 'Did you ever see such a terrible thing'? one cried. 'The strong young man rides while his poor father must walk'. So the boy dismounted and the father got on instead.

They hadn't gone very far when they met two women. 'Look at that heartless father!' exclaimed one of them, 'His poor little son must walk while he rides'. At that, the man said to his son, 'Come up here with me. We'll both ride'.

They both rode for a while until they reached a group of men. 'Aren't you ashamed'? they called out. 'Overloading a poor little donkey like that'. So the man and his son both climbed off the donkey.

They thought and thought. They couldn't walk along with the donkey, or ride it one at a time, or ride it both together. Then they had an idea. They got a tree and cut it into a long pole. Then they tied the donkey's feet to it, raised the pole to their shoulders, and went on their way, carrying the donkey.

As they crossed a bridge, the donkey – who didn't like being tied up – kicked one of his feet loose, causing the father and son to stumble. The donkey fell into the water. Because its feet were tied, it drowned.

Moral: If you try to please everyone, you'll end up pleasing no one.

THE ASS & THE FOX

An ass put on a Lion's skin, and roamed around the forest amusing himself by scaring all the foolish animals he met. Finally, he met a Fox, and tried to scare him, too – but as soon as the Fox heard the ass' voice, he said, 'Well, I might have been frightened…if I hadn't heard your bray'.

Moral: Clothes may disguise a fool, but his words give him away.

THE THIRSTY PIGEON

A pigeon, overcome by thirst, saw a glass of water painted on a sign. Not realizing it was only a picture, she quickly flew towards it and crashed into the sign. Her wings broken, she fell to the ground – and was captured by a bystander.

Moral: Zeal should not outrun discretion.

THE SERPENT & FILE

A serpent wandered into a carpenter's shop. As he glided over the floor he felt his skin pricked by a file lying there. In a rage he turned and attacked, trying to sink his fangs into the file; but he could do no harm to the heavy iron and soon had to give over his wrath.

Moral: It is useless attacking the insensible.

Mercury is the only metal that is liquid at room temperature.

CLASSIC HOAXES

Here are a few more of our favourite frauds.

THE PSALMANAZAR HOAX

The Set-Up: In 1703 a 'converted heathen from Formosa' (now Taiwan) named George Psalmanazar was introduced to the Bishop of London by a local cleric (who was really his partner in crime). 'In eighteenth-century London', as Laura Foreman writes in *Hoaxes and Deceptions*, 'a Formosan was as great a sensation as a Martian would be today', and Psalmanazar became the toast of English society.

People were fascinated with his stories. They were shocked to learn, for example, that before he joined the Anglican faith, he was a cannibal – and that snakes, snake blood and raw meat, including the flesh of executed criminals, were delicacies in Formosa. Divorce customs were similarly barbaric: if a Formosan man grew tired of his wife, 'he had only to accuse her of adultery, and he then was entitled to cut off her head and eat her'. Psalmanazar taught himself to eat raw meat, and whenever he dined with upper-class hosts, would insist on it.

The Bishop of London sent the 'reformed savage' to Oxford University to study and to lecture on the Formosan language and history. While he was there, the Anglican Church commissioned him to translate the Bible into Formosan (a language he promptly invented). The following year, Psalmanazar wrote his extremely popular *Historical and Geographical Description of Formosa*, complete with comprehensive descriptions of Formosan art, culture, diet, dress and language. Among his disclosures: Formosan religion demanded that the hearts of 18,000 Formosan boys under the age of nine were sacrificed to the gods every year, 'a population-depleting practice offset by the sparing of eldest sons, and polygamy'.

Why It Worked: No one in England had ever been to Formosa, and Psalmanazar was so inventive that when a doubting missionary who really had spent 18 years in China challenged him publicly, Psalmanazar made him look foolish. Plus, the English of the time were incredibly gullible about other cultures. When, for example, they asked why he didn't he look Oriental, Psalmanazar explained that the ruling class spent all their time in underground houses – it was only the workers whose skin turned 'yellow'. The public bought it.

Perhaps the real reason Psalmanazar was so successful was religious chauvinism. He roundly criticized Catholic missionary work in Asia and embraced the Anglican Church – confirming as an outsider what many English felt was true anyway. And in 1700, it was considered a real feather in the English church's cap to have converted a cannibal when Catholics couldn't.

What Happened: Psalmanazar's graphic descriptions of life in Formosa were at odds with everyone else's, and skeptics kept attacking until he was finally exposed as a fraud by Dr. Edmund Halley (of comet fame) in 1706. Halley quizzed Psalmanazar on just how much sunlight those underground houses got – and Psalmanazar got this, as well as other phenomena, wrong. He finally admitted having made everything up – including the 'language' he spoke – and confessed to being a Frenchman. But he never revealed his true identity – it remains a mystery to this day.

THE BARON OF ARIZONA

The Set-Up: In 1883 a man named James Addison Reavis filed legal papers claiming ownership of more than 44,000 sq km of territory in what is now Arizona and New Mexico.

This wasn't as far-fetched as it might sound: when the U.S. government purchased the Arizona Territory from Mexico in 1848, it agreed to honour all Spanish land grants, and according to Reavis, the land had been presented to Don Miguel de Peralta de la Cordoba in 1748 by the King of Spain. Reavis said he'd bought the land and title from the family that had inherited it, and now he was staking his claim.

If Reavis' claim was true, the thousands of people living and working in Arizona were there illegally – and could be forced to leave. At the time, there were thousands of land grants being processed and verified by the United States. Reavis' was just the biggest (and most outrageous). Astonishingly, government experts pronounced it real.

'The claim brought panic to the territory', writes one historian, 'and an outpouring of riches to the new baron'. Railroads, mines and other businesses began paying Reavis for the right to use his land. Over the next decade, he collected more than $10 million in ill-gotten revenues.

Why It Worked: Reavis was an extremely talented forger who had spent years laying the groundwork for his fraud. In particular, he had travelled to Spain where, after getting access to historic documents, he had skilfully altered them to create a record of the (nonexistent) Peralta family and their land grant. Then he produced impeccable copies of the grant itself.

What Happened: There are different accounts of how the hoax was eventually discovered. According to one source, a newspaper publisher noticed that the typestyle on one of the documents was too recent to be authentic, and that the watermark on the paper was from a Wisconsin paper mill that had not even been built when the document was supposedly written.

Another says that technology did Reavis in. When he planned his scheme, Reavis knew nothing of scientific innovations that would make it possible for investigators to test the age of paper and ink. By 1893, suspicious officials were able to have the tests done – and they revealed that the 135-year-old documents 'were written in the wrong kind of ink on 10-year-old parchment'. Reavis was sentenced to six years in prison for his crime, and died penniless in 1908.

* * *

THAT'S ART!

• How slow a painter was Paul Cézanne? So slow that when he painted a bowl of fruit, it wasn't uncommon for the fruit to begin to rot before he finished painting. So he used waxed fruit for models.

• In the 19th century a 26-year-old painter named Richard Dadd went insane, killed his father, and was confined to an asylum. The asylum let him continue his painting – and his insanity actually improved his painting ability: *Oberon and Titania*, one of the works he painted at the asylum, is considered one of the greatest paintings of the Victorian era.

Going down: bottle-nosed dolphins can dive 1,000 metres in two minutes.

THE MODERN ZOO, PART II

Zoos provide the only opportunity many of us will ever have to see exotic animals up close. London Zoo, for example, contains more than 5,000 beasts, spread across 526 different species. The story of the origin of the modern zoo is on page 104.

STATUS SYMBOL

In the late 1850s, Philadelphian Dr. William Camac visited the London Zoo. Inspired by what he saw, he founded the Philadelphia Zoological Society. His goal: to build a world-class zoological garden and the first scientific zoo in America.

By the late 1850s, major cities all over Europe either had zoos or were in the process of establishing them. They were status symbols: the citizens of Madrid, Hamburg and Dublin, for example, regarded zoos as a means of communicating to the rest of world that their cities were to be taken as seriously as London or Paris. Dr. Camac wanted the same thing for Philadelphia: 'When we see cities such as Amsterdam, Frankfurt, and Dublin – cities not so large as Philadelphia – supporting first-class zoological gardens', he wrote, 'we see no reason why Philadelphia, with all its taste, wealth, enterprise, and advantages, should not in time possess one of the finest institutions in the world'.

SIDESHOW

The U.S. lagged behind Europe in zoo development. Westward expansion brought pioneers in contact with animals they had never seen before – and many animals were captured and brought back to cities to be exhibited to curious crowds. But as late as the 1870s, most animal viewing was limited to spectacles like a bear chained up in the corner tavern, or travelling carnivals put on by sea captains to show off exotic animals captured overseas.

EARLY AMERICAN ZOOS

New York

By 1861 New York City had a menagerie in Central Park, but this jumble was little more than a dumping ground for private collec-

Total combined population of the North American colonies in 1610: 350.

tions and carnivals, including a black bear, two cows, deer, monkeys, raccoons, foxes, opossums, ducks, swans, eagles, pelicans and parrots. No rational thought was put into the collection; the keepers just accepted whatever animals people gave them and put them on display.

Still, the menagerie was a popular attraction. 'By the late 1800s', Linda Koebner writes in *Zoo*, 'it was a center of entertainment both for wealthy Fifth Avenue strollers and for the poor who were looking for a break from their daily working lives. Newly arrived immigrants lived in dark, crowded tenements on the Lower East Side of New York. A trip up to the green of Central Park to see the menagerie was well worth the walk or the nickel fare on the trolley'.

Chicago

The menagerie in Chicago's Lincoln Park wasn't much better than the one in Central Park. It got its start when the Central Park menagerie presented them with a gift of two swans. This prompted similar 'gifts', and by 1873 the park had 27 mammals and 48 birds.

GENUINE ARTICLE

While these zoos were popular attractions, neither Central Park nor Lincoln Park knew anything about animals or bothered to hire anyone who did; the care and feeding of the creatures was left to the parks department, whose main concern in reality was picking up rubbish and raking leaves. The park-keepers certainly weren't trained in how to look after animals.

As Dr. Camac proposed it, the Philadelphia Zoological Garden would be something completely different: a well-funded, intelligently planned collection of animals housed in permanent facilities and run by a professional, full-time staff. The public would be admitted into the zoo, but it would also serve a more serious purpose: scientists at the University of Pennsylvania, the Academy of Sciences, and other organizations would be able to study and observe the animals up close.

Planning for the facility began in March of 1859, but the outbreak of the American Civil War in 1861 (it ended in 1865) interfered with construction, so it was not completed until 1873.

In the 19th century, India imported ice harvested from ponds in the United States.

THE TOILET ERA

When it opened to the public on 1 July, 1874, the Philadelphia Zoo was a state-of-the-art facility, complete with a monkey house, bird house, prairie dog village and sea lion pool. But the early zookeepers had a lot to learn about caring for animals. Hunters and trappers who captured the animals knew next to nothing about how the animals lived in the wild or what they ate, and thousands died before they could be delivered to the zoo. The zookeepers didn't know much more, and animals that made it to the zoo didn't live much longer.

Because animal behaviour was so poorly understood, animals that lived in social or family groups in the wild were often acquired one at a time and placed in bare cages – no attempt was made to simulate their natural environment. Animals frequently had nowhere to hide, and climbing animals like monkeys and wildcats had nowhere to go to get off the floor. The emphasis in cage design was on preventing disease by making them easy to clean: enclosures were usually made of concrete and tile and looked so much like bathrooms, Koebner writes, that 'this manner of keeping the animals gave rise to the term "the toilet era"'.

Visitors to the zoos were similarly shortchanged: displays did little to educate the public other than give the name of the animal and the feeding schedule. Scientific aspects of the zoo were played down; the garden's workers were often poorly informed and so could do little to shed light on any of the exhibits.

Where the public was concerned, the emphasis was on entertainment. Elephants paraded, bears danced, and chimpanzees wore clothes and ate with silverware at dinner tables, part of the zoology garden's attempt to show how 'humanlike' they were.

A NEW ERA

Things began to improve at the turn of the century, thanks in large part to a German circus trainer named Carl Hagenbeck, considered the 'father of modern zoos'. For years Hagenbeck had made his living catching and training exotic animals for zoos. In 1907 he expanded his business by opening his own zoo, which he named the Hagenbeck Tierpark.

As an animal catcher, Hagenbeck had seen animals in the wild and was determined that the animals in his zoo would never live in cages that looked like public conveniences. 'I wished to exhibit them not as captives, confined to narrow spaces and looked at between bars, but as free to wander from place to place within as large limits as possible'.

Hagenbeck put his experience as an animal trainer to work, testing the animals to see how high and how far they could jump, and then dug moats so deep and wide that the animals would not try to escape. He also tried to give the cages and compounds an authentic appearance so that the animals would be as comfortable as possible.

Optical Illusion

Hagenbeck also arranged the exhibits to make them look as much like the animals' natural habitats as possible; it even seemed as if predators and their prey were part of the same exhibit. The lion exhibit was located just in front of the zebra, antelope and ostriches (safely separated by a moat that was concealed behind bushes and landscape.) All of the animals appeared to be together, just as they would be in their natural habitat in Africa. As a result, Koebner writes, 'the public could see the interrelationship of animals, begin to picture what the African landscape looked like and learn about predators, prey and habitats'.

The advantages of Hagenbeck's reforms were obvious, and soon most zoos began adopting his ideas to improve their exhibits. Still, his enclosures had drawbacks: they were expensive, took up more space than cages, and increased the distance between animals and the viewing public from 1.5 m to as much as 20 m. And some zoo directors felt they were too revolutionary. Dr. William Hornaday of the Bronx Zoo, for example, criticized the new enclosures as 'a half-baked German fad'. But Hornaday was in the minority. Zookeepers from all over the world began making pilgrimages to the Hagenbeck Tierpark to learn as much as they could.

CHANGING TIMES

Hagenbeck's reforms were part of a broader zoological trend: all over the world, zoos were beginning to take better care of their animals. In the old days, the supply of animals in the wild seemed inexhaustible – if an animal in a zoo died, they could just send a hunter into the jungle to get another one. Life was cheap, and

Touché! The gap between the front benches in the Commons is precisely two swords long.

animals were expendable.

By the early 1900s, zoos were already beginning to look different. Many animals had been driven to extinction or close to it. And foreign governments – realizing how valuable the surviving animals were – started charging zoos for the privilege of hunting in their territories. As the supply of animals went down and the cost of obtaining them went up, zoos became more interested in preserving and extending the lives of the animals they had.

But the practical aspects of running and maintaining a zoo didn't change as fast as the philosophy. 'Even with increased difficulties in capture and export, it would still be many decades before capture in the wild slowed significantly', Koebner writes in *Zoo*. Until about the early 1960s, zoos still obtained the majority of their animals from well-funded expeditions into the wild, which amounted to little more than raids upon wildlife areas in Africa and Asia. Barbaric practices, such as killing a mother elephant or hippopotamus in order to capture its child, were still commonplace and widely accepted.

ZOOS TODAY

In the 1960s and 1970s, however, zoos began to make substantive shifts toward conservation – not just of the animals in the zoo, but also those still in the wild. And instead of competing against one another, they began working together to accomplish these goals. This is critical in the case of endangered species that are extinct, or practically so, in the wild – and survive only in zoos today. In cases where only a few dozen animals survive and their numbers are scattered among several zoos, the only way to bring the species back from extinction is to manage the animals as one population.

'Today's zoos have a very specific message to preach', writes Allen Nyhuis in *The Zoo Book*. 'By introducing the public to the world's enormous variety of animals and their native habitats, they hope that people will better appreciate the animals and want to help preserve them'.

* * *

The hedgehog's name stems from its piglike foraging in hedgerows in search of food. While seeking food it maintains a steady whistling sound.

When you use your car's brakes, they generate enough heat to warm your house.

HOT STUFF!

Indian scientists claimed to have found the world's hottest chillies, the Naga Jolokia, spicier even than Mexico's famed Habanero chillies. If you love hot food, read on...

BLAME IT ON COLUMBUS

When Christopher Columbus arrived in the New World, he thought he'd landed in India. So he called the people he met there 'Indians'.

That wasn't the only mistake he made. When his hosts served a spicy food containing hot chillies, he assumed the chillies were related to *piper nigrum*, the plant that produces black pepper.

They're actually part of the *Solanaceae*, or nightshade, family and are more closely related to potatoes, tomatoes and aubergines. But chillies have been known as chilli 'peppers' ever since.

MADE IN BOLIVIA

All varieties of chilli peppers descended from prehistoric wild chilli plants that originated somewhere near present-day Bolivia. Scientists believe that most animals avoided the painfully hot plants, but birds ate them – apparently because they can't taste chillies – and spread the seeds all over Central and South America. Humans began eating the wild peppers as early as 7,000 B.C., and had domesticated them by 2,500 B.C.

South American and Latin American peoples, including the Aztecs, revered the peppers. They were used for everything from treating upper-respiratory disorders to ritualistic morning beverages. Montezuma, the last Aztec emperor, drank a concoction of chocolate and hot chillies for breakfast. The Incas took their reverence a step further: Agar-Uchu, or 'Brother Chilli Pepper' in English, is one of the four brothers of the Incan creation myth.

Chillies remained exclusive to the New World until the 1490s, when Columbus brought some to Europe. From there they spread via trade routes to every remaining corner of the globe, and within a century they were firmly established in the cuisines of India, China, and Africa.

Today an estimated 75 per cent of the world's population eats chillies on a daily basis. Mexico tops the list – Mexicans consume, on average, one chilli per person, every day.

What made the Dickin Medal for Valour unique during WWII? It was awarded to animals.

CHILLI SCIENCE

What Makes Them Hot?

• All chillies contain a powerful alkaloid called capsaicin (cap-SAY-a-sin), which gives chillies their heat – and which isn't found in any other plants. It's so potent that humans can detect it even when it's diluted to one part per million.

• The 'capsaicinoids', as they're also known, are produced in the plant by the placenta – the part just below the stem of the chilli. That's also where the seeds and the 'ribs' grow. On average, these parts are 16 times hotter than the rest of the plant, so it stands to reason that one way to cool down a chilli (if that's what you want) is to remove the placenta.

• How hot is capsaicin? It's so strong that it's the main ingredient in a product designed to drive grizzly bears away. It's also the 'pepper' in pepper spray, which has replaced tear gas in more than 1,200 police departments around the U.S. According to America's *Smithsonian* magazine, when sprayed in the face, 'it causes eyes to slam shut and creates a spasm in the respiratory system – an unpleasant experience that lasts 30 to 45 minutes'.

What Makes Them So Good?

• When you eat chillies, capsaicin irritates the pain receptor cells in your mouth.

• Some scientists believe the receptors then release something known as 'substance P', which rushes to 'alert' the brain to the pain. In response, the brain produces chemicals called endorphins that kill the pain and elicit feelings of well-being. Does hot, spicy food taste less hot to you after a couple of bites? Chilli enthusiasts say this is the endorphins at work.

• In fact, some experts think that it's the addictive nature of endorphins, not the taste of the chillies themselves, that makes the spice so popular.

Cooling Down

• Do you reach for cold water when you eat a hot pepper? It's not a great idea – it not only won't cool your mouth down, it will probably make things worse by spreading the capsaicin around. Beer might work (experts aren't sure), but the best way to put out the fire is to drink cold milk – or eat any dairy product (e.g., frozen yoghurt) with lactic acid. They contain casein, which acts

Bug rule of thumb: centipedes are carnivores, millipedes are vegetarians.

like a detergent to help wash away the capsaicin. Other recommended foods: sugar, salt, tortillas, rice, chunks of bread and corn.

THE SCOVILLE SCALE

In 1912 Wilbur Scoville, a pharmacologist with the Parke Davis pharmaceutical company, needed to test the potency of some chillies he was mixing into a muscle salve. He mixed pure ground chillies into sugar-water and had a panel of tasters drink the water, in increasingly diluted concentrations, until the liquid was so diluted that it no longer burned their mouths.

Next, Scoville assigned a number to each chilli based on how much it needed to be diluted before the tasters tasted no heat. The 'Scoville scale', as it's still known, measures potency in multiples of 100. Here's how some popular chillies are ranked:

Bell and sweet peppers:	0–100 Scoville Units
New Mexican peppers:	500–1000
Española peppers:	1,000–1,500
Ancho & pasilla peppers:	1,000–2,000
Cascabel & cherry peppers:	1,000–2,500
Jalapeno & mirasol peppers:	2,500–5,000
Serrano peppers:	5,000–15,000
De Arbol peppers:	15,000–30,000
Cayenne & Tabasco:	30,000–50,000
Chiltepin peppers:	50,000–100,000
Scotch bonnet & Thai peppers:	100,000–350,000
Habanero peppers:	200,000 to 300,000
Red savina habanero peppers:	up to 577,000
Indian Naga Jolokia chillies:	as high as 855,000
Pure capsaicin:	16,000,000

Today the potency of chillies is measured very precisely by machines that calculate the exact amount of capsaicin in each chilli. But the scale that is used is still named the Scoville scale in Wilbur Scoville's honour.

If you count things compulsively, you're an arithmomaniac.

HEALTH NOTES

Can eating chillies make you sick? Epidemiologists from Yale University and the Mexico National Institute of Public Health concluded that chilli peppers may cause stomach cancer. However, peppers also contain quercetin, a chemical shown to reduce cancer risk in laboratory animals, so who knows?

Other maladies to watch out for if you're a hardcore chilli eater:

- **Salsa sniffles.** 'Sweating and rhinitis (runny nose) caused by eating hot peppers'.
- **Hunan hand.** 'The skin irritation that comes from chopping chillies'.
- **Jaloprocitis.** 'The burn jalapeños leave as they exit the body.

On the other hand, according to a book called *The Healing Powers of Chili*:

- A 1986 experiment at Oxford University found that eating chillies may assist in burning calories.
- The popular muscle salve Heet is made mostly of capsaicin.
- Chilies are low in fat, high in fibre and loaded with beta carotene and vitamin C. One half cup of chopped chilli peppers offers more than twice the vitamin C of an orange.
- Capsaicin is a natural antibiotic, slowing down bacteria's growth.
- A few more ailments that have been treated with capsaicin: indigestion, acne, alcoholism, arthritis, bronchitis, cramps, haemorrhoids, herpes, low blood pressure, shingles, wounds.

MORE CHILLI FACTS

- Chilli is the Nahuatl, or Aztec, word for the plant.
- According to most accounts, chilli peppers were introduced into what is now the United States by Capitan General Juan de Oñante, who also founded Santa Fe in 1598.

Second most-published playwright in history, after Shakespeare: Neil Simon.

UNCLE JOHN'S 'STALL OF FAME'

More of Uncle John's bathroom heroes.

Nominee: Glen Dorenbush, formerly of San Francisco
Notable Achievement: Being flushed down the toilets of his favourite bars after he died
True Story: According to news reports, 'When Dorenbush died in the summer of 1996, his cronies ended up with eight pounds (nearly four kilograms) of his ashes and an interesting predicament. The amiable eccentric left no will when he checked out, but had made it clear to those who knew him best what he wanted done with his remains: he wanted most of his ashes flushed down the toilets of his favourite bars'.

The dilemma: 'It's technically illegal in California to sprinkle cremated remains down the can, not to mention bad for the plumbing'. His friends finally decided to improvize and 'scatter some ashes on a beach in Puerto Vallarta where he loved to vacation and some more in the ocean off Stinson Cafe on Hyde Street. The rest, it was decided, would go down the latrines at several undisclosed locations'.

Nominee: An unnamed homeowner in Fayetteville, Arkansas
Notable Achievement: Creative bathroom-based entrepreneurship
True Story: In 1995 the man bought American Football coach Jimmy Johnson's former house and had a great idea while rennovating his bathroom. He took out an ad in a local paper, offering 'a great deal for football fans': For only $250, they could own (and sit on) the toilet once used by the ex–Dallas Cowboys trainer.

Nominee: Richard List of Berkeley, California
Notable Achievement: Creating a museum (and philosophical statement) featuring painted toilets
True Story: 'New York has the MOMA', writes a San Francisco reporter, 'Paris has the Louvre. Berkeley has the New Sense Museum, where art is strictly in the eyes of the beholder. The

New Sense (say it fast) consists of a vacant, weed-strewn lot studded with weird objects, most notably a flotilla of commodes painted fluorescent pink, orange and green'.

According to Richard List, the museum's guiding force, 'People say, "I don't get the message". Well, that's the point. Life is a mystery'.

Nominee: St. Louis circuit judge Edward Peek
Notable Achievement: Presiding over the first murder trial ever instigated by an argument about toilet paper
True Story: There's nothing funny about this, of course, but it's too weird to leave out. In the late 1980s, a 36-year-old man admitted to the judge that he had shot and killed his younger brother. The reason: He was angry that his brother had 'used too much of a new eight-roll package of toilet paper'. The man was convicted of second-degree murder.

Nominee: Barney Smith of San Antonio, Texas
Notable Achievement: Created the Toilet Seat Museum in his garage
True Story: Smith, a plumber, asked his customers if he could keep the old toilet seat every time he installed a new one. 'Then', says the *Houston Post*, 'he would decorate each seat with something special, things like keepsakes from a vacation or mementos from a historic moment....Smith has decorated and dedicated about 400 toilet-seat lids, artistically altering the functional commode covers to become hanging history. And he has generously hung them for the world to see'.

Nominee: Nelson Camus of Hacienda Heights, California
Notable Achievement: Inventing the world's first urine-powered battery
True Story: The 'Argentine-born electrical engineer', says John Kohut in *Dumb, Dumber, Dumbest*, 'announced that his battery generates more power than standard acid-reaction batteries and is cheaper. His partner, Ed Aguayo, said 10 urine-powered batteries, each about half the size of a normal car battery, could power a normal house'. No word as yet on when the battery will become available to an undoubtedly eager public.

In 1912 the Archbishop of Paris declared dancing the tango a sin.

MORE IT'S A WEIRD, WEIRD WORLD

More proof that truth really is stranger than fiction.

PERFORMING UNDER PRESSURE

'On September 12, the Great Hurricane of 1938 devastated the New England states (of America). That morning a man in West Hampton Beach received a barometer in the mail. The needle was stuck on "hurricane". Disgusted, and thinking it was defective, he marched back to the Post Office and mailed the instrument back to the store from which he had purchased it. When he returned, his home was gone'.

– *Our Fascinating Earth*

DID HE CROAK?

'Doctors in a Mexican hospital were in the midst of open-heart surgery when a frog fell out of an overhead lamp and landed on the patient'.

– *The Fortean Times*

ROCK YOUR WORLD

'For years, maps have shown that northern Germany's highest mountain, the Brocken, was 1,139 metres tall. But recently, more precise measurements revealed that the peak is only 1,137 metres tall. To avoid correcting the world's maps, a construction company dumped 19 tonnes of granite on the summit, stacking the rocks in a 1.8-metre pile'.

– *Portland Oregonian*, 28 February≥, 1998

NEXT COMES A *STRAIT*JACKET

'Despite 18 years working at a Florida fishing camp, Freddie Padgett was so terrified of water that he wore a life jacket to bed on stormy nights. Friends made fun of him, until a twister sucked him out of his (mobile home) while he was sleeping and dropped him into Lake Harney a mile away. He suffered broken ribs and other injuries, but authorities say the life jacket probably saved his life'.

– *The Skeptic*

Face value of a Titanic boarding pass auctioned in 1999: £5. It sold for £60,000.

WORD ORIGINS

Here are some more interesting word origins.

AMBULANCE
Meaning: A specialized vehicle for transporting the injured to a hospital
Origin: 'The name comes from an invention of Napoleon Bonaparte's, *l'hôpital ambulant* (walking hospital), a litter fitted with bandages and other first-aid equipment that served as a field hospital for wounded soldiers. In time, the litters became elaborate and mechanized, yielding first to horse-drawn wagons, eventually to motorized ambulances'. (From *Fighting Words*, by Christine Ammer)

TABOO
Meaning: A behaviour or activity that is prohibited
Origin: 'Originally a Tongan word, tabu, meaning "marked as holy". The first taboos were prohibitions against the use or even the mention of certain things because of religious belief that to do so would invoke the wrath of the gods. The word gradually was extended in use to cover all sorts of prohibitions or bans based upon social convention'. (From *Dictionary of Word and Phrase Origins*, Vol. III, by William and Mary Morris)

BUMPKIN
Meaning: A loutish countryman
Origin: 'From the Dutch *boomkin*, small tree – hence, a countryman thought to possess the tree's intelligence'. (From *Loose Cannons and Red Herrings*, by Robert Claiborne)

SENATE
Meaning: A representative body in a republic or democracy
Origin: 'Literally, "a gathering of old men". Like most cultures, ancient Roman society respected age. In the days before the Roman Empire, tribes would gather. The representatives from these clans were usually elders, whose experience led to wiser, more thoughtful deliberation. When the empire flourished, the tradition of the council of elders continued. To this day there are age requirements for our Senate (in the U.S.)'. (From *Where in the Word?*, by David Muschell)

UNCLE JOHN'S TOP 10 AMAZING COINCIDENCES

We're constantly finding stories about amazing coincidences. Here, Uncle John lists his 10 favourites. Send us yours, and next edition, we'll do a readers' Top 10.

10. WHAT GOES AROUND...

'In 1965, at age four, Roger Lausier was saved from drowning off a beach at Salem, Mass., by a woman named Alice Blaise. Nine years later, in 1974, on the same beach, Roger paddled his raft into the water and pulled a drowning man from the water. The man was Alice Blaise's husband'.

– The Book of Lists

9. NUMBER NINE, NUMBER NINE...

BELOIT, Wisconsin – 'Nicholas Stephen Wadle was born at 9:09 a.m. on the ninth day of the ninth month of 1999. But the string of coincidences doesn't end there. He weighed 9 pounds, 9 ounces.

'A spokeswoman for Beloit Memorial Hospitals said the mother "couldn't believe it", but "the most surprised were the professionals involved....As the nines started to stack up, they were going crazy".

'The baby was due Sept. 15, but complications with the births of Mrs. Wadles's two older children led her doctor to schedule a cesarean section for Thursday, to be safe. The delivery was set for 8:00 a.m. but there was an emergency, which allowed the 9:09 birth'.

– Appleton, Wisconsin, *Post Crescent*, September 10, 1999
(Contributed by Julie Roeming)

8. ARE YOU MY DADDY?

'Wilf Hewitt, 86, a widower from Southport, wanted to look through a list of registered voters in the library, and asked the woman who had the list if she was going to be long. Vivien Fletoridis replied that she was looking for a man named Hewitt.

Farthest distance a pumpkin has been hurled without the use of explosives: 1,133 metres.

She was his daughter, whom he had not seen for 46 years. Wilf had had a wartime love affair with Vivien's mother, who had died in 1983. Their daughter was adopted in 1941 and went to live in Australia with her foster parents. In July 1987 she traced her two brothers and sister through an agency, and then set out to find her father'.

– The Fortean Times

7. REINCARNATED SURVIVOR

'On three separate occasions – in 1664, 1785, and 1860 – there were shipwrecks where only one person survived the accident. Each time that one person's name was Hugh Williams'.

– The Book of Useless Information

6. I DO, I THINK

'A woman in Kissimmee, Florida, should have no trouble remembering her new husband's name. But, following a bizarre chain of coincidences surrounding the couple's wedding, she might have trouble remembering what he looks like.

'Ronald Legendre married his girlfriend, Hope, in August 1995. The best man – who wasn't related to the groom in any way – was also named Ronald Legendre. And the ceremony was performed by someone who wasn't connected to either man: Judge Ronald Legendre'.

– Knuckleheads in the News

5. SECRET-AGENT KID

'James Bond, 15, a pupil at Argoed High School, North Wales, and a candidate for examinations in 1990, was given the examination number 007 by a computer quirk'.

– The World's Most Incredible Stories

4. HER NAME IS MY NAME, TOO

'A computer mix-up that gave two American women the same social security number was responsible for highlighting a further series of incredible coincidences. Patricia Kern of Colorado and Patricia di Biasi of Oregon were brought together by the blunder.

'The women discovered they had both been born Patricia Ann Campbell with fathers called Robert. They were born on the same date, too: 13 March, 1941. Both Patricias married military men in 1959, within eleven days of one another, and had children aged nineteen and twenty-one. They also shared an interest in painting with oils, had studied cosmetics and worked as bookkeepers'.

– One in a Million

3. AND HER NAME IS MY NAME, TOO

'Mother of two, Michelle Samways, was caught up in a spot of trouble – with mother of two Michelle Samways. The two women moved into numbers 5 and 6 Longstone Close, Portland, Dorset, in Oct. 1994 and hardly a day goes by without a mix-up of some kind. They discovered that they share the same name only when they entered a raffle at a toddlers' group. The two Michelles, aged 26 and 27, were both named after the 1965 Beatles song. They are the same height and build, [and have] similar hair colour'.

– The Fortean Times

2. BABIES KEEP FALLING ON MY HEAD

'Joseph Figlock was passing an apartment block in Detroit in 1975 when he was knocked unconscious. A baby had fallen fourteen stories and landed on him. Both survived. One year later, Figlock was passing the same apartment block – and once again he was hit by a falling child...and survived!'

– One in a Million

And the No.1 coincidence is:

1. CIVIL SERVANT

'One of the lesser-known figures of American history is Wilmer McLean, a Virginia farmer who took little interest in politics.

'In 1861, most of the Rebel army marched onto McLean's land. The Union forces attempted to bar their way, and the first full-scale battle of the Civil War (Battle of Bull Run), got underway – right on his farm. Thirteen months later, it happened again. The second battle at Bull Run destroyed McLean's land. McLean had had enough. He packed his wagons and moved two hundred miles away from the war.

'Three years later, in a weird twist of fate, two men confronted each other in Wilmer McLean's parlor. These two men talked and signed a document on McLean's best table; for he had moved to a little village called Appomattox Court House – where Robert E. Lee and Ulysses S. Grant negotiated the end of the Civil War'.

– Ripley's Believe It or Not

In the 1500s, Queen Elizabeth I outlawed wife beating after 10 p.m.

PUSS IN BOATS

In the days of sailing ships cats went to sea to keep rats and mice down, but Trim became a personal pet and companion to explorer Captain Matthew Flinders.

BIRTH

The timbers creak and the sails flap as the vessel pitches and tosses. We're aboard the good ship *Reliance* sailing eastward across the Indian Ocean from Cape Town to Botany Bay. The winds are howling and the waves are huge. The year is 1799.

Below deck (that's downstairs to anyone not *au fait* with sea speak) a birth is taking place. A birth in a berth, as it were.

A litter of mewing, blind, flat-eared kittens is arriving. But I don't suppose either mother or new arrivals are taking much notice of the noisy, heaving weather. Doubtless Mother cat just purposefully gets on with licking and suckling her kittens, purring.

CATS GALORE

It was nothing unusual of course. Cats and ships went together like sausages and mash. They were a form of rodenticide. Almost all vessels were badly infested with nibbling rats and mice. No doubt this particular mother cat had been born at sea herself and knew no other life.

No, what is unusual about this feline happy event is that it was chronicled. That's how we know about it. It's also why, nearly two hundred years later, it was solemnly commemorated in Sydney.

TRIM AND FLINDERS

One of the kittens was a nice little Tom named Trim. He became a personal pet and companion to Captain Matthew Flinders, British explorer. Together they shared some pretty hair-raising adventures. For five years the Captain and the cat were inseparable friends and, together, they travelled tens of thousands of pretty eventful miles.

Flinders, ably assisted by Trim, was the first bloke to chart much of the Australian coast. Eventually he recorded his doings

In the 1950s, Winston Churchill set up a secret inquiry to investigate flying saucers.

and deeds in a book called *Voyage to Terra Australis*, which was published in Britain after his death in 1814. The enterprising Captain also invented the Flinders Bar to offset the effects of iron on the compass needle and was the first person to use a barometer to predict wind changes. Clever chaps these early explorers!

Man and cat also saw service together on the *Investigator*. Then, in 1800, Trim and Flinders returned to England, a journey that would have taken many tedious and uncomfortable weeks. There Trim made the acquaintance of Mrs. Flinders, the Captain's wife. She would have seen a great deal less of her seadog of a husband than his cat did, although there are no records of her having minded particularly.

WAR

Between 1802 and 1815 Britain was again at war with France. But a little thing like that didn't stop Captain Flinders and his intrepid feline from sailing back to the Antipodes where they enjoyed (or at least survived) a 'friendly' meeting with French ships anchored at Encounter Bay on Australia's south coast. How did the conversation go? '*Bonjour. Permettez moi de vous present mon chat*, Trim'. Perhaps. The presence of a cat has always been a useful icebreaker in sticky situations. Perhaps Trim, had he known it, was doing a bit of international diplomatic work.

By 1803, Trim and Flinders were on the *Porpoise*. Unfortunately for them, it was shipwrecked shortly after they set sail and together the unlucky pair waited two months for rescuers before joining another ship, the *Cumberland*. Their destination was Britain, where Flinders hoped to find a better ship. Alas, the poor *Cumberland* was no more seaworthy than its predecessor and Flinders was forced to call in at the French (and therefore enemy) island of Mauritius and ask for help.

Oh dear. Luck had finally run out. There was no one to vouch for this Englishman on enemy territory in war time. Moreover the 'passport' given to Flinders by the French offering him French hospitality should he ever need it, was in the name of the *Investigator* not the *Cumberland*. One can just imagine the heated exchange and level of misunderstanding between the British sea captain and the French governor.

If you're an average sleeper, you'll roll over 12 times in bed tonight.

The results were grim for both man and cat. Flinders was held as a spy in captivity for seven years before his release to retirement in Britain, but Mauritius was the end for poor old Trim. He disappeared in mysterious circumstances. 'An untimely death, being devoured by the Catopophagi of that island', surmised his master, sadly.

FLINDERS KEEPS RECORD

We know all this because Flinders kept boredom at bay during his period of detention by writing a journal. The original manuscript is now held at the National Maritime Museum in Greenwich, but an extract was published in Australia. In his journal Flinders was very affectionate about his good mate, Trim. Flinders hoped that there would one day be a memorial to Trim which would call attention to the cat's 'little merriment with delight and his superior intelligence with surprise', and to remind us all that, 'Never will his like be ever seen again!'

TRIM'S MEMORIAL

It took nearly two centuries, but the State Library of New South Wales, Sydney, finally got round to fulfilling Flinders' wishes in 1996. There's been a statue of Captain Flinders outside the library in Macquarie Street in Sydney since 1925. In 1996, the explorer was joined by a beautiful life-sized statue of this cat, Trim, cast in bronze by the sculptor John Cornwell. It was the idea of a keen amateur maritime historian, Vaughan Evans, who worked as a volunteer at the library. Trim now stands, nose up and best paw forward, inside the building on a sunny windowsill. So that loyal and much loved puss has found a warm, peaceful and permanent resting place.

Money for the 'Trim Project' was raised by public subscription. Many donors sent gifts in the names of their own cats: Sir Basil, Stripey, Smokey and Jellicle to name but a few. The feline monument was unveiled on 28 March 1996 by Rear-Admiral David Campbell, AM RAN Naval Command, Sydney, in the presence of 400 admirers and the Naval Reserve Band.

In France, it's considered good taste to spread your bread with pig brain paté.

SUPERSTITIONS

Here's where some common superstitions come from.

FINDING A FOUR-LEAF CLOVER

The belief that four-leaf clovers are good luck comes from the Druids, ancient residents of the British Isles. Several times a year, they gathered in oak groves to settle legal disputes and offer sacrifices – then they ended their rituals by hunting for four-leaf clovers. Why? They believed a four-leaf clover enabled its owner to see evil spirits and witches – and therefore avoid them.

THROWING PENNIES INTO A WELL

Ancient people believed spirits living in springs and fountains demanded tribute – usually flesh. Young Mayan girls, for example, were sometimes tossed into the Well of Sacrifice (where they would 'marry' the spirits). Today we just toss the spirits a coin or two for luck.

KNOCKING ON WOOD

In the Middle Ages, churchmen insisted that knocking on wood was part of their tradition of prayer, since Christ was crucified on a wooden cross. They were right…but the tradition started several thousands of years earlier, with a different deity. Both Native Americans and ancient Greeks developed the belief (independently) that oak trees were the domain of an important god. By knocking on an oak, they were communicating with him and asking for his forgiveness. The Greeks passed their tradition on to the Romans, and it became part of European lore. The oak's 'power' was eventually transferred to all wood.

NAILING A HORSESHOE OVER A DOOR

This 'good luck charm' is a combination of two superstitions:

1. In early times, horses were considered magical. Because they can find their way in the dark, for example, people believed they could foresee danger or could guide souls through the underworld so anything connected with a horse was lucky.

2. Horseshoes are made of iron, which was considered protective.

The Norse god of battle wore iron gloves and carried an iron hammer. Romans nailed pieces of iron over their doors, believing it could ward off evil spirits.

In the 10th century, Christians added their own twist to the superstition – the tale of a blacksmith named Dunstan, who later became Archbishop of Canterbury. Dunstan had an unusual customer one day, a man with cloven feet who requested iron shoes. Dunstan pretended not to recognize him and agreed to make the shoes. But he knew who the fellow was – he shackled the Devil to the wall, treating him so brutally that Satan cried for mercy. Dunstan released him only after extracting a promise to never enter a dwelling with a horseshoe on the door.

OPENING AN UMBRELLA INDOORS

One of the few superstitions that isn't ancient or irrelevant. In the 18th century, spring-loaded, metal-spoked umbrellas were new and unpredictable. Opening one indoors was courting disaster – it could fly out of control and damage property – or people. It was a practical impulse to regard it as bad luck.

PULLING ON A WISHBONE

Over 2,000 years ago, the Etruscans (an early Italian civilization) believed that chickens – which squawk before they lay their eggs – could tell the future. The powers extended to part of the chicken's skeleton, too, so when a sacred hen died, the Etruscans put its collarbone in the sun until it dried out. Then people would pick it up, rub it, and make a wish. It became known as the 'wishbone'. Why this particular bone? Apparently because the V-shape looks a little like a human crotch.

Later, as more people wanted to get in on the wishing, the rubbing turned into a symbolic tug-of-war. Not everyone was going to get their wish; it became a contest to see whom the gods favored.

THE STORK BRINGING BABIES

In Scandinavia, storks – gentle birds with strong family ties – habitually nested on top of people's chimneys. So when Scandinavian parents needed to explain to youngsters how babies arrived, the stork was a handy answer. This traditional tale was spread in the 1800s by Hans Christian Andersen, in his fairy tales.

Your body gives off enough heat in 30 minutes to bring half a gallon of water to the boil.

OOPS!

Everyone's amused by tales of outrageous blunders – probably because it's comforting to know that someone's screwing up even worse than we are. So go ahead and feel superior for a few minutes.

HOT CLUE

PHILADELPHIA – 'A former Philadelphia fireman, in Federal Court here trying to overturn his dismissal for long hair, set his head on fire.

'William Michini apparently tried to dramatize that his locks were not a safety threat to his job. "Hair is self-extinguishing. It doesn't burn", he boasted. With that he struck a match and held it to his head, which caught fire. "It must have been the hairspray I used", said the sheepish firefighter'.

– *Remarkabilia,* by John Train

...AND HOW'S YOUR WIFE, CARLY?

'Kathie Lee Gifford inadvertently stumbled into talk-show hell on a recent *Live with Regis and Kathie Lee.*

'Singer-songwriter James Taylor was one of the guests, and the perky one, just making conversation, asked how his older brother, Alex, was doing. Sweet Baby James replied: "I wish I could say he was doing well....Alex died about four years ago".

'The *Washington Post* noted: "Mortification hung in the air for a few long moments". Blues singer Alex Taylor died of a heart attack in 1993, at age 46'.

– *The Portland Oregonian,* 1 May, 1997

WHAT ARE YOU DOING HERE?

'The Aldo Oliveri Stadium was meant to be the perfect memorial for one of Italy's greatest sports heroes: a stadium in Verona, dedicated to the memory of the goalie who led Italy to victory in the 1938 World Cup. Everything went smoothly right up to the weekend before it was due to open, when a small problem was discovered. Aldo Oliveri wasn't dead; he was alive, 86, and by all accounts, in the best of health. Plans are now afoot to open the stadium later, under a different name'.

– *The Fortean Times,* 1997

AND WHAT ARE YOU DOING HERE?

'In 1964 Gary Grannai escorted Tricia Nixon to the International Debutante Ball in New York City. Seven years later President Nixon was justifying his prosecution of the Vietnam War, despite the family's loss of a friend: "Gary was a second lieutenant. He was on patrol duty when it happened. You feel the personal tragedy when it comes into your own home. Yet there is no alternative to the war's going on". Publication of these remarks was followed by the (embarrassing) reappearance of Gary Grannai, who was very much alive and happily married'.

– *Oops,* by Richard Smith and Edward Recter

WELL, IN FRANCE KIDS LIKE IT

'French broadcasting system Canal France International blamed a "technical glitch" that sent an X-rated film instead of children's programming to Arab countries last Saturday. "We deeply regret this unacceptable incident, and we share in the high feelings prompted in Saudi Arabia and more widely in the Arab world", a foreign ministry spokesman said. An investigation is under way'.

– *USA Today,* 23 July, 1997

SURE IT WAS A MISTAKE

TORONTO – 'Proofreaders at Canada's postal service let a royal error slip through in the production of a souvenir stamp book – a reference to "the Prince of Whales".

'Much to Canada Post's chagrin, the book was printed with a passage describing a visit by the "Prince of Whales" to the snowy shores in 1860. He eventually became King Edward VII.

'It was human error and there was no intended slight to the Royal Family or to Prince Charles, said a spokesman. He also said Canada Post will not pull the book from shelves'.

– *Reuters News Service,* 1997

ALPHABET SOUP

In the 1980s, the Pfeiffer Brewing Company decided to use its successful print ad campaign on the radio. They realized it was a mistake when they heard the announcer say their written slogan aloud: 'Pfeiffer's – the beer with the silent P'.

REEL QUOTES

Here are some of our favourite lines from the silver screen.

ON DATING
Allen: 'What are you doing Saturday night'?
Diana: 'Committing suicide'.
Allen: 'What are you doing Friday night'?

– Play It Again, Sam

ON LOVE
Darrow: 'You ever been in love, Hornbeck'?
Hornbeck: 'Only with the sound of my own voice, thank God'.

– Inherit the Wind

'Jane, since I've met you, I've noticed things I never knew were there before: birds singing...dew glistening on a newly formed leaf...stoplights...'

– Lt. Frank Drebin,
Naked Gun

ON ANATOMY
Nick Charles: 'I'm a hero. I was shot twice in the *Tribune*'.
Nora Charles: 'I read where you were shot five times in the tabloids'.
Nick: 'It's not true. They didn't come anywhere near my tabloids'.

– The Thin Man

ON GOLF
'A golf course is nothing but a poolroom moved outdoors'.

– Barry Fitzgerald,
Going My Way

ON RELIGION
Sonja: 'Of course there's a God. We're made in his image'.
Boris: 'You think I was made in God's image? Take a look at me. Do you think he wears glasses'?
Sonja: 'Not with those frames... Boris, we must believe in God'.
Boris: 'If I could just see a miracle. Just one miracle. If I could see a burning bush, or the seas part, or my Uncle Sasha pick up a check (bill)'.

– Woody Allen's
Love and Death

ON BEING CLEAR
Ted Striker: 'Surely, you can't be serious'.
Dr. Rumack: 'I am serious. And don't call me Shirley'.

– Airplane!

Ollie: 'You never met my wife, did you'?
Stan: 'Yes, I never did'.

– Helpmates

THE FREEPLAY RADIO STORY

A hand-cranked radio? Surely it's a wind-up. Exactly! And the story of its invention is a classic tale of British ingenuity…

In a world that prizes ever-more technologically-advanced gizmos, it takes courage to go the other way and not only create a hand-cranked radio but also market it successfully to the digital generation. Charismatic British inventor Trevor Baylis had the agile mind and boundless energy to make that leap.

A NATURAL-BORN RISK TAKER

Born in 1937 in Kilburn, London, Baylis had already lived a full life before he came up with the design that made him a household name. By 15, Baylis was already swimming for Britain. He went on to study engineering at the local technical college and, after National Service, got into the swimming pool business, initially as a salesman – albeit one who was happy to give a personal demonstration of pool use to the astonishment of potential purchasers.

Baylis then decided on an abrupt career change and became a stunt man! This line of work included a stint with the Berlin State Circus, performing underwater feats of Houdini-like escapology. Peter Cook and Dudley Moore were among those who featured him on television. This early success paid for a house, appropriately enough on the eccentric little enclave of Eel Pie Island, in the middle of the Thames near Richmond.

DISABILITY BENEFITS

Passionate about inventing from childhood, Baylis continued to indulge his creative instincts while a stuntman, primarily through making aids for fellow circus performers who had been injured in their line of work. He claimed to have come up with something like 200 devices to allow the disabled to do anything from read a book to operate a camera whilst in a wheelchair. However, Baylis' greatest inspiration came to him after watching a documentary one day in 1991.

RADIO FREE AFRICA

In the 1990s the poverty, civil wars and the plight of AIDS affecting Africa was recognized as a major world problem. One of the major problems faced by the continent's governments was the lack of a reliable way to get information to their citizens. Shortwave radio was the best medium, but electricity supplies in many parts of Africa were at best erratic, and the cost of batteries was equivalent to a week's wages.

It was while watching a TV programme about this problem that Trevor had his 'eureka' moment. He thought back to the design of the gramophone record player, which had a handle that was turned to wind up a spring. When released, it had enough power to play discs at 78 rpm. Baylis set to work with a hand drill, a 6-volt DC motor run in reverse and an ordinary radio. The brace turned the motor, which acted as a generator. He added a clockwork mechanism which wound up a spring. As it unwound, the radio played for 15 minutes after just two minutes of winding. The next step was for Baylis to find backers to help him manufacture and market his device. He didn't get very far until 1994, when his invention was featured on the BBC science programme *Tomorrow's World*. Suddenly, offers of finance began to roll in, and Baylis set up business as BayGen Power Industries, based in Cape Town, South Africa.The aim was to make Freeplay wind-up radios, with labour supplied by local disabled people.

WINDING UP THE WORLD

The radios were not only a hit in Africa, but sold well in Europe and America. A range of models followed, including a solar-powered version (clearly not for the UK market). Even Bill Clinton once let slip that he had one of the radios! Baylis became a natural media star, a jovial, twinkly-eyed figure who looked and sounded every inch the archetypal madcap inventor, bursting with ideas and enthusiasm. Design awards followed – as did praise from aid agencies and environmental groups for Baylis' cheap and eco-friendly device. In 1997 he was awarded an O.B.E. Unfazed by success, Baylis went on to develop hand-cranked torches, mobile phone chargers and a clockwork computer. By 2000 he was using his considerable influence to call for the creation of a Royal Academy of Inventors in the UK – and that's not a wind-up.

A: Seaweed.

IN DREAMS...

People have always been fascinated by dreams. Where do they come from? What do they mean? D. H. Lawrence put it perfectly when he said, 'I can never decide whether my dreams are the result of my thoughts or my thoughts are the result of my dreams'. On occasion, art, music and even discoveries and inventions have resulted directly from information received in a dream. Here are some examples.

THE SEWING MACHINE

Elias Howe had been trying to invent a practical lock-stitch sewing machine for years, but had been unsuccessful. One night in the 1840s, he had a nightmare in which he was captured by a primitive tribe who were threatening to kill him with their spears. Curiously, all the spears had holes in them at the pointed ends. When Howe woke up, he realized that a needle with a hole at its tip – rather than at the base or middle (which is what he'd been working with) – was the solution to his problem.

DR. JEKYLL AND MR. HYDE

Since childhood, novelist Robert Louis Stevenson had always remembered his dreams and believed that they gave him inspiration for his writing. In 1884, he was in dire need of money and was trying to come up with a book. He had already spent two days racking his brain for a new plot when he had a nightmare about a man with a dual personality. In the dream, 'Mr. Hyde' was being pursued for a crime he'd committed; he took a strange powder and changed into someone else as his pursuers watched. Stevenson screamed in his sleep, and his wife woke him. The next morning he began writing *The Strange Case of Dr. Jekyll and Mr. Hyde*.

INSULIN

Frederick Banting, a Canadian doctor, had been doing research into the cause of diabetes, but had not come close to a cure. One night he had a strange dream. When he awoke, he quickly wrote down a few words that he remembered: 'Tie up the duct of the pancreas of a dog...wait for the glands to shrivel up...then cut it out, wash it...and filter the precipitation'. This new approach to extracting the substance led to the isolation of the hormone now known as insulin, which has saved millions of diabetics' lives. Banting was knighted for his discovery.

With at least 16 spooks, Pluckley in Kent is probably the most haunted village in the UK.

LEAD SHOT

James Watt is remembered for inventing the steam engine, but he also came up with the process for making lead shot used in shotguns. This process was revealed to him in a dream. At the time, making the shot was costly and unpredictable – the lead was rolled into sheets by hand, then chopped into bits. Watt had the same dream each night for a week: He was walking along in a heavy rainstorm – but instead of rain, he was being showered with tiny pellets of lead, which he could see rolling around his feet. The dream haunted him; did it mean that molten lead falling through the air would harden into round pellets? He decided to experiment. He melted about a kilogram of lead and tossed it out of the tower of a church that had a water-filled moat at its base. When he removed the lead from the water, he found that it had hardened into tiny globules. To this day, lead shot is made using this process.

THE BENZENE MOLECULE

Friedrich A. Kekule, a Belgian chemistry professor, had been working for some time to solve the structural riddle of the benzene molecule. One night while working late, he fell asleep on a chair and dreamed of atoms dancing before him, forming various patterns and structures. He saw long rows of atoms begin to twist like snakes until one of the snakes seized its own tail and began to whirl in a circle. Kekule woke up 'as if by a flash of lightning' and began to work out the meaning of his dream image. His discovery of a closed ring with an atom of carbon and hydrogen at each point of a hexagon revolutionized organic chemistry.

JESUS *(as many people think of Him)*

Warner E. Sallman was an illustrator for religious magazines. In 1924 he needed a picture for a deadline the next day, but was coming up blank. Finally, he went to bed – then suddenly awoke with 'a picture of the Christ in my mind's eye just as if it were on my drawing board'. He quickly sketched a portrait of Jesus with long brown hair, blue eyes, a neatly trimmed beard, and a beatific look – which has now become the common image of Christ around the world. Since 1940, more than 500 million copies of Sallman's *Head of Christ* have been sold. It has been reproduced billions of times on calendars, lamps, posters, etc.

UNCLE ALBERT SAYS...

Cosmic question: what would Albert Einstein think if he knew we consider his comments great bathroom reading?

'Only two things are infinite, the universe and stupidity – and I'm not sure about the former'.

'God is subtle, but He is not malicious'.

'"Common sense" is the set of prejudices acquired by age eighteen'.

'Nationalism is an infantile disease. It is the measles of mankind'.

'I never think of the future. It comes soon enough'.

'Try not to become a man of success, but rather, a man of value'.

'I experience the greatest degree of pleasure in having contact with works of art. They furnish me with happy feelings of an intensity such as I cannot drive from other realms'.

'To punish me for my contempt for authority, Fate made me an authority myself'.

'Why is it that nobody understands me, and everybody likes me'?

'A life directed chiefly toward fulfilment of personal desires sooner or later always leads to bitter disappointment'.

'My political ideal is that of democracy. Let every man be respected as an individual, and no man idolized'.

'Whatever there is of God and goodness in the Universe, it must work itself out and express itself through us. We cannot stand aside and let God do it'.

'Science without religion is lame, religion without science is blind'.

'I am a deeply religious nonbeliever...This is a somewhat new kind of religion'.

'With fame I become more and more stupid, which of course is a very common phenomenon'.

HEADLINE HOWLERS

These are 100 per cent honest-to-goodness headlines. Can you figure out what they were trying to say?

Kids Make Nutritious Snacks

ENRAGED COW INJURES FARMER WITH AXE

Red Tape Holds Up New Bridge

BILKE-A-THON NETS $1,000 FOR ILL BOY

PANDA MATING FAILS; VETERINARIAN TAKES OVER

School taxpayers revolting

Eye Drops Off Shelf

HELICOPTER POWERED BY HUMAN FLIES

Circumcisions Cut Back

POPE TO BE ARRAIGNED FOR ALLEGEDLY BURGLARIZING CLINIC

City wants Dead to pay for cleanup

MOORPARK RESIDENTS ENJOY A COMMUNAL DUMP

Montana Traded to Kansas City

Area man wins award for nuclear accident

International Scientific Group Elects Bimbo As Its Chairman

Storm delayed by bad weather

LEGISLATORS TAX BRAINS TO CUT DEFICIT

DEAD GUITARIST NOW SLIMMER AND TRIMMER

Study Finds Sex, Pregnancy Link

Include Your Children When Baking Cookies

Trees can break wind

RANGERS TO TEST PEETERS FOR RUST

Cockroach Slain, Husband Badly Hurt

Living Together Linked to Divorce

ECUADOR'S PRESIDENT DECLARES HE'S NOT DEAD

LACK OF BRAINS HINDERS RESEARCH

Two Sisters Reunited After 18 Years At Checkout Counter

Man, Shot Twice in Head, Gets Mad

MISSOURI WOMAN BIG WINNER AT HOG SHOW

Teacher Dies; Board Accepts His Resignation

PANTS MAN TO EXPAND AT THE REAR

Largest cast ever assembled for a film: 300,000, for the funeral scene in Gandhi.

THE HISTORY OF ROCK: QUIZ #1

How much do you know about the early days of rock 'n' roll? Here's a test to find out. Answers are on page 463.

1. The song that made Elvis a mega-star was the 1956 smash '(You Ain't Nothin' but a) Hound Dog'. How did he come up the song in the first place?
a) He used to sing it to his real hound dog, 'Buster'.
b) He copied it from a Las Vegas lounge act.
c) He overheard a woman singing it in a Memphis bus station.

2. The flip side of 'Hound Dog', 'Don't Be Cruel', was also a big hit. Elvis not only sang it, but co-wrote it with Otis Blackwell. How did Elvis and Otis wind up working together?
a) They were sitting next to each other on an aeroplane in 1955. To kill time, they started playing a rhyming game that turned into a hit song.
b) Otis was a nephew of Colonel Tom Parker (Elvis' manager) and needed money to get married. Elvis co-wrote the song with him as a 'wedding present'.
c) They didn't. Elvis just insisted on getting a writing credit (and half the royalties) as his 'reward' for singing the song.

3. In the 1950s, Pat Boone was known as a 'cover artist' – which meant he copied black artists' new songs and usually outsold them (because white artists' records got more airplay). In 1956, he covered Fats Domino's classic 'Ain't That a Shame'. How did he try to change it?
a) He tried to take the word 'ain't' out and replace it with 'isn't' because he thought it would reflect badly on his education.
b) He tried to slow it down. 'It sounds too much like jungle music', he explained.
c) He tried to turn the sax solo into a tuba solo because his parents were polka fans.

4. The Platters were one of the biggest vocal groups in the early days of rock. Their hits were often new versions of old standards. Their biggest hit was the 1955 version of Jerome Kern's 'Smoke Gets in Your Eyes'. Kern was dead when the song was released, but his wife…
a) Threatened a lawsuit to stop the record.
b) Helped the group become the first rock artists with their own TV show.
c) Tried to get them to record three songs she'd written.

5. Chuck Berry is one of the fathers of rock 'n' roll. He had more than a dozen hits – but only one of them hit No. 1 on the U.S. chart. It was…
a) 'Johnny B. Goode'
b) 'Roll Over Beethoven'
c) 'My Ding-a-Ling'

6. Jerry Lee Lewis was one of the wildmen of early rock 'n' roll. His first hit, 'Whole Lotta Shakin' Goin' On' (1957), was banned from the radio because…
a) His line, 'All you gotta do is stand in one place and wiggle your hips', was considered obscene.
b) It was creating riots. Whenever it played on the radio – even in school – teenagers would jump up and start doing a new dance they called 'The Shake'.
c) A fundamentalist minister claimed he'd played it backward and heard satanic messages – the first time anyone ever said that.

7. Another crazy man of 1950s rock 'n' roll was Little Richard, who recorded classics like 'Tutti Frutti' and 'Rip It Up'. When he recorded 'Long Tall Sally', he had one particular thing in mind. What was it?
a) He sang it as fast as he could, so censors wouldn't be able to distinguish the 'dirty' lyrics.
b) He sang it as fast as he could, so Pat Boone wouldn't be able to do a cover version of it.
c) He sang it as fast as he could, because he was absolutely desperate to go to the loo!

Camel rule of thumb: one-hump camels run faster than two-humped camels.

THE TRUTH ABOUT LOVE

If you want to know something important, ask a kid. These quotes about love were submitted by BRI member Alan Reder, who got them from the Internet and e-mailed them to us.

HOW DO TWO PEOPLE WIND UP FALLING IN LOVE?

Andrew, age 6: 'One of the people has freckles and so he finds somebody else who has freckles too'.

Mae, age 9: 'No one is sure why it happens, but I heard it has something to do with how you smell....That's why perfume and deodorant are so popular'.

Manuel, age 8: 'I think you're supposed to get shot with an arrow or something, but the rest of it isn't supposed to be so painful'.

WHAT IS FALLING IN LOVE LIKE?

John, age 9: 'Like an avalanche where you have to run for your life'.

Glenn, age 7: 'If falling in love is anything like learning how to spell, I don't want to do it. It takes too long'.

HOW IMPORTANT IS BEAUTY IN LOVE?

Anita, age 8: 'If you want to be loved by somebody who isn't already in your family, it doesn't hurt to be beautiful'.

Brian, age 7: 'It isn't always just how you look. Look at me. I'm handsome like anything and I haven't got anybody to marry me yet'.

Christine, age 9: 'Beauty is skin deep. But how rich you are can last a long time'.

Coldest towns on earth: Verkyoyanks and Oymyakon, Siberia, with temps as low as –95° F.

WHY DO LOVERS HOLD HANDS?

Gavin, age 8: 'They want to make sure their rings don't fall off because they paid good money for them'.

John, age 9: 'They are just practising for when they might have to walk down the aisle someday and do the matchimony thing'.

WHAT'S YOUR PERSONAL OPINION ABOUT LOVE?

Jill, age 6: 'I'm in favour of love as long as it doesn't happen when *Dinosaurs* is on television'.

Floyd, age 9: 'Love is foolish…but I still might try it sometime'.

Dave, age 8: 'Love will find you, even if you are trying to hide from it. I been trying to hide from it since I was five, but the girls keep finding me'.

Regina, age 10: 'I'm not rushing into being in love. I'm finding the fourth grade hard enough'.

WHAT'S A SUREFIRE WAY TO MAKE A PERSON FALL IN LOVE WITH YOU?

Del, age 6: 'Tell them that you own a whole bunch of [sweet shops]'.

Camille, age 9: 'Shake your hips and hope for the best'.

Carey, age 7: 'Yesterday I kissed a girl in a private place….We were behind a tree'.

REFLECTIONS ON THE NATURE OF LOVE

Greg, age 8: 'Love is the most important thing in the world, but baseball is pretty good, too'.

* * *

'To love a thing means wanting it to live'. – ***Confucius***

CURSES!

Even if you're not superstitious, it's hard to resist tales of 'cursed' ships, tombs and other creepy places. Who knows – maybe there's something to them. Here are some of our favourites.

THE CURSE OF JAMES DEAN'S PORSCHE

Curse: Disaster may be ahead for anyone connected with James Dean's 'death car'. It seems to attack people at random.

Origin: In 1955, Dean smashed his red Porsche into a another car and was killed. The wreckage was bought by George Barris, a friend of Dean's (and the man who customized cars like the Munsters' coffin-mobile for Hollywood). But as one writer put it, 'the car proved deadly even after it was dismantled'. Barris noticed weird things happening immediately.

Among Its Victims:

• The car slipped while being unloaded from the truck that delivered it to Barris, and broke a mechanic's legs.

• Barris put its engine into a race car. It crashed in the race, killing the driver. A second car in the same race was equipped with the Porsche's drive shaft – it overturned and injured its driver.

• The shell of the Porsche was being used in a Highway Safety display in San Francisco. It fell off its pedestal and broke a teenager's hip. Later, a truck carrying the display to another demonstration was involved in an accident. 'The truck driver', says one account, 'was thrown out of the cab of the truck and killed when the Porsche shell rolled off the back of the truck and crushed him'

Status: The Porsche finally vanished in 1960, while on a train en route to Los Angeles.

THE PRESIDENTIAL DEATH CYCLE

Curse: Between 1840 and 1960, every U.S. president elected in a year ending in a zero either died in office of natural causes or was assassinated. By contrast: Since 1840, of the 29 presidents who were not elected in the 20-year cycle, only one has died in office and not one has been assassinated.

Origin: The first president to die in office was William Henry Harrison, elected in 1840. In 1960, when John Kennedy was shot, people began to realize the eerie 'coincidence' involved.

Victims:

- William Henry Harrison, dead in 1841 after one month in office
- Abraham Lincoln (elected in 1860), fatally shot in 1865
- James Garfield (1880), assassinated in 1881
- William McKinley (re-elected in 1900), fatally shot in 1901
- Warren G. Harding (1920), died in 1923
- Franklin D. Roosevelt (elected for the third time in 1940), died in 1945
- JFK (1960), assassinated in 1963
- Ronald Reagan (1980) was nearly the eighth victim. He was shot and badly wounded by John Hinckley in 1983

Status: Astrologers insist that 1980 was an aberration because 'Jupiter and Saturn met in an air sign, Libra'. That gave Reagan some kind of exemption. They say we still have to wait to find out if the curse is over.

THE CURSE OF THE INCAN MUMMY

Curse: By disturbing a frozen mummy's remains, authorities brought bad luck to the region where it had been buried.

Origin: Three Andean mummies were discovered by an archaeologist/mountaineer in October 1995. They had been undisturbed in snow at the top of 6,096 metre Mount Ampato, in Southern Peru, for at least 500 years. Then an earthquake exposed them. One of the mummies was the remains of a young woman, referred to by local shamans as 'Juanita'. She had apparently been sacrificed to Incan gods.

Among Its Victims:

- Within a year of the discovery, a Peruvian commercial jet crashed and killed 123 people near the discovery site.
- Thirty-five people were electrocuted when a high-tension cable fell on a crowd celebrating the founding of the city of Arequipa (which is near the discovery site).

Status: Local shamans said these were the acts of the angered 'Ice Princess'. To break the curse, they gathered in the city of Arequipa in August 1996 and chanted: 'Juanita, calm your ire. Do not continue to damn innocent people who have done nothing to you'. Apparently it worked – we've heard nothing of it since 1996.

Q: What do olives and tomatoes have in common?

THE BIRTH OF THE MICROWAVE

To a lot of us, microwave ovens are 'magical mystery boxes'. We're not sure how they work – but after a while we can't live without them. Uncle John swore he'd never use one – until he had children. Now he blesses it every time he hauls out an emergency frozen pizza and manages to feed the kids before they kill each other. If you use a microwave, you might be interested to know more about it.

Chances are, you'll use a microwave oven at least once this week – probably (according to research) for heating up leftovers or defrosting something.

Microwave ovens are so common today that it's easy to forget how rare they once were. As late as 1977, only 10 per cent of U.S. homes had one. By 1995, 85 per cent of households had *at least* one. Today, more people own microwaves than own dishwashers.

MICROWAVE HISTORY

Magnetrons, the tubes that produce microwaves, were invented by British scientists in 1940. They were used in radar systems during World War II – and were instrumental in detecting German planes during the Battle of Britain.

These tubes – which are similar to TV picture tubes – might still be strictly military hardware if Percy Spencer, an engineer at Raytheon (a U.S. defence contractor), hadn't stepped in front of one in 1946. He had a chocolate bar in his pocket; when he went to eat it a few minutes later, he found that the chocolate had almost completely melted.

That didn't make sense. Spencer himself wasn't hot – how could the chocolate bar be? He suspected the magnetron was responsible. So he tried an experiment: he held a bag of popcorn kernels up to the tube. Seconds later they popped.

The next day Spencer brought eggs and an old tea kettle to work. He cut a hole in the side of the kettle, stuck an egg in it, and placed it next to the magnetron. Just as a colleague looked into the kettle to see what was happening, the egg exploded.

BRINGING MICROWAVES TO MARKET

Spencer shared his discovery with his employers at Raytheon and suggested manufacturing magnetron-powered ovens to sell to the public. Raytheon was interested. They had the capacity to produce 10,000 magnetron tubes a week – but with World War II over, military purchases had been cut back to almost nothing. 'What better way to recover lost sales', Ira Flatow writes in *They All Laughed*, 'than to put a radar set disguised as a microwave oven in every American home'?

Raytheon agreed to back the project. (According to legend, Spencer had to repeat the egg experiment in front of the board of directors, splattering them with egg, before they okayed it.) The company patented the first 'high-frequency dielectric heating apparatus' in 1953. Then they held a contest to find a name for their product. Someone came up with 'Radar Range', which was later combined into the single word – *Radarange*.

DEVELOPING THE PRODUCT

Raytheon had a fantastic product idea and a great name, but they didn't have an oven anyone could afford. The 1953 model was 1.7 metres tall, weighed more than 340 kilos, and cost £1,800. Over the next 20 years, trains, ocean liners and expensive restaurants were virtually the only Radarange customers.

• In 1955, a company called Tappan introduced the first microwave oven aimed at average consumers; it was smaller than the Radarange, but still cost (£800 – more than some cars.

• Then in 1964, a Japanese company perfected a miniaturized magnetron. For the first time, Raytheon could build a microwave oven that fitted on a kitchen countertop. In 1967, they introduced a Radarange that used the new magnetron. It sold for £300. But that was still too expensive for the average family.

• Finally, in the 1980s, technical improvements made it possible to lower the price and improve the quality enough to make microwave ovens both affordable and practical. By 1988, 10 per cent of all new food products in the United States were microwaveable. Surveys showed that the microwave oven was America's favourite new appliance – and it still is today.

How does a microwave oven work? See page 317 to find out.

Prince Philip was born on the dining room table of his parents' house in Corfu.

Q&A: ASK THE EXPERTS

Everyone's got a question or two they'd like answered. Here are a few of those questions, with answers from some top trivia experts.

HOLY COW!

Q: Why are there holes in Swiss cheese?

A: Because of air bubbles. 'During one of the stages of preparation, while it is still "plastic", the cheese is kneaded and stirred. Inevitably, air bubbles are formed in the cheese as it is twisted and moved about, but the viscous nature of the cheese prevents the air bubbles from rising to the surface and getting out. As the cheese hardens, these air pockets remain, and we see them as the familiar "holes" when we slice the wheel of cheese'. (From *A Book of Curiosities*, compiled by Roberta Kramer)

PHOTO FINISH

Q: Why do eyes come out red in photographs?

A: 'The flash from the camera is being reflected on the rear of the eyeball, which is red from all the blood vessels'. The solution: 'Use a flash at a distance from the camera, or get your subjects to look somewhere else. Another trick is to turn up the lights in the room, making them as bright as possible, which causes the subject's pupil to contract and admit less of the light from the subsequent flash'. (From *Why Things Are*, by Joel Aschenbach)

HOT STUFF

Q: How can you cool off your mouth after eating hot chillies?

A: 'Drink milk', says Dr. Robert Henkin, director of the Taste and Smell Clinic in Washington, D.C. 'Casein, the main protein in milk, acts like a detergent, washing away capsaicin, the substance in [chillies] responsible for their "fire"'. (From *Parade* magazine, 14 November, 1993)

SOMETHING FISHY

Q: Do fish sleep?

A: Hard to tell if they sleep in the same sense we do. They never look like they're sleeping, because they don't have eyelids. 'But they do seem to have regular rest periods....Some fish just stay more or less motionless in the water, while others rest directly on the bottom, even turning over on their side. Some species...dig or burrow into bottom sediment to make a sort of "bed". Some fish even...prefer privacy when they rest; their schools disperse at night to rest and then reassemble in the morning'. (From *Science Trivia*, by Charles Cazeau)

PICK A BALL OF COTTON

Q: Should you toss out the cotton after opening a bottle of pills?
A: Yep. 'The cotton keeps the pills from breaking in transit, but once you open the bottle, it can attract moisture and thus damage the pills or become contaminated'. (From *Davies Gazette*, a newsletter from Davies Medical Centre in San Francisco)

SLIPPERY QUESTION

Q: A few years ago, we started seeing foods containing 'canola oil'. What is it?
A: A variety of rapeseed – which, until recently, was only grown for industrial oils. 'Scientists in Canada were able to breed new varieties of rapeseed that were suitable for cooking. They named their creation canola to honour Canada. Canola seed contains 40 per cent to 45 per cent oil, of which 6 per cent is saturated fatty acids. Canola oil contains less fat than any other oil: 50 per cent less than corn oil and olive oil, 60 per cent less than soybean oil'. (From *Why Does Popcorn Pop?*, by Don Voorhees)

* * *

SAMUEL JOHNSON'S DICTIONARY

Cuckingstool: Engine to punish scolds and unquiet women
Eructation: Belching
Fopdoodle: Fool
Looby: Clown
Muckender: Handkerchief
Slubberdegullion: Dirty, sorry wretch
Urinator: Underwater diver

MORE STRANGE LAWSUITS

Here are a few more real-life examples of unusual legal battles.

THE PLAINTIFF: Janet R.
THE DEFENDANT: Kay-Bee Toys at Valley View Mall, Roanoke, Virginia
THE CASE: She claimed that while shopping in the mall in 1996, she was hit by a truck – a toy truck. Apparently a customer, playing with a radio-controlled 4 x 4, bumped Robinson in the ankle. She sued for $100,000, asking compensation for 'pain, humiliation, aggravation and disability'.
THE VERDICT: Suit dropped by plaintiff.

THE PLAINTIFF: Etta Stephens of Tampa, Florida
THE DEFENDANT: The Barnett Bank
THE CASE: In 1995 Stephens opened the envelope containing her monthly money market statement – and found the account balance listed as zero, instead of $20,000 as she expected. 'Upon seeing this', says one report, 'Stephens clutched her bosom and fell to the ground' with a heart attack. Officials of the bank said it was a mistake caused by a 'printing error' and apologized. But Stephens still sued them for nearly killing her.
THE VERDICT: Unknown.

THE PLAINTIFF: Katherine Balog, 60-year-old Californian
THE DEFENDANTS: Bill Clinton and the Democratic Party
THE CASE: In 1992 Balog sued 'to recover damages for the trauma of Clinton's candidacy'. She claimed she was suffering 'serious emotional and mental stress' because Clinton, a 'Communist sympathizer' and 'draft dodger', was about to be elected president.
THE VERDICT: Unknown.

THE PLAINTIFF: Bennie Casson
THE DEFENDANT: PT's Show Club, an Illinois strip joint

THE CASE: In 1997 a stripper named Busty Heart allegedly approached Casson during her act and 'slammed' her 2.2-metre bust (a reported 18 kilos per breast) into his head and neck. He sued for 'emotional distress' and claimed an old neck injury had been aggravated by the attack.
THE VERDICT: No lawyer would take the case, so the judge had to dismiss it.

THE PLAINTIFF: Debra Lee Benagh, 44, of Denver
THE DEFENDANT: Elitch Gardens, an amusement park
THE CASE: In 1997, according to Benagh's suit, she rode on the Mind Eraser roller coaster – and actually suffered memory loss. Benagh sued for negligence, contending that the park operators should have known of the ride's hazards.
THE VERDICT: Unknown.

THE PLAINTIFF: Swee Ho, a Chinese merchant in Thailand
THE DEFENDANT: Pu Lin, a rival merchant
THE CASE: As reported by Gerald Sparrow, once a judge in Bangkok: 'Pu Lin had stated sneeringly at a party that Swee Ho's new wife, Li Bua, was merely a decoration to show how rich her husband was. Swee Ho, he said, could no longer "please the ladies". Swee Ho sued his rival for slander in the British Consular Court, claiming that Li Bua was his wife in every sense'.
THE VERDICT: Swee Ho won – without a word of testimony. Swee Ho's lawyer 'simply put the blushing Li Bua in the witness box. She was quite obviously pregnant'.

* * *

IRONIC TWIST

The Ramses brand condom is named after the great Pharaoh Ramses II, who fathered over 160 children.

THE BIG DIPPER

What's the one constellation everyone knows? The Big Dipper. After you read this article you'll be able to sound like a know-it-all the next time you're star-gazing with someone.

THE NIGHT SKY

The Big and Little Dippers are probably the best-known star groups in the northern hemisphere. They're both parts of larger star groups, or constellations, named after bears. The Big Dipper belongs to the constellation Ursa Major, 'The Greater Bear', and the Little Dipper is part of Ursa Minor, 'The Lesser Bear'.

• Ursa Major is the most ancient of all the constellations. For some reason, early civilizations all over the world seem to have thought of it as a bear. This is remarkable, since Ursa Major doesn't look anything like a bear. It's even more remarkable when you consider that most of the ancient world had never seen a bear

THE NATIVE AMERICAN SKY

In the New World, the Iroquois, who had seen plenty of bears, called it Okouari, which means – bear. The Algonquin and Black-foot tribes called it 'The Bear and the Hunters'. For them, the three stars in the handle of the Big Dipper were three hunters going after the bear.

• In a typical Native American story, a party of hunters set out on a bear hunt. The first hunter carried a bow and arrow. The second hunter brought along a pot or kettle to cook the bear in. The faint star Alcor, which you can just see above the middle star of the Dipper's handle, was the pot. The third hunter carried a bundle of sticks with which to build a fire to cook the bear.

• The bear hunt lasted from spring until autumn. In the autumn, the first hunter shot the bear. Blood from the wounded animal stained the autumn leaves in the forest. The bear died, was cooked, and was eaten. The skeleton lay on its back in the den through the winter months. The bear's life, meanwhile, had entered into another bear, which also lay on its back, deep asleep for the winter.

• When spring returned, the bear came out of the den and the hunters started to chase her again, and so it went from year to year.

THE GREEK SKY

Greek mythology offers another version of how the Bears got into the sky. Calisto, the beautiful daughter of the King of Arcadia, caught the eye of Zeus, the king of the gods. Zeus took her by surprise, leaving her to become the mother of his child. In time, Calisto gave birth to a son, whom she named Arcas. Hera, queen of the gods, changed Calisto into a bear in a jealous rage.

After a number of years had passed, Arcas was out hunting when he saw a bear. Not knowing the bear was his mother, Arcas raised his spear, ready to kill the animal. Before Arcas could throw his spear, Zeus quickly rescued Calisto by placing her in the skies – where she remains today. Arcas also became a constellation, Ursa Minor, next to his mother.

• Some say Zeus swung both bears around by their tails and flung them into the sky, which explains why their tails are so long.

• The Greeks called Ursa Major Arktos, which means 'Bear'. This is where we get out word Arctic. The Greek poet, Homer, described the Bear as keeping watch from its Arctic den looking out for the hunter Orion. Homer also remarked that in his day, the Bear never sank into the ocean, which meant that it never set. Hera was responsible for this, having persuaded the ocean gods not to allow the two Bears to bathe in their waters.

HIPPOS AND PLOUGHS

But not everyone has thought of these constellations as bears. The Egyptians saw the seven stars of the Big Dipper as a bull's thigh or a hippopotamus. Because its stars circled around the north pole of the sky without setting, or 'dying', below the horizon, this constellation was a symbol of immortality and figured in rebirth rituals at funerals. Ursa Minor was the Jackal of the god Set that participated in rites for the dead taking place in the Egyptian underworld.

In Mesopotamia, Scandinavia, Italy and Germany, people referred to the Big Dipper as a wagon, chariot, or cart. In England

Bagpipes were invented in Iran and brought to Scotland by the Romans.

it was 'Charles' Wain' (the word wain meant 'wagon' and Charles stood for Charles the Great). The Little Dipper was the 'Smaller Chariot', or 'Little Wain'. The four stars that make up the bowl of the dipper are the carriage part of the wain, and the dipper's handle is the part of the wain attached to the horses that pull it.

In some parts of England (and elsewhere), people saw the Big Dipper as 'The Plough'. The four stars of the dipper's bowl form the blade of the plough, behind which stretches its three-starred handle.

DIPPER DIRECTIONS

At the tip of the handle of the Little Dipper is the most celebrated star in the sky, Polaris, the North Star. While not the brightest star in the heavens, Polaris is certainly the most valuable. It has provided directions to countless travellers. The two stars at the end of the bowl of the Big Dipper, called 'The Pointers', point to the North Star.

The Greeks used the Greater Bear and the Phoenicians used the Lesser Bear to find north. American slaves called the Big Dipper 'The Drinking Gourd' and followed it northward to freedom. Seen from the spinning Earth, the sky appears to move during the night, carrying all the stars along with it. Only the North Star stands in the same spot at the hub of the dome of the sky. The Greeks called this star Cynosure, a word that has found its way into our language meaning the centre of attraction or interest. Others called the North Star the 'Lodestar', most likely referring to the magnetic rock lodestone, used in mariners' compass needles to find north.

* * * *

'It is easier to accept the message of the stars than the message of the salt desert. The stars speak of man's insignificance in the long eternity of time. The desert speaks of his insignificance right now'.

– *Edwin Way Teale*

GO ASK ALICE

When Charles Lutwidge Dodgson met a four-year-old girl named Alice Liddell in 1856, he wrote in his diary, 'I mark this day with a white stone' – which meant it was a particularly wonderful day for him. It turned out to be a pretty good day for children all over the world: Charles Dodgson became famous as Lewis Carroll – and Alice Liddell was the child who inspired him to write Alice in Wonderland.

BACKGROUND

• Charles Lutwidge Dodgson was a deacon and professor of mathematics at Christ Church College in Oxford. He was also a poet and photographer who drew his inspiration from children – especially little girls. In fact, he chose teaching as a career because it left him time to pursue photography and poetry.

• In 1856, the same year Dodgson began teaching at Christ Church, a new dean arrived – Henry George Liddell. He had four children, and Dodgson quickly became friendly with them. He especially enjoyed taking them on outings and photographing the girls. The youngest, 4-year-old Alice, had a special relationship with Reverend Dodgson – perhaps because her favourite expression was 'let's pretend'.

DOWN THE RABBIT HOLE

On what he recalled as a 'golden July afternoon' in 1862, Dodgson took the three Liddell girls boating on the river for a picnic.

• As they rowed lazily downstream, Alice begged Dodgson to tell them a story – so he made one up.

• He called his heroine Alice to please her. Then he 'sent her straight down a rabbit-hole to begin', he later explained, 'without the least idea what was to happen afterwards'.

• Amazingly, he made up most of *Alice in Wonderland* on the spot.

SAVING A TREASURE

Alice liked the story so much that she asked Dodgson to write it down. He agreed. In fact, that night – as a gift for his favourite little girl – he sat up and wrote the whole thing out in longhand, adding his own illustrations. He called it *Alice's Adventures Underground*.

• Dodgson had already decided he needed a pseudonym for the humorous poems and stories he'd been contributing to magazines. (He also wrote academic articles on mathematics, and was afraid people wouldn't take him seriously if they knew he was writing nonsense rhymes.)
• He came up with the name Lewis Carroll by scrambling letters in his first two names, and used it for the first time when he signed *Alice's Adventures Underground* for Alice.

A BOOK IS BORN

Fortunately for us, before Dodgson brought the handwritten manuscript to Alice, he happened to show it to a friend named George MacDonald, who read it to his children. If he hadn't, Alice's adventures might have been nothing more than a personal gift to one little girl. But the entire MacDonald family loved the story so much that they urged Carroll to publish it.
• After giving the original to Alice Liddell as promised, Dodgson decided to take their advice. He revised the story, added to it, then hired John Tenniel, a well-known cartoonist, to illustrate it.
• The book was published in 1865 as *Alice's Adventures in Wonderland*. It became so popular that in 1871 Carroll published the further adventures of Alice, entitled *Through the Looking Glass*.

THE ALICE MYSTERY

Shortly after Dodgson presented Alice with the handwritten story, something happened that ended his relationship with the Liddell family. No one knows what it was. But the abruptness of the split has led to speculation about Carroll's sexuality. Why was he so interested in little girls in the first place?
• In fact, however, there's no evidence that his relationships with children were in any way improper. His biographers interviewed many of the women Carroll entertained as children and they always spoke of him with great respect and fondness. It's more likely, say some biographers, that Carroll broached the subject of marriage to one of the Liddell girls and was rejected.
• At any rate, the lazy days of games and stories were over for Alice and Dodgson. By the time Alice received her copy of the published edition of *Alice's Adventures in Wonderland*, the author was no longer a part of her life.

In her entire life, Queen Berengaria of England never once visited England.

In 1926, Alice Liddell sold the original manuscript of *Alice's Adventures Underground* to an American book dealer for $25,000. He resold it to a group of Americans. They took it to England and presented it as a gift to the British people in gratitude for their bravery in World War II. It remains there today, in the British Museum.

* * *

FAMILIAR FACES

Many of the now-classic characters in Carroll's stories were easily recognizable to the Liddell children. For example:

The White Rabbit: Was modelled after Carroll himself. Like the rabbit, he was very proper, usually dressed in an old-fashioned formal black suit and top hat. He always wore gloves – no matter what the weather – which he frequently misplaced.

The Dodo: Carroll had taken the girls to a museum, where they were fascinated by a stuffed Dodo bird. He incorporated the bird into the story as himself because he stammered and his name came out: as 'Do-Do-Dodgson'.

The Duck, Lory and Eaglet: The Duck was Carroll's friend, Robinson Duckworth, who'd accompanied him on many of the outings with the children. The Lory was Lorina Liddell, the Eaglet, Edith Liddell. The three sisters show up again in the Dormouse's story as Elsie (from L.C., Lorina's initials), Lacie (an anagram for Alice), and Tillie (a family nickname for Edith).

The Mock Turtle's Song: 'Beautiful Soup' was a parody of one of the children's favourite songs, 'Star of Evening', and the way they sang in their childish voices.

The Mad Hatter: Supposedly modelled after an eccentric man named Theophilus Carter, who'd been at Christ Church but became a furniture dealer.

Marks & Spencer shift 18 tonnes of chicken tikka masala sandwiches every week.

THE WORLD ACCORDING TO ALICE

The Alice books are among the most quotable children's stories ever written. There's a gem on practically every page – and some passages in particular are packed with them. Here are some of our favourite bits – see if you agree with our choices.

In that direction", the Cheshire Cat said, waving its right paw round, "lives a Hatter: and in that direction", waving the other paw, "lives a March Hare. Visit either you like: they're both mad".

"But I don't want to go among mad people", Alice remarked.

"Oh, you can't help that", said the Cat: "we're all mad here. I'm mad. You're mad".

"How do you know I'm mad!" said Alice.

"You must be", said the Cat, "or you wouldn't have come here"'.

* * *

'"It was much pleasanter at home", thought poor Alice, "when one wasn't always growing larger and smaller, and being ordered about by mice and rabbits. I almost wish I hadn't gone down that rabbit hole and yet it's rather curious, you know, this sort of life! I do wonder what can have happened to me! When I used to read fairy tales, I fancied that kind of thing never happened, and now here I am in the middle of one! There ought to be a book written about me, that there ought! And when I grow up, I'll write one but I'm grown up now", she added in a sorrowful tone, "at least there's no room to grow up any more here"'.

* * *

'Alice took up the fan and gloves, and, as the hall was very hot, she kept fanning herself all the time she went on talking: "Dear, dear! How queer everything is today! And yesterday things went on just as usual. I wonder if I've been changed in the night? Let

It isn't a 'big band' unless it has 14 different instruments.

me think: was I the same when I got up this morning? I almost think I can remember feeling a little different. But if I'm not the same, the next question is, Who in the world am I? Ah, that's the great puzzle!" And she began thinking over all the children she knew, that were of the same age as herself to see if she could have been changed for any of them'.

* * *

'"Who are you?" said the Caterpillar.

'This was not an encouraging opening for a conversation. Alice replied, rather shyly, "I, I hardly know, sir, just at present at least I know who I was when I got up this morning, but I think I must have been changed several times since then".

"What do you mean by that"? said the Caterpillar sternly. "Explain yourself!"

"I can't explain myself, I'm afraid, sir", said Alice, "because I'm not myself, you see".

"I don't see", said the Caterpillar. "I'm afraid I can't put it more clearly", Alice replied very politely, "for I can't understand it myself to begin with; and being so many different sizes in a day is very confusing".

"It isn't", said the Caterpillar.

"Well, perhaps you haven't found it so yet", said Alice; "but when you have to turn into a chrysalis – you will some day, you know – and then after that into a butterfly, I should think you'll feel a little queer, won't you?"

"Not a bit", said the Caterpillar.

"Well, perhaps your feelings may be different", said Alice; "all I know is, it would feel very queer to me".

"You!" said the Caterpillar contemptuously. "Who are you?"'

* * *

'The two *Alices* are not books for children; they are the only books in which we *become* children'.

– Virginia Woolf

IT'S A MIRACLE!

They say the Lord works in mysterious ways. Do you believe it? These people obviously do – in fact, they may be the proof.

THE GLASS MENAGERIE

The Sighting: An 11-metre image of the Virgin Mary on the side of a building in Clearwater, Florida

Revelation: In 1996, workers chopped down a palm tree in front of the Seminole Finance Company building. Not long afterward, a customer noticed a discolouration in the building's tinted windows that resembled the Madonna. The discovery was reported on the afternoon news. By the end of the week, an estimated 100,000 people visited the site – including a Baptist minister who was ejected after he 'condemned the crowd for worshipping an image on glass'.

Impact: The city set up a 'Miracle Management Task Force' to install portable toilets at the site, arrange police patrols, and erect a pedestrian walkway over the adjacent road (Route 19) to stop the faithful from dodging in and out of traffic. 'That's the busiest highway in Florida', one policeman told reporters. 'You want to know the real miracle? Half a million people have crossed that intersection and nobody's been injured or killed'.

STRANGE FRUIT

The Sighting: The words of Allah in a sliced tomato in Huddersfield, England

Revelation: In June 1997, 14-year-old Shasta Aslam sliced a tomato in half for her grandparents' salad and saw what appeared to be the Koranic message 'There is no God but Allah' spelled out in Arabic in the veins of one half of the tomato, and the words 'Mohammed is the messenger' written in the other half.

'There were some letters missing and it was hard to decipher', her grandmother told reporters, 'but the message was clear'.

Impact: Hundreds of Muslims from all over the United Kingdom went to view the tomato. 'They knock on the door and I take them through to the kitchen and open the fridge door for them to have a look', the grandmother explained. The tomato has since been moved to the freezer.

NICE BUN

The Sighting: The face of Mother Teresa in a cinnamon bun in Nashville, Tennessee

Revelation: In the autumn of 1996, bakers at the Bongo Java coffee-house were baking cinnamon buns when they noticed one that bore a striking resemblance to Mother Teresa.

Impact: Bongo Java owner Bob Bernstein preserved the bun and put it in a display case beneath the coffeehouse's cash register. The story was reported in newspapers and on national television. The coffeehouse, now a tourist attraction, set up a Web site and began selling 'Immaculate Confection' T-shirts, mugs, cards and 'Mother Teresa's Special Roast' coffee beans. More than 2 million people from 80 different countries have visited the Web site, and many have left messages. 'I hate to burst your bubble', one visitor wrote, 'but to me, it looks more like Abe Vigoda [a U.S. comedy actor] in a hooded sweatshirt'.

When Mother Teresa – who didn't even allow her own order to use her image in fundraising – learned of the bun, her lawyers asked the coffeehouse to remove it from display. 'If it were sacrilege, we'd stop', a Bongo spokesman said. 'But it's not'.

THIRSTY FOR ENLIGHTENMENT

The Sighting: A statue of Lord Ganesh, the elephant-headed Hindu god of wealth and power, drinking milk through its trunk

Revelation: On 21 September, 1995, a Hindu in India had a dream that Ganesh, the god of wealth and power, 'wanted some milk'. So he held an offering of a teaspoonful of milk up to the trunk of his Ganesh statue – and it drank it. As word spread over the next few days, the same phenomenon was observed in Hindu communities in England, Hong Kong, Malaysia, Nepal, the Netherlands and the United States. (Sceptics point to capillary action – the ability of porous stone and metals to absorb liquids – as a likely culprit.)

Impact: According to Indian news reports, 'So many Hindus were caught up in the mass hysteria that milk supplies were depleted and shopkeepers raised the price of milk 20 times. The military used bamboo canes to control the worshippers flooding Hindu temples'. The phenomenon spread to other religions, too. 'After reading news reports', one man in Kuala Lumpur wrote, 'I tried the same thing on Mother Mary and baby Jesus. They drank a whole spoonful'.

On average, your left hand does 56 per cent of your typing.

OLYMPIC MYTHS

Every four years, we're treated to another round of Olympics. Whether you watch them or not, it's impossible to avoid all the hype – which, it turns out, isn't all true. Next time someone refers to 'Olympic tradition', read them this.

THE MYTH: Athletes who competed in the ancient Greek Olympics were amateurs.

THE TRUTH: Technically, maybe. But in fact, they were handsomely rewarded for their victories. 'Contrary to popular belief', says David Wallechinsky in his *Complete Book of the Olympics*, 'the Ancient Greek athletes were not amateurs. Not only were they fully supported throughout their training, but even though the winner received only an olive wreath at the Games, at home he was amply rewarded and could become quite rich'. Eventually, top athletes demanded cash and appearance fees – even back then.

THE MYTH: In ancient Greece, the Olympics were so important that everything stopped for them – even wars.

THE TRUTH: No war ever stopped because of the Olympics. But wars didn't interfere with the games because: 1) participants were given night-time safe-conduct passes that allowed them to cross battlefields after a day's fighting was done and 2) the Olympics were part of a religious ceremony, so the four olympic sites – including Delphi and Olympia – were off-limits to fighting.

THE MYTH: To honour ancient tradition and discourage commercialism, organizers of the modern Olympics decided that only amateur athletes could compete.

THE TRUTH: Not even close. It was 'amateurs only' strictly to keep the riff-raff out. Baron Coubertin, the man responsible for bringing back the Olympics in 1896, was a French aristocrat who wanted to limit competitors to others of his social class. 'He saw the Olympics as a way to reinforce class distinctions rather than overcome them', writes one historian. Since only the rich could afford to spend their time training for the games without outside support, the best way to keep lower classes out was to restrict them to amateurs.

THE MYTH: The torch-lighting ceremony that opens the games originated with the ancient Greeks.
THE TRUTH: It has no ancient precedent – it was invented by the Nazis. The 1936 Olympics took place in Berlin, under Hitler's watchful eye. Carl Diem, who organized the event for the Führer, created the first lighting of the Olympic flame to give the proceedings 'an ancient aura'. Since then, the ceremony has become part of Olympic tradition – and people just assume it's much older than it really is.

THE MYTH: The five-ring Olympic symbol is from ancient Greece.
THE TRUTH: The Nazis are responsible for that myth, too. According to David Young's book, *The Modern Olympics*, it was spread in a Nazi propaganda film about the Berlin Games.

THE MYTH: Adolf Hitler snubbed U.S. runner Jesse Owens at the 1936 Olympics in Berlin.
THE TRUTH: This is one of the enduring American Olympic myths. Hitler, the story goes, was frustrated in his attempt to prove Aryan superiority when Owens – an African American – took the gold. The furious Führer supposedly refused to acknowledge Owens's victories. But according to Owens himself, it never happened. Hitler didn't congratulate anyone that day because the International Olympic Committee had warned him he had to congratulate 'all winners or no winners'. He chose to keep mum.

THE MYTH: The Olympic marathon distance was established in ancient times to honour a messenger who ran from Marathon to Athens – about 26 miles – to deliver vital news – then died.
THE TRUTH: The marathon distance – 42,195 metres – was established at the 1908 Games in London. It's the distance from Shepherd's Bush Stadium to the Queen's bedroom window.

THE MYTH: Drugs have always been taboo in the Olympics.
THE TRUTH: Drugs weren't outlawed until 1967. In fact, according to the *Complete Book of the Olympics*, drugs were already in use by the third modern Olympic Games: 'The winner of the 1904 marathon, Thomas Hicks, was administered multiple doses of strychnine and brandy during the race'.

The English sparrow isn't a sparrow. And it comes from Africa, not England.

THE EIFFEL TOWER, PART I

It's hard to believe now, but when the Eiffel Tower was proposed in the late 1800s, a lot of Parisians – and French citizens in general – opposed it. Here's a look at the story behind one of the most recognizable architectural structures on earth.

REVOLUTIONARY THINKING

In 1885, French officials began planning the Great Exposition of 1889, a celebration of the 100th anniversary of the French Revolution. They wanted to build some kind of monument that would be as glorious as France itself.

The Washington Monument, a masonry and marble obelisk, had recently been completed. At 170 metres high, it was the tallest building on earth. The French decided to top it by constructing a 305-metre tall tower right in the heart of Paris.

Now all they had to do was find somebody who could design and build it.

OPEN SEASON

On 2 May, 1886, the French government announced a design contest: French engineers and architects were invited to 'study the possibility of erecting on the Champ de Mars an iron tower with a base 125 metres square and 300 metres high'.

Whatever the contestants decided to propose, their designs had to meet two other criteria: 1) the structure had to be self-financing – it had to attract enough ticket-buying visitors to the exposition to pay for its own construction; and 2) it had to be a temporary structure that could be torn down easily at the end of the Exposition.

MERCI...BUT NON, MERCI

More than 100 proposals were submitted by the 18 May deadline. Most were fairly conventional, but some were downright weird. One person proposed building a huge guillotine; another suggested erecting a 305-metre tall sprinkler to water all of Paris during droughts; a third suggested putting a huge electric light atop the tower that – with the help of strategically placed parabolic mirrors – would provide the entire city with 'eight times as much light as is necessary to read a newspaper'.

NO CONTEST

The truth was, none of them had a chance. By the time the contest was announced, Alexandre-Gustave Eiffel – a 53-year-old structural engineer already considered France's 'master builder in metal' had the job sewn up. (He would later become known as *le Magicien du Fer* – 'the Iron Magician'.)

Weeks earlier, he had met with French minister Edouard Lockroy and presented plans for a wrought iron tower he was ready to build. Eiffel had already commissioned 5,329 mechanical drawings representing the 18,038 different components that would be used. Lockroy was so impressed that he rigged the contest so only Eiffel's design would win.

JOINT VENTURE

In January 1887, Eiffel signed a contract with the French government and the City of Paris. Eiffel & Company, his engineering firm, agreed to contribute £800,000 of the tower's estimated £1 million construction cost. In exchange, Eiffel would receive all revenues generated by the tower during the Exposition – and for 20 years afterward. (The government agreed to leave the tower up after the Exposition.) Afterward, full ownership reverted to the City of Paris. They could tear it down if they wanted.

MONEY MACHINE

Unlike other public monuments, the Eiffel Tower was designed to make money from the very beginning. If you wanted to take the lift or the stairs to the first storey, you had to pay 2 francs; going all the way to the top cost 5 francs (Sundays were cheaper). That was just the beginning: restaurants, cafes, and shops were planned for the first storey; a post office, telegraph office, bakery and printing press were planned for the second storey. In all, the tower was designed to accommodate up to 10,416 paying customers at a time.

Even if baboons wanted to, they couldn't play cricket – they can't throw overhand.

GROUNDBREAKING

Construction began on 26 January, with not a moment to spare. With barely two years left to build the tower in time for the opening of the Exposition, Eiffel would have to build the tower more quickly than any similar structure had been built before. The Washington Monument, just over half the Eiffel Tower's size, had taken 36 years to complete.

PARISIAN PARTY POOPERS

A 305-metre tower would dwarf the Parisian skyline and overpower the city's other landmarks, including Notre Dame, the Louvre and the Arc de Triomphe. When digging started on the foundation, more than 300 prominent Parisians signed a petition protesting against the building of the tower. They claimed that Eiffel's 'hollow candlestick' would 'disfigure and dishonour' the city. But Eiffel and the city ignored the petition, and work continued uninterrupted.

OTHER FEARS

The tower still had its critics. A French mathematics professor predicted that when the structure passed the 228-metre mark, it would inevitably collapse; another 'expert' predicted that the tower's lightning rods would kill all the fish in the Seine.

The Paris edition of the New York *Herald* claimed the tower was changing the weather; and the daily newspaper *Le Matin* ran a headline story claiming 'The Tower Is Sinking'. 'If it has really begun to sink', *Le Matin* pontificated, 'any further building should stop and sections already built should be demolished as quickly as possible'. As the tower's progress continued unabated, however, a sense of awe began to replace the fear.

Part II of the story begins on page 372.

* * *

Interesting Sidelight

August Eiffel also designed and built the iron skeleton that holds up the Statue of Liberty.

CANINE QUOTES

A few thoughts about man's best friend.

'You can say any fool thing to a dog, and the dog will give you this look that says, "My God, you're right! I never would have thought of that!"'

– Dave Barry

'They say the dog is man's best friend. I don't believe that. How many friends have you had neutered'?

– Larry Reeb

'My dog is half pit bull, half poodle. Not much of a guard dog, but a vicious gossip'.

– Craig Shoemaker

'Outside a dog, a book is man's best friend. Inside a dog it's too dark to read'.

– Groucho Marx

'If a dog will not come to you after he has looked you in the face, you should go home and examine your conscience'.

– Woodrow Wilson

'Dogs laugh, but they laugh with their tails'.

– Max Eastman

'Acquiring a dog may be the only opportunity a human ever has to choose a relative'.

– Morecai Siegal

'Every dog should have a man of his own. There is nothing like a well-behaved person around the house to spread the dog's blanket for him, or bring him his supper when he comes home man-tired at night'.

– Corey Ford

'To his dog, every man is Napoleon; hence the constant popularity of dogs'.

– Aldous Huxley

'To err is human, to forgive canine'.

– Anonymous

'Dogs have more love than integrity. They've been true to us, yes, but they haven't been true to themselves'.

– Clarence Day

'Every dog is entitled to one bite'.

– English proverb

Lions are the only cats that live in packs.

AFTER THE FUNERAL

Your grave is supposed to be your final resting place. But that isn't always the case, especially if you're famous. Take a look at what happened to these unfortunate souls.

ABRAHAM LINCOLN
Claim to Fame: 16th President of the United States
How He Died: Assassinated by John Wilkes Booth on 14 April, 1865
After the Funeral: On 21 April, his body was laid to rest in a temporary vault in Springfield, Illinois, while a permanent mausoleum was under construction. The body was moved three more times, then entombed in the National Lincoln Monument in Washington D.C. on 15 October, 1874. But in 1876 a ring of counterfeiters made two attempts to kidnap the body and hold it hostage until an accomplice was freed from prison; the second attempt was nearly successful – it was foiled just as the conspirators were prying open the sarcophagus.

Between 1876 and 1901, Lincoln's body was moved 14 more times – sometimes for security reasons, other times to repair the dilapidated crypt. In 1901 Old Abe was laid to rest a final (so far) time. As his son Robert supervized, the coffin was encased in steel bars and buried under tons of cement. As far as anyone can tell, Abe hasn't been moved since.

FRANCISCO PIZARRO
Claim to Fame: 16th-century Spanish explorer and conqueror of the Incas
How He Died: Stabbed to death by his countrymen in 1541 in a feud over Incan riches
After the Funeral: Pizarro's body was buried behind the cathedral in Lima, Peru, on the night he died, where it remained for 2½ years. In 1544, his bones were exhumed, placed in a velvet-lined box, and deposited under the main altar of the cathedral.

Pizarro's remains were moved repeatedly over the next 350 years because of earthquakes, repair work on the cathedral and other reasons. On the 350th anniversary of his death, in 1891, a mummified body authenticated as his was placed in a glass and marble sarcophagus, which was set out for public display.

Then in 1977, some workers repairing a crypt beneath the main altar found two boxes – one lined with velvet and filled with human bones. The other box bore the Spanish inscription, 'Here is the skull of the Marquis Don Francisco Pizarro who discovered and won Peru and placed it under the crown of Castile'.

Which body was Pizarro's? In 1984, forensics experts from the United States flew to Peru to compare the two sets of remains and determined that the bones in the boxes were those of Pizarro. (The boxes fitted the historical description, and of the two sets of bones, the ones in the boxes were the only ones with stab wounds.)

Aftermath: When Pizarro's bones were positively identified, they were placed in a box in the glass sarcophagus, and the 'impostor' mummy (who was never identified) was returned to the crypt underneath the altar.

* * *

FROM THE 'WEIRD FUNERAL LAWSUIT' FILES

THE PLAINTIFF: Mrs. Margaret Taylor

THE DEFENDANT: Randle & Sons Funeral Home, St. Louis, Missouri, USA

THE CASE: The casket for William Taylor's 1997 funeral was closed until after the pastor finished his eulogy. Then it was opened…and people yelled 'That's not Willie, you got the wrong man!' Mrs. Taylor called the police to keep the funeral home 'from literally burying their mistake', and the body was taken to the morgue. It was identified as Frederick Ware – whose own funeral had passed without anyone noticing he wasn't really there. Taylor's body was finally located, but Mrs. Taylor was enraged. She sued for $2.2 million for emotional distress and 'fear of not knowing the whereabouts of her husband's body for more than one week'.

THE VERDICT: Unknown.

WILDE ABOUT OSCAR

Wit and wisdom from Oscar Wilde, one of the most popular and controversial writers of the 19th century.

'When people agree with me I always feel that I must be wrong'.

'I never put off till tomorrow what I can possibly do the day after'.

'I sometimes think that God, in creating man, somewhat overestimated His ability'.

'As long as a woman can look ten years younger than her own daughter, she is perfectly happy'.

'Women are meant to be loved, not to be understood'.

'After a good dinner one can forgive anybody, even one's own relations'.

'I like men who have a future, and women with a past'.

'Women give to men the very gold of their lives, but they invariably want it back in small change'.

'Nowadays people know the price of everything and the value of nothing'.

'The Americans are certainly great hero-worshippers, and always take their heroes from the criminal classes'.

'No great artist sees things as they really are. If he did he would cease to be an artist'.

'In this world there are only two tragedies. One is not getting what one wants and the other is getting it'.

'Experience is the name everyone gives to their mistakes'.

'A gentleman is one who never hurts anyone's feelings unintentionally'.

'The one duty we owe to history is to rewrite it'.

'The basis of action is lack of imagination. It is the last resource of those who know not how to dream'.

Folk wisdom: if you refrigerate your elastic bands, they'll last longer.

FART FACTS

You won't find trivia like this in any ordinary book.

THE NAME

The word fart comes from the Old English term *foertan*, to explode. *Foertan* is also the origin of the word petard, an early type of bomb. Petard, in turn, is the origin of a more obscure term for fart – ped, or pet, which was once used by military men. (In Shakespeare's *Henry IV*, there's a character whose name means fart – Peto.)

WHY DO YOU FART?

Wind has many causes – for example, swallowing air as you eat and lactose intolerance. (Lactose is a sugar molecule in milk, and many people lack the enzyme needed to digest it.) But the most common cause is food that ferments in the gastrointestinal tract.

• A simple explanation: The fats, proteins, and carbohydrates you eat become a 'gastric soup' in your stomach. This soup then passes into the small intestine, where much of it is absorbed through the intestinal walls into the bloodstream to feed the body.

• But the small intestine can't absorb everything, especially complex carbohydrates. Some complex carbohydrates – the ones made up of several sugar molecules (beans, some milk products, fibre, etc.) can't be broken down. So they're simply passed along to the colon, where bacteria living in your intestine feed off the fermenting brew. If that sounds revolting, try this: the bacteria then excrete gases into your colon. Farting is how your colon rids itself of the pressure the gas creates.

FRUIT OF THE VINE

So why not just stop eating complex carbohydrates?

• First, complex carbohydrates – which include fruit, vegetables, and whole grains – are crucial for a healthy diet. 'Put it this way', explains Jeff Rank, an associate professor of gastroenterology at the University of Minnesota. 'Cabbage and beans are bad for [wind], but they are good for you'.

• Second, they're not the culprits when it comes to the least desirable aspect of farting: smell.

It's techno-madness: gadgets worth £5bn have been discarded in UK homes.

• Farts are about 99 per cent odourless gases – hydrogen, nitrogen, carbon dioxide, oxygen and methane (it's the methane that makes farts flammable). So why the odour? Blame it on those millions of bacteria living in your colon. Their waste gases usually contain sulphur molecules – which smell like rotten eggs. This is the remaining 1 per cent that clears rooms in a hurry.

AM I NORMAL?

• Johnson & Johnson, which produces drugs for wind and indigestion, once conducted a survey and found that almost one-third of those interviewed believe they have a flatulence problem.

• However, according to Terry Bolin and Rosemary Stanton, authors of *Wind Breaks: Coming to Terms with Flatulence*, doctors say most flatulence is healthy. What's unhealthy is worrying about it so much.

NOTABLE FARTERS

• Le Petomane, a 19th-century music hall performer, had the singular ability to control his farts. He could play tunes, as well as imitate animal and machinery sounds rectally. Le Petomane's popularity briefly rivalled that of Sarah Bernhardt.

• A computer factory in England, built on the site of a 19th-century chapel, is reportedly inhabited by a farting ghost. Workers think it might be the embarrassed spirit of a girl who farted while singing in church. 'On several occasions', said an employee, 'there has been a faint girlish voice singing faint hymns, followed by a loud raspberry sound and then a deathly hush'.

• Joseph Stalin was afraid of farting in public. He kept glasses and a jug of water on his desk so that if he felt a blast coming on, he could mask the sound by clinking the glasses while pouring water.

• Martin Luther believed, 'on the basis of personal experience, that farts could scare off Satan himself'.

* * *

True Story: In 1991, the scientists Simon Brassell, Karen Chin and Robert Harman published a paper proposing that millions of years' worth of dinosaur farts may have helped make the Earth more hospitable for humans and other mammals. How? The methane gas passed by dinosaurs, they suggested, 'may have been a...contributor to global warming'.

The average woman has 1.5 sq metres of skin. It stretches to 5.5 metres feet during pregnancy.

NOW HEAR THIS!

If you weren't reading right now, you might be listening to a 'personal stereo' – like a Walkman. But then when people start banging on the door, asking what you were doing in there, you wouldn't hear them. Maybe they'd panic and think you were dead, like Elvis. They'd run outside and get a group of people to help break down the door. Wham! And there you'd be, completely oblivious. They'd get so mad that they'd attack you with the toilet plunger, which would get stuck to the top of your head. You'd end up in hospital, and... well, aren't you glad you're reading Uncle John's Bathroom Reader *instead? Since it's obviously not safe to listen to a Walkman, we'll print a story about one instead. It's by Jack Mingo.*

THE PRESSMAN

In the mid-1970s, a team of Sony engineers headed by Mitsuro Ida created the Pressman – a portable tape recorder that could fit into a shirt pocket. As Sony expected, it quickly became standard equipment for journalists. But there was one small problem: the Pressman recorded in mono, and radio journalists preferred working in stereo. They requested a stereo version.

Sony's engineers put their best into it, shrinking stereo components, trying to get them into a small, pocket-sized case. They almost made it – but could only fit in the playback parts and two tiny speakers. Since the whole point was to come up with a tape recorder, the attempt was an embarrassing and expensive failure. Still, the quality of the sound was surprisingly good. So Ida kept the prototype around the shop instead of dismantling it. Some of the engineers started playing cassettes on it while they worked.

THE MISSING LINK

One day Masaru Ibuka wandered by. Although he'd co-founded the company with Akio Morita, he was considered too quirky and creative to fit into day-to-day operations. So he was made 'honourary chairman' – a title that gave him much respect, little authority, and lots of time to wander the halls of Sony.

Ibuka stopped to watch the Pressman engineers working on their design problem. He heard music coming from the unsuccessful prototype and asked, 'Where did you get this great little tape player'? Ida explained that it was a failure because it couldn't record.

Ibuka spent a lot of his time roaming around, so he knew what was going on all over the company. He suddenly remembered another project he'd seen that was being developed on the other side of the building – a set of lightweight portable headphones.

'What if you got rid of the speakers and added the headphones'? he asked Ida. 'They'd use less power and increase the quality of the sound. Who knows, maybe we can sell this thing even if you can't record on it'. The engineers listened politely and respectfully – while privately thinking the old man had finally lost it. Why make a tape recorder that can't record?

LISTENING WELL

Ibuka took the gadget, with headphones attached, to Morita. He too was skeptical – until he heard the quality of the stereo music. To the shock of the engineering team, Morita gave it a green light. It was dubbed the Walkman, to go along with the Pressman.

The marketing department thought it was a terrible idea They projected that the company would lose money on every unit sold. Even the name seemed wrong. According to American distributors, 'Walkman' sounded 'funny' to English ears. So Sony rolled the product out as the 'Stowaway' in England and the 'Soundabout' in the U.S.. Their 1979 publicity campaign – a low-budget, lukewarm affair aimed at teens – got virtually no results. It seemed as though the Walkman's critics were right.

As it turned out, though, Sony had just targeted the wrong market. Teenagers had their ghetto blasters – it was adults who wanted the Walkman. The little unit was perfect for listening to Mozart while jogging or the Stones while commuting, and was small enough to fit into a briefcase or the pocket of a business suit. To Sony's surprise, white collar workers discovered the Walkman on their own. It became a sudden, raging success. Sony had prepared an initial run of 60,000 units; when the first wave hit, they sold out instantly.

The world still loves the Walkman and its offspring. By 1997, four million personal cassette players were sold a year.

If you never trimmed your fingernails, on your 80th birthday they'd be about 5 metres long.

HERE COMES THE SUN

Some facts about that big lightbulb in the sky, from astronomer (and BRI member) Richard Moeschl.

It takes 8.3 minutes for the sun's light – travelling at 299,791 km per second – to reach Earth. (At that speed, light can travel around the Earth seven times a second.)

The sun looks yellow-gold because we're viewing it through the Earth's atmosphere. Judging from its surface temperature, the sun's colour is probably closer to white.

The temperature of the sun at its core is around 40 million degrees C (73 million degrees F). It takes 50 years for this energy to reach the sun's surface, where we can see it as light.

The English astronomer James Jeans calculated that if you placed a piece of the sun's core the size of the head of a pin on Earth, its heat would kill a person 150 km away.

The temperature of the sun's photosphere, the part that sends us light, is about 5,500 degrees C (10,000 degrees F).

The sun contains 99.9 per cent of all the matter in the solar system.

The sun produces more energy in one second than human beings have produced in all of our history. In less than a week, the sun sends out more energy than we could make by burning all the natural gas, oil, coal and wood on Earth.

The total energy output of the sun is 1.92 calories per minute per square centimetre, or 3.83 x 1,000,000,000,000,000, 000,000-000,000 watts.

The Earth receives 2 one-billionths of the sun's power.

The surface gravity on the sun is 28 times that of Earth. If you weigh 54 kilograms on Earth, on the sun you would weigh 1,524 kilograms.

The sun rotates once every 26.8 days.

With every passing day, the sun is losing energy – but it still has about 5 billion years of life left in it.

There are 250,000 sweat glands in a pair of human feet.

CELEBRITY GOSSIP

Here's the BRI's trashy tabloid section – a load of gossip about famous people.

ALBERT EINSTEIN
• He applied to the Federal Polytechnic Academy in Zurich, but failed the entrance exam. When his father asked his headmaster what profession Albert should adopt, he got the answer, 'It doesn't matter, he'll never amount to anything'.
• For many years, Einstein thought of his work in physics as something of a hobby. He regarded himself as a failure because what he really wanted to do was play concert violin. Einstein was uncharacteristically intense when he played his violin, swearing like a trooper whenever he made a mistake. One evening, while playing violin duets with the queen (our queen, that is), Einstein suddenly stopped in the middle of the piece and unceremoniously told her she was playing too loudly.

MUHAMMAD ALI
• For some reason, as a child, he always walked on his tiptoes. When he got older, he played American Football, but wouldn't play tackle because he thought it was too rough.
• Because he was afraid to fly, Ali (then going by his original name, Cassius Clay) almost didn't make it to the 1960 Rome Olympics, where he won the gold medal that launched his career.

JANIS JOPLIN
• In 1965, when she was on the verge of becoming a blues star, strung out on heavy drugs, hanging out with Hell's Angels, Joplin wrote to her parents and asked them to send her one present for Christmas: 'a *Betty Crocker* or *Better Homes and Gardens* cookbook'.
• She once went on a blind date with one William Bennett. He was apparently so traumatized that he eventually became drug czar under Ronald Reagan, and a conservative 'family values' advocate.

Worldwide, the average woman is 15 cm shorter than the average man.

GENERAL GEORGE PATTON

• On the way through Europe during World War II with his troops, Patton was continuously in danger from shelling, strafing and bombing. In the middle of one scorched, scarred, and burning landscape, with the sound of explosions around him, he threw out his arms and looked to the skies as if bathing in a warm spring rain. 'Could anything be more magnificent'? he shouted to the soldiers endeavouring to shrink to insignificance. 'God, how I love it!'

MICHAEL JACKSON

• Jackson's favourite song? He told a group of reporters that it was 'My Favourite Things', performed by Julie Andrews.
• His opinion of other singers: Paul McCartney? Okay writer, not much of an entertainer. 'I do better box office than he does'. Frank Sinatra? 'I don't know what people see in the guy. He's legend, but he isn't much of a singer. He doesn't even have hits anymore'. Mick Jagger? 'He sings flat. How did he ever get to be a star? I just don't get it. He doesn't sell as many records as I do'. Madonna? 'She just isn't that good...She can't sing. She's just an OK dancer...She knows how to market herself. That's about it'.

FIDEL CASTRO

• For Castro's first revolutionary attack on a military post, he forgot his glasses. As a result, he could barely drive to the post, much less aim his gun accurately.
• Castro fancies himself as quite a ladies man. In fact, there are dozens of children in Cuba who claim him as father. His technique? One purported lover, a dancer at the Tropicana Hotel, said he read while making love. A French actress complained that he 'smoked his damned cigar'. An American woman said he never took his boots off. Other women said he took them to romantic spots and then talked for hours on end about things like agricultural reform.

ALFRED HITCHCOCK

• When he sat on a public toilet and another man entered the room, he'd quickly raise his legs in the stall 'so that no one could tell anyone was there'.

It takes 345 squirts from a cow's udder to get a gallon of milk.

LUCKY FINDS

You'd be amazed at some of the valuables and hidden treasures you can pick up at car boot sales, or even hidden away in your own attic. Here's a selection of really lucky strikes.

BOOT TREASURE

The Find: Two Shaker 'gift' paintings
Where They Were Found: Inside a picture frame
The Story: In 1994, a retired couple from New England, USA, bought an old picture frame for a few dollars at a garage sale. When they took the frame apart to restore it, two watercolour drawings – dated 1845 and 1854 – fell out.

A few months later, the couple was travelling in Massachusetts and noticed a watercolour on a poster advertising the Hancock Shaker Village Museum. It was similar to the two they'd found. Curious, they did some research and found out the works were called 'gift paintings'.

It turns out that the Shakers, a New England religious sect of the 1800s, did not allow decorations on their walls; Shaker sisters, however, were permitted to paint 'trees, flowers, fruits and birds…to depict the glory of heaven'. The paintings were then 'gifted' to other sisters and put away as holy relics. And one of the couple's paintings was signed by the most famous of all 'gift' artists, Hannah Cohoon.

They called a curator of the Hancock Museum with the news, but he didn't believe them. Only 200 Shaker 'gift' paintings still exist – and very few are of the quality they described. Moreover, all known paintings were in museums – none in private hands. Nonetheless, in January 1996, the couple brought the paintings to the museum, where they were examined and declared authentic. A year later, in January 1997, Sotheby's sold them for $473,000.

BIZARRE BITE

The Find: A diamond
Where It Was Found: In a plate of pasta
The Story: In October 1996, Liliana Parodi of Genoa, Italy, went to her favourite restaurant for some pasta. The meal was uneventful – until she bit down on something hard and it wedged

painfully between her teeth. She complained to the management, then left. The next morning, she went to a dentist, who extracted the object – a one-carat, uncut diamond worth about £1,800. Parodi took it to a jeweller and had it set in a ring. How it got into the pasta is still a mystery.

A BEATLE'S LEGACY

The Find: Dozens of sketches by John Lennon
Where They Were Found: In a notebook
The Story: In 1996, a man named John Dunbar – who'd been married to singer/actress Marianne Faithfull in the 1960s – was going through some old belongings and came across a notebook he hadn't seen in over 25 years. He'd had it with him at a London party in 1967, on a night when he and his friend John Lennon were taking LSD together. But he'd stashed it away and forgotten about it.

During that week in 1967, Lennon had seen an ad in the newspaper offering 'an island off Ireland', for about £1,200. At the party, the drugged-out Beatle suddenly decided to buy it. He and Dunbar immediately flew to Dublin, travelled across Ireland in a limousine, and hired a boat to get there. 'The island was more like a couple of small hills joined by a gravelly bar with a cottage on it', Durbar recalled. 'When we got there, John sat down and started drawing'. The pair stayed on the island for a few days. Lennon did buy it, but never lived there. (In fact, he gave it away a few years later, to a stranger who showed up at Apple Records.)

Dunbar kept the notebook as a memento of the trip, and today, experts estimate the drawings to be worth about £100,000. The incredulous Dunbar can always look as it as a belated 'thank you' – he was the fellow, it turns out, who introduced Lennon to Yoko Ono.

LOTTERY TICKET

The Find: A wallet with £135.
Where It Was Found: On a street in Adelaide, Australia
The Story: In the 1970s, Joan Campbell found a wallet and tracked down the owner, hoping for a nice reward. She was disappointed – all the man gave her was a single lottery ticket. Later, she cheered up: the ticket paid £27,000.

The highest value bank note issued in the UK was the £1000, last produced in 1943.

BOND – JAMES BOND

Here's a shaken – not stirred – history of the most popular (and profitable) British secret agent in Hollywood history – and of the former World War II intelligence officer who brought the character to life.

SPY STORY

Even before World War II started, Great Britain knew it would never be able to patrol the entire northern Atlantic and defend all its ships against the German Navy. But the British also knew that if they could learn the locations of Nazi ships and submarines by deciphering coded German radio communications, they'd be able to reroute convoys of food and weapons around German patrols. In 1939 they launched a massive effort, code-named Ultra, to do just that.

The Enigma. The Germans sent coded messages using an encryption machine called the 'Enigma'. By September 1940 the British had managed to put together a working model of the Enigma using parts captured in several raids on German ships. But the Enigma was so sophisticated that even when the British had one in their possession, they couldn't crack the German codes. They needed a copy of the Nazis' special codebook.

FLEMING – IAN FLEMING

How were they going to get one? The wildest suggestion came from the assistant to the Director of Naval Intelligence, a man named Ian Fleming. On 12 September, 1940, Fleming wrote the following memo to his boss:

> Director of Naval Intelligence:
>
> I suggest we obtain the loot (codebook) by the following means:
>
> 1. Obtain from Air Ministry an air-worthy German bomber.
>
> 2. Pick a tough crew of five, including a pilot, wireless telegraph operator and a fluent German speaker. Dress them in German Air Force uniform, add blood and bandages to suit.
>
> 3. Crash plane in the Channel after making S.O.S. to rescue service in plain language.

Indian government statistic: 99 per cent of India's lorry drivers can't read road signs.

> 4. Once abroad the rescue boat, shoot German crew, dump overboard, bring rescue boat back to English port.

In order to increase the chances of capturing a small or large minesweeper, with their richer booty, a crash might be staged in mid-Channel. The Germans would presumably employ one of this type for the longer and more hazardous journey.

OPERATION RUTHLESS

The Director of Naval Intelligence passed the plan along to Winston Churchill, who gave it his personal approval. A German twin-engine Heinkell 111, shot down during a raid over Scotland, was restored to flying condition and a crew was recruited to fly it. 'Operation Ruthless' was ready to go. But as David Kahn writes in *Seizing the Enigma*,

> In October, Fleming went to Dover to await his chance. None came. Air reconnaissance found no suitable German ships operating at night, and radio reconnaissance likewise found nothing... The navy awaited favorable circumstances. But they never materialized, and the plan faded away.

Even though Great Britain never did attempt a raid as daring as Fleming proposed, it did manage to capture codebooks from German ships. By 1943 they were cracking Enigma codes regularly; and by May of that year the Battle of the Atlantic was effectively over.

A NOVEL IDEA

After the war Fleming got out of the intelligence business and became an executive with the company that owned the *Sunday Times*. He never forgot his wartime experiences.

First Person. By 1952 Fleming was in his forties and was just about to be married for the first time. He was apparently tense at the thought of giving up his bachelorhood, and his future wife suggested he try writing a novel to ease the strain. Fleming had wanted to write a novel for years, so he decided to give it a try. Drawing on his war-time intelligence background, he wrote a spy thriller called *Casino Royale* during a two-month winter holiday in Jamaica.

Picking a Name. The book was filled with murders, torture, and lots of action. It was an autobiographical fantasy, the adventures of a British secret agent named James Bond that Fleming – who spent World War II stuck behind a desk in London – wanted to be, but couldn't.

Fleming thought that giving the agent an unexciting name would play off well against the plot. But what name? As Fleming later recounted, he found it 'in one of my Jamaican bibles, *Birds of the West Indies* by James Bond, an ornithological classic. I wanted the simplest, dullest, plainest-sounding name that I could find. James Bond seemed perfect'.

ON HIS WAY

Casino Royale was published in England in April 1953, and in the U.S. a year later. The book was a critical success, but sales were slow. Luckily for Fleming, he took a two-month holiday in Jamaica every year, and in each of the next several years he wrote a new Bond novel during his vacation, including *Live and Let Die* (1954), *Moonraker* (1955) and *Diamonds are Forever* (1956).

Live and Let Die became a bestseller in England, and Fleming began building a considerable following in the UK But in America, sales remained sluggish for the rest of the 1950s.

Thanks, JFK. The Bond bandwagon got rolling in the U.S. in 1961, when *Life* magazine published a list of President John F. Kennedy's favourite books. Listed among the scholarly tomes was one work of popular fiction – *From Russia, With Love*. 'This literally made Bond in America overnight', Raymond Benson writes in *The James Bond Bedside Companion*. 'From then on, sales improved almost immediately....It was good public relations for Kennedy as well – it showed that even a President can enjoy a little 'sex, sadism, and snobbery'.'

How did a little-known Scottish actor named Sean Connery land the role of the most famous secret agent in Hollywood history? *The story continues on page 302.*

* * * * *

Happy Anniversary! The first push-button phones were installed Nov. 18, 1963. They were put into service between Carnegie and Greensburg, Pennsylvania.

DUMB CROOKS

Many people are worried about the growing threat of crime, but the good news is that there are plenty of crooks who are their own worst enemies. Want proof? Check out these news reports.

CAREFUL, THIS FINGER'S LOADED

MERCED, California – 'A man tried to rob a bank by pointing his finger at a teller, police said.

'Steven Richard King just held up his finger and thumb in plain sight and demanded money. The Bank of America teller told Mr. King to wait, then just walked away. Mr. King then went across the street to another bank...jumped over the counter, and tried to get the key to the cash drawer. But an employee grabbed the key and told him to "get out of here".

'Police officers found Mr. King sitting in the shrubs outside the bank and arrested him'.

– *New York Times*, April 1997

STRANGE RESEMBLANCE

OROVILLE, California – 'Thomas Martin, former manager of a Jack In the Box restaurant, reported that he'd been robbed of $307 as the store was closing. He provided police sketch artist Jack Lee with a detailed description of the suspect. When Lee put his pad down, he observed that the drawing looked just like Martin. When questioned, Martin confessed'.

– *Parade* magazine, December 1996

KEYSTONE KROOK

OAKLAND, California – 'According to the Alameda County District Attorney's office, in 1995 a man walked into an Oakland bank and handed the teller a note reading: *This is a stikkup. Hand over all yer mony fast.*

'Guessing from this that the guy was no rocket scientist, the teller replied, "I'll hand over the cash as long as you sign for it. It's a bank policy: All robbers have to sign for their money".

'The would-be robber thought this over, then said, "I guess that's OK". And he signed his full name and address.

'That's where the cops found him a few hours later'.

– *Jay Leno's Police Blotter*

SHAKE YOUR BOOTIES

WICHITA, Kansas – 'Charles Taylor was on trial for robbing a shoe store at knifepoint, accused of taking a pair of tan hiking boots and $69. As he listened to testimony in court, he propped his feet on the defence table. He was wearing a pair of tan boots.

"'I leaned over and stared", the judge told a reporter later. "I thought, surely nobody would be so stupid as to wear the boots he stole to his own trial". But when an FBI agent called the shoe store, he found out that the stolen boots were size 10, from lot no. 1046 – the same size and lot number as the boots Taylor was wearing. The jury found Taylor guilty, and officers confiscated the boots. "We sent him back to jail in his stocking feet", the judge said'.

– From wire service reports, March 1997

NEXT WEEK HE'S COMING BACK FOR BRAINS

'In March 1995, a twenty-six-year-old inmate walked away from his community release facility in South Carolina. He was recaptured a week later when he went back to pick up his (pay)'.

– *Knuckleheads in the News*, by John Machay

OH, JUST BAG IT

'Not wishing to attract attention to himself, a bank robber in 1969 in Portland, Oregon, wrote all his instruction on a piece of paper rather than shouting.

"'This is a hold-up and I've got a gun", he wrote and then held the paper up for the cashier to read.

'The bemused bank official waited while he wrote out, "Put all the money in a paper bag".

'This message was pushed through the grille. The cashier read it and then wrote on the bottom, "I don't have a paper bag", and passed it back. The robber fled'.

– *The Book of Heroic Failures*, by Stephen Pile

VIDEO TREASURES

How many times have you found yourself at a video store staring at the thousands of films you've never heard of, wondering which ones are worth watching? It happens to us all the time – so we decided to offer a few recommendations for relatively obscure, quirky videos you might like.

DREAMCHILD (1985) *Drama*
Review: 'A poignant story of the autumn years of Alice (Liddell), the model for Lewis Carroll's *Alice in Wonderland*. Film follows her on a visit to New York in the 1930s, with fantasy sequences by Jim Henson's Creature Shop'. *(Video Hound's Golden Movie Retriever) Stars:* Coral Brown, Ian Holm, Peter Gallagher. *Director:* Gavin Millar.

THE STUNT MAN (1980) *Mystery / Suspense*
Review: 'Nothing is ever quite what it seems in this fast-paced, superbly crafted film. It's a Chinese puzzle of a movie and, therefore, may not please all viewers. Nevertheless, this directorial *tour de force* by Richard Rush has ample thrills, chills, suspense, and surprises for those with a taste for something different'. *(Video Movie Guide) Stars:* Peter O'Toole, Steve Railsback, Barbara Hershey. *Director:* Richard Rush.

SUGAR CANE ALLEY (1984. French, with subtitles) *Drama*
Review: 'Beautifully made drama about an 11-year-old boy and his all-sacrificing grandmother, surviving in a Martinique shantytown in the 1930s. Rich, memorable characterizations; a humanist drama of the highest order'. *(Leonard Maltin's Movie & Video Guide) Stars:* Gary Cadenat, Darling Legitimus. *Director:* Edwin L. Marian.

SMILE (1975) *Satire*
Review: 'Hilarious, perceptive satire centring around the behind-the-scenes activity at a California "Young American Miss" beauty pageant, presented as a symbol for the emptiness of American middle-class existence'. *(Leonard Maltin's Movie & Video Guide) Stars:* Bruce Dern, Barbara Feldon. *Director:* Michael Ritchie.

In 2002, £933 million of notes were issued in the UK in £5, £10, £20 and £50 notes.

WRONG IS RIGHT (1982) *Comedy*
Review: 'Sean Connery, as a globe-trotting television reporter, gives what may be the best performance of his career, in this outrageous, thoroughly entertaining end-of-the-world black comedy, written, produced, and directed by Richard Brooks. An updated version of *Network* and *Dr. Strangelove*'. (*Video Movie Guide*) *Stars:* Sean Connery, Robert Conrad. *Director:* Richard Brooks.

MIRACLE MILE (1989) *Thriller*
Review: 'A riveting, apocalyptic thriller about a mild-mannered misfit who...standing on a street corner at 2 a.m., answers a ringing pay phone. The caller...announces that bombs have been launched for an all-out nuclear war....A surreal, wicked farce sadly overlooked in theatrical release'. *(Video Hound's Golden Movie Retriever) Stars:* Anthony Edwards, Mare Winningham. *Director:* Steve DeJamatt.

TIME BANDITS (1981) *Fantasy*
Review: 'This subversive kid's adventure teams a youngster with a criminally minded pack of dwarves on the run from the Supreme Being through holes in time. A highly imaginative, quirky mix of Monty Python humour, historical swashbuckler, and kid's gee-whiz adventure'. *(Seen That, Now What?) Stars:* Sean Connery, David Warner. *Director:* Terry Gilliam.

DEFENCE OF THE REALM (1985) *Thriller*
Review: 'A British politician is accused of selling secrets to the KGB through his mistress and only a pair of dedicated newspapermen believe he is innocent....They discover a national cover-up conspiracy. An acclaimed, taut thriller'. *(Video Hound's Golden Movie Retriever) Stars:* Gabriel Byrne, Greta Scacchi. *Director:* David Drury.

NIGHT MOVES (1975) *Mystery*
Review: 'While trying to deal with his own sour private life, a P.I. is hired by a fading Hollywood star to track down her reckless daughter, involving him in art smuggling, murder, and sex on Florida's Gulf Coast. This incisive psychological drama manages to be both intelligent and entertaining'. *(Seen That, Now What?) Stars:* Gene Hackman, Jenifer Warren. *Director:* Arthur Penn.

Oldest vehicle in human history: a floating log. Second oldest: a sled.

LITTLE SHOP OF HORRORS

In this chapter, we feed you the story of one of the most unlikely – but most popular – cult films of all time.

ALL SET TO GO

A few days after he finished work on a film called *A Bucket of Blood* in 1959, director Roger Corman had lunch with the manager of Producers Studio, the company that rented him office space. The manager mentioned that another company had just finished work on a film, and the sets were still standing.

'I said, just as a joke, "If you leave the sets up, I'll come in for a couple of days and see if I can just invent a picture, because I have a little bit of money now and some free time"', Corman recalled years later. 'And he said, "Fine". The whole thing was kind of a whim. I booked the studio for a week'.

TO B OR NOT TO B

Corman, 32, had only been directing films for five years (*The Monster from the Ocean Floor* and *Attack of the Crab Monsters* were two early titles). But he was already developing a reputation for making profitable movies very quickly on minuscule budgets – a skill that would later earn him the title 'King of the B films'.

He had filmed *A Bucket of Blood*, a 'beatnik-styled horror comedy' in only five days, a personal record. He bet his friend at Producers Studio that he could make this next film in 48 hours.

COMING UP WITH A SCRIPT

Corman called scriptwriter Chuck Griffith, who'd written *A Bucket of Blood*, and told him to write a new variation of the same story. The only limitations: it had to be written for the existing sets, and Corman had to be able to rehearse all the scenes in three days...and then film them in two.

Griffith took the assignment. He and Corman went bar-hopping to brainstorm and outline for the film. It was a long night: Griffith got drunk, then got into a barroom brawl. Somehow, he and Corman still managed to come up with a story about a nerdy flower shop employee and his man-eating plant.

In Germany, making the 'Shhhh' sound means 'hurry up'.

DEJA VU

Griffith turned in the final script a week later. It was essentially a warmed-over version of *A Bucket of Blood*.

• In *A Bucket of Blood*, a well-meaning sculptor accidentally kills his landlord's cat, then hides the evidence by turning it into a sculpture, which he titles 'Dead Cat'. When the sculpture brings him the notoriety he's always sought, he starts killing people and making them into sculptures, too.

• In *Little Shop of Horrors*, a well-meaning flower shop employee becomes a local hero after he accidentally creates a man-eating plant (which he names Audrey Jr., after his girlfriend) by cross-breeding a Venus flytrap with a buttercup. He then begins killing people to keep the plant – and his fame – alive.

LOW BUDGET

• The filming took place between Christmas and New Year's Eve 1959. Corman spent a total of $23,000 on the film, including $800 for the finished script and $750 for three different models of Audrey Jr.: a 30-centimetre version, a 1.8-metre version, and a full-grown 2.4-metre version.

• Corman pinched pennies wherever he could. Jack Nicholson, 23 years old when Corman hired him to play a masochistic dental patient named Wilbur Force, remembers that Corman wouldn't even spend money making copies of the script: 'Roger took the script apart and gave me only the pages for my scenes. That way he could give the rest of the script to another actor or actors'.

• Corman also paid a musician named Fred Kat $317.34 for the musical score – but as John McCarty and Mark McGee write in *The Little Shop of Horrors* book,

> Katz simply used the same score he'd written for *A Bucket of Blood*, which has also been used in another Corman film, *The Wasp Woman* and would be used yet again in Corman's *Creature from the Haunted Sea*. Whether or not Corman was aware he was buying the same score three times is unknown.

• Even if a shot wasn't perfect, Corman would use it if he could. In the first day of shooting, Jackie Haze and Jack Nicholson accidentally knocked over the dentist's chair, spoiling the shot and breaking the chair. When the property master said it would take an hour to fix the chair so they could reshoot the scene, Corman changed the script to read, 'The scene ends with the dentist's chair falling over'.

• Corman was legendary for getting as much work out of his actors and writers as he could. One example: Chuck Griffith, who wrote the script, also played a shadow on a wall, the man who runs out of the dentist's office with his ear bitten, and the thief who robs the flower shop. He also directed the Skid Row exterior shots and provided the voice for Audrey Jr. (Griffith's voice wasn't supposed to make it into the final film – he was just the guy who stood off camera and read the plant's lines so the actors would have something to react to. Corman had planned to dub in another actor's voice later. 'But it got laughs', Griffith says, 'so Corman decided to leave it the way it was'.)

• Corman also saved money by filming all of the Skid Row exteriors actually in Skid Row, and using 'real bums to play the bums'. Griffith, who directed the scenes, paid them 10¢ per scene, using the change he had in his pocket.

THAT'S A WRAP

• Corman finished all of the interior shots in the required two days, then spent a couple more evenings filming the exterior shots. To this day, *Little Shop of Horrors* is listed in the *Guinness Book of World Records* for 'the shortest shooting schedule for a full-length, commercial feature film made without the use of stock footage'.

• In this original release, *Little Shop of Horrors* was only a modest success. It didn't develop its cult following until the late 1960s, when it became a Creature Feature classic on late-night TV. It was adapted into an off-Broadway musical in 1982, which was itself adapted into a new $20 million film in 1987.

• '*Little Shop of Horrors* is the film that established me as an underground legend in film circles', Corman says. 'People come up to me on the street who have memorized parts of the dialogue. I suppose you could say it was *The Rocky Horror Picture Show* of its time'.

In Finland, saunas outnumber cars.

BRAND NAMES

Here are some origins of commercial names.

ADIDAS. Adolph and Rudi Dassler formed Dassler Brothers Shoes in Germany in 1925. After World War II, the partnership broke up, but each brother kept a piece of the shoe business: Rudi called his new company Puma; Adolph, whose nickname was 'Adi', renamed the old company after himself – *Adi Das*sler.

PENNZOIL. In the early 1900s, two motor oil companies – Merit Oil and Panama Oil – joined forces and created a brand name they could both use: Pennsoil (short for William Penn's Oil). It didn't work – consumers kept calling it Penn-soil. So in 1914 they changed the **s** to a **z**.

DIAL SOAP. The name refers to a clock or watch dial. The reason: it was the first deodorant soap, and Lever Bros. wanted to suggest that it would prevent B.O. 'all around the clock'.

WD-40. In the 1950s, the Rocket Chemical Company was working on a product for the aerospace industry that would reduce rust and corrosion by removing moisture from metals. It took them 40 tries to come up with a workable Water Displacement formula.

LYSOL. Short for lye solvent.

MAZDA. The Zoroastrian god of light.

NISSAN. Derived from the phrase *Nissan snagyo*, which means 'Japanese industry'.

ISUZU. Japanese for '50 bells'.

MAGNAVOX. In 1915 the Commercial Wireless and Development Co. created a speaker that offered the clearest sound of any on the market. They called it the *Magna Vox* – which means *great voice* in Latin.

Is your entire family overweight? If so, odds are your dog is, too.

FAMOUS FOR BEING NAKED

We know – this sounds a little off-colour. Butt – er – we mean but *– it's just another way to look at history.*

LADY GODIVA, wife of Earl Leofric, Lord of Coventry, in the 1100s
Famous for: Riding her horse through Coventry, covered only by her long blonde hair.
The bare facts: Lady Godiva was upset by the heavy taxes her husband had imposed on poor people in his domain. When she asked him to give the peasants a break, he laughingly replied that he'd cut the taxes if she would ride through the town naked. To his shock, she agreed. But she requested that townspeople stay indoors and not peek while she rode through the streets. Legend has it that they all complied except for one young man named Tom, who secretly watched through a shutter – which gave us the term 'peeping Tom'.

ARCHIMEDES (287–212 B.C.), a 'classic absent-minded professor' and one of the most brilliant thinkers of the Ancient World
Famous for: Running naked through the streets of ancient Syracuse, screaming 'Eureka!'
The bare facts: Archimedes' friend, King Hieron II of Syracuse, Sicily, was suspicious that his new crown wasn't solid gold. Had the goldsmith secretly mixed in silver? He asked Archimedes to find out. As Peter Lafferty recounts in book, *Archimedes:*

> Archimedes took the crown home and sat looking at it. What was he to do? He weighed the crown. He weighed a piece of pure gold just like the piece the goldsmith had been given. Sure enough, the crown weighed the same as the gold. For many days, he puzzled over the crown. Then one evening…the answer came to him.
>
> That night, his servants filled his bath to the brim with water. As Archimedes lowered himself into the tub, the water overflowed onto the floor. Suddenly, he gave a shout and jumped out. Forgetting that he was

> naked, he ran down the street to the palace shouting *'Eureka'* ('I have found it!')

Archimedes, presumably still wearing his birthday suit, explained his discovery to the king: 'When an object is placed in water', he said, 'it displaces an amount of water equal to its own volume'.

To demonstrate, he put the crown in a bowl of water and measured the overflow. Then he put a lump of gold that weighed the same as the crown into the bowl. 'The amount of water was measured', writes Lafferty, 'and to the king's surprise, the gold had spilled less than the crown'. It was proof that the goldsmith really had tried to cheat the king. The secret: 'Silver is lighter than gold, so to make up the correct weight, extra silver was needed. This meant that the volume of the crown was slightly larger than the gold, so the crown spilled more water'.

Archimedes became famous for his discovery. We can only guess what happened to the goldsmith.

RED BUTTONS, popular red-headed American actor of the 1940s and 1950s
Famous for: Being the first person ever to appear naked on TV
The bare facts: In the early 1950s, Red did a guest spot on the *Milton Berle Show*, which was broadcast live. One skit featured Berle as a doctor and Buttons as a shy patient who wouldn't disrobe for his exam. Buttons wore a special 'breakaway' suit – the coat, shirt and trousers were sewn together so they'd all come off when Berle yanked on the shirt collar. As he explained in *The Hollywood Walk of Shame:*

> When my character refused to get undressed, Milton was supposed to grab my shirt front and rip the entire thing off – and I'd be left standing there in old-fashioned, knee-to-neck piece underwear.
>
> Well, Milton reached for my shirt and accidentally grabbed me under the collar. And when he yanked at my breakaway suit, everything came off – including my underwear! We were on live television and there I stood – nude in front of a studio audience and all the people watching at home. When I realized what had happened, I got behind Milton, who was as shocked as I was, but had the presence of mind to announce the next act and have the curtain closed.

Buttons said he turned 'as red as my hair'.

A gozzard is a person who owns geese.

THE SPIDER DANCE

Here's an interesting little tale about a classic folk dance.

DANCE FEVER

Over the last 2,000 years there have been occasional instances of mass hysteria that scientists call 'epidemic dancing'. Entire towns or provinces will begin a wild, spontaneous dancing, often accompanied by hallucinations.

Perhaps the most serious outbreak took place in July 1374, in the French town of Aix-la-Chapelle. As Frederick Cartwright writes in *Disease and History*,

> The sufferers began to dance uncontrollably in the streets, screaming and foaming at the mouth. Some declared they were immersed in a sea of blood, others claimed to have seen the heavens open to reveal Christ enthroned with the Virgin Mary....Streams of dancers invaded the Low Countries, moved along the Rhine, and appeared throughout Germany....In the later stages, the dancers often appeared to be entirely insensible to pain, a symptom of hysteria.

Today, scientists and historians speculate the dancing was caused by eating rye bread contaminated with 'ergot', a fungus that infects bread cereals. One of the chemical compounds created by ergot is lysergic acid diethylamide – LSD. So the dancers were essentially high on LSD. And long after the effects of the drug had worn off, mass hysteria kept them going.

We know about the hallucinogenic effects of LSD today – but until a few decades ago, no one had any idea what caused the mysterious outbreaks. In the 16th century, when a similar incident took place near Taranto, Italy, the townspeople blamed the *tarantula*, a local spider named after the town.

The tarantula was known for its painful bite, which was thought to be deadly. So when the dancers survived, the Tarantans were surprised. 'In due course', John Ayto notes in *The Dictionary of Word Origins*, 'the dancing came to be rationalized as a method of counteracting the effects of the spider's bite, and so the dance was named the *tarantella*'.

Italians don't dance away their spider bites anymore, but they still have a lively folk dance called the *tarantella*.

THE CURSE OF DRACULA

In every film about Dracula, there's a curse. But did the curse extend beyond the screen...and actually affect the people involved with bringing the character to life? Don't dismiss the idea. Read these stories...and then decide.

Horace Liveright. The stage producer who brought *Dracula* – and later *Frankenstein* – to America made a fortune doing it. But he was a terrible businessman and spent money as fast as it came in. He made more than $2 million on *Dracula* alone, but was so slow to pay author Bram Stoker's widow, Florence, the royalties she was due that he lost control of the stage rights in a dispute over a late payment...of a mere $678.01. He died drunk, broke, and alone in New York in September 1933.

Helen Chandler. She was only 20 when she signed on to play the female lead Mina Murray in the 1931 film version of *Dracula*, but she was already close to the end of her film career. It was tragically shortened by a bad marriage and addictions to alcohol and sleeping pills. By the mid-1930s she was no longer able to find work in Hollywood, and in 1940 she was committed to a sanitarium. Ten years later she was severely burned after smoking and drinking in bed, in what may have been a suicide attempt. She died in 1965.

Dwight Frye. In the 1931 film, Frye played Renfield, the character who goes insane after meeting Dracula and spends the rest of the movie as Dracula's slave. He performed so well in that part that he was offered a similar role in the movie version of *Frankenstein*, as Dr. Frankenstein's hunchback assistant Igor.

Unfortunately for him, he took it – and was promptly typecast as the monster's/mad scientist's assistant for the rest of his career. He didn't get a chance to play any other type of role until 1944, when he was cast as the Secretary of War in the film *Wilson*. Not long after he won the part, Frye had a heart attack on a Los Angeles bus and died before he was able to appear in the film.

Carl Laemmle, Jr. As president of Universal Pictures, he did more than anyone else to establish Universal as the horror movie studio of the 1930s. He left the studio after it was sold in 1936 and tried to establish himself as an independent producer. He never succeeded. A notorious hypochondriac, Laemmle eventually did come down with a debilitating disease – multiple sclerosis – in the early 1960s. He died in 1979 – 40 years to the day after the death of his father.

Bela Lugosi. Worn out by years of playing Dracula in New York and on the road, Lugosi was already sick of the vampire character by the time he began work on the film version; the indignity of being paid less than his supporting cast only made things worse. Reporter Lillian Shirley recounted one incident that took place in Lugosi's dressing room between scenes:

> I was with him when a telegram arrived. It was from Henry Duffy, the Pacific Coast theatre impresario, who wanted Mr. Lugosi to play Dracula for sixteen weeks. 'No! Not at any price', he yelled. 'When I am through with this picture I hope never to hear of Dracula again. I cannot stand it…I do not intend that it shall possess me. No one knows what I suffer for this role'.

But like a real vampire, Lugosi was trapped in his role. *Dracula* was a box-office smash when it premiered in 1931 and Universal, eager to repeat its success, offered Lugosi the part of the monster in *Frankenstein*. It was the first in a series of planned monster movie roles for Lugosi that Universal hoped would turn Lugosi into 'the new Lon Chaney', man of a thousand monsters.

Stubborn Kind of Fellow

Foolishly, Lugosi turned down the role of the Frankenstein monster because there was no dialogue – Frankenstein spoke only in grunts – and the make-up would have obscured his features, which he feared would prevent fans from knowing that he was the one under all that make-up.

The role went instead to an unknown actor named William Henry Pratt…who changed his name to Boris Karloff and within a year he had eclipsed Lugosi to become Hollywood's most famous horror star of the 1930s.

Still life: your body uses 300 muscles to balance itself when you're standing still.

'Thereafter', David Skal writes in *V Is for Vampire*, 'Lugosi was never able to negotiate a lucrative Hollywood contract. *Dracula* was the height of his Hollywood career, and also the beginning of its end'. His last good role was as the monster keeper Igor in the 1939 film *Son of Frankenstein*, considered to be the finest performance of his entire career.

Count on Him

Lugosi played Count Dracula for a second and final time in the 1948 Universal film *Abbot and Costello Meet Frankenstein*, his last major-studio film. After that he was reduced to appearing in a string of low-budget films, including the Ed Wood film *Bride of the Monster* (1956). Wood also had cast Lugosi in his film *Plan 9 From Outer Space* (1958), but Lugosi died on 16 August, 1956 (and was buried in full Dracula costume cape, and make-up)...so Wood recycled some old footage of Lugosi and hired a stand-in, who covered his face with his cape so that viewers would think he was Lugosi. When he died, Lugosi left an estate valued at $2,900.

...LAST, BUT NOT LEAST

Florence Stoker. Mrs. Stoker was nearly broke when she sold Universal the movie rights to *Dracula*, a sale that, combined with the royalties from the novel and the London and American plays, enabled her to live in modest comfort for the rest of her life. But she never did get rich off of the property that would bring wealth to so many others. When she died in 1937, she left an estate valued at £6,913.

Then again, Mrs. Stoker may have been luckier than she knew: After her death it was discovered that when Bram Stoker was issued a copyright for *Dracula* in 1897, he or his agents neglected to turn over two copies of the work to the American copyright office as was required by law; and the Stoker estate failed to do so again in the 1920s when the copyright was renewed in the UK. Since Stoker failed to comply with the requirements of the law, *Dracula* was technically in the public domain, which meant that anyone in the United States could have published the novel or adapted it into plays, movies or any other form without Mrs. Stoker's permission and without having to pay her a cent in royalties.

If you take a plant with you on a long airplane flight, it, too, will suffer from jet lag.

MR MOONLIGHT

Some facts about our night-light in the sky, from astronomer (and BRI member) Richard Moeschl.

It takes 29 days, 12 hours, 44 minutes and 3 seconds for the moon to go through all of its phases (from one full moon to the next). This is close to the length of a month – which is why the word *month* means 'moon'.

The light that comes from the moon is sunlight reflected off the moon's surface. It takes 1¼ seconds for the light to travel to Earth.

The moon is smaller than any planet in the solar system, but relative to the size of the planets the other moons orbit, our moon is the largest of the moons.

The moon is 3,457 kilometres in diameter – about a quarter of the Earth's diameter.

If the Earth was as big as a fist, the moon would be the size of a stamp – placed 3 metres away.

The average temperature on the Moon is –175° to –165°C (–283° to 266°F).

Since the moon spins once on its axis every 27⅓ days – the same amount of time it takes to go around the Earth once – we end up seeing only one side of the moon (about 59 per cent of its surface). We never see the 'dark side of the moon'.

The side of the moon we always see is called 'the near side'. The side we never see from Earth is 'the far side'. That's probably where Gary Larsen got the name of his comic strip.

There is no sound on the moon. Nor is there weather, wind, clouds or colours at sunrise and sunset.

If you weigh 54 kilograms on Earth, you would weigh 9 kilograms on the Moon – ⅙ of your Earth weight. This is because there is less gravity on the Moon.

A 1-metre jump on Earth would carry you 5.7 metres on the moon.

Astronauts have brought over 382 kilograms of moon samples back to Earth.

The moon is moving away from the Earth at the rate of about 3 millimetres a year. So, we don't have to worry about losing sight of it just yet.

If you feed beer to a rat, it will live six times longer than a rat that drinks only water.

THE WRITING ON THE WALL

At some time, all bathroom readers have found themselves in a public toilet with nothing to read. Your eye starts to wander…and then you spot – graffiti! Here's a tribute to that emergency reading material.

You might be surprised to learn that graffiti is not something new. The term comes from the Italian word for 'scribbling'…and it was coined by archaeologists to describe wall-writing found in ancient ruins. It has been discovered in the catacombs of Rome, the Tower of London, medieval English alehouses and even Mayan pyramids.

Some of the earliest examples of graffiti were preserved on the walls of Pompeii when Mt. Vesuvius erupted in 79 A.D. As you can see from the following examples, it hasn't changed much in nearly 2,000 years:

Appolinaris, doctor to the Emperor Titus, had a crap here

NO ONE'S A HANDSOME FELLOW UNLESS HE HAS LOVED

Whoever loves, goes to hell. I want to break Venus' ribs with blows and deform her hips. If she can break my tender heart, why can't I hit her over the head?

HULLO, WE'RE WINESKINS

Artimetus got me pregnant

In Nuceria, near Porta Romana, is the district of Venus. Ask for Novellia Primigenia

He who sits here, read this before anything else: If you want to make love ask for Attice. The price is 16 asses.

LOVERS, LIKE BEES, ENJOY A LIFE OF HONEY

Wishful thinking

O Chius, I hope your ulcerous pustules reopen and burn even more than they did before

IN NUCERIA VOTE FOR LUCIUS MUNATIUS CAESARNINUS: HE IS AN HONEST MAN

Romula tarried here with Staphylus

The Olympics have been hosted twice by the UK, in 1908 and 1944, both times in London.

A RECORD OF HISTORY

People have been studying and collecting graffiti for centuries. Hurlo Thrumbo, an English publisher, put out the first printed collection in the 1700s. In the early 1900s, German sociologists collected scrawls from public toilets and turned them into the first academic study of graffiti. In America, the Kinsey researchers collected bathroom messages as part of their study of men's and women's sex habits. But it wasn't until the 1960s, when graffiti became an outlet for the counterculture and anti-Vietnam protest movement, that academics really started to pay attention.

Now these 'scribblings' are regarded as important adjuncts to the 'official' history of a culture. They provide a look at what the average person was thinking and give evidence of the social unrest, political trends and inner psychology of a society.

COLLECTING INFO

After decades of study, experts have decided that graffiti fits into four major categories.

• **Identity graffitists:** Want to immortalize themselves or a part of their lives (a romance, an accomplishment)

• **Opinion or message graffitists:** Want to let the world know what they think: 'UFOs are real – the Air Force doesn't exist'.

• **Dialogue graffitists:** Talk back to other graffitists. 'I've got what every woman wants'...*(underneath:)* 'You must be in the fur coat business'.

• **'Art' graffitists:** The most recent trend, with spray cans of paint used to create intricate designs signed with pseudonyms. Either vandalism or modern design, depending on your point of view.

THE GRAFFITI HERO

The most famous graffitist in history was Kilroy. Beginning in World War II, the line 'Kilroy was here' started showing up in outrageous places. Kilroy left his signature on the top of the torch of the Statue of Liberty, on the Marco Polo Bridge in China, and even on a Bikini atoll where an atomic bomb was to be tested. The original Kilroy was an infantry soldier who was sick of hearing the Air Force brag about always being first on the spot. But the phrase has appeared for so many years in so many places that 'Kilroy was here' has become synonymous with graffiti.

In her entire lifetime, Spain's Queen Isabella (1451–1504) bathed twice.

MORE WRITING ON THE WALL

A sampling of contemporary graffiti, collected since the 1960s.

Q: How do you tell the sex of a chromosome?
A: Pull down its genes.

If Love is blind, and God is love, and Ray Charles is blind, then God plays the piano.

Mafia: Organized Crime
Government: Disorganized Crime

Flush twice, it's a long way to Washington.

Death is just nature's way of telling you to slow down.

How come nobody ever writes on the toilet seats?

Things are more like they are now than they have ever been before.

I can't stand labels, after all, I'm a liberal.

Although the moon is smaller than the earth, it's farther away.

Free Chile!
...Free tacos!
...Free burritos!

Only Jackie knows what her Onassis worth.

Did you ever feel like the whole world was a white wedding gown, and you were a pair of muddy hiking boots?

Standing room only. (written on top of a men's urinal)

The chicken is an egg's way of producing another egg.

If you think you have someone eating out of your hands, it's a good idea of count your fingers.

The typical Stanford undergrad is like a milkshake: thick and rich.

Blessed is he who sits on a bee, for he shall rise again.

Please remain seated during the entire program.
– The Management

There are those who shun elitism. Why?
...Because it is there.
...It's the elitist thing to do.

Please do not throw cigarette butts in the toilet, as they become hard to light.

You can lead a horticulture, but you can't make her think.

Both poison oak and poison ivy are members of the cashew family.

MOTHERS OF INVENTION

There have always been women inventors – even if they've been overlooked in history books. Here are a few you may not have heard of.

MELITTA BENTZ, *a housewife in Dresden, Germany*
Invention: Drip coffeemakers
Background: At the beginning of the 20th century, people made coffee by dumping a cloth bag full of coffee grounds into boiling water. It was an ugly process – the grounds inevitably leaked into the water, leaving it gritty and bitter.

One morning in 1908, Frau Bentz decided to try something different: she tore a piece of blotting paper (used to mop up after runny fountain pens) from her son's schoolbook and put it in the bottom of a brass pot she'd poked with holes. She put coffee on top of the paper and poured boiling water over it. It was the birth of 'drip' coffeemakers – and the Melitta company. Today, Melitta sells its coffeemakers in 150 countries around the world.

LADY ADA LOVELACE, *daughter of British poet Lord Byron*
Invention: Computer programming
Background: The forerunner of modern computers – called the 'analytical engine' – was the brainchild of a mathematical engineer named George Babbage. In 1834 Babbage met Lady Lovelace, and the two formed a partnership, working together on the engine's prototype. In the process, Lovelace created the first programming method, which used punch cards. Unfortunately, tools available to Babbage and Lovelace in the mid-1800s weren't sophisticated enough to complete the machine (though it worked in theory). Lovelace spent the rest of her life studying cybernetics.

LADY MARY MONTAGU, *a British noblewoman*
Invention: Smallpox vaccine
Background: In 1717, while travelling in Turkey, she observed a curious custom known as *ingrafting*. Families would call for the services of old women, who would bring nutshells full of 'virulent' – live smallpox – to a home. Then it would be 'ingrafted' into a patient's open vein. The patient would spend a few days in bed with a slight illness but was rendered immune to smallpox. This tech-

nique was unknown in England, where 30 per cent of smallpox victims died. Montagu convinced Caroline, Princess of Wales, to try it on her own daughters. When it worked, she anonymously published *The Plain Account of the Inoculating of the Small-pox by a Turkish Merchant*. Despite vehement opposition from the church and medical establishments, the idea took hold. Lady Montagu lived to see England's smallpox death rate drop to 2 per cent.

MARGARET KNIGHT, *an employee of the Columbia Paper Bag Company in the late 1800s*
Invention: The modern paper bag
Background: Knight grew so tired of making paper bags by hand that she began experimenting with machines that could make them automatically. She came up with one that made square-bottomed, folding paper bags (until then, paper bags all had V-shaped bottoms). But her idea was stolen by a man who'd seen her building her prototype. A court battle followed in which the main argument used against Knight was her 'womanhood'. But she proved beyond a doubt that the invention was hers and received her patent in 1870. Knight was awarded 27 patents in her lifetime, but was no businesswoman – she died in 1914 leaving an estate of only $275.05.

BETTE NESMITH GRAHAM, *a secretary at the Texas Bank & Trust in Dallas in the early 1950s*
Invention: Liquid Paper
Background: Graham was a terrible typist...but when she tried to erase her mistakes, the ink on her IBM typewriter just smeared. One afternoon in 1951, while watching sign painters letter the bank's windows, she got a brilliant idea: 'With lettering, an artist never corrects by erasing but always paints over the error. So I decided to use what artists use. I put some waterbase paint in a bottle and took my watercolour brush to the office. And I used that to correct my typing mistakes'. So many other secretaries asked for bottles of 'Mistake Out' that in 1956 she started a small business selling it. A year later, she changed the formula and founded Liquid Paper, Inc. In 1966 her son, Michael Nesmith, made more money as a member of the Monkees than she did with Liquid Paper. But in 1979, Bette Nesmith Graham sold her company to Gillette for $47 million.

Bathroom readers beware: the fine for leaving a public toilet unflushed in Singapore: £100.

MISSED IT BY *THAT* MUCH

Often success and disaster are a lot closer than we'd like to think. Here are some classic 'near misses'.

AN ASSASSINATION

Theodore Roosevelt: On 14 October, 1912, the former president was on his way to give a speech in Milwaukee when a man named John Schrank drew a revolver, pointed it at Roosevelt, and pulled the trigger. Roosevelt staggered but didn't fall. No blood could be detected, but Roosevelt's handlers begged him to go to the hospital. He refused and delivered a 50-minute speech to a cheering throng. However, when he pulled the 100-page speech out of his vest, he noticed a bullet hole in it. It turned out that the bullet had ripped through the paper and penetrated 10 centimetres into Roosevelt's body, right below his right nipple. If the written speech hadn't slowed the bullet down, he would have been killed. After speaking, Roosevelt was treated for shock and loss of blood.

A PLACE IN HISTORY

Elisha Gray: Gray was an electrical genius who independently developed his own telephone. Incredibly, he filed a patent for the invention on 14 February, 1876 – the *exact same day* that Alexander Graham Bell did – but a few hours *after* Bell. 'If Bell had been a few hours late', says one historian, 'what we know of as the Bell System would have been the Gray System'. Gray was successful with other inventions, but was bitter for the rest of his life about not receiving credit for the telephone.

James Swinburne: Leo Baekeland patented the first modern plastic on 14 June, 1907; he called it 'Bakelite'. A day later, a Scottish electrical engineer named James Swinburne filed a patent for almost exactly the same thing. He'd been experimenting with the same chemicals on his own halfway around the world, and had come up with the same substance completely independently. Unlike Gray, though, he made peace with his near-miss and wound up chairman of the Bakelite company.

A CAREER-ENDING 'INJURY'

Frank Sinatra: 'Gangster Sam Giancana once ordered a hit on Frank Sinatra. He was going to have Sinatra's throat cut to ruin his voice. But on the night the hit was supposed to go down, Giancana was enjoying an intimate moment with (his girlfriend) Phyllis McGuire, who played Sinatra records to heighten the romantic mood. After listening for a while, Giancana decided he couldn't in good conscience silence that voice. He cancelled the hit'. (The Portland *Oregonian*, 29 August, 1997)

MILITARY DEFEAT

George Washington: 'On Christmas night, 1776, Washington was preparing to cross the Delaware with his army to attack the British. The commander of the British forces at Trenton, Colonel Rall, was German. He was drinking and playing cards when he received a note from a British loyalist warning him of the attack. But the note was in English, which Rall couldn't read, and he was groggy anyway, so he put it in his pocket. At dawn, Washington attacked and because the British were unprepared, he won. As Rall lay dying on the battlefield, the note was translated into German and Rall admitted if he'd read it, 'I would not be here'.' (From *Oh Say Can You See?*)

THE PRESIDENCY

John Janney: 'In 1840, Janney was Chairman of the Whig Party Convention in Virginia. This convention nominated William Henry Harrison for President. John Janney and John Tyler were the nominees for Vice President. When the vote of the convention was a tie, Janney, as Chairman, did the 'honourable' thing and voted for Tyler. Harrison won the election but died soon after, and John Tyler became President. John Janney lost the presidency by one vote – his own'. (From *Dear Abby*, 17 December, 1996)

Sen. Ben Wade: When Lincoln was shot in 1865, Andrew Johnson became president. In 1867 the Republican Congress tried to impeach him, but was one vote shy of the two-thirds majority needed to remove him from office. Wade, as president of the Senate, would have become the 18th American president. He became the second man in history to miss the U.S. presidency by one vote.

GOING DOWN THE TUBE

How did the world's first underground railway come to be. More importantly, will they ever get it to work properly? They've only had 100 years to fix it. Mind the gap!

Travelling on London's tube network is something that once experienced is not lightly forgotten. It is noisy, confusing, dirty, a bit scary, and subject to its own skewed laws of time, space and speed. Love it or hate it (or should that be hate it or *really* hate it) it's a fascinating subterranean world with a more than interesting history.

ALL BLOCKED UP

In the mid-1800s traffic was threatening to choke London to a standstill (no change there then). And this was even before the car was invented! Victorian gentlemen would quietly steam under their top hats as they sat for hours in horse-drawn-carriage-jams. Something had to be done to relieve the pressure on the capital's roads – and reduce the mountainous piles of horse dung that were being deposited on them. The recently-opened overground railways had been a hit, allowing people to move out to the new suburbs. So, some asked, why not build railways in the city?

As Londoners did not want a railway running *through* their city, it was decided to build one *under* it, between Farringdon Street in the City and the mainline station of Paddington. The driving force behind the scheme was Charles Pearson, Solicitor to the City of London. He help to set up the Metropolitan Railway Company in 1854, and did much to raise the £1 million needed to build the first underground railway line.

GOING UNDERGROUND

The idea was frighteningly new and radical – would people be frightened by the dark, or asphyxiated by the fumes? Until electric trains were introduced in 1890 (with the opening of the City & South London Railway), underground steam trains diverted smoke to their own water tanks. When they reached specially-built ventilation shafts that led from the tunnel to the world above, they would pump out the remainder. There's still a ventilation shaft at Great Portland Street station near Euston.

To lay the track, streets were dug up and either re-covered later or left open – as at Farringdon Road station, which is still open to the elements to this day. The first train ran on what was called the Metropolitan Line on 10 January, 1863, along the 6 km of track from Farringdon Street to Paddington Station. It was an instant success, the trains carrying 40,000 passengers on the first day alone. The one sad element was that Charles Pearson was not there to enjoy it – he died four months before the grand opening.

THE NEXT TRAIN DEPARTS IN 100 YEARS

The opening of the Metropolitan Line was the start of a massive programme of building by a number of companies. It took 150 years to complete the entire tube network we have today, but all the main lines were in place by the start of the 20th century. In 1890, the City & South London Railway (now part of the Northern line) was the first in the world to be electrically operated, although its trains were at first supposed to be hauled along the tracks by cables, like the cable cars of San Francisco.

One odd fact about the first tube trains was that they didn't have any windows: the railway companies thought there was no need for them, as a guard was employed to yell out the name of each station as the train pulled in. However, the fact that the guards couldn't be heard over the noise the trains created soon caused the train companies to change their minds.

PICK OF THE BUNCH

The tube network was brought together when the London Passenger Transport Board was formed in 1933. The new authority ensured a uniform corporate style, with bright, modern stations featuring good lighting and handy ticket machines. An official named Frank Pick, in charge of planning and improving routes, made a highly visible contribution through his design and PR work. The Underground had found someone passionate about style, who even believed it had a civilizing effect. The look and feel of the Underground, even today, is largely Pick's work.

Even the network's map became a design icon. Harry Beck, a

Call waiting: nearly 6 per cent of all marriage proposals are made over the telephone.

29-year-old electrical draughtsman, produced a simple representation of the tube network based on circuit diagrams. Until his masterstroke, tubs maps showed every complicated twist and turn that the tubes took. Beck simplified the map down to its bare essentials. His first design was rejected as being too revolutionary, but in 1933 his next effort was accepted and is still in use today.

GIMME SHELTER

During World War II London's tube stations were pressed into action for a dramatic new use – as bomb shelters in which Londoners could hide during the Blitz. At the height of the bombing campaign, 177,000 citizens were sleeping in tube stations every night. The war left the Underground largely intact and fully operational, but in urgent need of new signals, escalators and rolling stock. Yet 1930s vintage trains were still running well into the early 1980s. It said much for their original build and design that they ran millions of miles virtually non-stop for 50 years.

TRAVELLING IN STYLE?

The latest addition to the tube network is the Jubilee Line, which was completed in 2000, just in time for the opening of the Millennium Dome (the Jubilee Line station of North Greenwich stops just outside the Dome).

But in contrast to the shiny, new Jubilee line, much of the rest of the network has suffered years of neglect, lack of investment and falling staff levels. A journey on a rush hour tube is akin to a journey to hell and back: the tubes are massively overcrowded, and boiling hot in the summer and freezing cold in winter. Delays and random track closures only add to passenger stress levels. A tube train at 8.30 a.m on a weekday morning is not a place where you will see Lononders at their best.

But as pioneers of the underground railway, Londoners can be proud of a system that has been emulated around the world, from Moscow to New York, and from Tokyo to Berlin. Despite competition from buses and cars and the introduction of new and often wacky alternative forms of transport – from rickshaws to rollerskates – the Tube is still the quickest (if not the most comfortable) way to get around the capital.

Scotland was once part of a continent called Laurentia, which included North America.

TUNNEL VISION

So, when you're next stuck on the tube, waiting patiently for the train to crawl into the next station, impress your fellow passengers with some of these Underground statistics:

Ongar on the Central Line is the start point for measuring the network. Every 200 metres there is a reference marker for engineers and other workers.

The 27 km of the Northern Line makes it the longest continuous tunnel in the UK (for many years it was the longest tunnel in the world).

Epping to West Ruislip on the Central Line is the longest continuous journey – 54 km. It takes about 90 minutes to get from one end to the other – on a good day!

Gillespie Road was the only station to be renamed after a football club. Since 1932 it's been called Arsenal.

There are 475 km of Underground routes, of which 235 km are in the open, 150 km in tunnels and just 32 km in cut-and-cover tunnels.

There are 2.8 million trips taken on the tube each day. Some 866 million journeys were made in the last two years of the 1990s.

Hampstead is the deepest station in the tube network, being 58 metres under ground. Its escalators are also the longest in the system, at 55 metres.

At night, a Tunnel Cleaning Train runs through the tube network, sucking up tonnes of dust a debris from the track. Experts estimate that due to the build-up of dust in tunnels and stations, for the average passenger a 20 minute tube journey is the equivalent to smoking a cigarette.

Julian Lloyd Webber was the first licensed busker allowed to perform on the Underground.

Drama! Cornwall's Minack Theatre is carved into the granite cliffs of Porthcurno Bay.

BOND ON FILM

Sean Connery is so closely associated with the role of James Bond that it's hard to believe he was initially a longshot for the part. Here's the story of how Ian Fleming's 007 thrillers found their way onto film.

BOND-AGE FILMS

In the late 1950s Albert R. 'Cubby' Broccoli and Harry Saltzman, two movie producers, teamed up to turn Ian Fleming's Bond novels into action films. *Thunderball* was their choice for the first Bond film, but it was tied up in a lawsuit between Fleming and some other writers. So they settled on *Dr. No*. They shopped the idea around to every film studio in Hollywood...and were rejected by nearly everyone. Finally, United Artists agreed to back the film – as long as they didn't have to spend a lot of money. *Dr. No's* budget was set at a paltry $1 million.

Casting Call

The first task was to find the right James Bond. Broccoli and Saltzman knew what kind of actor they were looking for: a top-notch British performer who was willing to work for low-budget wages, and who would commit to making several sequels (in the unlikely event that *Dr. No* was successful).

But as Broccoli and Saltzman quickly realized, no actor like that existed. Broccoli's friend Cary Grant was one of the first people to say no; many others followed. Stage actor Patrick McGoohan rejected the role on moral grounds (too violent); and up-and-coming British actor Richard Johnson refused to commit to a multi-picture deal, fearing it would hurt his career. (Both men later ended up playing James Bond knock-offs on TV and in film.) Ian Fleming suggested either David Niven or Roger Moore; Niven wasn't interested, and Moore was already committed to *The Saint*, a TV detective/spy series.

SERENDIPITY

Not long after it was announced that Dr. No was being made into a film, the *Daily Express*, which ran the James Bond comic strip, held a readers' poll to see who should be cast as Bond. The winner was Sean Connery, a little-known Scottish actor and former Mr.

First person to refer to a coward as a 'chicken': William Shakespeare.

Universe contestant. Connery was beginning to build a following in Great Britain, and had recently been interviewed by the paper.

At about the same time, Cubby Broccoli and his wife saw the Disney film *Darby O'Gill and the Little People*, in which Connery played a 'farmer and country bumpkin'. Neither of the Broccolis was particularly impressed with Connery's acting, but Cubby Broccoli liked his accent, and Mrs. Broccoli thought he had the raw sex appeal that the Bond part needed.

Coincidentally, a short time later, film editor Peter Hunt sent Broccoli several reels of a film he was working on called *Operation Snafu*, with the recommendation that one of the stars – Sean Connery again – would make a great Bond.

TOUGH GUY

Connery's career prior to the Bond films was nothing to brag about, but he still played hard to get. When Broccoli asked him to test for the part, he refused, telling Broccoli 'Either take me as I am or not at all'.

'He pounded the desk and told us what he wanted', Broccoli recounted years later. 'What impressed us was that he had balls'. The producers finally tricked him into auditioning on film by telling him they were experimenting with camera setups.

Mr. Right

Connery came from a working-class background and he showed up at the audition wearing grubby clothes, but by the time he finished his screen test Broccoli and Saltzman knew the search for Eton-educated Bond was over. 'He walked like he was Superman', Broccoli recalled, 'and I believed we had to go along with him. The difference between him and the other young actors was like the difference between a still photo and film. We knew we had our Bond'. Connery recalls his casting somewhat less romantically:

> Originally, they were considering all sorts of stars to play James Bond. Trevor Howard was one. Rex Harrison was another. The character was to be a shining example of British upper-crust elegance, but they couldn't afford a major name. Luckily, I was available at a price they could afford.

Casting an unknown in the lead part did not go down well at the studio – one executive rejected him and told the producers to, 'see if you can do better'. Connery did not impress Ian Fleming, either. 'I'm looking for Commander James Bond', he complained, 'not an overgrown stuntman'. But Connery stayed.

THE BOND THEME

Composer Monty Norman created the musical score for *Dr. No*, and while Broccoli and Saltzman were happy with his work on the rest of the film, they didn't like his theme song. So they hired a new composer named John Barry. They told him they needed a song exactly 2½ minutes long to fit into the soundtrack where the old song had gone. Without even seeing the film, Barry composed the 'James Bond Theme', one of the most recognizable themes in Hollywood history. He was paid £200 for his effort.

BOND MANIA

Dr. No premiered in 1962 and was a smash hit. The film earned huge returns for Broccoli, Saltzman, and United Artists and launched the most successful film series in history. By 1997 a total of 20 Bond films had been made, including seven with Sean Connery, one with George Lazenby, one with David Niven, seven with Roger Moore, two with Timothy Dalton, and two with Pierce Brosnan, who signed on for two more through the 21st century.

Dr. No and the second Bond film, *From Russia with Love*, also launched a 'Bond mania' complete with 007 toys, board games, spy kits, decoder rings, cartoons, toiletries, clock radios and even lingerie. The fad peaked in 1965, but continued well into the 1970s, inspiring numerous TV knock-offs such as *The Man from U.N.C.L.E.*, *I Spy*, and *The Avengers*.

For the Boys

But the success of *Dr. No* went beyond launching a spy fad or a film series, as Suzanna Andrews writes in the *New York Times*.

> *Dr. No* also marked the beginning of the big-budget 'boy' movies that today dominate the film industry, movies marked by action, special effects, and, men who never fail. In spirit and style, Bond is godfather to such movies as *Lethal Weapon* and *Die Hard*, and many films that star Sylvester Stallone or Arnold Schwarzenegger.

In the Middle Ages, you were supposed to throw eggs at the bride and groom.

UNTIMELY END

James Bond's creator, Ian Fleming, did not live to see the full impact of the genre he created. In 1964, after only two Bond films had been completed, he died from a massive heart attack brought on by years of heavy drinking and a 70-cigarette-a-day smoking habit. He was 56.

In his lifetime Fleming earned nearly £1.8 million in book royalties; but his heirs would lose out on many of the profits his work generated after he died. Less than a month before his death, Fleming, who suspected the end was near, sold 51 per cent of his interest in the James Bond character to reduce the inheritance taxes on his estate. He collected only £170,000, even though it was worth millions.

* * * * *

FOOD NOTES

Ian Fleming made James Bond into a connoisseur of fine wine, women, weapons and food, but Fleming's own tastes left a lot to be desired, especially when it came to food. As his friend and neighbour on Jamaica, Noel Coward, recounted years later,

> Whenever I ate with Ian at Goldeneye (Fleming's Jamaican hideaway) the food was so abominable I used to cross myself before I took a mouthful....I used to say, 'Ian, it tastes like armpits'. And all the time you were eating there was old Ian smacking his lips for more while his guests remembered all those delicious meals he had put into the books.

BOND'S FIRST MARTINI

> 'A dry Martini', (Bond) said. 'One. In a deep champagne goblet'. 'Oui, Monsieur'.
>
> 'Just a moment. Three measures of Gordon's, one of vodka, half a measure of Kina Lillet. Shake it very well until it's ice cold, then add a large thin slice of lemon peel. Got it'?
>
> 'Certainly, Monsieur'. The barman seemed pleased with the idea.
>
> – ***Casino Royale*, 1953**

THE DISCOVERY OF THE PLANETS

As early as nursery school, we're taught that there are nine planets. but 200 years ago, even scholars were sure there were only six planets. Here's how we got the three new ones.

THE END OF THE SOLAR SYSTEM

People have always known about Mercury, Venus, Mars, Jupiter and Saturn. Early civilizations named the days of the week after each of these planets, plus the sun and moon. The Greeks watched them move through the night sky, passing in front of the stars that make up the constellations of the zodiac, and called them *planetes* – which means 'wanderers'.

As recently as the 1700s, people still believed that the planet Saturn was at the farthest extent of the solar system. That there might be other planets wasn't even a respectable idea. But as technology and science became more sophisticated, other members of the solar system were discovered.

URANUS

In 1781 a self-taught astronomer, William Herschel, was 'sweeping the skies' with his telescope. By March, he had reached the section that included the constellation Gemini, and he spotted an object that appeared as a disk rather than a glowing star. Because it moved slightly from week to week, Herschel thought it was circular...and came to the shocking conclusion that it wasn't a comet, but an unknown planet. People were astonished.

Finding a Name

No one since ancient times had named a planet. Herschel felt that it should be called 'Georgium Sidus' (George's Star) in honour of his patron, George III (if there was one thing Herschel was good at, it was sucking up to those in power). Some people wanted to name it 'Herschel' after its discoverer. But one influential astronomer suggested they call it 'Uranus', after the Greek god of the heavens. That made sense, since this new planet was certainly the limit of the skies of the solar system. Or so they thought.

In Equatorial Guinea, it's illegal to name your child Monica.

NEPTUNE

The newly found planet had a slight variation in its orbit, almost as if something were tugging at it. Could there be another planet affecting Uranus? A century earlier, Isaac Newton had come up with laws describing the effects that the gravitational forces of planets have on one another. Using Newton's laws, two young scientists set out independently in 1840 to find the unknown planet whose gravitational forces might be pulling on Uranus. One of the scientists was a French mathematician, Jean Leverrier. The other was an English astronomer, John Couch Adams. Both hoped the unknown planet would be where their calculations said they should be able to find it.

The Hidden Planet

Adams finished his calculations first, in September 1845. The following August, Leverrier completed his. Neither had access to a large telescope, so they couldn't verify their projections – and no one would make one available to them. Finally, Leverrier travelled to the Berlin Observatory in Germany, and the young assistant manager, Johann Gottfried Galle, agreed to help search for the as yet unverified planet.

That was 23 September, 1846. That night, Galle looked through the telescope, calling out stars and their positions while a young student astronomer, Heinrich Louis d'Arrest, looked at a star chart, seaching for the stars Galle described. Finally Galle called out an eighth-magnitude star that d'Arrest couldn't locate on the charts. They had found the unknown planet! It had taken two years of research – but only a half hour at the telescope. The honour of the discovery belongs to both Adams and Leverrier, who had essentially discovered the new planet with just a pen and a new set of mathematical laws. The greenish planet was named after Neptune, god of the sea.

VULCAN

Leverrier was on a roll. He started looking for other planets...and became convinced that there was one between the Sun and Mercury. He called his planet 'Vulcan', the god of fire, because it was so close to the Sun. Leverrier noted that, like Uranus, Mercury experienced disturbances that caused it to travel farther in one point in its orbit. Since Neptune was one of the causes of similar pulls on Uranus, it made sense that another planet was affecting Mercury.

Leverrier never found Vulcan, but people believed it was there until 1916, when Einstein's general theory of relativity was published. Einstein gave a satisfactory explanation for the discrepancies in Mercury's orbit, so scientists no longer needed Vulcan. It thereby ceased to exist...until decades later, when Gene Roddenberry, creator of *Star Trek*, appropriated the planet and made it the home of Spock.

PLUTO

The discovery of Neptune did not completely account for the peculiar movements of Uranus. Once again, scientists considered the pull of another planet as a cause and set out to find 'Planet X'. Using the telescope at his observatory in Flagstaff, Arizona, Percival Lowell searched for Planet X for 10 years. After he died in 1916, his brother gave the observatory a donation that enabled it to buy a telescope-camera. The light-sensitive process of photography allowed astronomers to capture images of dim and distant stars that they couldn't see, even with the aid of a telescope.

In 1929 the Lowell Observatory hired Clyde Tombaugh, a young self-taught astronomer from Kansas, to continue the search for Planet X. Lowell had suggested that the unknown planet was in the Gemini region of the sky. Using an instrument called the blink microscope, Tombaugh took two photographs of that area of the sky a few days apart and placed them side by side under the microscope. If something moved in the sky, as planets do, it would appear as a speck of light jumping back and forth as Tombaugh's eyes moved from one photograph to the other, looking through the microscope.

That's just what happened. The observatory announced the discovery of the ninth planet on 13 March, 1930. An 11-year-old girl, the daughter of an Oxford astronomy professor, chose the name Pluto – the god of the underworld – for the new planet.

For years before his death, Tombaugh repeatedly declared that there were no more planets in our solar system. If there were, he said, he would have found them.

It's impossible to snore in the weightlessness of space.

OOPS!

More cock-ups, blunders and idiotic mistakes.

CHURCH MUSIC

'A funeral in 1996 in an English church ended with Rod Stewart singing:

If you want my body,
And you think I'm sexy,
C'mon baby let me know.

The vicar admitted that when he was recording the deceased's last request – a hymn – he'd apparently failed to erase the entire cassette tape'.

– *Fortean Times*, 1996

UNPLUGGED

'In 1978 workers were sent to dredge a murky stretch of the Chesterfied-Stockwith Canal. Their task was to remove all the rubbish and leave the canal clear.... They were disturbed during their tea-break by a policeman who said he was investigating a giant whirlpool in the canal. When they got back, however, the whirlpool had gone...and so had a 1½-mile [2.4-kilometre] stretch of the canal.... A flotilla of irate holidaymakers were stranded on their boats in brown sludge.

Among the first pieces of junk the workers had hauled out had been the 200-year-old plug that ensured the canal's continued existence. "We didn't know there was a plug", said one bewildered workman.... All the records had been lost in a fire during the war'.

– *The Book of Heroic Failures*, by Stephen Pile

YIKES!

'Defense lawyer Phillip Robertson, trying to make a dramatic point in front of the jury at his client's recent robbery trial in Dallas pointed the pistol used in the crime at the jury box, causing two jurors to fling their arms in front of their faces and others to gasp. Though Robertson was arguing that his client should be sentenced only to probation, the horrified jury gave him 13 years'.

**– 'The Edge', in the *Portland Oregonian*,
10 September, 1997**

Siberia means 'sleeping land'.

GREAT MOMENTS IN TELEPHONE HISTORY

Everyone's got at least one telephone – but it seems the only thing anyone knows about it is that Alexander Graham Bell invented it. But when exactly did Bell invent the telephone? And what happened next? Read on to find out.

February, 1876. Beating a competing inventor by only a few hours on Valentine's Day, Alexander Graham Bell arrives at the U.S. patent office and patents the telephone in his name. Three days later, he builds the first telephone that actually works. Hoping to earn a page in the history books, he memorizes lines from Shakespeare to use in the world's first telephone conversation. But when the magic moment arrives, he spills acid on himself and barks out 'Mr. Watson, come here. I want you'.

Autumn 1876. Bell offers to sell the rights to his invention to the Western Union Telegraph Co. for $100,000. He is laughed out of the office.

• Stage fright becomes a significant obstacle in expanding telephone sales. To reassure the public, Bell takes out ads claiming that 'Conversations can be easily carried on after slight practice and with occasional repetitions of a word or sentence'.

1877. Charles Williams of Somerville, Massachusetts, becomes the first American to install a telephone in his house. (But since no one else had a phone, he couldn't call anyone. So he installed a telephone in his office, where his wife could reach him during the day.)

1877. A woman named Emma Nutt becomes the first female telephone operator in the United States. Initially the phone company preferred to hire young boys as operators, but eventually had to phase them out because of their foul language and penchant for practical jokes.

1879. In the middle of a measles epidemic in Lowell, Massachusetts, a doctor, worried about what would happen if the town's operators succumbed to the disease, suggests to the local phone company that it begin issuing the nation's first phone numbers to telephone subscribers. At first the public resists the idea, attacking phone numbers as being too impersonal.

1881. Thomas Edison comes up with a new way to answer the telephone. 'Originally', writes Margaret Cousins in *The Story of Thomas Edison*, 'people wound the phone with a crank, which rang a bell, and then said: "Are you there?" This took too much time for Edison. During one of the hundreds of tests made in his laboratory, he picked up the phone one day, twisted the crank and shouted: "Hello!" This became the way to answer the telephone all over [the world], and it still is'.

* * *

GREAT MOMENTS IN EMERGENCY DIALLING

In 1995, a woman in Devizes was awakened from a sound sleep by a phone ringing.

> Upon answering it, she was greeted by moans, groans and yelling. The woman dismissed the call as a prank and hung up.
>
> A short while later the phone rang again. This time the woman heard outright screaming, followed by a female shouting, 'Oh my God!' Terrified, the woman hung up. There was no mistaking it: the voice on the other end belonged to her daughter, who lived about a hundred miles away

The woman phoned the police. They sent squad cars to the daughter's house, broke down the door, and stormed the bedroom.

> There they found the daughter making love to her boyfriend on the bed.
>
> Apparently, during two wild moments of passion, the daughter's big toe accidentally hit the speed-dial button on the phone, which was on a table next to the bed.
>
> 'This is a warning for other people', a police spokesman said. 'If you're going to indulge in that sort of thing, move the phone'.

– ***Knuckleheads in the News***

THE LEANINGEST TOWER ON EARTH

The Leaning Tower of Pisa is one of the most recognizable buildings in the world, a visual symbol of Italy itself. Here's a look at its unusual history.

CIVIC RIVALRY

In 1155, builders in Venice finished work on a bell tower next to the Cathedral of San Marco. Legend has it that citizens in the seaport town of Pisa – determined not to be outdone by the Venetians – decided to build their own bell tower next to the Cathedral of Pisa.

Work began in 1173. The plans called for a seven-storey marble tower with more than 200 columns, plus a belfry with seven large bells at the top. The building would be 56 metres tall but only 16 metres in diameter.

The entire building was supposed to stand on a foundation less than 683 metres deep. But as it turned out, the ground – largely sandy soil and waterlogged clay – was too spongy to support it.

BACK AND FORTH

By the time the second floor was finished, the building had already begun leaning slightly to the north. But rather than start again, the builders just lengthened the northern walls on the third floor and shortened the southern ones, levelling off the top of the building in the process. That way, they supposed, the rest of the building would be level, too.

STOP AND GO

As luck would have it, political unrest in Pisa forced the builders to stop work on the building for 90 years. That meant the clay soil beneath the tower was allowed to compact and strengthen over time. Soil experts now believe that if it hadn't, the tower would have collapsed when the upper floors were added.

But they didn't. Six more storeys were successfully added between 1270 and 1278. This time, however, the added weight caused the building to lean to the *south*, the direction in which it still leans today. The builders applied the same solution to the fifth floor that they'd used on the third, only in reverse: they lengthened the southern walls and shortened the northern ones, giving the building a slight banana shape. Once again, the top was level.

FINAL ADDITION

Political unrest halted construction again, this time until 1360. By now the building was terribly off-centre, but builders added the belfry anyway – again making the southern walls taller than the northern ones, to level out the roof. One hundred and eighty-seven years after it was begun, the tower was finally finished.

But the tilt was only beginning. Over the next six centuries, the building moved a tiny amount each year. By the early 1990s, it was more than 4 metres off-centre.

SAVING THE TOWER

By 1900, the Leaning Tower of Pisa had already become one of the world's great tourist attractions. So the Italian government appointed a commission to work out if there was a way to keep it from falling over.

The commission wasn't much help – except to the government, which was able to take credit for actively trying to save the tower. After that, whenever scientists speculated that the tower was falling, the government just appointed another commission. The only one that had any lasting impact was the 1933 commission...which made things worse. They drilled 361 holes in the ground surrounding the tower and filled them with 1,800 tonnes of concrete. Instead of stabilizing the ground, the concrete added weight to the tower's foundation, causing it to tip six times faster.

THE FINAL FIX

In 1989, the Italian government appointed its 15th commission. This time, it actually helped. In 1992, scientists began implementing a three-phase plan to halt the tilting:

1. In April 1992, five steel bands were strapped around the second floor of the building (the weakest part). The belts act like girdles – when a building collapses at the base, the part that gives way bursts *outward*, not inward. The bands hold everything in place.

2. In the summer of 1993, scientists began placing 75 8-tonne weights on the north side of the tower, hoping that by compressing the earth to the north, the building would stop leaning so much to the south. By November, the tower had actually straightened up about 6 mm.
3. In 1995, the scientists began removing clay soil from beneath the tower, extracting the water and replacing it all in a process they called 'controlled subsistence'. The goal: to have the tower resting on a drier, firmer soil base that will be better able to support the building.

THE END?

In April 1997, John Burland, the British soil mechanics expert who devised the plan, announced that the Leaning Tower of Pisa had finally stopped its tilt. However, in 2001, the tower was continuing to increase its tilt at about 1.2 mm per year. Has the tower been saved? Only time – a lot of it – will tell.

TOWER FACTS

• Six of the tower's eight floors are without safety rails. More than 250 people have fallen to their deaths since 1174.
• According to Italian officials, there's little danger anyone will be hurt if the tower does come crashing down. They predict that a collapse won't be sudden – that there will be plenty of rumbling and groaning in the building ahead of time to warn people. The point was moot for several years; the building was closed to the public in 1990 – though after extensive safety improvements, it reopened in 2001.
• Restoration officials get an average of two letters a week with suggestions on how to keep the tower upright. Some of the weirdest: building an identical tower to lean against the first one; building a huge statue of a man who looks like he's holding the tower up; tying helium balloons to the roof; anchoring the top of the tower to a hillside several kilometres away with a large steel cable.
• Of course, officials could tear the tower down, stone by stone, and rebuild it – this time perfectly vertical – on a strengthened foundation. But there's no chance of that – the tower brings in £180 million a year from tourists. 'Let's face it, the tower would have no significance if it were straight', caretaker Spartacom Campani admitted in 1983. 'Its lean is Pisa's bread-and-butter'.

Some shellfish can live as long as 150 years.

IT'S SO BAD, IT'S...

...Well...funny, anyway. Here's some dialogue from a few truly awful sci-fi B-moviess. No kidding, someone actually got paid to write this stuff.

Scientist: 'They took five death row inmates and injected them with a genetic code of sorts, taken from different species of fish, primarily salmon. It essentially fuses with the genetic material already existing'.
Astonished Listener: 'Fish-men!'?
Scientist: 'You could say that. The goal was to create an amphibious soldier, but...something went wrong'.

– Humanoids from the Deep

Dr. Wagner: 'But you're sacrificing a human life!'
Dr. Brandon (mad scientist): 'Do you cry over a guinea pig? This boy is a free police case. We're probably saving him from the gas chamber'.
Dr. Wagner: 'But the boy is so young, the transformation horrible...'
Dr. Brandon: 'And you call yourself a scientist! That's why you've never been more than an assistant'.

– I Was a Teenage Werewolf

Teenager: 'You know something? Those things, whatever they are – they're smarter than all of us put together'.

– The Eye Creatures

Dr. Durea: 'Oh, she's a lucky young woman, (Dr.) Groton. We have desperate need of her blood. She has survived decapitation and is manufacturing the right type of vital fluid for us. We are not butchers, Groton! We don't have this young lady here to merely drain her body and cast her aside! No. We are scientists! And we must have others to experiment with!'

– Dracula vs. Frankenstein

Galileo's best telescope was about as powerful as a good pair of binoculars are today.

First Scientist: 'You say you made a close examination of this light'?
Second Scientist: 'Not as close as I would have liked. It was being guarded by a…a sea serpent! A hideous beast that defies description!'
First Scientist: 'Oh, doctor, if I didn't know you were a scientist of high standards, I'd say you were a victim of the ridiculous "Phantom" stories that are running wild around the village!'

– ***The Phantom from 10,000 Leagues***

Steve (the hero scientist): 'Who are you? What do you want'?
Evil alien brain: 'I am Gor! I need your body as a dwelling-place while I am here on your planet Earth!'
Steve: 'Why me'?
Gor: 'Because you are a recognized nuclear scientist. Because you have entrée to places on Earth I want to go. I chose your body very carefully, even before I knew about Sally – a very exciting female!'
Steve: 'Leave Sally out of this!'
Gor: 'Why? She appeals to me! There are some aspects of the life of an Earth savage that are exciting and rewarding! Things that are missed by the brains on my planet, Arous'.

– ***The Brain from Planet Arous***

Dr. Marvin (hero scientist): 'General, we saw a strange thing this afternoon. We saw what appeared to be a flying saucer'.
General Hanley: 'A flying saucer!'?
Carol Marvin (scientist's new wife): 'It nearly ran us off the road'.
Hanley: 'You're sure of that'?
Dr. Marvin: 'Both Carol and I are subject to the same atmospheric disturbances that may have affected other observers, but there is a quantitative difference, when you're a scientist'.

Dr. Marvin: 'What do you want with me'?
Alien: 'Arrange for your world leaders to confer with us in the city of Washington D.C'.
Dr. Marvin: 'They may not listen! I'm only a scientist!'

– ***Earth Versus the Flying Saucers***

HOW A MICROWAVE WORKS

We gave you a brief history of the microwave oven on page 239. Now here's the rest of the story – the science that makes it work.

WHAT ARE MICROWAVES?

Here's the first thing you should know about 'microwaves': like visible light, radio waves and X-rays, they are waves of electromagnetic energy. What makes the four waves different from each other? Each has a different length *(wavelength)* and vibrates at a different speed *(frequency)*.

• Microwaves get their name because their wavelength is much shorter than electromagnetic waves that carry TV and radio signals.

• The microwaves in a microwave oven have a wavelength of about 10 centimetres, and they vibrate 2.5 billion times per second – about the same natural frequency as water molecules. That's what makes them so effective at heating food.

• A conventional oven heats the air in the oven, which then cooks the food. But microwaves cause water molecules in the food to vibrate at high speeds, creating heat. The heated water molecules are what cook the food.

• Glass, ceramic and plastic plates contain virtually no water molecules, which is why they don't heat up in the microwave.

MICROWAVE MECHANICS

• When the microwave oven is turned on, electricty passes through the magnetron, the tube which produces microwaves. The microwaves are then channelled down a metal tube *(wave-guide)* and through a slow rotating metal fan *(stirrer)*, which scatters them into the part of the oven where the food is placed.

• The walls of the oven are made of metal, which reflects microwaves the same way that a mirror reflects visible light. So when the microwaves hit the stirrer and are scattered into the food chamber, they bounce off the metal walls and penetrate the food from every direction. Some ovens have a rotating turntable that helps food cook more evenly.

• Do microwave ovens cook food from the inside out? Some people think so, but the answer seems to be no. Microwaves cook food from the outside in, like conventional ovens. But the microwave energy only penetrates a couple of centimetres into the food. The heat that's created by the water molecules then penetrates deeper into the food, cooking it all the way through. This secondary cooking process is known as 'conduction'.

• The metal holes in the glass door of the microwave oven are large enough to let out visible light (which has a small wavelength), but too small to allow the microwaves (which have a larger wavelength) to escape. So you can see what's cooking without getting cooked yourself.

YOU CALL THAT COOKING?

According to legend, shortly after Raytheon perfected its first microwave oven in the 1950s, Charles Adams, the chairman of Raytheon, had one installed in his kitchen so he could taste for himself what microwave-cooked food was like. But as Adams' cook quickly discovered, meat didn't brown in the oven, chips stayed limp and damp, and cakes didn't rise. The cook, condemning the oven as 'black magic', resigned in a huff.

When sales of microwave ovens took off in the late 1980s, millions of cooks discovered the same thing: microwaves just don't cook some foods as well as normal ovens do. The reason: Because microwaves cook by exciting the water molecules in food, the food inside a microwave oven rarely cooks at temperatures higher than 100°C (212°F), which is the temperature at which water turns to steam.

Conventional ovens, on the other hand, cook at temperatures as high as 287°C (550°F). High temperatures are needed to caramelize sugars and break down proteins, carbohydrates and other substances and combine them into more complex flavours. So microwave ovens can't do any of this, and they can't bake, either. Some people feel this is the microwave's Achilles' heel. 'The name 'microwave oven' is a misnomer', argues Cindy Ayers,

Sark, a Channel Island, is run by a Seigneur with a 400-year-old feudal constitution.

an executive with the company that makes Campbell's Soup. 'It doesn't do what an oven does'.

'It's a glorified popcorn popper', says Tom Vierhile, a researcher with *Marketing Intelligence*, a newsletter that tracks microwave sales. 'When the microwave first came out, people thought they had stumbled on nirvana. It's not the appliance the food industry thought it would be. It's a major disappointment'.

Adds one cooking critic: 'Microwave sales are still strong, but time will tell whether they have a future in the American kitchen'. In the meantime, Uncle John isn't holding his breath – he's too busy heating up leftovers.

MICROWAVE FACTS

• Have you heard that microwave ovens are dangerous? In 1968 the Walter Reed Hospital tested them to see if the microwaves leaked out. They did – and the U.S. government stepped in to set the first federal standards for microwave construction. Today all microwaves sold in the U.S. must be manufactured according to federal safety standards.

• If you microwave your foods in a square container and aren't happy with the results, try cooking them in a round one. 'Food cooks better in a round container than in a square one', says Jim Watkins, president of the company that makes Healthy Choice microwave food products. 'No one really knows why'.

• Irregularly shaped foods, such as a leg of chicken that is thick at one end and thin at the other end, cook unevenly.

• Food that has been cut up will also cook faster than a single, large piece of food, for the same reason: the microwaves penetrate completely through smaller pieces of food, but not through larger pieces.

• Aluminium foil reflects microwave energy the same way mirrors reflect light energy. That's why you can't use foil in a microwave...unless, for example, you're using it to shield some food items on a plate while others are being cooked. But be careful: if too much food is shielded with foil, the microwaves can overload the oven and damage the magnetron.

MYTH-CONCEPTIONS

Common knowledge is frequently wrong. Here are a few examples of things that most people believe...but just aren't true.

Myth: Watching television in a dark room is bad for your eyesight.
Fact: As Paul Dickson and Joseph C. Goulden write in *Myth-Informed:* 'The myth was created in the early 1950s by an innovative Philadelphia public relations man named J. Robert Mendte, on behalf of a client who manufactured lamps'.

Myth: For every cockroach you see in your house, there are 10 more you didn't see.
Fact: According to studies conducted by the Insects Affecting Man and Animals Labouratory of the U.S. Department of Agriculture, the number is actually closer to 1,000 to 1.

Myth: Flamingos are naturally pink.
Fact: Flamingos are grey when chicks. They turn pink as adults because the sea creatures they eat turn pink during digestion. The pigment is then absorbed by the bird's body and colours its feathers. If flamingos are fed a different diet, they're white.

Myth: Johnny Weissmuller's famous Tarzan yell was his own voice.
Fact: His voice was combined with a high C sung by a soprano, and a hyena's howl recorded on tape and played backward.

Myth: All your fingernails grow at the same rate.
Fact: If you're right-handed, nails on your right hand grow faster; if you're left-handed, nails on your left will.

Myth: Tonto's nickname for the Lone Ranger, Kemo Sabe, means 'faithful friend'.
Fact: In Apache *Kemo Sabe* means 'white shirt', and in Navaho it means 'soggy shrub'. But George Trendle, who created the Lone Ranger, didn't know that. He took the name from a summer camp he went to as a boy.

It takes about 10 kilos of milk to make half a kilo of butter.

Myth: The artist Vincent van Gogh cut off his entire ear.
Fact: The famous episode followed two months of hard work, hard drinking and an argument with his best friend and fellow artist, Paul Gauguin. Van Gogh was despondent and cut off only a small part of his earlobe.

Myth: Hens cannot lay eggs without a rooster.
Fact: Almost all eggs we buy are unfertile eggs, laid by hens with no help from a rooster.

Myth: More women in the U.S. have had face lifts than any other type of cosmetic surgery.
Fact: 'Fraid not. The cosmetic surgery performed most frequently on women in the U.S. is liposuction. The second most popular process is collagen injections.

Myth: John F. Kennedy is one of many presidents buried in Arlington National Cemetery in Virginia.
Fact: Actually, there are only three. William Howard Taft (27th president) and Woodrow Wilson (28th president) are the others.

Myth: The largest pyramid in the world is in Egypt.
Fact: The Quetzalcoatl pyramid southeast of Mexico City is 54 metres tall, with a base covering 18 hectares and a volume of 3.4 million cubic metres. Cheops, the largest in Egypt, though originally 147 metres tall, has a base covering only 5.26 hectares and a volume of only 2.5 million cubic metres.

Myth: Giraffes have more vertebrae in their necks than any other mammals.
Fact: They're the same as the rest of us. Although giraffes have the longest neck of any animal – 3 to 4 metres – they have the same number of vertebrae as all mammals, including humans. The giraffe's neck bones are farther apart, though.

Myth: Air fresheners remove offending odours from the air.
Fact: Not even close. Actually, they either cover smells up with a stronger scent, or make your nose numb so you can't smell the bad stuff. The only way you can get *rid* of odours is with expensive absorption agents like charcoal or silica gel.

LOVE POTION No. 9

People have been looking for aphrodisiacs since the beginning of recorded time. Most of the concoctions they've come up with are pretty weird and basically worthless. But some, it turns out, may actually work.

ORIGIN OF THE TERM

The word *aphrodisiac* comes from Aphrodite, the Greek goddess of love and beauty (also known as *Kallipygos*, or 'Beautiful Buttocks' in Greek).

• Aphrodite was originally supposed to be the embodiment of pure beauty and heavenly love. But over the years she came to represent great prowess in sexuality and seduction as well.

• Eventually, according to the *Dictionary of Word and Phrase Origins*, her name was used 'to describe any drug or other substances used to heighten one's amatory desires'.

APHRODISIACS IN HISTORY

As sex therapist Dr. Ruth Westheimer says – and history proves – 'an aphrodisiac is anything you think it is'.

• In the Middle Ages people believed that 'eating an apple soaked in your lover's armpit is a sure means of seduction'. Others drank the urine of powerful animals to increase sexual powers.

• A 15th-century Middle Eastern book entitled *The Perfumed Garden for the Soul's Delectation* suggested that lovers eat a sparrow's tongue, and chase it down with a cocktail made of honey, 20 almonds and parts of a pine tree.

• People once thought that eating any plant that looks phallic would increase male virility – carrots, asparagus and mandrake root were especially popular. Bulbs and tubers – e.g., onions – which people thought resembled testicles, were also believed to increase sexual potency, And peaches, tomatoes, mangoes, or other soft, moist fruits were considered aphrodisiacs for women.

• In *Consuming Passions*, Peter Farb and George Armelagos write that during the 1500s and 1600s, 'Europe was suddenly flooded with exotic plants whose very strangeness suggested the existence of secret powers'. For example:

> Tomatoes brought back from South America were at first thought to be the forbidden fruit of Eden, and were known as 'love apples'. And when potatoes first

> arrived in Europe – the sweet potato probably brought back by Columbus and the white potato somewhat later – they were immediately celebrated as potent sexual stimulants....A work dated 1850 tells the English reader that the white potato will 'incite to Venus'.

• In the 20th century, everything from green M&Ms to products like Cleopatra Oil and Indian Love Powder have been passed off as aphrodisiacs. Even in 1989, a British mail-order firm called Comet Scientific was offering an aerosol spray that it claimed made men 'irresistible to women'.

DANGEROUS APHRODISIACS

• Spanish fly, one of the most famous aphrodisiacs, is also one of the most dangerous. It has nothing to do with Spain or flies. It's really the dried, crushed remains of an insect known as the 'blister beetle'. Although it can constrict blood vessels, and thus may appear to be a sexual stimulant, it's actually a deadly poison. It can do irreparable damage to the kidneys.

• For thousands of years, people (especially in the Far East) have believed that by eating part of a powerful animal, a man can absorb its sexual vitality. This has led to the ingestion of such weird stuff as dried and powdered bear gallbladders, camel humps and rhinoceros horns. (In fact, animal horns have been considered sexual stimulants for so long that the term 'horny' became slang for feeling turned on.) It has also had a drastic effect on some endangered species. *U.S. News & World Report* noted in 1989 that 'with a kilo of rhino horn fetching $42,800 in Taiwan, poachers have slaughtered rhinos so relentlessly that barely 11,000 survive'. And in North America, poachers have killed thousands of black bears to get their golf ball sized gallbladders.

THE REAL THING

Traditionally, scientists have dismissed aphrodisiacs as frauds. But new research into medicinal herbs and pheromones (chemical messengers) has produced some interesting results. Experts now believe that some aphrodisiacs may really work. Here are seven 'maybe's'.

1. Yohimbe: The bark of a West African tree thought for centuries to produce passion in African men. Research has found that the chemical yohimbine can in fact excite men by increasing blood flow. The drug was approved by America's Federal Drug Administration in the 1990s as a treatment for impotence.

2. Oysters: Traditionally considered an aphrodisiac because of their association with the sea and their resemblance to female sex organs. However, now we also know that they're very rich in zinc – a mineral necessary to male sexual health. A man deficient in zinc is at high risk for infertility and loss of libido.

3. Chocolate: Contains PEA, a neurotransmitter that is a natural form of the stimulant amphetamine. It has been shown that either love or lust increases the level of PEA in the bloodstream and that with heartbreak, the levels drop automatically.

4. Caffeine: Research has shown that coffee drinkers are more sexually active than non-drinkers, but no one's sure if that's because of something in the caffeine, or just because it keeps people awake, and therefore interested, after bedtime.

5. DHEA: This hormone has been called the 'natural aphrodisiac' by doctors. It's been shown in studies that blood levels of DHEA predict sexual thoughts and desire. DHEA became a food-supplement fad when it was hyped in the media as a way to increase energy and maybe even prevent cancer or heart disease (as well as boosting the libido).

6. Cinnamon: According to Dr. Alan Hirsch, director of the Smell and Taste Research Foundation, the aroma of cinnamon has the ability to arouse lust. As reported in *Psychology Today*, 'Hirsch fitted male medical students with gauges that detected their excitement level, and then exposed them to dozens of fragrances. The only one that got a rise was the smell of hot cinnamon buns'.

7. Androstenone: This is a pheromone. Scientists conducting research with animals found that androstenone produced by boars had a very positive effect on the sexual receptivity of sows. Androstenone is also found in human sweat.

FINAL THOUGHT

'Power is the great aphrodisiac'.
– Henry Kissinger

Brain food: you can think 625 thoughts on the caloric energy of one Corn Flake.

WHAT HAPPENED AT ROSWELL?

The 'incident at Roswell' is probably the biggest UFO story in history. Was it a military balloon…or an alien spacecraft? You be the judge…

THE FIRST FLYING SAUCERS

In 1947, a U.S Forest Service pilot name Kenneth Arnold was flying over the Cascade Mountains in Washington State in search of a missing plane when he spotted what he claimed were nine 'disc-shaped craft'. He calculated them to be moving at speeds of nearly 2,000 kilometers per hour, far faster than any human-built aircraft of the 1940s could manage.

When he talked to reporters after the flight, Arnold said the crafts moved 'like a *saucer* skipping over water', and a newspaper editor, hearing the description, called the objects 'flying saucers'. Thus, the expression 'flying saucer' entered the English language, and a UFO craze much like the one that followed Orson Welles' 1938 broadcast of *War of the Worlds* swept the country. 'Almost instantly', Dava Sobel writes in her article *The Truth About Roswell*, 'believable witnesses from other states and several countries reported similar sightings, enlivening wire-service dispatches for days'.

THE ROSWELL DISCOVERY

It was in this atmosphere that William 'Mac' Brazel made an unusual discovery. On 8 July, 1947, while riding across his ranch 42 kilometres outside of Roswell, New Mexico, he came across some mysterious wreckage – sticks, foil paper, tape and other debris. Brazel had never seen anything like it, but UFOs were on his mind. He'd read about Arnold's sighting in the newspaper and had heard about a national contest offering $3,000 to anyone who recovered a flying saucer. He wondered if he'd stumbled across just the kind of evidence the contest organizers were looking for.

Brazel gathered a few pieces of the stuff and showed it to his neighbours, Floyd and Loretta Proctor. The Proctors didn't know what it was, either. And neither did George Wilcox, the county sheriff. So Brazel contacted officials at the nearby Roswell Army

Air Force base to see if they could help.

The next day, an Army Intelligence Officer named Jesse Marcel went out to Brazel's ranch to have a look. He was as baffled as everyone else. 'I saw…small bits of metal', he recalled to reporters years later, 'but mostly we found some material that's hard to describe'. Some of it 'looked very much like parchment' and some of it consisted of square sticks as much as 1.2 metres long. Much of it was metallic.

The stuff was also surprisingly light – Brazel later estimated that all the scraps together didn't weigh more than 2.3 kilograms. Marcel and his assistant had no trouble loading all the debris into their cars and driving it back to the Roswell base. The next day, Marcel took it to another base, in Fort Worth, Texas, where it was examined further.

SUSPICIOUS FACTS

Was the Wreckage from Outer Space?

• Brazel and the Proctors examined some of the debris before surrendering it to the military. Although it seemed flimsy at first, it was extremely resilient. 'We tried to burn it, but it wouldn't ignite', Loretta recalls. 'We tried to cut it and scrape at it, but a knife wouldn't touch it….It looked like wood or plastic, but back then we didn't have plastic. Back then, we figured it doesn't look like a weather balloon. I don't think it was something from this Earth'.

The Military's About-Face

• The morning after the military took possession of the wreckage, the media relations officer at Roswell hand-delivered a press release to the two radio stations and newspapers in town. The release stated that the object found in Brazel's field was a 'flying disc', which in the 1940s was synonymous with 'flying saucer'. It was the first time in history that the U.S. military had ever made such a claim.

• A few hours later, though, the military changed its story. It issued a new press release claiming that the wreckage was that of a weather balloon carrying a radar target, not a 'flying disc'. But it was too late – the newspaper deadline had already passed. They ran the first news release on the front page, under the headline:

AIR FORCE CAPTURES FLYING SAUCER
ON RANCH IN ROSWELL REGION

A light-year (the distance light travels in a year) is about 6 trillion miles.

Other newspapers picked up the story and ran it as well; within 24 hours, news of the military's 'capture' spread around the globe.

• Interest in the story was so great that the next day, Brig. Gen. Roger Ramey, commander of the U.S. Eighth Air Force, had to hold a press conference in Fort Worth in which he again stated that the recovered object was only a weather balloon and a radar target that was suspended from it. He even displayed the wreckage for reporters and allowed them to photograph it.

Mr. Brazel's Unusual Behaviour

• Mac Brazel refused to talk about the incident for the rest of his life, even with members of his immediate family, except to say that 'whatever the wreckage was, it wasn't any type of balloon'. Why the silence? His son Bill explains: 'The Air Force asked him to take an oath that he wouldn't tell anybody in detail about it. My dad was such a guy that he went to his grave and he *never* told anyone'.

• Kevin Randle and Donald Schmitt, authors of *UFO Crash at Roswell*, claim that shortly after Brazel made his famous discovery, 'His neighbours noticed a change in his lifestyle... He suddenly seemed to have more money...When he returned, he drove a new pickup truck...he also had the money to buy a new house in Tularosa, New Mexico, and a meat locker in Las Cruces'. Randle and Schmitt believe the military may have paid Brazel handsomely for his silence.

TRUST ME

Today, if a government announced it had captured a UFO – even if it was mistaken – and tried to change its story a few hours later by claiming it was really a weather balloon, nobody would believe it. But people were more trusting in the years just following World War II. Amazingly, the story died away. As Dava Sobel writes:

> The Army's announcement of the 'weather balloon' explanation ended the flying saucer excitement. All mention of the craft dropped from the newspapers, from military records, from the national consciousness, and even from the talk of the town in Roswell.

Even the *Roswell Daily Record* – which broke the story in the first place – was satisfied with the military's explanation. A few days later, it ran a headline that was even bigger than the first one:

GENERAL RAMEY EMPTIES ROSWELL SAUCER

THE NAKED TRUTH

Here's a BRI collection of 'Nudes in the News'.

THE NAKED USHERETTE

RIO DE JANEIRO, Brazil – 'During a screening of *The Exorcist* at La Pampa Cinema in 1974, the audience was distracted by an usherette scampering backward and forward across the screen pursuing a rat with a mop. To cries of "Get 'em off!" she started to disrobe. It was while dancing naked in front of the screen that she noticed the auditorium being cleared by armed police. Explaining her behaviour, the usherette said later: "I thought the audience was calling for me. I was as surprised as anyone"'.

– *Star Billing,* by David Brown

WHAT, NO DERBYS?

SEDGLEY, England – 'Last May, police investigated claims that smartly dressed men were stripping off their suits and dancing naked in woodland near Penn Common, on the edge of the Black Country. "We just do not know what these men are up to", said Superintendent Malcolm Gough.

'"It's been going on and off for about a year now, although it seems to stop after November", said resident Judy Bardburn. She added: "People who have seen them say that all they wear are black shoes and black socks"'.

– *Fortean Times*

COUNTRY COMFORT

NASHVILLE, Tennessee – 'When singer-songwriter Kristi Lockwood said she was looking for a little exposure, she meant it.

'Wearing only cowboy boots and a cowboy hat...Lockwood strolled down the city's famous Music Row, stunning other onlookers.

'"Yeah, I saw Lady Godiva walking around", said George McLain, who works at a recording company. "She looked at us, and said 'Hi guys'. It was pretty amazing".

'The singer admitted she was doing it all for the publicity. She said she'd been in Nashville for three years, "working real hard on

In the 1600s in Europe, 'fashion' wigs were often made of plaster of Paris.

my voice and getting good feedback on my songs, but nobody was paying much attention".

'The police did. After getting a few calls, they found Lockwood, covered her, cited her for indecent exposure, and took her home'.

– *Nashville Banner*, 15 February, 1996

GENERAL BUTT NAKED

MONROVIA, Liberia – 'In the annals of Liberia's civil war, nothing tops the tale of Gen. Butt Naked. Nude except for lace-up leather shoes and a gun, the general would lead his Butt Naked Battalion – which was famed for its fearlessness and brutality – into battle. Why no clothes? The general says he believed "it ensured protection from his enemies".

'As the war wound down, so did Gen. Butt Naked's commitment to kill, until he gave it up and became an evangelical preacher. Today he wears a suit and tie as he roams the battered capital with a microphone preaching peace and reconciliation'.

– Wire service reports, 3 August, 1997

NAKED LUNCH

MELBOURNE, Australia – 'Daring shoppers escaped the heat by taking off their clothes today in an Australian music store. About 50 patrons crowded Gaslight Music for its annual Nude Day promotion.

'The nude customers won free compact discs and were served buffet lunch by a waiter and waitress and entertained by a pianist and an orator, all wearing only a smile…as the media looked on'.

– *Reuters News Service*, 18 October, 1994

NAKED LUNCH II

STOCKHOLM, Sweden – 'A tourist in Stockholm could not catch the restaurant waiter's eyes, so he stepped outside, took all his clothes off and reentered, shouting: "You Swedes only pay attention to nudes. Now will you serve me?" He was arrested for indecent behaviour'.

– *The World's Greatest Mistakes*, by Steve Brummett

THE DANCING MARQUESS

The history of Britain's aristocracy is littered with odd tales of barking mad ne'er-do-wells. And here's one of them...

Almost lost to history is one of the most flamboyant figures in the annals of aristocracy: Henry Cyril Paget, the Fifth Marquess of Anglesey (1875-1905). After leading a dissolute life dedicated to the pursuit of pleasure, his successors sought to erase Henry's life and memory from the history books. Fortunately, they didn't quite succeed.

TOO MUCH OF A GOOD THING

The grandson of Sir Henry William 'One Leg' Paget, the general who famously had his leg blown off while talking to Wellington at Waterloo, Henry inherited a huge fortune while still in his twenties. Within four years he had blown the lot, and in 1905 died in Monaco, burnt out and bankrupt from his excesses. But it wasn't wine, women and song that did it for Henry – it was amateur dramatics! Within four short years he managed to fritter away today's equivalent of £50 million on his love for the theatre.

AN ACTOR'S LIFE FOR ME

Henry's family seat was at Plas Newydd, in Angelsey, just down the road from Llanfairpwllgwyngyllgogerychwyrndrobwllllantysiliogogogoch, the village with Britain's longest place name. The Paget home had its own 18th-century chapel, which Henry wasted no time in converting into a small theatre when he inherited the place in 1901.

Henry had been raised mostly in France, among theatre people, and grew up with a passion for treading the boards. But it would be safe to say that Henry's artistic vision was not exactly conventional. Displaying a taste for stage wear that would make Liberace blush, Henry liked his productions to be big, brash and beautiful. Typically, there would be casts of 50 or 60 performers, all elaborately kitted out in hand-made, jewel-encrusted designer costumes. One costume for a production of *Henry V*, for example,

In Italy, James Bond is known as 'Mr. Kiss-Kiss-Bang-Bang'.

cost £40,000 – that's around £4 million pounds in today's prices. Eat your heart out Elton John!

LORD OF THE DANCE

Light opera was Henry's forte. As well as staging shows at Plas Newydd, Henry also paid for his productions (starring himself, naturally) to tour Britain and the Continent – at enormous expense. His favourite piece was *Aladdin*. During the interval of this particular production, Henry would appear on stage and perform his famous 'Butterfly Dance', resplendent in bejewelled costume complete with silky, gossamer-light wings. Henry was probably called many things by his contemporaries, but this particular act earned him the nickname 'The Dancing Marquess'.

In one rare picture of Henry in full costume, you get some idea of the kind of figure he cut: there he sits, one white stockinged leg provocatively exposed from beneath a plush, striped cape; giant, gilded shoulderpads, worthy of Joan Collins in her *Dynasty* prime; all topped-off by a kind of jewel-encrusted crash helmet – with wings sprouting out from the sides. Add to this Henry's sultry pout, just visible beneath his luxuriant handlebar moustache, and he resembles nothing less than an Edwardian Freddie Mercury.

EXIT, STAGE LEFT

Not surprisingly, Henry's louche lifestyle didn't endear him to his family – especially his habit of squandering the family millions on some of the most expensive clothing ever made. When Henry died in Monaco in 1905 (the cause of death is not known), his successor as Marquess of Angelsey straight away set about erasing his ancestor from history. The theatre at Plas Newydd was converted back into a chapel, and all of Henry's correspondence, diaries, itineraries and theatrical plans were destroyed. It was an ignominious end for such a flamboyant character. But it seems he just wasn't made for the times in which he lived. Although Henry was much loved by his staff and in his local village, one newspaper obituary more accurately summed up the general feeling of the day when it concluded: 'His example will remain one of the strongest arguments against our hereditary system that the most ardent revolutionary would wish for.'

As a boy, young Ian Fleming also gave his mother the nickname 'M'.

YOU CALL *THAT* ART?

It's interesting to study the paintings of the great masters – but sometimes it's even more fun to study the work of the great fakers. Like these people.

HANS VAN MEEGEREN

Background: At the end of World War II, Dutch authorities began investigating the sale of Dutch national treasures to Nazi officials. They learned that Hans Van Meegeren, a struggling Dutch artist, had sold a priceless 17th-century Vermeer called *Christ and the Adulteress* to Nazi leader Hermann Goering for £156,000. Once the painting was repossessed and authenticated as a work painted during Vermeer's 'middle period', Van Meegeren was arrested and charged with collabourating with the Nazis – a crime punishable by death.

The Truth: Van Meegeren defended himself by saying that there was no Vermeer 'middle period', and that he had faked all six of the paintings attributed to those years of the artist's life. Van Meegeren also claimed to have painted two works by Dieter de Hoochs, and one by Terborch.

The judge didn't believe him. But to be sure, he sent the artist back to his studio [under guard] and told him to 'paint another Vermeer'. Van Meegeren quickly created something he called *The Young Christ Teaching at the Temple*. It was, by all appearances, painted in the style of Vermeer.

What Happened: The judge dropped the treason charges. But as each of the paintings Van Meegeren took credit for were tested and proven to be fakes, he was arrested again – this time for forgery and fraud. He was convicted and sentenced to a year in prison; he died from a heart attack one month after the trial.

DAVID STEIN

Background: In the mid-60s, a 31-year-old art collector named David Stein walked into the shop of one of New York's top art dealers with three watercolour paintings by Russian painter Marc Chagall. The dealer bought all three for $10,000.

The Truth: Stein had painted all three 'Chagalls' that morning before lunch. He made the new canvases look old by soaking them in Lipton's tea, and forged letters of authentication at the frame shop while waiting for the paintings to be framed.

What Happened: As Stein put it, 'I should have stuck to dead men'. By pure coincidence, Marc Chagall happened to be in New York that very same day...and the art dealer who bought the paintings had an appointment to meet with him. The dealer brought the paintings to the meeting, and Chagall immediately denounced them as fakes. Stein was arrested and spent nearly four years in American and French prisons. But the case was such a boost to his reputation that when he got out of prison, he was able to make a living from his own original paintings.

PAVEL JERDANOWICH

Background: In the spring of 1925, the Russian-born Jerdanowich submitted a painting called *Exaltation* to a New York art exhibition. The red and green colours were unusual for the period, and the face of the woman in the painting was distorted, but art critics admired the work, and Jerdanowich was invited to exhibit at a New York show in 1926. He did – this time displaying a painting called *Aspiration* and explaining that he was the founder of the 'Disumbrationist' school of painting. The following year, he showed two more paintings, *Adoration* and *Illumination*. Jerdanowich's groundbreaking work caused a storm, and he was hailed as a visionary.

The Truth: 'Pavel Jerdanowich' was actually Paul Jordan Smith, a Latin scholar who hated abstract and modernist trends in art. When an art critic criticized his wife's realistic paintings as 'definitely of the old school' in 1925, he set out to prove that critics would praise any painting they couldn't understand. 'I asked my wife for paint and canvas', he recounted after admitting the hoax. 'I'd never tried to paint anything in my life'. The Disumbrationist School was born.

What Happened: Smith admitted the ruse to the *Los Angles Times* in 1927, but the confession only fuelled interest in his work. A Chicago gallery owner displayed the paintings in 1928, and later called the show 'the most widely noticed exhibition I have ever heard of'.

The most costumes ever used for one film: 32,000 – for Quo Vadis in 1951.

HAR-HAR! RAH-RAH!

Palindromes are phrases or sentences that are spelled the same way backward or forward. Some people spend their whole lives making new ones up. Here are some of Uncle John's favourites.

A dog! A panic in a pagoda!

I'm a boob, am I?

Dog doo! Good god!

'Do orbits all last'? I brood.

Ed, I saw Harpo Marx ram Oprah W. aside.

An admirer! I'm Dana!

Oh no! Don Ho!

Emil, a sleepy baby, peels a lime.

Party boobytrap.

He spots one last sale. No stops, eh?

Neil, an alien.

Go hang a salami! I'm a lasagna hog!

Tarzan raised Desi Arnaz' rat.

All erotic, I lose solicitor Ella.

Madame, not one man is self-less; I name not one, Madam.

Ron, I'm a minor.

Stressed was I ere I saw desserts.

So, Ed, I vow to do two videos.

Yo! Bozo boy!

Wonton? Not now.

Sis, ask Costner to not rent socks 'as is'.

Cigar? Toss it in a can, it is so tragic.

Too far, Edna, we wander afoot.

Diana saw I was an aid.

Mad? Am I, madam?

Angola balogna.

Tennis set won, now Tess in net.

Stella wondered: 'No wallets'?

Star comedy: Democrats.

I Love Me, vol. I

Now, Ned, I am a maiden won!

Ma is a nun, as I am.

Did I do, O God, did I as I said I'd do? Good, I did!

Amoral aroma.

Alan Alda stops race car, spots ad: 'Lana – L.A'.

CURSES AGAIN!

We've all heard of one curse or another. Usually, we laugh about them. But perhaps sometimes there's a good reason for believing.

THE CURSE OF TOSCA

Curse: Nasty things happen to actors during performances of this opera.

Origin: Unknown, but productions have been plagued with problems at least as far back as the 1920s.

Among Its Victims:

• During a production in New York in the 1920s, the knife with which Tosca 'murdered' Scarpia at the end of Act II failed to retract. Singer Antonio Scotti was stabbed.

• In 1965 at Covent Garden, Maria Callas' hair caught fire while she was singing the title role. It had to be put out by a quick-thinking Tito Gobbi, who was playing Scarpia.

• In a production in Rome in 1965, Gionni Raimondi's face was scorched during the firing squad scene.

• In 1993, Elisabeth Knighton Printy jumped off the wrong side of the stage in St. Paul, Minnesota, and plunged more than 9 metres to the ground, breaking both her legs.

Status: Ongoing. Last reported incident was in 1995, when Fabio Armiliatu, starring in a Roman production, was hit in the leg by debris from blanks fired in the execution scene. He was taken off in a stretcher. Two weeks later he returned to the stage; he fell and broke his other leg in two places while standing in the wings at the end of the first act.

THE *SPORTS ILLUSTRATED* JINX

Curse: If you appear on the cover of America's *Sports Illustrated* magazine, you're in for a slump or a defeat.

Origin: Unknown. For decades, sports stars have claimed that making *SI's* cover was the fastest way to a slump in form.

Among its Victims:

• Studying the records of 58 baseball players going back to 1955 (because there are sufficient records to check in baseball), researchers found that 'there was a distinct tendency for batting performance to decline...about 50 points from immediately before appearing on the cover until three weeks after the appearance'.

Status: Scientists say that if there is anything to the *SI* jinx, it's because it spooks players and thus is self-fulfilling. Also: 'This extra attention and effort might cause more injuries, fatigue, or other interruptions to the hitter's natural flow, with the result that performance suffers'.

THE OSCAR CURSE

Curse: Winning the gold statuette can ruin, rather than help, an actor's career.

Origin: Luise Rainer won back-to-back Oscars for *The Great Zeigfield* (1936) and *The Good Earth* (1937). Two years and five horrible movies later, she was considered a has-been. Hollywood columnist Louella Parsons wrote that it was 'the Oscar curse'. Parsons said her Ouija board had warned, 'Beware, beware, the Oscar will get you if you don't watch out'.

Among its Victims:

• Rita Morena and George Chakiris (Best Supporting Actor and Actress, 1961, *West Side Story)*. Disappeared from films after winning.

• Richard Dreyfuss (Best actor, 1978, *The Goodbye Girl)*. His weight rose to 82 kilograms, he stopped bathing, and he started bingeing on booze and drugs.

• Michael Cimino (Best Director, 1979, *The Deer Hunter)*. Followed Oscar with three losers: *Heaven's Gate*, *Year of the Dragon* and *The Sicilian*.

• Linda Hunt (Best Supporting Actress, 1983, *The Year of Living Dangerously)*. Last seen in the short-lived sci-fi TV series, *Space Rangers*.

Status: Considered credible in Hollywood. High expectations that can't always be fulfilled accompany an Oscar. It's also attributed to salary demands, type-casting, greedy agents or studio bosses, and stars who believe their own press and become hard to work with.

A: Walt Disney – 20 statuettes, 12 plaques and certificates.

WORD GEOGRAPHY

A few more words that were derived from the names of real places.

SUEDE
From: Sweden
Explanation: *Gants de Suede* is French for 'gloves of Sweden'. It was in Sweden that the first leather was buffed to a fine softness, and the French bought the *gants de Suede*. Suede now refers to the buffing processes – not to any particular kind of leather.

TURKEY
From: Turkey
Explanation: *Turk* means 'strength' in Turkish. The turkey bird is a large European fowl named after the country of its origin. American colonists mistakenly thought that a big bird they found in the New World was the same animal – so they called it a turkey

CHEAP
From: Cheapside, a market in London
Explanation: The Old English word was *ceap* (pronounced 'keep'), which meant 'to sell or barter'. Because *Cheapside* was a major market where people went to barter for low prices, the word gradually took on a new pronunciation…and meaning.

MAYONNAISE
From: Port Mahon, Spain (according to legend)
Explanation: The *-aise* suffix is French for 'native to' or 'originating in'. *Mahonnaise* was supposedly created to celebrate a 1756 French battle victory over the British on the Spanish isle of Port Mahon.

COFFEE
From: Kaffa, Ethiopia
Explanation: According to legend, coffee beans were first discovered in the town of Kaffia. By the thirteenth century, the Kaffa beans had travelled, becoming *qahwah* in Arabia, *café* in Europe, and finally *coffee* in the New World.

Most-performed rock song in history: 'You've Lost That Lovin' Feeling'.

COLOGNE
From: Cologne, Germany
Explanation: Scented water that was produced there beginning in 1709 was named for the city.

DENIM
From: Nimes, France
Explanation: The tough cloth used in jeans was also made in Nimes. It was called *serge di Nimes* – later shortened to *di nimes*, which became *denim*.

SLAVE
From: Slavonia, Yugoslavia
Explanation: After large parts of Slavonia were subjugated by Europeans in the Middle Ages, a *Slav* become synonomous with someone who lived in servitude. Eventually *Slav* became *Slave*.

LIMERICK
From: Limerick, Ireland
Explanation: The town was popularly associated with humorous verses that had five lines, the first two rhyming with the last, the middle two rhyming with each other. The poems became an English fad in the mid-19th century, and people naturally identified them with the town's name.

HAMBURGER
From: Hamburg, Germany
Explanation: People in the immigration-port city of Hamburg – called Hamburgers – liked to eat raw meat with salt, pepper and onion-juice seasoning, a treat brought to them via Russia that we call *steak tartare* today. A grilled version using minced meat eventually became popular in America.

TURQUOISE
From: Turkey/Europe
Explanation: Another Turkish origin. Turquoise comes from a number of places, but was probably first imported to Europe from Turkey. So it was called *turquoise*, which means 'Turkish stone'.

OH, WHAT A TANGLED WEB

Some cultures consider the spider a sign of good luck: 'If you wish to live and thrive, let a spider run alive'. This old English rhyme may be a recognition of the important role spiders play in insect control. In fact, that's what webs – those amazingly beautiful tapestries strung between branches, leaves, doorways, etc. – are for. They're deadly traps. Here's some info on the spider webs to make them even more interesting.

WEB CONSTRUCTION

- Only about half of all spiders spin webs.
- All spider webs are made of silk.
- Although it's only about .003 millimetres in diameter, a spider's silk is stronger than steel of equal diameter. It is more elastic than nylon, more difficult to break than rubber, and is bacteria and fungi resistant.
- These qualities explain why at one time web was used to pack wounds to help mend them and stop bleeding.
- Spiders have 1–6 kinds of spinning glands, each producing a different type of silk. For instance, the cylindrical gland produces silk used for egg sacs (males often lack this) and the aciniform gland produces silk used for wrapping prey. Some spiders have glands that produce very fine silk. They comb and tease the fine strands until it's like velcro – tiny loops and hooks which entrap insect feet.
- Silk is extruded through special pores called *spinneretes* which consist of different sized 'spigots'. Silk starts out as a liquid. As the liquid silk contacts the air, it hardens. The spider may need different silk for different purposes. By changing how fast the liquid is extruded or by using a different silk gland, it can control the strength and quality of the silk.
- Why doesn't a spider get stuck on its own web? The spider weaves in non-sticky silk strands and only walks on those. Also, spiders have a special oil on their legs which keeps them from sticking.

The average lightning bolt is only two centimetres in diameter.

THE WELL-BRED SPIDER

• A spider can often be identified by the type of web it weaves. The ability to weave is inherited, so specific types of spiders build specific types of webs. In addition, individual spiders sometimes develop a personal style; sort of like a signature.

• The spider is a hunter and its web is a snare, designed to hold its prey. So the design of its web and the place where the spider builds it depends on the kind of insects it is trying to catch.

• The determining factor: there are more insects, especially crawling ones, closer to the ground. Strong flying insects are usually higher, so the web is stronger.

WEB-SPINNERS

There are five different types of webspinners.

Cobweb spiders: (example: black widows)

• Use 'trip lines' to snare prey. From their web, several vertical lines are drawn down and secured tautly to a surface with globs of 'glue'.

• Some unfortunate insect becomes stuck to the glue and breaks the line. The tension of the elastic trip lines, once released, flings the victim up to the spider waiting in its web.

• Cobweb weavers usually build only one web and so, with time, the web becomes tattered and littered with bits of debris.

Sheet-builders: (example: filmy dome spiders)

• Construct a horizontal mat beneath a horizontal trip line, much like a trampoline under an invisible wire.

• Flying or jumping insects that are stopped midair by the line are flung to the net below.

• As the prey struggles to regain its balance, the agile spider pounces and inflicts a deadly bite.

Web-casting spiders: (example: ogre-faced spiders)

• Use 'web snares' much differently than others: Instead of attaching the web to a bush or wall, the spider carries it.

• The spider uses it much like a fishing net and casts it on passing prey. Each night it hunts. Afterwards, it may either tuck the web away until the next day's hunt, or spin a new one.

The single most common object involved in choking is toothpicks.

Angle lines: (example: the bola spider)

• It first suspends itself from a trapeze line and hangs there upside down. Then it sends down a single line baited with a glob of glue.

• When an insect moves by, the bola takes careful aim and casts the line towards the moving insect. If successful, it will reel in its prize.

Orb weavers: (the most familiar webs)

• Spin the largest and strongest webs. Some span more than one metre. Natives of New Guinea and the Solomon Islands used the webs of the orb weaving spiders as fishing nets. They were reportedly strong enough to hold a fish weighing as much as half a kilogram.

• These webs are especially tailored to capture flying insects – which is why they're vertically suspended.

• Orb weavers weave such intricate webs that they are often the focus of behavioural studies. For example: two orb weavers went along on *Sky Lab II* on 28 July, 1973. Researchers were interested to know the effects of zero gravity on weaving. After some adjustments, the spiders were able to weave fairly normal webs. One curious difference: the space webs were symmetrical while earth webs tend to be asymmetrical.

WEB FACTS

Researchers have covered the eyes of web-spinning spiders and discovered that it did not keep them from finding their prey in the web. The secret: a web spinner uses its web as a giant feeler. Based on vibrations it feels in the web, a spider can determine the size and energy of prey, environmental conditions and even the presence of another spider.

• Male spiders of some species use vibrations to communicate to the female. They strum the female's web – and must send just the right vibration to convince the female that they are mates…and not dinner.

F.Y.I.: In old English, the word 'cob' meant spider.

OOPS – FALSE ALARM!

With people so nervous about bomb threats these days, it's inevitable that there are going to be some pretty bizarre false alarms. At the BRI, we've been keeping a file on them. Here's what we've collected so far.

A DRINKING PROBLEM

Background: In 1978, security personnel at Pan American Airlines suspected that either maintenance crews or flight attendants were stealing miniature bottles of booze, which cost 35¢ apiece, from aeroplanes. So they attached a clock device to the drinks cabinet to record the times of the alleged thefts.
False Alarm: 'While airborne', write Nash and Zullo in *The Misfortune 500*, 'a flight attendant heard the ticking and thought it was a bomb. She alerted the captain, who re-routed the plane to the nearest airport, where passengers were quickly evacuated by emergency exits. The unscheduled landing cost Pan Am $15,000'.

DIAL B FOR BOMB

Background: In November 1995, a Royal Jordanian Airlines plane en route to Chicago was forced to land in Iceland when it received a bomb threat.
False Alarm: It turned out that the culprit was a Chicago woman who was trying to keep her mother-in-law, a passenger on the plane, from visiting her.

HIT OR MISSILE

Background: On 17 October,1995, Joanna Ashworth heard a thud outside her Level Plains, Alabama, home. 'She opened the door', reported the local Daleville *News Ledger*, 'and saw a white object sticking out from the roof of the shed behind her home'. It was a 46-centimetre missile. She called the police.

Level Plains officer Lt. Ralph Reed arrived shortly after 6 a.m. and climbed a ladder to look at the missile. He saw markings that could have been military, so he decided to leave it where it was. 'My mother didn't raise no fool', Reed proclaimed. 'I wasn't gonna touch it'.

Reed contacted officials at nearby Fort Rucker, who decided to evacuate people from the area. They closed the roads nearby

and called the bomb squad from Fort Benning in Georgia.
False Alarm: Fort Benning's Ordnance Explosive Detachment (OED) arrived four hours later. For about half an hour, they carefully worked on getting the object out of Ashworth's roof. Then they announced to the press that it was a cardboard model that could be purchased at any toy store.

Local police vowed to get to the bottom of things. 'The investigation is not closed', Lt. Reed said, as the story made national news. A few days later a 14-year-old dropped by the police station to let them know it was his rocket. He'd shot it off at a nearby playground and had been wondering what happened to it.

BRITISH FARCE

Background: According to the *Fortean Times:* 'A suspicious-looking cardboard box was found outside a Territorial Army centre in Bristol in 1993'.
False Alarm: 'The TA called the police, who in turn called an Army bomb-disposal unit, who blew up the box – to find it full of leaflets on how to deal with suspicious-looking packages'.

ANIMAL CRACKERS

Background: On 28 May, 1996, an employee at the Wal-Mart Superstore in Enterprise, Alabama, found a suspicious-looking box in the car park. Police were called. Taking no chances, they roped off the area, then called the bomb squad at Fort Benning, Georgia.
False Alarm: A few hours later, their Ordnance Explosive Detachment (the same ones who showed up in Level Plains) arrived by helicopter. They X-rayed the package and determined that it contained suspicious-looking wires. The store and surrounding area were evacuated. Then the package was blown up. It turned out to contain a dead armadillo.

* * * * *

'My licence plate says PMS. Nobody cuts me off'.

– Wendy Liebman

A horse expends more energy lying down than it does standing up.

RUMOURS: BASED ON A TRUE STORY

Some rumours are straight fiction, but some have a kernel of truth at the core – which makes them a little more believable. Have you heard any of these?

Rumour: After World War II the Japanese renamed one of their cities Usa, so products manufactured there could be exported with labels that read, 'made in USA'.

Hidden fact: There really is a town in Japan called Usa, just as there are Usas in Russia, Tanzania and Mozambique.

The truth: Usa predates the war. The town is very small, so it doesn't show up on every map of the country – which may contribute to the notion that it suddenly 'popped up' out of nowhere. But even if a country wanted to pull such a stunt, U.S. Customs regulations wouldn't allow it: Imported goods must be stamped with the *country* of origin, not the city.

Rumour: In the 1960s the U.S. military forced the recall of *U.S.S. Nautilus* plastic submarine models. The models were so accurate that the government feared Soviet spies would buy them and learn America's submarine secrets.

Hidden fact: In 1961 Vice Admiral Hyman Rickover *did* complain that a model kit of the Polaris nuclear submarine, made by the Revell Toy Company, revealed too much – including detailed floor plans of the engine and missile compartments. (Defence contractors that made the real submarine's missiles even used the models to demonstrate how their weapons systems worked.)

The truth: The military complained...but the model was never recalled. Super-accurate models annoy the military even today. In 1986 the Testor Model Company offered a surprisingly accurate model of the F-19 Stealth fighter – even before the U.S. Air Force acknowledged the plane existed.

A HISTORY OF THE YO-YO

What's it like being in the yo-yo business? They say it has its ups and downs. Here's a brief history of one of the world's most enduring toys.

WHODUNNIT?

• The yo-yo is believed to be the second-oldest toy in the world, after dolls. No one knows for sure when or where it was invented: some think China, others the Philippines.

• Most yo-yo experts agree that a version of the yo-yo was used as a weapon in the Philippines as far back as prehistoric times. Hunters wrapped 6-metre leather straps around heavy pieces of flint and hurled the rock at prey. If a hunter missed, he could pull the rock back and try again. (The name 'yo-yo' comes from a Filipino expression that means 'come come' or 'come back'.)

• Even when it fell into disuse as a weapon, the yo-yo retained an important role in Filipino culture: people used yo-yo contests to settle disputes. Yo-yoing became the national pastime of the islands. 'To this day', says one game historian, 'young, rural Filipinos spend weeks creating their own custom yo-yos out of rare wood or a piece of buffalo horn'.

YO-YOS IN EUROPE

• The ancient Greeks played with yo-yos as far back as 500 B.C. They even portrayed yo-yoers in their art. In *World on a String*, Heliane Zeiger writes that terra-cota yo-yos and a 'piece of decorated pottery showing a youngster in a headband and tunic, playing with a yo-yo – both from the classical period in Greece – are currently on display in the Museum of Athens'.

• 'In 1790', Zeiger continues, 'the yo-yo made its way from the Orient to Europe, where it became popular among the British and French aristocracies...and inherited some new names. In England the yo-yo was known as the *bandalore*, *quiz*, or *Prince of Wales' toy*. (A painting from the 1700s shows King George IV, then Prince of Wales, whirling a bandalore.)'

• 'In France, the yo-yo picked up the nicknames *incroyable*, *l'emigrette*, and *jou-jou*'. One contemporary account of the French

Among other things, ancient Egyptian embalmers preserved mummies with cinnamon.

Revolution notes that several French noblemen were seen yo-yoing in the carts hauling them off to the guillotine'. And Napoleon's soldiers amused themselves by fiddling with yo-yos between battles.

Coming to America

Bandalores appeared in the United States in the 19th century. For about 100 years, they occasionally popped up as local fads in areas on the East Coast…then faded in popularity each time. They never disappeared completely but didn't attain greater success until the early 20th century.

ENTER DONALD DUNCAN

The turning point for the yo-yo came in 1928, when a businessman named Donald Duncan happened to see Pedro Flores, owner of the Flores Yo-Yo Corporation, demonstrating yo-yos in front of his store. Duncan was impressed with the huge crowds that had gathered to watch the tricks. He estimated that a mass-produced yo-yo, if heavily promoted, would make a lot of money – so in 1929 he and Flores began manufacturing yo-yos on a larger scale. A year later Duncan bought Flores out for $25,000 and renamed the company after himself.

No Strings Attached

Yo-yo historians disagree on whether Flores or Duncan deserves credit for the innovation, but the yo-yos that Duncan manufactured in 1929 boasted an important new feature: the yo-yo string was looped loosely *around* the axle (the centre post between the two halves of the yo-yo), rather than being firmly secured to it. This allowed a Duncan Yo-Yo to spin freely at the end of the string. It transformed the yo-yo from a device that could only to up and down to one that could perform an endless number of tricks.

Duncan started out with just one model – the O-Boy Yo-Yo Top – but by the early 1930s had a whole line of yo-yo products… and a trademark on the name 'yo-yo'. Legally, his company was the only one in the United States that could call its toy a yo-yo.

SALES HYPE

But it took more than a technical innovation to make the yo-yo a national fad. It took promotion – and Duncan was a promotional genius. He immediately created…

• **The 'Yo-Yo Champion'.** Many Filipinos living in the United States had played with yo-yos since they were kids. Duncan hired 42 of them (including his former business partner, Pedro Flores), gave them each the title 'Champion', and sent them on tour to demonstrate yo-yos all over the country. At its peak, the company had one demonstrator on the road for every 100,000 people in America.

• **The yo-yo contest.** To drum up local support, Duncan sponsored neighbourhood yo-yo contests all over the country, awarding new yo-yos, 'All American Yo-Yo Sweaters', baseballs, gloves, bicycles, and other prizes to winners.

HELP FROM HEARST

But Duncan's most productive effort came one afternoon in 1929, when he walked uninvited into the San Simeon mansion of newspaper press baron William Randolph Hearst, talked his way past the butler, and made a quick sales pitch to Hearst, telling him how he could use yo-yo contests to boost newspaper circulation.

Duncan's idea was simple: Hearst's newspapers would publicize his yo-yo competitions, and in exchange for the free publicity, Duncan would require all entrants to sell three Hearst newspaper subscriptions as the price of admission to the contests. Hearst knew a good idea – and a good product – when he saw one. He took Duncan up on the offer. The promotions worked; in 1931, for example, one month-long effort in Philadelphia helped sell three million yo-yos.

Picture Perfect

To make newspaper coverage of his product as exciting as possible, Duncan arranged to photograph as many actors, professional athletes and other celebrities playing with yo-yos as he could. He got lucky: two of the first stars who agreed to the photos were Douglas Fairbanks and Mary Pickford – then Hollywood's biggest stars. Their superstar status guaranteed that other celebrities would enthusiastically follow suit.

Some celebrity endorsements went beyond mere photographs: he got Bob Hope to perform yo-yo tricks for U.S. troops during World War II, and talked a young singer named Bing Crosby into singing promotional songs for the company, including this one:

What is the dearest thing on earth,
that fills my soul with joy and mirth? My yo-yo.
What keeps my senses in a whirl,
and makes me break dates with my best girl? My yo-yo.

THAT'S A LOT OF YO-YOS

These promotional efforts paid off. By the early 1930s, annual sales had shot from thousands of yo-yos to millions. The yo-yo craze spread all over the world. Demand became so great that in 1946 Duncan had to build a huge plant in Luck, Wisconsin, to keep up. The factory could turn out 3,600 yo-yos an hour – but at times Duncan still couldn't fill all the orders…even running the plant 24 hours a day.

Still, long-term sales were unpredictable. In boom years, the demand for yo-yos was insatiable. Other years, the demand declined by as much as 90 per cent.

UPS AND DOWNS

The biggest yo-yo craze in history took place in the 1960s. In 1962 alone, according to news reports, 45 million were sold in America – despite the fact that there were only 40 million kids in the country. This should have been the Duncan Yo-Yo Company's finest hour – but it was their undoing. Why?

1. To meet the demand, they expanded and got too far into debt.

2. They stuck with wood when they should have switched to plastic. Wood had to dry for as long as six months, so they couldn't increase production fast enough.

3. They lost their 'yo-yo' trademark. There was so much money to be made selling yo-yos that competitors challenged the trademark in court. As proof that the term had become generic, they pointed to a billboard Duncan itself had erected near its factory: *Welcome to Luck, Wisconsin, Yo-yo Capital of the World.* If there was a yo-yo *capital*, that must mean yo-yos were made elsewhere, too. In 1962 a Federal Court of Appeals ruled that the trademark was invalid because the word yo-yo was the name of the toy itself.

These problems, combined with increasing costs and competition from Frisbees, skateboards and other toys, sent the company into a tailspin. In 1965 the Duncan Co. filed for bankruptcy.

The world's oceans have risen an average of six inches in the past 100 years.

Three years later, the Flambeau Plastics Corporation bought the rights to the Duncan name and began cranking out plastic yo-yos. The Duncan name survives to this day (its yo-yos still have an 80 per cent to 85 per cent market share), and yo-yo fads still come and go; Donald Duncan, Jr. is even still in the business, producing yo-yos for the educational market under the name Playmaxx. But for purists, the end of the era came in 1965.

YO-YO FACTS

• Donald Duncan applied his promotional genius to other products: he also invented the Eskimo Pie, originated the Good Humour ice cream truck, co-patented the first four-wheel hydraulic automobile brake, and was the first person to successfully market the parking meter to cities and towns. (At one point, his parking meter company manufactured 80 per cent of all meters in the United States.)

• In the early 1900s Hubert Meyer of Toledo, Ohio, patented an edible yo-yo.

• The Lego company built yo-yos for sale in the 1930s, but like Duncan, it sometimes found itself with huge inventories and low demand. One year it had so many unsold yo-yos in its warehouses that it sawed them in half and used them for wheels on toy trucks and cars.

• In 1984 astronaut David Griggs brought a yo-yo on board the Space Shuttle as part of NASA's 'Toys in Space' experiments. His finding: yo-yos don't 'sleep' in space – they just reach the end of their string and bounce right back up.

• The world's record for yo-yoing was set by John Winslow of Gloucester, Virginia. He started on 23 November, 1977 and didn't stop for five days – 120 hours.

• The world's largest yo-yo, Big-Yo, is 127 cm tall and 80 cm wide, and weighs 115 kg. The string is 2 cm of braided rope. In 1980 the *You Asked for It* TV show launched it off Pier 39 in San Francisco. But the string accidentally got wet before the launch and Big-Yo kept spinning in a 'sleeper' position until its axle overheated and the string burned through. The yo-yo plunged 9 metres into San Francisco Bay and frogmen had to keep it from drifting away until it could be retrieved and towed to shore.

The Swiss spend more money per capita on insurance than citizens of any other country.

CELEBRITY SUPERSTITIONS

They're only human, after all.

John Madden: An American Football coach, he wouldn't let his team leave the locker room until running back Mark van Eeghen burped.

Confederate General Stonewall Jackson: Jackson always charged into battle with his left hand held over his head, for 'psychic balance'.

Alfred Hitchcock: The cameo appearance he made in each film he directed was for good luck.

Michael Jordan: Always wears his North Carolina shorts under his uniform. 'As long as I have these shorts on...I feel confident', he says.

The Barrymores: Lionel, Ethel and John always gave each other an apple on the night of a show's prémiere.

Jimmy Connors: Wouldn't compete in a tennis match without a little note from his grandma tucked into his sock.

Jack Lemmon: Whispered 'magic time' as filming started.

Thomas Edison: Carried a staurolite, a stone that forms naturally in the shape of a cross. Legend has it that when fairies heard of Christ's crucifixion, their tears fell as 'fairy cross' stones. Also a lucky piece for Theodore Roosevelt and Woodrow Wilson.

Greta Garbo: Wore a lucky string of pearls.

Mario Andretti: Won't use a green pen to sign autographs.

Kichiro Toyoda: A fortuneteller told him it was good luck to change his product's name to *Toyota* and only use car names beginning with 'C' (Celica, Camry, etc.).

John Wayne: Considered it lucky to be in a movie with actor Ward Bond.

John McEnroe: Thinks it's bad luck to play on a Thursday the 12th. Carefully avoids stepping on a white line on the tennis court.

The right whale's eyeball is about as big as an orange.

THE MAN WHO BUILT BRITAIN

Isambard Kingdom Brunel. Crazy name, crazy guy? Maybe not, but the great Victorian builder didn't always get it right.

Isambard Kingdom Brunel (1806-1859) is responsible for some of the Victorian age's most stupendous feats of engineering, from the Clifton Suspension Bridge to the Great Western Railway. But did you know that many of his great achievements were built on a false assumption? He created a giant system of railways, bridges, tunnels and ships all designed to transport hundreds of thousands of people from London to America, via Bristol. But once his grand vision was complete, the expected rush of travellers never materialized. Oh well, we all make mistakes.

TUNNEL VISION

Brunel was born in Britain but was educated in France at the instigation of his father, Marc, a UK-based French engineer. In 1826, Brunel Sr. made his 20-year-old son chief engineer on his ambitious Thames Tunnel project, a scheme to build a walkway under the river from Rotherhithe in the south to the Isle of Dogs in the north. It was a dangerous undertaking – the tunnel flooded twice while Isambard was working on it. After the flood, in May 1827, Isambard went down in a diving bell to supervize the repair work.; during the second flood Brunel Jr. was nearly drowned as he helped to rescue several workers.

The Thames Tunnel made Isambard's name. As well as his feats of derring-do, it also saw him establish the work pattern that he would follow for the rest of his life: 18-hour days, with little or no time for a social or personal life.

LITTLE MAN WITH BIG IDEAS

Standing just five feet four, Brunel liked to wear an almost comically elongated top hat to make himself seem taller. But his choice of headgear wasn't his only towering achievement. After his work on the Thames Tunnel, Isambard embarked on his first big solo project – the Clifton Suspension Bridge, over the River Avon.

However, while the bridge that looms over the Avon today was designed by Brunel, it wasn't built by him. After he drew up plans for the bridge, the project ran out of money. The bridge was finally built in 1864 – five years after Isambard's death. So while work on the Suspension Bridge was... er... suspended, Isambard busied himself on less glamorous projects, such as dock designs for Bristol, Milford Haven and Plymouth. Then, in 1833, aged 27, he got his big break when he was appointed chief engineer to the Great Western Railway project.

NOT QUITE ON THE RIGHT TRACK

This was a scheme to build a railway from London right across western England and into Wales. Brunel ended up building over 1,500 km of track in Britain, as well as in Italy, Australia and India. He handled every aspect of railway engineering, building bridges and tunnels, and designing the track, the rolling stock and even the lamp-posts for the stations. One of his greatest feats of railway engineering in Britain was the famous 4.5 km Box Tunnel, between Bath and Swindon, which took six years to build. When the two digging teams met in the middle, their tunnels were aligned to within 2 cm. However, Isambard's measurements weren't always precise: all the railway track he ever laid had to be ripped up and re-laid later, as he'd insisted on using a different gauge from the norm!

Apart from railways, Brunel's name was associated with steamships. Three times he built the world's then-biggest ship: the *Great Western* in 1837, a paddle steamer that provided the world's first regular transatlantic steamship service; the *Great Britain* in 1843, the first large ship to use a screw propeller; and the *Great Eastern* in 1858, the first double-hulled iron ship, which also laid the first transatlantic cable.

BRISTOL OR BUST

His other work included a collapsible, pre-fabricated field hospital for use in the Crimean War, and experimental vacuum propulsion systems for trains that were years ahead of their time. While Brunel never succeeded in making Bristol the great mass transit point for travel to America (Liverpool always retained that honour), the work he put in to try and make it so at least ensured his place as Britain's greatest-ever engineer.

It takes about 2 1/2 gallons of oil to make a car tyre.

FAMILIAR PHRASES

More unusual origins of everyday words.

PARTING SHOT

Meaning: A final cutting remark or severe look at the end of an argument.

Origin: Unlikely as it seems, this term apparently evolved from the term *Parthian shot* or *Parthian shaft*. In about 1 B.C. in Western Asia, Parthian warriors were known for firing arrows *backwards* as they were retreating from an enemy.

TO LICK SOMETHING (OR SOMEONE) INTO SHAPE

Meaning: Improve something/someone; make them presentable

Origin: Comes from the old belief that bear cubs were born featureless, as 'shapeless masses of flesh and fur' and needed constant licking from their parents to achieve their final shape.

NO-MAN'S LAND

Meaning: Any desolate or dangerous place.

Origin: A thousand years ago in London, retribution for criminal acts was swift and severe. Most crimes were punishable by death. It was customary to transport condemned men just outside of the north wall of the city, where they would be hanged, impaled, or beheaded, and their bodies disposed of. Long after the surrounding territory was settled, no one laid a claim to the land where the executions had been held. Since no one owned it, it was designated as *no-man's land*.

TAKE WITH A GRAIN OF SALT

Meaning: Be skeptical; examine something carefully before accepting a statement's accuracy.

Origin: In ancient times, salt was rare and people thought it had special powers. Among other uses, they sprinkled it on food suspected of containing poison. It became customary to eat a questionable dish only if it was accompanied with a dash of salt.

Q&A: ASK THE EXPERTS

More random questions, with answers from leading trivia experts.

A LOT OF BULL

Q: *Do animals see colour?*

A: We often act as if they do, but the truth is, most don't. 'Apes and some monkeys perceive the full spectrum of colour, as may some fish and birds. But most mammals view colour only as shades of grey'. So, for example, 'bulls don't charge because a cape is red. They charge because of the *movement* of the cape'. (From *The Book of Answers*, by Barbara Berliner)

CARROT TRICK

Q: *What are the 'baby carrots' sold in plastic bags at supermarkets?*

A: 'Take a closer look. Right there on the bag, it says clearly: "baby-cut". These aren't now and never were baby carrots. In the early 1990s, a carrot packer…thought of a clever way to use his misshapen culls. Mechanically he cut them into short pieces, then ground and polished them until they looked like sweet, tender young carrots.

'Baby-cut packers today don't rely on culls…They use a hybrid carrot called "Caropak" that grow long and slender; it doesn't taper much and has little or no core. In the processing shed, the carrots are cleaned, cut into pieces, sorted by size, peeled in abrasive drums, then polished. Bagged with a little water and kept cold, they stay crisp and bright orange'. (From the *S.F. Chronicle*)

THREAD OF TRUTH

Q: *Is fibreglass really made of glass?*

A: 'It is, literally, tiny strands of glass that are anywhere from .0004 inches (.01 mm) to two-millionths of an inch (0.00005 mm) in diameter. They can be from six inches (15 cm) to more than a mile (nearly two kilometres) long.

'It's made by either of two processes. The longer, thicker fibres are made by melting glass marbles, then drawing melted strands through holes in a platinum bushing. Shorter, thinner fibres are made by an *air-stream* or *flame blowing* process that pulls bits of melted glass into tiny fibres. As the glass fibres cool, they are sprayed with a polymer that protects their surface and keeps the fibres strong'. (From *Everything You Pretend to Know and Are Afraid Someone Will Ask*, by Lynette Padwa)

THAT JUMPY FEELING

Q: *How far can a kangaroo jump?*

A: 'One large kangaroo, at a single desperate bound, is reported to have cleared a pile of timber 10½ feet [over three metres] high and 27 feet [over eight metres] long'. (From *Can Elephants Swim?*, compiled by Robert M. Jones)

STEEL AWAY

Q: *What makes stainless steel stainless?*

A: 'Stainless steel is coated with a thin, transparent film of iron oxide and chromium. This prevents soap, food, water, and air from getting to the metal below and eating it away. Since its coating is smooth, stainless steel is [also] very sanitary. Bacteria, fungi, and dirt have nowhere to hide and are easily washed away...[Ironically, the metal] was developed in 1913 by British metallurgist Harry Brearly, who was searching for a better lining for cannons'. (From *The Book of Totally Useless Information*, by Don Voorhees)

QUESTION WITH A-PEEL

Q: *Are most of a potato's nutrients in the peel?*

A: 'In most cases, the vitamins are spread evenly throughout the potato. But eating the peel is still a good idea. Certain minerals that your body needs, such as calcium and zinc, are found in larger amounts in the peel.... In baked potatoes, the peel does contain more than its share of vitamins. Baking causes vitamins and other nutrients to pile up in the peel.... [However], potatoes are members of the nightshade family. The stems, seeds and skins of this family are poisonous – some more so than others.... While the flesh of the potato (the white part) is okay, the leaves and skin contain [a small amount of] substances called glycoalkaloids.... That's why you should never eat potato eyes – that's where the glycoalkaloids concentrate'. (From *Know It All*, by Ed Zotti)

NEAR-DEATH EXPERIENCES

Death may be lurking closer than you think. Judging from these stories, it might be a good idea to have a box of groceries on hand, just in case. Here are a few classic 'near misses'.

TUNA SURPRISE

'During a robbery at a grocery store in Chicago, employee Vincente Arriaga was shot by the robber at a distance of 20 feet (6 metres). According to a report in the *Chicago Sun-Times*, the bullet barely broke Arriaga's skin because it was slowed down as it passed through a box of Tuna Helper he was holding'.

– *News of the Weird*, 10 January, 1996

A STIRRING STORY

'Someone fired a .45 caliber bullet into Ava Donner's kitchen. Luckily, she was holding a spoon. Donner was stirring a pot of macaroni and cheese when a bullet hit the stem of the stainless steel spoon, ricocheted off the refrigerator and landed on the kitchen counter... "If it had been an inch either way, it would have been in her chest", said Donner's husband. Police suspect the shot was fired by youths target shooting in a nearby vacant lot'.

– *San Francisco Chronicle*, 20 February, 1996

RADAR RANGE

'Two members of the British traffic police were in Berwickshire with a radar gun, checking for speeding motorists, when suddenly their equipment locked up with a reading of over 300 miles (480 km) per hour. Seconds later a low flying Harrier jet flew over their heads and explained the mystery. When the policemen complained to the RAF, they were informed they were lucky to be alive. The jet's target-seeker had locked onto their radar gun as "enemy" radar...which triggered an automatic retaliatory air-to-surface missile attack. Luckily for the traffic cops, the Harrier was unarmed'.

– *Pilot* magazine

REEL QUOTES

Here are some of our favourite lines from the Silver Screen.

ON INTELLIGENCE

Doc: 'This kid is so dumb he doesn't know what time it is'.
Golfer: 'By the way, what time is it'?
Doc: 'I don't know'.

– W.C. Fields,
The Dentist

ON MARRIAGE

'If love is blind…marriage must be like having a stroke'.

– Danny De Vito,
War of the Roses

'What's marriage anyhow? Just a tradition started by cavemen and encouraged by florists'.

– Olivia de Haviland,
The Strawberry Blonde

'Marriage is forever – like cement'.

– Peter Sellers,
What's New Pussycat?

ON SEX

'I like my sex the way I play basketball: one on one, and with as little dribbling as possible'.

– Leslie Nielsen,
The Naked Gun

ON RELIGION

Luna: 'Do you believe in God'?
Miles: 'Do I believe in God? I'm what you'd call a theological atheist. I believe that there is intelligence to the universe, with the exception of certain parts of New Jersey. Do YOU believe in God'?
Luna: 'Well, I believe that there's somebody out there who watches over us'.
Miles: 'Unfortunately, it's the government'.

– Woody Allen's *Sleeper*

ON RELATIONSHIPS

'She dumped me cause she said I wasn't paying enough attention to her, or something. I don't know, I wasn't really listening'.

– Jeff Daniels,
Dumb & Dumber

'A guy'll listen to anything if he thinks it's foreplay'.

– Susan Sarandon,
Bull Durham

'I'm not livin' with you. We occupy the same cage, that's all'.

– Elizabeth Taylor,
Cat on a Hot Tin Roof

THE DISAPPEARANCE OF THE *MARY CELESTE*

One of the most famous unexplained disappearances ever recorded is the case of the Mary Celeste. *In 1872 it was found drifting aimlessly in the Atlantic, in seaworthy condition and fully provisioned. But the entire crew had vanished without a trace. To this day, no one knows what happened.*

BACKGROUND

On 5 November, 1872, the *Mary Celeste* set off from New York carrying a cargo of 1,701 barrels of commercial alcohol. Her captain was Benjamin Spooner Briggs, a well-known seaman who allowed no drinking on his ship and regularly read the Bible to his men. The crew had been carefully chosen for their character and seamanship, especially because the captain had brought along his wife and two-year-old daughter. He was looking forward to a safe and pleasant voyage.

DISAPPEARANCE

One month later, on 5 December, Captain Morehouse of the *Dei Gratia* – another cargo ship bound for Gibraltar – noticed a vessel on the horizon. It looked like it was in trouble, so he changed course to see if he could be of assistance. After calling out to the ship and getting no reply, Morehouse lowered a boat and sent two men to board. It was immediately evident that the ship, which turned out to be the *Mary Celeste*, was deserted. The men looked for underwater damage, but the vessel was not leaking, and was in no danger of sinking. There was evidence that the *Mary Celeste* had encountered bad weather, but on the whole she was in perfectly good condition and should have had no problem continuing her journey.

Stranger yet, there were six months' worth of provisions aboard and plenty of fresh water. All of the crew's personal possessions were intact – even the ship's strongbox. In fact, absolutely nothing was missing except some of the ship's papers and the ship's lifeboat. Captain Briggs, his family, and the crew had obviously abandoned the ship in hurry...but why? What could have

Einstein couldn't read until the age of nine.

frightened them so much that they'd desert a perfectly seaworthy vessel for an overcrowded lifeboat and take their chances in the stormy Atlantic?

INVESTIGATION

Still puzzled by the disappearance of the crew, Captain Morehouse decided to claim the *Mary Celeste* as salvage. He put three men aboard her and proceeded with both ships to Gibraltar.

Officials in Gibraltar were suspicious of Morehouse when he showed up with a 'salvage' ship in such good condition, still carrying valuable cargo. They investigated and discovered that:

- The *Mary Celeste*'s hull was perfectly sound, indicting she had not been in a collision. Nor was there any evidence of explosion or fire.

- The cargo of commercial alcohol seemed to be intact and complete.

- A phial of sewing machine oil was standing upright, spare panes of glass were found unbroken, and the furniture in the captain's cabin was in its proper place – all indications that the ship hadn't endured particularly rough weather.

- The fact that the crew had left behind all their possessions – even their tobacco – indicated that they had left the ship in a panic, afraid for their lives, but the investigators could see no reason for this.

- The most mysterious item aboard was a sword found under the captain's bed. It seemed to be smeared with blood, then wiped. Blood was also found on the railing, and both bows of the ship had strange cuts in them which could not be explained.

THE OFFICIAL WORD

Solly Flood, Attorney General for Gibraltar, found the bloodstains suspicious and was convinced there had been violence aboard the *Mary Celeste*. However, the Vice Admiralty Court issued a verdict clearing Morehouse and his crew of any suspicion. After the ship's owners paid Morehouse a reward, the *Mary Celeste* was given a new crew, and went on to Italy, where her cargo was delivered. She continued to sail for 12 years but was known as a 'hoodoo ship', so most seamen refused to set foot on her.

WHAT HAPPENED?

The mysterious disappearance of the *Mary Celeste's* crew had people all over the world imagining possible scenarios.

•Some believed a mutiny had occurred – the crew murdered the captain and his family, then took the ship. But if that were true, why did they abandon their prize?

•Perhaps an outbreak of disease panicked those left alive. But why would they subject themselves to the close quarters of the smaller boat, where the crowding would *guarantee* that everyone caught the disease?

•The most outrageous explanation offered was that the ship had been attacked by a giant squid several times, until everyone was killed. But a squid wouldn't have been interested in the ship's papers. And a Squid wouldn't need the ship's lifeboat.

•Because the story of the *Mary Celeste* got so much publicity, fake survivors started popping up and selling their stories to newspapers and magazines. But they all checked out false – no one who claimed to have been on board had their facts straight.

ONLY ONE EXPLANATION?

The mystery of the *Mary Celeste* has puzzled people for over a century. In all that time, say experts, only one feasible explanation has been proposed. This postulates that four things happened, in succession:

1. The captain died of natural causes while the ship was caught in bad weather.

2. A crew member misread the depth of the water in the hold, and everyone panicked, thinking the ship was going down.

3. They abandoned ship in such a hurry that they took no food or water.

4. Everyone in the lifeboat either starved or drowned.

Is that what happened? No one will ever know.

Start counting: on average, an adult laughs about 15 times a day; a child laughs 400 times.

QUEEN OF THE NILE

She's one of the most famous queens in history...but how much do you really know about her?

For centuries, people have been enthralled by stories of Cleopatra. She was a tragic heroine in Shakespeare's *Antony and Cleopatra*; a scheming vamp in *Cleopatra*, Theda Bara's classic 1917 silent film; a buxom babe in Elizabeth Taylor's 1963 film flop. But most people know very little about the real Queen of the Nile. And much of what they *think* they know is false.

Belief: There was only one Cleopatra.
Truth: There were seven Queen Cleopatras in the Egyptian dynasty that began with King Ptolemy I in 323 B.C.; Cleopatra, who reigned from 15 B.C.–30 B.C. was the seventh and last. Her eldest sister was Queen Cleopatra VI, and her daughter (who never became queen) was also named Cleopatra.

Belief: She was Egyptian.
Truth: She was considered Greek. Cleopatra was one of king Ptolemy I's direct descendants; *he* had been a Greek staff officer of Alexander the Great before becoming king of Egypt following Alexander's death. Like the Egyptian pharaohs before them, the Ptolemaic dynasty adopted incestuous brother-sister marriages as a way to keep their bloodline 'pure'; historians believe it's unlikely Cleopatra had any Egyptian blood at all. For that matter, she was the first Ptolemaic ruler who could even *speak* Egyptian.

Belief: She was one of the most beautiful women in the world.
Truth: At best, she had ordinary features; at worst, she was decidedly unattractive. 'Her coins', Lucy Hughes-Hallett writes in *Cleopatra: History, Dreams and Distortions*, 'minted on her orders and therefore more likely to flatter than otherwise, show a strong, bony face with a hooked nose and a jutting chin, pretty neither by the standards of Cleopatra's day nor by those of ours'. The ancient Roman historian Plutarch describes her as being not particularly good-looking, although her intellect, beautiful voice and strong character made her desirable and enjoyable company.

Watches get their name because they were originally worn by night watchmen.

Belief: She was a great seductress.
Truth: This is based on her well-known affairs with Julius Caesar and Marc Antony. But in the days of ancient Rome, affairs between rulers were a common means of cementing alliances. Caesar is known to have had liaisons with several other queens and at least one king (one of his contemporaries described him as 'every woman's man and every man's woman'); Mark Antony was also a notorious womanizer. Cleopatra, on the other hand, was completely celibate for more than half her adult life and is believed to have had only two lovers: Caesar and Marc Antony.

Belief: Caesar and Marc Antony were madly in love with her.
Truth: It is possible Caesar fell in love with Cleopatra (no one knows); but he really stayed in Egypt to get his hands on her fortune. And historians say he made her queen of Egypt because he didn't want to appoint a Roman who might become his rival.

Cleopatra's relationship with Marc Antony was also based on politics. At their first meeting, when they supposedly fell in love, they made a deal: Antony agreed to kill Cleopatra's sister so she'd have no challenge to her authority; Cleopatra became a loyal ally. Then he went back to Rome and his wife. When his wife died, he didn't marry Cleopatra – he shacked up with the sister of a political rival. Years later, he finally visited Cleopatra and the twins he'd fathered with her. Coincidentally, he also needed her treasure and her navy at the time.

Antony did commit suicide and die in Cleopatra's arms, but it wasn't for love; he was despondent because they'd been defeated in battle. Cleopatra committed suicide, too. For love? No. The Romans told her she was going to be paraded in disgrace through Rome in chains, and she couldn't take that.

Belief: She committed suicide by getting herself bitten by an asp.
Truth: Nobody knows for sure how she killed herself. 'Plutarch had read the memoirs of her private physician, but even he was not sure', Hughes-Hallett writes in *Cleopatra: History, Dreams and Distortions:* 'It seems likely to have been the bite of a snake brought to her in a basket of figs, but it may be that she had some poison ready prepared and hidden in a hollow hair comb, or that she pricked herself with a poisoned hairpin. The only marks found on her body were two tiny scratches on her arm'.

The most common word spoken by a dying person is 'Mother' or 'Mommy'.

LUCKY FINDS

Here are three more stories of people who found something valuable. It could happen to you…

A HIDDEN VALUE

The Find: An 1830 painting

Where It Was Found: At an auction

The Story: In the mid-1990s, American Wanda Bell paid $25 for an old print depicting the signing of the Declaration of Independence. One day, as she was cleaning the print, she noticed something underneath it. She removed it…and found an oil painting of a man. Bell was curious to know more about it. In August 1997, she heard that an antiques roadshow was offering free appraisals with experts from Sotheby's, so she took the painting there. Their assessment: it's an early portrait painted by a famous New England artist named Sheldon Peck. Estimated value: $250,000.

A ROLL OF FILM

The Find: The pilot show of *I Love Lucy*

Where It Was Found: Under a bed

The Story: In 1949, CBS offered Lucille Ball her own TV show, to be based on her successful radio program, *My Favorite Husband*. She agreed – as long as they'd let her real-life husband, Desi Arnaz, co-star. CBS called the idea preposterous. 'Who'd believe you were married to a Cuban bandleader?' they said.

Lucy was determined. She and Desi decided to create a live show and take it on the road to prove that audiences would accept them together. 'Desi moved quickly to assemble a first-rate vaudeville act', write Steven Coyne Sanders and Tom Gilbert in their book, *Desilu*.

> He called in an old friend, the renowned international Spanish clown Pepito, to devise some physical-comedy sketch material. Pepito rigorously coached the couple, as Desi recalled, 'eight to ten hours a day' at the Coronado Hotel in San Diego.

The stage show was a huge success, so CBS agreed to film a sitcom pilot. The synopsis: 'Ricky goes to a TV audition. Pepito the

Clown, due to an accident, fails to appear and Lucy takes his place for the show'. It was filmed on 2 March, 1951.

I Love Lucy, of course, became one of the most successful TV programs in history. But along the way, the pilot episode was lost. Fans and TV historians tried over the years to locate it, but it appeared to be gone for good. Then one day in 1989, Pepito's 84-year-old widow (he'd died in 1975) looked under a bed in her Orange County home and came across a can of film labelled 'Lucy-Desi-Pepito' audition. It was the long-lost *Lucy* pilot. Desi, it turns out, had given it to Pepito as a thank-you for his help. The film, with an estimated value of over $1 million, was quickly turned into a TV special and home video.

A LUCKY MISTAKE

The Find: A unique coin

Where It Was Found: At a flea market

The Story: In 1970, Guy Giamo came across an interesting 1969 penny at a Northern California flea market. 'What made it intriguing', reported the *San Francisco Chronicle*, 'was that it seemed to be a "double die" stamping, a Bureau of the Mint manufacturing error that gave the legends *Liberty* and *In God We Trust* a blurred, double-image look'.

There are a lot of double-dies from 1955, worth more than $500 apiece. But double-die coins are easy to fake, and many are counterfeit. Giamo bought it anyway Cost: about $100.

In 1978, he sent it to the U.S. Mint to find out if it was real. A few months later a Secret Service agent called and said simply: 'The Treasury Department has determined your coin to be counterfeit, and it will be confiscated and destroyed'. 'That's it?' Giamo asked. 'Affirmative', the agent replied, and hung up.

But that's not the end. A year later, Giamo was surprised by another call from the Treasury Department. 'What the hell do you want now?' he asked bitterly. 'We have a coin for you', he was told. Someone had re-examined his penny before it was melted down, and decided it was genuine. 'We goofed', they told him.

Giamo's coin is the only double-die 1969 penny in existence. Its estimated value: as much as $50,000.

Smokers need to ingest 40 per cent more vitamin C than non-smokers just to stay even.

STRANGE CELEBRITY LAWSUITS

Here's a great selection of truly bizarre court cases involving the rich and famous.

THE PLAINTIFF: Elton John
THE DEFENDANT: The *Sunday Mirror*, an English newspaper
THE CASE: In 1992, the *Sunday Mirror* claimed that John had been spitting out chewed hors d'oeuvres at a Hollywood party, calling it a 'new diet'. The singer had recently gone public about his bulimia; he sued because 'the story implied he was a sham'... and because he wasn't even at the party.
THE VERDICT: The singer was awarded £315,000 in damages. The *Mirror* issued a formal apology admitting the story was bogus.

THE PLAINTIFF: Catherine Deneuve, French movie star
THE DEFENDANT: Outspoken Enterprises, Inc., a San Francisco magazine publisher
THE CASE: For five years, Outspoken Enterprises published *Deneuve* magazine. By 1996, it had 200,000 readers – making it one of the largest magazines for lesbians in the United States. The editor claimed the title was inspired by 'the name of her first love', not the actress. But Catherine Deneuve didn't believe it. In January, 1996, she sued for trademark infringement.
THE VERDICT: The suit was apparently dropped when the magazine voluntarily changed its name to *Curve*.

THE PLAINTIFFS: French sexpot Brigitte Bardot and her neighbour, Jean-Pierre Manivet
THE DEFENDANTS: Jean-Pierre Manivet and Brigitte Bardot
THE CASE: Not surprisingly, it's about sex. In 1989, Bardot and Manivet lived next to each other on the French Riviera. Bardot owned a female donkey, Mimosa, and a mare, Duchesse; Manivet had a male donkey, Charly. Bardot, an animal activist, agreed to let Charly graze with her animals. But when Charly 'began to show male instincts toward the old mare', he lost his grazing

The word 'love' appears in more film titles than any other word. Second place: 'Paris'.

rights, and a bit more than he bargained for – Bardot had him castrated. Manivet was out of town at the time; when he returned, he sued Bardot for 4,500 francs (about £450) in damages, plus 10,000 francs (£1,000) for 'moral prejudice'. Bardot countersued, claiming Manivet's publicity about the case harmed her image.
THE VERDICT: Everyone lost. The court ruled it was within Bardot's rights to 'fix' the donkey, but not to protect her 'image'.

THE PLAINTIFF: Richard Belzer, of TV's *Homicide: Life on the Street*
THE DEFENDANTS: Hulk Hogan and Mr. T., professional wrestlers
THE CASE: In 1985, Belzer hosted a cable talk show called *Hot Properties*. Hogan and Mr. T. appeared on one program as guests. According to news reports, the interview was 'merely awkward' until Belzer asked them to show him some wrestling moves.

> 'I'm going to make him squeal', Hogan chuckled as he stood up. Mr. T. urged 'the Hulkster' to show Belzer a 'Pipsqueak Sandwich'.
>
> While the band played Chopin's funeral march in the background – and a Manhattan studio audience, including 50 children in wheelchairs, who had been invited to the show, watched in horror – Hogan demonstrated his 'front chin lock'. After a few seconds, the comedian collapsed. He recovered briefly – long enough to break for a commercial – and then he was taken by ambulance to Mount Sinai Hospital where nine stitches were taken in his scalp.

Belzer sued the two wrestlers for $5 million.
THE VERDICT: In 1988, the case was settled out of court.

THE PLAINTIFF: Michael B. Mukasey, stepfather of singer Mariah Carey
THE DEFENDANT: Mariah Carey
THE CASE: in 1993, Mukasey sued his step-daughter claiming that Carey had promised to let him market 'singing dolls that looked like her'. Underlying the lawsuit: his contention that he deserved a share of her earnings because 'he helped her achieve stardom by…providing transportation to rehearsals and paying for dental work'.
THE VERDICT: Case dismissed.

Only pharaohs were allowed to eat mushrooms in ancient Egypt.

THE HISTORY OF ROCK: QUIZ #2

Now it's time to find out how much you know about oldies from the 1960s. See page 466 for the answers.

1. The Jefferson Airplane's 'White Rabbit' – inspired by *Alice in Wonderland* – was one of the rock classics of the 1960s. What prompted singer Grace Slick to write it?

a) The rest of the group locked her in a room and told her not to come out until she'd written some songs.

b) She read *Alice* to her niece and couldn't get over how 'psychedelic' the story was.

c) She went to a Halloween party and saw Janis Joplin dressed as Alice.

2. 'Summer in the City' was the Lovin' Spoonful's biggest hit, a No.1 song in 1966. It was co-written by Spoonful leader John Sebastian and...

a) Tommy Gershwin, nephew of composer George Gershwin. He adapted it from an unpublished piece of music his uncle had left him.

b) Mark Sebastian, John's brother. According to legend, Mark submitted the lyrics as a poem in his high school English class...and got an 'F' on them. John didn't think they were so bad and put them to music

c) Grace Slick. She'd just finished 'White Rabbit' and was looking for something new to work on.

3. Roy Orbison hit No.1 in 1964 with 'Pretty Woman'. How did he come up with the idea for the song?

a) His wife announced she was going to buy groceries.

b) His wife announced she was pregnant.

c) His wife announced she was leaving him.

4. In 1962, Frankie Valli and the Four Seasons were rudely interrupted while recording their soon-to-be No.1 song, 'Walk Like a Man'. What happened?

a) The studio was robbed. The thieves took their money, jewellery – and all the instruments.

b) The building was on fire – fire fighters were smashing down the studio door as the group desperately tried to finish the recording.

c) A gang of fans broke down the door and chased the group all over the studio – finally cornering them in the men's toilet. Police had to rescue them.

5. In 1969, a group called Steam hit No.1 with a pop tune called 'Na Na Hey Hey Kiss Him Goodbye'. How did they wind up with that title (which is also the chorus)?

a) One of the musicians was a Native American whose tribal name was 'Nah nah hay-hay'.

b) They couldn't think of any words, so they just stuck in some nonsense syllables.

c) One of the musician's kids, a three-year-old, came up with it.

6. In 1964, jazz trumpeter Louis Armstrong became the oldest artist ever to have a No.1 song when his version of 'Hello, Dolly' topped the charts. Why did he record the song?

a) 'Dolly' was his first wife's name.

b) It was a publicity gimmick. He cut a deal with David Merrick, the show's producer: if Armstrong's record made the Top 10, Merrick said he'd pay the trumpeter an extra $100,000.

c) Someone gave it to Armstrong at the recording session. He'd never heard of the musical or the song, but thought it was decent enough to record.

7. Which of these classic 1960s rock songs was made up spontaneously – right in the middle of a live performance?

a) 'When a Man Loves a Woman', by Percy Sledge

b) 'All You Need Is Love', by the Beatles

c) 'My Boyfriend's Back', by the Angels

KING TUT'S CURSE

When he died in 1352 B.C., Tutankhamun had been a minor, short-lived Pharaoh. But the curse around his name has ensured his fame. But what of the man who survived the dreaded curse?

According to popular legend, everyone who came into contact with the tomb or the mummified body of the boy king of Ancient Egypt died mysteriously. From Lord Carnarvon's death from a mosquito bite in 1923, down to the caretaker at the Cairo museum's deadly car accident, every fatality was blamed on the curse. So what became of the man who found the tomb and opened the sarcophagus containing Tutankhamun's body? Surely he would have been the most cursed of all?

HOWARD DIGS EGYPT

Howard Carter was born in 1874. His father was a professional artist and Howard also had artistic talent. He trained as a painter and draughtsman, and first went to Egypt as an assistant draughtsman on an English archaeological survey in 1891. He was just 17, but was soon hooked on Egyptology. Carter stayed in Egypt for several years, making detailed drawings of tombs and artifacts, and was eventually appointed inspector-in-chief of the monuments of Upper Egypt by the Egyptian government.

In 1908 he joined an expedition funded by the Earl of Carnarvon, which was digging at the necropolis (city of the dead) at Thebes. While Carter helped uncover a number of tombs, nearly all the best burial sites in Egypt had already been opened and cleaned out by tomb raiders over the centuries. Carnarvon was a collector of antiquities not an archaeologist, so was mainly interested in finding a tomb that still contained its treasures – he was, in effect, a modern-day tomb raider himself.

ON TUT'S TRAIL

After years of research, Carter came to believe that the tomb of the virtually unknown boy king Tutankhamun may never have been opened. All he had to do was find it. He found other tombs on his digs during and after World War I, but none were the perfect tomb he sought. In 1922, Lord Carnarvon summoned him back to England to call off the search, but Carter managed to convince him that he was close to a find, and needed just one more season.

Then, on 14 November, 1922, Carter discovered some stone stairs hidden by the rubble from another tomb. When uncovered, the stairs lead to an ancient doorway, still intact. On the door was inscribed the three hieroglyphs that spelt out the name Tut-ankh-amun. This discovery began Carter's most famous work of Egyptology. His survey of the tomb and its treasures is a masterpiece that took him 10 years to complete.

CURSES, FOILED AGAIN

The popular press of the day (and right up to the present), have always loved the story of the curse. Anyone remotely connected with the find who died in suspicious circumstances was added to the list of victims. The deaths of Lord Carnarvon, Carter's secretary, Carter's secretary's father, museum attendants and their families, the child of a scientist who wrote about the mummy, even Carnarvon's dog, were all attributed to the curse.

Carter carried on regardless of the mounting body count. He always denied that there was a curse carved above the door of the tomb. He should have known – he was the one who broke the seals on the tomb, was the first to look inside, and the first to go in. In spite of all of this, he lived and worked in Egypt and England until 1939, when he died of natural causes, in his mid-60s. The curse got many people, but it didn't get Carter.

Many others who were present at the dig and the tomb's opening, who catalogued the artifacts and who unwrapped and studied the mummified remains died of natural causes, too. In fact, of those who were present, a high percentage lived for decades after the discovery and showed no signs of being cursed at all.

MUMMY, I'M FRIGHTENED

There are many explanations for the story of the curse. The first mummified bodies of Egyptians arrived in London in the 1820s, 100 years before Carter's find. These remains were unwrapped in side-shows and for paying audiences (and probably rewrapped between performances!). Horror and ghost stories were enjoyed in the 1800s as much as they are today. Before long, stories involving mummies taking revenge on the living for disturbing their rest

Only 2 per cent of women think they should keep their maiden name when they marry.

became popular: even Louisa May Alcott, the normally demure and wholesome author of *Little Women*, wrote one. Thus, the idea of a curse was already fixed in the public's mind when King Tut was rediscovered. So when Lord Carnarvon died only one year after the tomb was opened, of a seemingly innocuous mosquito bite, everyone was ready to believe in the revenge of the long-dead king.

So how did Carter survive the 'curse'? Simple: he just didn't believe in it!

* * *

And while we're on the subject of mummy's curses...

Have you ever heard the story of the Princess Amen-Ra? It's been circulating for years, and is now doing the rounds on e-mail.

It's the one about the mummified princess whose curse killed or ruined the four men who found her, caused all sorts of death and mayhem at the British Museum and, for an encore, while in transit to a new owner in the U.S., sank the *Titanic*!

If you ever come across the story: don't believe a word of it. It's just a long-running hoax. And unlike Tutankhamun, the princess never even existed. The British Museum even has an official denial that it sends out to people who enquire about the curse.

* * *

SOME RANDOM THOUGHTS

Ufffington's White Horse is said to be the oldest UK hill figure, dating back to the Bronze Age.

The tallest fence in the Grand National is the Chair, at five feet and two inches.

In the 1920s, Essex saw the formation of the first Gymnosophist Society (that's nudist club to you).

The two lines that connect the bottom of your nose to your lip are called the philtrum.

THE EIFFEL TOWER, PART II

Room with a view: among amenities that Gustave Eiffel designed for the tower was a penthouse apartment at the top, complete with a grand piano and spotlights for shining on other Paris monuments. He built it for his own use.
Part I begins on page 257.

EIGHTH WONDER OF THE WORLD

Most advances in architecture and engineering are incremental. If, for instance, you wanted to build the world's first ten-storey building, you'd expect to study the construction techniques of eight- and nine-storey buildings first.

But Gustave Eiffel didn't have that luxury. No one had ever built an iron tower like his of *any* size – let alone one that was twice as tall as the tallest building on earth.

AN ENGINEERING GENIUS

To accomplish his task, Eiffel devised some incredibly ingenious techniques:

- Unlike other massive engineering projects of the day, he had nearly all of the parts used in the tower prefabricated off-site in his workshops. This meant that when they arrived at the tower, the parts could be quickly riveted into place with a minimum of fuss.
- The rivet holes themselves were pre-drilled to a tolerance of one-tenth of one millimetre, making it possible for the twenty riveting teams to drive an average of 1,650 rivets a day.
- None of the girders used in the tower was permitted to weigh more than three tonnes. This made it possible to use smaller cranes to lift everything into place. As Joseph Harris writes in *The Tallest Tower:*

> Eiffel had learned that using small components was faster and safer, even if this method did require more riveting, for cranes could be smaller and more mobile. The chances of accidents were reduced, and if one did occur the consequences were less serious. Use of bigger girders would have slowed the entire operation

and required more expensive and complicated construction methods.

Thanks to these and other safety measures, the Eiffel Tower – the world's tallest construction site – was also one of the safest. Of the hundreds of people who worked on the tower, only one, a riveter's assistant named Dussardin, fell to his death.

THE PIERS

In the early days of the project there were actually four construction sites at the Eiffel Tower, one for each foot, or 'pier'. These piers did not join together until the 55-metre level – and once this point was reached, they had to be set *perfectly* level with one another to create a perfectly horizontal platform on which the remaining 244 metres of the tower could be built. If the piers were even slightly out of alignment, the tiniest discrepancy at the base of the tower would be magnified at the top: the whole tower would appear to lean.

Eiffel knew there was no way he could *guarantee* the piers would be vertical when finished – the margin for error was too great. So he installed temporary hydraulic pistons in the base of each of the feet. That way, as work on the tower progressed, he could fine-tune the entire tower into perfect alignment by slightly raising or lowering each foot. When the tower was properly aligned, workers could drive iron wedges into the piers to secure them permanently.

As it turned out, Eiffel had little to worry about. Even at the 55-metre level, the worst of the four piers was less than 6.5 centimetres out of line. All four were easily adjusted and secured in place. Even today, the tower is perfectly vertical.

FINIS

The Eiffel Tower was a marvel – not just for its ingenuity of design, but also because it was completed ahead of schedule and under budget. The Exposition was scheduled to open on 6 May; work on the tower was finished on 31 March.

Eiffel & Company earned back its money in record time. During the six months of the Exposition, the tower recouped more than £850,000 of its £975,000 construction cost; that, combined with the £180,000 subsidy provided by the French government, pushed the tower into the black even before the Exposition closed.

The tower was such a magnificent structure that it won over many of its earlier critics. Among them was French Prime Minister Tirard. He had opposed the project at its inception, but awarded Eiffel the Legion of Honour, France's most prestigious medal, after it was finished. The tower, a symbol of France's unrivalled technical expertise, became the symbol of France itself.

Not everyone who hated the tower experienced a change of heart. Guy de Maupassant, the novelist best known for *The Necklace*, was said to eat regularly at a restaurant on the tower's second floor. His reason: it was the only place in Paris where he was sure he wouldn't see the tower. (Even some of the characters in his novels hated the tower.)

TOWER FACTS

• Every seven years, the Eiffel Tower receives a fresh coat of more than 300 tonnes of reddish-green paint. Why reddish-green? Because, tower officials say, it is the colour that clashes least with the blue sky over Paris, and the green landscape of the Champ de Mars below.

• The positions of the Eiffel Tower's four 'feet' correspond to the 'cardinal' points of a compass: they point exactly north, south, west, and east.

• In 1925 the City of Paris wanted to decorate the tower with electric lights as part of an arts exposition being held nearby, but the cost, estimated at £300,000, was too high. When car manufacturer André Citroën learned of the project, he offered to pay for it himself – in exchange for the right to put his company name and corporate symbol in lights as well. The City agreed. 'The Eiffel Tower', Blake Ehrlich writes in *Paris on the Seine*, 'became the world's largest electric sign, its outlines traced in lights'. The lights were so popular that the tower remained lit with various designs until 1937.

• There is one sad fact, though. The Eiffel Tower is the most popular landmark for suicides in France. In an average year, four people commit suicide by jumping off the tower or, occasionally, by hanging themselves from its wrought iron beams. The first person killed in a jump from the tower, in 1911, was not an intentional suicide – the man was a tailor named Teichelt who had sewn himself a 'spring-loaded bat-wing cape' that he thought would enable him to fly. It didn't.

THE FIRST CENTREFOLD

Whether you approve of the magazine or not, Playboy *represents a significant part of Western culture. One of its trademarks is the centrefold. Here's the tale of the first one.*

THE BARE FACTS

In the late 1940s, Marilyn Monroe was still an unknown actress, struggling to pay the rent. One day in 1948 she borrowed a car to get to an audition, but had an accident on the way. As bystanders gathered, she announced she was late for an appointment and had no money for a cab. Tom Kelley, a photographer, gave her $5 and his business card.

A year later when Marilyn needed money, she went to Kelley's studio to ask if he had any work for her. He did – he was doing a photo shoot for poster advertising Pabst Blue Ribbon Beer and his model had failed to show up. Marilyn happily stepped in and took the job.

A few weeks later Kelley called Monroe with more work. A Chicago calendar manufacturer named John Baumgarth had seen the Pabst poster and wanted a few 'tasteful' nude pinup shots.

According to Anthony Spoto in *Marilyn*:

> (She) accepted at once. Two nights later she returned to Kelley's studio and signed a release form as 'Mona Monroe'.
>
> A red velvet drape was spread on the studio floor, and for two hours Marilyn posed nude, moving easily from one position to another as the photographer, perched ten feet (three metres) above her on a ladder, clicked away.

Baumgarth paid Kelley $500 for all rights to the photos from the session, and Kelley gave Marilyn $50. They never met again.

PIN-UP GIRL

Baumgarth did nothing with the photos until 1950, when Marilyn began to get attention for her role in *The Asphalt Jungle*. He decided to use her picture on a pinup calendar. It was only meant to be a giveaway for service stations, tool dealers, contractors, etc. But in April 1952, *Life* magazine included a tiny reproduction of

More strange stats: In one day, an average typist's hands travel 20 km.

the calendar in a cover story they did on Marilyn. As a result, the picture became world-famous. And Marilyn became infamous.

'Marilyn blunted the potential effect on her career', says Spoto, 'by giving interviews in which she explained that she had desperately needed money. The public bought it. But the saga of the pinup calendar wasn't over'.

PUBLIC EXPOSURE

Just as the furore surrounding Marilyn's pinup shot was dying down, Baumgarth got a visit from a fellow Chicagoan who wanted to use it. According to Russell Miller in *Bunny, the Real Story of Playboy*:

> Because of the risk of prosecution for obscenity, Baumgarth believed there was probably no other use to which the pictures could be put. He was surprised, therefore, when (a young man) showed up at his office, without an appointment, on the morning of 13 June, 1953, and asked if he could buy the rights to publish the Monroe nude pictures in a magazine he was planning to launch.

The man was Hugh Hefner; the magazine was *Stag Party* (soon to be renamed *Playboy)*. Baumgarth not only sold Hefner the magazine rights, but threw in the colour separations as well – which saved the struggling Hefner – who'd barely scraped up enough money for the 48-page first issue – a bundle.

Hefner knew his magazine was finally on its way. Monroe – featured that year in *How to Marry a Millionaire* – was now a star. And Hefner could announce that she would be his first 'centrefold'. In December 1953, the première issue of *Playboy* hit the stands, with Marilyn beckoning from the front cover. Due in part to the famous pinup, *Playboy* was an instant success. Ironically, this exposure made the photos even more famous – and more valuable. Spoto concludes:

> More than any other portraits of a nude woman in the history of photography, those of Marilyn Monroe taken in 1949 became virtual icons, everywhere recognizable, ever in demand. Landmarks in the union of art with commerce, the photographs have appeared in calendars, playing cards, keychains, pens, clothing, accessories, linens and household items; for decades, entrepreneurs have become wealthy by claiming or purchasing rights to their dissemination.

No surprise: people laugh least in the first hour after waking up in the morning.

THE ACME ANTI-CASTRO SPY KIT

Like the Coyote and Road Runner, the CIA was obsessively trying to kill Fidel Castro in the 1960s. But like Coyote, they just couldn't seem to do it. Was it because Castro was so wily…or because the CIA was so imcompetent? Here are some examples of how the anti-Castro super-spies spent their time and the taxpayers' money.

CONCOCTING WEIRD PLOTS

Here are seven strange-but-true plots against Castro that the CIA actually considered.

1. Use agents in Cuba to spread rumours that the second coming of Christ is imminent and that Castro is the anti-Christ.

2. Surprise him at the beach with an exploding conch shell.

3. Put thallium salts in his shoes or cigars during an appearance on *The David Susskind Show*, to make his beard and hair fall out.

4. Put itching powder in his scuba suit and LSD on his mouth-piece so he would be driven crazy and drown.

5. Offer him exploding cigars designed to blow his head off.

6. Shoot him with a TV camera that has a machine gun inside.

7. Spray his broadcasting studio with hallucinogens.

EMBARGOING BASEBALLS

In its war against Fidel Castro during the 1960s, the CIA literally tried to play hardball politics. 'The CIA tried to cut off the supply of baseballs to Cuba. Agents persuaded suppliers in other countries not to ship them. (U.S. baseballs were already banned by the trade embargo the U.S. had declared.)' The bizarre embargo was effective. Some balls got through, 'but the supply was so limited that the government had to ask fans to throw foul balls and home runs back onto the field for continued play'.

– Jonathan Kwitny, *Endless Enemies*

A bee has 5,000 nostrils. It can smell an apple tree 3 km away.

CONSULTING JAMES BOND

How out-of-control was the CIA in its anti-Castro frenzy? They even took Ian Fleming's jokes seriously. This anecdote from Deadly Secrets, *by Warren Hinkle and William Turner, says it all.*

'It was, even by Georgetown standards, one helluva dinner party. It was the spring 1960. The hosts were Senator and Mrs. John F. Kennedy. The guest of honour was John Kennedy's favourite author, Ian Fleming.

'Kennedy asked Fleming what his man James Bond might do if M assigned him to get rid of Castro. Fleming had been in British intelligence....He was quick to answer. According to his biographer, John Pearson, Fleming thought he would have himself some fun...

'[He] said there were three things which really mattered to the Cubans – money, religion, and sex. Therefore, he suggested a triple whammy. First the United States should send planes to scatter [counterfeit] Cuban money over Havana. Second, using the Guantanamo base, the United States should conjure up some religious manifestation, say a cross of sorts in the sky which would induce the Cubans to look constantly skyward. And third, the United States should send planes over Cuba dropping pamphlets to the effect that owing to American atom bomb tests the atmosphere over the island had become radioactive; that radioactivity is held longest in beards, and that radioactivity makes men impotent. As a consequence the Cubans would shave off their beards, and without bearded Cubans there would be no revolution.

'Fleming was staying at the house of British newsman Henry Brandon. The next day CIA director Allen Dulles called Brandon to speak to Fleming. Brandon said his guest had already left Washington. Dulles expressed great regret. He had heard about Fleming's terrific ideas for doing in Castro and was sorry he wouldn't be able to discuss them with him in person.

'It is testimony to the resounding good sense exercised by the CIA during the Secret War that all three of Fleming's spoof ideas were in one form or another attempted – or at least seriously considered'.

Rather than sell the first story he wrote, Charles Dickens swapped it for a bag of marbles.

FAMOUS FOR 15 MINUTES

Pop artist Andy Warhol once famously announced that 'in the future, everyone will be famous for 15 minutes'. Here are a few examples to prove his point.

THE STAR: Shawn Christopher Ryan, 7-year-old resident of Castro Valley, California
THE HEADLINE: *Second-Grader Smells Smoke, Saves Sixteen*
WHAT HAPPENED: At 4 a.m. on 9 February, 1984, Shawn awoke and smelled smoke. He ran into his mother's room, saw that her mattress had caught fire (she'd fallen asleep smoking), and woke her up. He helped her escape, then ran back into the apartment building and knocked on every door, waking up and saving all 16 neighbours. For a few weeks, he was a national hero. He was honoured at the state capitol by the Governor of California, received a commendation from President Reagan, and was lauded on the floor of the U.S. House of Representatives.
AFTERMATH: Ryan wasn't in the news again until 1995, eleven years later. Ironically, it was because he pleaded guilty to the murder of two acquaintances (alleged drug dealers) while they were all high on methamphetamine. 'I can't explain it', he said. 'I'm not the kind of person to take a life, not for any reason'. He was sentenced to 32 years in prison.

THE STAR: Diane King, a 33-year-old night-shift manager at a Portland, Oregon, Taco Bell
THE HEADLINE: *Good Samaritan Gets Heave-ho from Taco Bell*
WHAT HAPPENED: On 16 August, 1995, a fight broke out in a Taco Bell car park, leaving one teenager dead and one lying motionless in the street. King, a former nurse's aide, rushed to help. She left another employee in charge of the restaurant, even though she knew it was against company policy. Later, she explained, 'I was worried he might die out there'. When the police arrived, she went back to work. A few weeks later, she was unceremoniously fired. Newspapers reported the story as an example of both corporate insensitivity and a screwed-up society that discourages good samaritans.

AFTERMATH: Hundreds of people offered King jobs and money. *People* magazine ran a story on the incident. Oprah Winfrey flew King to Chicago for a show titled 'Would You Help a Stranger in Distress'? Finally, Taco Bell – which had tried to reinstate King without admitting it had done anything wrong (she refused) – ran a full-page apology in the Portland *Oregonian*. 'Sometimes big corporations make mistakes', it said. 'In this case, we did, and we've learned it'. King ignored them and took a job at a convenience store. She also filed a $149,500 suit against Taco Bell for 'shock, outrage, and emotional distress'. No word as yet on the outcome.

THE STAR: Nicholas Daniloff, Moscow bureau chief for *U.S. News and World Report*
THE HEADLINE: *U.S. Reporter Held Hostage by Soviets*
WHAT HAPPENED: In 1986 Gennadi Zakharov, a member of the Soviet Union's mission to the United Nations, was arrested in New York for spying. A few weeks later, the Soviets retaliated, arresting Daniloff in Moscow and charging *him* with espionage – with a possible death penalty. His arrest was front-page news. President Reagan and Secretary of State George Schultz called it 'an outrage', but swore they'd never swap a spy (Zakharov) for a hostage (Daniloff). The matter was so serious that it jeopardized the upcoming Summit meeting in Iceland between Ronald Reagan and Mikhail Gorbachev. The United States even announced it was expelling 25 members of the Soviet delegation to the U.N. because they worked for the KGB.

Some fancy manoeuvering followed. Daniloff was released. The United States waited a while (so it didn't seem like there was any connection) then released Zakharov in exchange for a Russian dissident and allowed some of the expelled U.N. workers to stay. Daniloff was welcomed home – but a *day* after his release, he was already old news. The Reagan administration changed the subject. Their new focus – it was to avoid scrutiny of the deal they'd made, some suggested – was details of the Summit meeting.
AFTERMATH: Daniloff surfaced again in 1988 when he toured the country promoting his autobiography, *Two Lives, One Russia* (published on the second anniversary of his imprisonment). He became a professor at Northeastern University in Boston and a respected expert on Russia.

THE STAR: Lucy De Barbin, Dallas clothes designer who claimed to be Elvis's lover and mother of his child
THE HEADLINE: *Dallas Designer's Daughter Royal Descendant?*
WHAT HAPPENED: In 1987 De Barbin revealed her secret 24-year affair with Elvis in a book entitled *Are You Lonesome Tonight?: The Untold True Story of Elvis Presley's One True Love – and the Child He Never Knew.* She said they kept their involvement a secret so it wouldn't mess up his career. Later, she kept it quiet to protect Lisa Marie and the daughter she had with Elvis, Desir'ee. 'I was so afraid of what was going to happen (if the secret got out)', she told a reporter. 'I thought if one person found out, everybody would know'. She didn't even tell Elvis they had a child, she said, although she hinted at it in a phone conversation just before the King's death: 'I just said things like, "I have a wonderful secret to tell you" and "Her name is Desir'ee", things like that. And he said, "I hope what I'm thinking is true"'.
De Barbin's publisher, Random House, believed her. And several experts confirmed that a poem the King had reportedly written for De Barbin was in his handwriting. But neither the public nor the Presley estate bought the story.
AFTERMATH: De Barbin never produced blood samples to prove that her daughter was Elvis'. Apparently, she offered no real evidence that they'd been lovers. The Presley estate claimed that because the book was not a success (it actually was), they didn't need to bother suing De Barbin.

THE STAR: Matthias Jung, a German tourist in Dubrovnik, Croatia
THE HEADLINE: *Brazen Tourist Has Dubrovnik All to Himself*
WHAT HAPPENED: Dubrovnik, Croatia, was one of the world's loveliest towns and a major tourist resort. But for seven months, from autumn 1991 to spring 1992, the Serbs bombarded it with mortar shells. Tourism fell off, then disappeared. In August 1995, tourists warily started returning – only to be greeted with more shelling. They all fled, except one – Jung, a 32-year-old shopkeeper from Hanover. He wasn't a thrill-seeker; he just wanted peace and quiet for his vacation.
AFTERMATH: After a while, things got *so* quiet that Jung admitted he was bored and went north.

Human beings have 46 chromosomes. Goldfish have 96.

MYTH-SPOKEN

Everyone knows that Captain Kirk said, 'Beam me up, Scotty' in every episode of Star Trek *and that Bogart said, 'Play it again, Sam' in* Casablanca. *But everyone's wrong. Here are a few common misquotes.*

Line: 'Beam me up, Scotty'.
Supposedly Said By: Captain Kirk
Actually: That line was *never* spoken on *Star Trek*. Not once. What Kirk usually said was, 'Beam us up, Mr. Scott', or 'Enterprise, beam us up'. According to Trekkies –who really know about this sort of stuff – he came pretty close just once. In the fourth episode, he said, 'Scotty, beam me up'.

Line: 'Don't fire till you see the whites of their eyes'.
Supposedly Said By: Colonel William Prescott to American soldiers at the Battle of Bunker Hill, as they lay in wait for the British during the American War of Independence.
Actually: Sounds like another American myth. There's no record of Prescott ever saying it, but there are records of both Prince Charles of Prussia (in 1745) and Frederick the Great (in 1757) using the command.

Line: 'You dirty rat'.
Supposedly Said By: James Cagney in one of his movies
Actually: Every Cagney impressionist says it, but Cagney himself never did. He made over 70 movies but never spoke this line in any of them.

Line: 'Nice guys finish last'.
Supposedly Said By: Leo Durocher in 1946, when he was manager of the Brooklyn Dodgers.
Actually: While being interviewed, he waved toward the Giants' dugout and said, 'The nice guys are all over there. In seventh place'. When the article came out, reporters had changed his statement to 'The nice guys are all over there in last place'. As it was repeated, it was shortened to 'Nice guys finish last'. Durocher protested that he'd never made the remark but couldn't shake it. Finally he gave in, and eventually used it as the title of his autobiography.

The world's first recorded tonsillectomy was performed in the year 1000 B.C.

Line: 'Gerry Ford (U.S. president, 1974-77) is so dumb he can't walk and chew gum at the same time'.
Supposedly Said By: President Lyndon Johnson
Actually: This remark was cleaned up for the public – what Johnson really said was, 'Gerry Ford is so dumb he can't fart and chew gum at the same time'.

Line: 'How I wish I had not expressed my theory of evolution as I have done'.
Supposedly Said By: Charles Darwin, on his deathbed
Actually: The Christian evangelist, Jimmy Swaggart, announced in a speech in 1985 that Darwin had spoken the words as he lay dying, and asked that the Bible be read to him. But it was an old lie started shortly after Darwin's death by a Christian fanatic who was speaking to seminary students. Darwin's daughter and son both deny that their father ever had any change of heart about his scientific theory. According to his son, his last words were, 'I am not the least afraid to die'.

Line: 'I rob banks because that's where the money is'.
Supposedly Said By: Infamous bank robber Willie Sutton
Actually: According to Sutton, it was a reporter who thought up this statement and printed it. 'I can't even remember when I first read it', Sutton once remarked. 'It just seemed to appear one day, and then it was everywhere'.

Line: 'Play it again, Sam'.
Supposedly Said By: Humphrey Bogart, in the classic film *Casablanca*
Actually: This may be the most famous movie line ever, but it wasn't in the movie. Ingrid Bergman said, 'Play it, Sam. Play "As Time Goes By".' And Bogart said 'If she can stand it, I can. Play it!' But the only person who ever used 'Play it again, Sam' was Woody Allen – who jokingly called his theatrical homage to Bogart *Play It Again, Sam* because he knew it was a misquote.

Line: 'Elementary, my dear Watson'.
Supposedly Said By: Sherlock Holmes, in Arthur Conan Doyle's books
Actually: Holmes never said it in any of the stories. It was a movie standard, however, beginning in 1929 with *The Return of Sherlock Holmes*.

The word hussy originally meant 'housekeeper'.

BOND(S) – *JAMES* BONDS

Every 007 fan has their own opinion of which actor – Sean Connery, George Lazenby, Roger Moore, Timothy Dalton or Pierce Brosnan – made the best James Bond…but do you know how each actor landed the role? Here are their stories.

SEAN CONNERY (See page 302 for the whole story.)

The role of James Bond turned Connery from a nobody into an international sex symbol in less than five years – but as Connery's fame grew with each Bond film, so did his frustration with the part. He worried about being typecast, he hated reporters, and he was annoyed by the crowds of fans that followed him wherever he went. And since his image was inextricably linked with the Bond character, he was angry that Cubby Broccoli and Harry Saltzman wouldn't make him a full partner in the 007 films and merchandising deals. He left the series in 1967 after making *You Only Live Twice*, his sixth Bond film.

GEORGE LAZENBY

In 1967 a friend asked George Lazenby, a part-time actor from Australia, to substitute for him on a blind date when his girlfriend suddenly came back to town.

The blind date 'was supposed to be some up-and-coming agent, which was why he wanted to go out with her', Lazenby recounted years later, 'but I didn't care. I was running a health studio in Belgium'. Some months later, the agent remembered Lazenby and contacted him when the search for Connery's replacement in *On Her Majesty's Secret Service* got underway. 'I got the part', Lazenby remembers, 'and my friend's career fizzled'.

So did Lazenby's: after fighting with the producers, the director and co-star Diana Rigg during the making of *On Her Majesty's Secret Service*, he either resigned or was fired, depending on who you ask.

When it premièred in 1969, *On Her Majesty's Secret Service* was panned by the critics and was a box-office disappointment; today it is considered one of the best of the Bond films.

SEAN CONNERY (II)

Panicked by the drubbing *On Her Majesty's Secret Service* took at the box office, Broccoli and Saltzman paid a reluctant Sean Connery $1.25 million plus a huge share of the profits to return to the series in the 1971 film *Diamonds Are Forever*.

Connery needed the boost – most of his post-Bond films were box-office flops – but he quit the series again after just one film, turning down a reported $5 million for *Live and Let Die*. The role went instead to his old friend Roger Moore. (Burt Reynolds was also considered, but Broccoli insisted on an Englishman.)

Connery returned for a seventh, and last, time in the 1983 film *Never Say Never Again*.

ROGER MOORE

Moore was one of Ian Fleming's original choices for the Bond role, and he finally got his shot in *Live and Let Die*. Unlike Lazenby, Moore succeeded – largely by complementing, not imitating, Connery's interpretation of the role. As Raymond Benson writes in *The James Bond Bedside Companion*,

> From *Live and Let Die* on, the scriptwriters tailored the screenplays to fit Roger Moore's personality. As a result, James Bond lost much of the *machismo* image which was so prominent in the sixties. It seems Bond never gets hurt in any of the subsequent films – the Roger Moore Bond uses his wits rather than fists to escape dangerous situations.

Moore's departure from Connery's Bond was so dramatic that it inspired a Beatles-vs.-Rolling Stones-type rivalry among 007 fans over who was the best Bond. 'People who saw their first Bond with Sean never took to Roger', says 007 marketing executive Charles Juroe, 'and people who saw their first Bond with Roger never took to Sean. Roger's movies grossed more than Sean's'. Moore made a total of seven Bond films between 1973 and 1985, tying Sean Connery. His last was *A View to a Kill*.

TIMOTHY DALTON

First choice for Moore's replacement was Irish actor Pierce Brosnan, star of the recently cancelled American TV series *Remington Steele*. Brosnan was given the unofficial nod for the role, but when word of the deal leaked, it generated so much publicity for the failing *Remington Steele* that the show's ratings skyrocketed to

The Netherlands used to be known as the United States.

fifth place in the U.S. ratings, their highest in history, promoting NBC to *un*-cancel the show and force Brosnan to serve out the remainder of his contract. With Brosnan out of the running, the job went to British actor Timothy Dalton, who appeared in *The Living Daylights* and *Licence to Kill*.

Dalton was considered by many 007 purists to be the best Bond since Connery; but he never dodged the stigma of being runner-up to Pierce Brosnan, and both films were box-office disappointments. In April 1994, amid rumours he was being fired, Dalton quit the series.

PIERCE BROSNAN

Two moths after Dalton quit, Brosnan finally won the nod to play 007 in *Goldeneye*, the 18th film in the series. 'Most of today's biggest male stars were eliminated from consideration for the role', the *New York Times* reported in 1994. 'Hugh Grant was thought too wimpy, Liam Neeson too icy. Mel Gibson…was deemed not quite right. Even Sharon Stone was talked about for the part of Bond'. Brosnan turned out to be a wise choice:
Goldeneye was the highest-grossing Bond film in history, with more than $350 million in ticket sales around the world. He signed on for three more films.

DAVID NIVEN

There will always be debates over which Bond movie is the best, but there isn't much disagreement over which one was the worst: *Casino Royale*, starring David Niven as James Bond. By the time Cubby Broccoli and Harry Saltzman bought the film rights to Ian Fleming's other novels, the rights to his first book, *Casino Royale*, had already been sold to someone else.

Work on the film version of *Casino Royale* did not begin until 1967, when Sean Connery's Bond image was already well established. Rather than compete against Connery directly, the producers decided to make a Bond spoof starring Niven, Peter Sellers and Woody Allen.

Budgeted at $8 million, *Casino Royale* was the most expensive Bond film to date, as well as one of the messiest. Seven different writers wrote the screenplay, five different directors worked on various parts of the film, and seven of the characters are named James Bond. 'What might have begun as a great idea ends up a

J, the youngest letter in the English alphabet, was not added until the 1600s.

total mess', Raymond Benson writes in *The James Bond Bedside Companion*. 'The film should not be considered part of the James Bond series'.

POISON GAS

One of the ways the U.S. intelligence community protected itself against adverse publicity and budget cuts in the early 1960s was by sending agents to Hollywood to act as 'technical advisers' in spy films, thereby making the spy business appear vital and heroic to the public. *Dr. No* and other early Bond films were no exception: they had real-life secret agents working on the set.

The agents turned out to be quite useful, as Bond scriptwriter Richard Mailbum recalls:

> Before we got done, we had literally about ten technical agents, all telling us marvellous stories of what had happened to them all over the world which we incorporated into the plot. There were foreshadowings of things in the Bond films – the pipe that was a gun, and other gadgets. There were some things that we couldn't use, such as foul stuff smelling like an enormous fart that the OSS agents used to spray on people they wished to discredit.

* * *

PRESENTING – THE FEJEE MERMAID

Background: In 1842 P.T. Barnum began displaying the body of what he claimed was an actual mermaid, which he said had been found by sailors near the faraway island of 'Feejee'. (That's how Barnum spelled Fiji.) He put the mermaid on display in August 1842, printing up more than 10,000 flyers, leading up to opening day.

What Happened: The 'mermaid', one of the biggest hoaxes of Barnum's long career, was actually 'an ingenious sewing together of a large fish's body and tail with the head, shoulders, arms, and rather pendulous breasts of a female orangutan and the head of a baboon'. But it did the trick – at the peak of New York's 'mermaid fever', ticket sales at Barnum's Museum hit nearly $1,000 a week. 'In truth, by the close of 1843', says a biographer, 'with the help of…a dried up old mermaid, Barnum had become the most famous showman in America'.

THE CURSE OF THE HOPE DIAMOND

The Hope Diamond is probably the most famous jewel in the Western world – and it carries with it one of the most famous curses. How much of it is legend, and how much of it is fact? Even historians can't agree.

BACKGROUND

In 1668, a French diamond merchant named Jean-Baptiste Tavernier returned from India with a magnificent 112.5-carat blue diamond. No one knew exactly where he'd found it – but rumours spread that it was stolen from the eye of a sacred Indian idol – and people said it was cursed.

Nonetheless, King Louis XIV bought the Great Blue and added it to his crown jewels. Four years later, he had it re-cut into the shape of a heart (which reduced it to 67.5 carats).

In 1774, the diamond was inherited by Louis XVI. His wife, Marie Antoinette, apparently wore it; she was also said to have loaned it on one occasion to the Princesse de Lamballe.

> 'When the French Revolution broke out, the Princesse de Lamballe was murdered by a mob and her head paraded under the window where Louis the XVI and his family awaited execution.
>
> Marie Antoinette herself was executed in October 1793'.

– *The Book of Curses*, by Gordon Stuart

THE HOPE DIAMOND

In 1792, in the midst of the French Revolution, the Great Blue diamond was stolen. It was never seen whole again.

> 'Thirty years later it emerged in Holland, owned now by an Amsterdam lapidary named Fals. His son stole the diamond and left Fals to die in poverty. After giving it to a Frenchman, named Beaulieu, Fal's son killed himself. Beaulieu brought it to London, where he died mysteriously'.

– *The Book of Curses*

In Nepal, Mt. Everest is known as 'Gauriosankar'.

In 1830, an oval-shaped blue diamond weighing 44.5 carats turned up in a London auction house. Experts recognized it as a piece of the Great Blue, re-cut to conceal its identity.

A wealthy banker named Henry Philip Hope bought the jewel for about £55,000, and it henceforth became known as the Hope Diamond.

WAS IT CURSED?

Hope was warned about the gem's 'sinister influence', but owning it didn't seem to have any effect on his life. He died peacefully.

However, in the early 1900s terrible things began happening again. Lord Francis Hope, a distant relative who'd inherited it, went bankrupt. Then his marriage fell apart. 'His wife prophesied', says Colin Wilson in *Unsolved Mysteries*, 'that it would bring bad luck to all who owned it, and she died in poverty'.

She seemed to know what she was talking about. According to Colin Wilson, over the next few years:

- Lord Francis sold it to a French jewel dealer named Jacques Colot. He ultimately went insane and committed suicide.
- Colot sold it to a Russian prince. He lent it to his mistress, a dancer at the Folies Bergere. The first night she wore it, he shot her from his box in the theatre. Later, the prince was reportedly stabbed by Russian revolutionaries.
- A Greek jewel dealer named Simon Manthadides bought it. He later fell (or was pushed) over a precipice.
- A Turkish sultan named Abdul Hamid bought it in 1908. He was forced into exile the following year and went insane.

TEMPTING FATE?

One wonders why anyone would want the diamond at this point. But French jeweller Jacques Cartier took possession. He quickly resold it to Edward McClean (owner of the *Washington Post)* and his wife, Evalyn. A fascinated public watched to see if the 'curse' would affect them. Did it?

- According to some accounts, McLean's mother and two servants in his household died soon after he purchased the jewel.

> After her mother-in-law's death, Evalyn McLean had a priest bless the gem. In her autobiography she writes about the experience: 'Just as he blessed it – without any wind or rain – this tree right across the street was

> struck by lightning. My maid Maggie fainted dead away. The old fellow was scared to death and my knees were shaking. By the time we got home the sun was out, bright as anything'.

– *Vanity Fair* magazine

Over the next 30 years, Evalyn McLean's family was decimated. Her father soon became an alcoholic and died. Her father-in-law went insane. The McLeans' beloved 10-year-old son, Vinson, was hit and killed by a car in front of their house. Their marriage broke up and Edward McLean went insane; he died in a mental institution. McLean's daughter Emily – who had worn the Hope Diamond at her wedding – committed suicide.

AFTERMATH

Through all the tragedy and even her own gradual financial ruin, Evalyn McLean scoffed at the 'curse'. She continued to wear the Hope Diamond until her death in 1947. Two years later, her children sold it to the famous diamond dealer Harry Winston, to pay estate taxes. He kept it (with no apparent ill effect) until 1958, then decided to give it away. He put it in a box with $2.44 in postage, paid $155 for $1 million insurance, and sent it to the Smithsonian Institution, in Washington D.C., via U.S. mail. 'Letters of protest poured in to the museum', writes Gary Cohen in *Vanity Fair*. 'Some reasoned that the curse would be transferred to its new owners – the American people'.

> 'Within a year, James Todd, the mailman who had delivered the gem, had one of his legs crushed by a truck, injured his head in a car crash, and lost his wife and dog. Then his house burned down. When asked if he blamed his ill fortune on the diamond, he said, 'I don't believe any of that stuff'.'

– *Vanity Fair* magazine

Today, the diamond is owned by the U.S. government. And we all know what kind of luck the United States has had since 1959.

* * * * *

WHAT ABOUT LIZ? It's widely believed that Elizabeth Taylor once owned the Hope. Not true. She owns a larger diamond, often compared to the Hope, but now known as the Burton Diamond.

READ ALL ABOUT IT!

We've all heard the expression 'Don't believe everything you hear'. Here are a few more reasons not to believe everything you read, either. Take a look at these newspaper hoaxes, for example:

BRITISH SCIENTIST FINDS LIFE ON THE MOON!
(New York Sun, 1835)

The Story: In 1835 the *Sun* reprinted a series of articles from the *Edinburgh Journal of Science*, based on reports sent in by Sir John Herschel, a respected astronomer. He was at the Cape of Good Hope at the time, trying out a powerful new telescope.

In the first three instalments, Herschel wrote that with his super-telescope, he could see amazing things on the moon: lakes, fields of poppies, 38 species of forest trees, herds of buffalo with heavy eyelids, bears with horns, two-footed beavers, etc.

In the fourth instalment (28 August, 1835), he made the biggest revelation of all: he had seen furry, bat-winged people on the lunar surface. He wrote:

> They averaged four feet [1.2 metres] in height, were covered, except in the face, with short and glossy copper coloured hair, and had wings composed of a thin membrane, without hair, lying snugly upon their backs from the top of their shoulders to the calves of the legs.

He said their faces looked like baboons' and officially named them 'Vespertilio-homo', or 'bat-man'.

Reaction: People were lined up at newsstands, waiting for the next issue. Rival newspapers claimed to have access to the original *Edinburgh Journal* articles and began reprinting the series. By the fourth instalment, the *Sun's* publisher announced his paper had the largest circulation in the world – about 20,000. A book about the moon discoveries sold more than 60,000 copies. A committee of scientists from Yale University arrived at the offices of the *Sun* to inspect the source writings by Herschel (they were given the runaround until they gave up). One group of society ladies even began raising money to send Christian missionaries there.

The Truth: There was no *Edinburgh Journal of Science* – and the *Edinburgh Philosophical Journal* (which is what they meant to quote) had gone out of business two years earlier. The whole thing was concocted by a young reporter named Richard Adams Locke, who said later that he'd written it as a 'satire on absurd scientific speculations that had gotten out of hand'. When the *Sun's* editors realized how out of control their scheme had gotten, they admitted it was a fake – and scolded other newspapers for copying the story without giving them credit.

CIVIL WAR WOES: LINCOLN DRAFTS 400,000 MEN!
(Brooklyn Eagle, 18 May, 1864)

The Story: On the morning of May 18th, two New York newspapers, the *World* and the *Journal of Commerce*, reprinted an Associated Press dispatch in which President Abraham Lincoln, lamenting recent Union setbacks in the Civil War, called for a national day of 'fasting, humiliation, and prayer', and announced the drafting of 400,000 additional troops to fight in the war.

Reaction: Wall Street was rocked by the pessimistic proclamation: stock prices plummeted and gold prices soared as panicked investors looked for safe places to put their money. According to one Lincoln confidant, the story 'angered Lincoln more than almost any other occurrence of the war period'.

The Truth: The story was planted by Joseph Howard, the city editor of the *Brooklyn Eagle*, who hoped to get rich by buying gold cheap before the story broke and selling it at inflated prices afterward. Howard wrote the fake AP report with an accomplice, then paid copy boys to deliver it to every newspaper in New York. Only two papers, the *World* and the *Journal of Commerce*, printed it without bothering to check if it was true. Howard and his accomplice were arrested two days after the story broke; they spent three months interned at an Army fort without trial before Lincoln personally ordered their release.

The Hidden Truth: As Carl Sifakis writes in *Hoaxes and Scams*,

> At the very time the phony proclamation was released, Lincoln had a real one on his desk, calling for the drafting of 300,000 men.
>
> When the president saw the impact of the false proclamation on the public and the financial markets, he delayed the real call up for 60 days until the situation cooled.

About 75 per cent of all the gold mined each year is made into jewellery.

MY MATE MARMITE?

Be prepared for a battle to the death, for in this war there can be no sitting on the fence. It has split families and ruined romances. What is it? Marmite. And you either love it or hate it.

In 1902, the Marmite Food Extract Company Limited was set up in a factory in Burton-on-Trent, at the heart of Britain's brewing industry. There was a good reason for the location. Believe it or not – and if you're eating a slice of Marmite-coated toast as you read this, you might want to put it down – the main ingredient in Marmite is recycled (i.e., used) brewer's yeast. Still, if you are a Marmite lover, that probably doesn't bother you – if you like Marmite, you like it no matter what.

A SLOW SPREADING YEAST INFECTION

Given its main ingredient, it's no wonder the product was slow to take off, especially when you add to that its sharp taste and the tar-like gloopy look of the stuff. Sales were boosted when it was discovered that yeast is a good source of vitamin B. Since then, the recipe for Marmite has remained largely unchanged over the years, despite the company changing hands many times. Marmite is the quintessential English food, the misfit we love to champion (or the oddball we love to hate). At least it's natural and vegan. The name came from the French word for pot, as in a cooking pot, which the bulb-shaped bottle resembles. The major permanent change to the Marmite look came in 1984, when the lid was changed from metal to yellow plastic.

THE TASTE OF BRITAIN

Until Internet sellers made it easy to get, Brits abroad often found that Marmite was one of the things they missed the most when they left the UK. There are imitators: Singaporean Marmite, Vegemite (from Australia) and a New Zealand brand, made by the appetizing-sounding Sanitarium Health Food Company. But for true Marmite lovers nothing compares to the real thing.

A British backpacker kidnapped in India in 1994 said it was the first thing he ate on his release. It's even a must-have item for expectant celebrities. Both Michael Douglas and David Beckham were snapped buying pots of the stuff for their pregnant spouses, Catherine Zeta-Jones and Posh Spice. Like everyone else, they knew there were no substitutes. Bovril, Promite and the low-cost, does-exactly-what-it-says-on-the-tin brand, Yeast Extract, have never inspired the devotion attached to Marmite. There are even Marmite-flavoured crisps and twiglets, designed to satisfy the cravings of yeast-addicts with a bad case of the munchies.

DIGGING FOR BLACK GOLD

Marmite is properly eaten on toast, spread thinly. Very thinly. Its taste can quickly overpower. If you use butter, make sure you don't get buttery crumbs in the jar. Let's face it, it looks bad enough to begin with. It's a good flavouring: a teaspoon can brighten up soups and casseroles, or be a substitute meat stock for a vegetarian dish. The main problem comes when the end of the jar is in sight. There's usually just enough under the broad shoulders of the bottle to warrant fiddling around with a knife, but it takes quite a bit of poking around to get it out to make a decent snack. Still, that's half the fun. Use a bendy knife and you'll get it all out (or, if no-one's looking, use your finger).

A LOVE-HATE RELATIONSHIP

Marmite has played on its controversial status. For a while it was 'the growing-up spread you never grow out of' and then there was the chant of 'My mate. Marmite'. By the centenary year of 2002, sales were booming, and Marmite's manufacturers launched a crafty advertising campaign, finally acknowledging that 'you either love it or you hate it'.

Marmite will continue to divide friends and families, pitting brother against brother and husband against wife. The taste of this spread is so distinctive that everyone knows what you mean if you say something is 'Marmite'. Margaret Thatcher, for example, was a Marmite politician. You thought she was awful or you loved her, there was definitely no middle ground. Although, unlike Marmite, even if you loved her you probably still wouldn't want to find her sitting at your breakfast table as you emerge bleary-eyed from the bedroom one morning!

WISE WOMEN

Some thoughtful observations from members of the stronger sex.

'If the world were a logical place, men would ride side-saddle'.

– *Rita Mae Brown*

'Creative minds have always been known to survive any kind of bad training'.

– *Anna Freud*

'Blessed is the man who, having nothing to say, abstains from giving worthy evidence of the fact'.

– *George Eliot*

'If you just set out to be liked, you would be prepared to compromise on anything at any time, and you would achieve nothing'.

– *Margaret Thatcher*

'If you don't risk anything, you risk even more'.

– *Erica Jong*

'How wonderful it is that nobody need wait a single moment before starting to improve the world'.

– *Anne Frank*

'It is not true that life is one damn thing after another. It's one damn thing over and over'.

– *Edna St. Vincent Millay*

'The heresy of one age becomes the orthodoxy of the next'.

– *Helen Keller*

'Regret is an appalling waste of energy; you can't build on it; it is only good for wallowing in'.

– *Katherine Mansfield*

'In the face of an obstacle which is impossible to overcome, stubbornness is stupid'.

– *Simone de Beauvoir*

'Spend the afternoon. You can't take it with you'.

– *Annie Dillard*

'You can be up to your boobies in white satin, with gardenias in your hair and no sugarcane for miles, but you can still be working on a plantation'.

– *Billie Holiday*

'You take your life in your own hands, and what happens? A terrible thing: no one to blame'.

– *Erica Jong*

'Just remember, we're all in this alone'.

– *Lily Tomlin*

Q: Why are boxing rings called rings?

RANDOM ORIGINS

Once again, the B.R.I. asks – and answers – the question: where did all this stuff come from?

THE TELEPHONE BOOTH

Alexander Graham Bell invented the telephone, but it was his assistant, Thomas Watson ('Come here, Mr. Watson'), who invented the phone booth. The reason: his landlady complained that he made too much noise shouting into the phone during his calls. Watson remedied the situation by throwing blankets over some furniture and climbing underneath whenever he needed to make a call; by 1883 he'd upgraded to an enclosed wooden booth with a domed top, screened windows, a writing desk and even a ventilator.

THE SLOT MACHINE

Other types of gambling machines date back as far as the 1890s, but the first one to really catch on was a vending machine for chewing gum introduced by the Mills Novelty Company in 1910. Their machine dispensed three flavours of gum – cherry, orange and plum – depending on which fruits appeared on three randomly spinning wheels. If three bars reading '1910 Fruit Gum' appeared in a row, the machine gave *extra* gum; if a lemon appeared, it gave no gum at all (which is why 'lemon' came to mean something unsatisfactory or defective.) You can't get gum in a slot machine anymore – the 1910 Fruit Gum machine was so popular that the company converted them to cash payouts – but the same fruit symbols are still used in slot machines today.

THE CINEMA MULTIPLEX

Invented by accident by theater owner Stan Durwood in 1963, when he tried to open a large theatre in a Kansas City, Missouri, shopping mall. The mall's developer told Durwood that the support columns in the building could not be removed to build a single large theatre...so Durwood built two smaller theatres instead. He showed the same movie on both screens – until it dawned on him that he'd sell more tickets if he showed two different films. It was a huge success; the national attention he got spurred a 'multiplex boom' in other cities.

MADE IN SWITZERLAND

If you've ever owned a Swiss Army knife, chances are you've asked yourself these two questions: Is there a Swiss army? And if so, do they really use these knives? The short answer is yes...and yes. The long answer is...

BACKGROUND. In 1891 Karl Elsner, owner of a company that made surgical instruments, got a rude shock – he found out that the pocket knives used by the Swiss Army were made in Germany. Outraged, he founded the Association of Swiss Master Cutlers. Their purpose: the manufacture of Swiss knives for Swiss soldiers.

Elsner designed a wood-handled knife that also contained a screwdriver, a punch and a can-opener. He called it 'the Soldier's Knife' and sold it to the Swiss Army.

But Elsner wasn't finished yet – he also wanted to develop a better knife for officers. It took five years, but he finally found a way to put blades on both sides of the handle, using the same spring to hold them in place – something no one had done before This made it possible to put roughly twice as many features on the knife. Elsner replaced the wood handle with red fibre (which lasted longer), then added a second blade and a corkscrew.

CHANGES.

Elsner had the market all to himself until 1908. Then a preacher named Theordore Wenger, from the French-speaking region of the country, started selling a similar product. The Swiss government, sensitive to regional favouritism, started buying half their pocket knives from him...and they still do. Today, the two companies are rivals. Elsner's company, Victorinox (after his mother, Victoria) calls its knife the 'original' Swiss Army Knife. The Wenger Company calls its knife the 'genuine' Swiss Army Knife. Each is allowed to put the Swiss White Cross on its knife – but no other company is.

Swiss Army knives became popular in the United States after World War II; returning G.I'.s brought them home by the thousands. Today, the U.S. is the world's largest market for them. And ironically, Victorinox, founded to prevent the Swiss Army from buying German pocket knives, is now the official supplier of pocket knives to the German Army.

In 2003, some 300,000 women and just 271,000 men had £200,000 in cash, shares and bonds.

A TOY IS BORN

Here are the origins of some toys you may have played with.

THE ERECTOR SET

Inventor: A.C. Gilbert, an Olympic pole-vaulter who owned the Mysto Company, which sold magic tricks and magicians' equipment

Origin: The market for magic tricks was pretty narrow, and Gilbert was hoping to break into the toy business. But he couldn't think of a product. Then one day in 1911, while riding a commuter train to New York City, Gilbert saw some new power lines being strung from steel girders. It suddenly occurred to him that kids might enjoy building things out of miniaturized girders. So he went home, cut out prototype girders from cardboard, and gave them to a machinist to make out of steel. 'When I saw the samples', Gilbert wrote in his autobiography, 'I knew I had something'.

Selling It: Gilbert brought the prototypes to the big toy fairs of the year, in Chicago and New York...and walked out with enough orders to keep his factory busy for a year. So Gilbert took a chance and the following year, he made the Erector Set the first major toy ever to be advertised nationally. It sold so well that overnight, the Gilbert Toy Company became one of America's largest toy manufacturers.

THE BABY ALIVE DOLL

Inventor: The Kenner Products Company

Origin: Baby dolls that wet themselves were nothing new in the early 1970s, and they were popular sellers. So in 1972 Kenner decided to take the concept to the next level with a doll called Baby Alive. When someone held a spoon or a bottle up to the doll's mouth, she took in the food...and after 'a suitable interval', she pooped it back out again. The baby's 'food' consisted of cherry, banana, and lime 'food packets' that were actually colored gel. 'And to answer the obvious question', writes Sydney Stem in *Toyland,* 'yes, what went in red, yellow, or green came out red, yellow or green'.

Selling It: At the time, Kenner was owned by food giant General Mills – which meant that Kenner president Bernie Loomis had to get approval from the Chairman of General Mills before he could put the doll into production. He nearly blew it, Stem writes:

> Unfortunately, he forgot to put a disposable diaper on the doll before feeding it, and it extruded poo-poo gel all over his boss's arm. 'Who in the world would ever want such a messy thing', asked the disgruntled chairman. As it turned out, there were fast hordes of children eager to own a defecating dolly. Baby Alive was the number-one-selling doll in 1973, and Kenner went on to sell three million of them.

RISK

Inventor: Albert Lamorisse, a French filmmaker

Origin: In 1957, a year after winning an Academy Award for his (now-classic) film, *The Red Balloon*, Lamorisse created the game he called *La Conquête du Monde* (Conquest of the World).

Sales Tales: *La Conquête du Monde* was a big hit in France, prompting U.S. game maker Parker Brothers to snap up the rights to the American version. They immediately ran into a problem: many of the executives at Parker Brothers were veterans of World War II and the Korean War, and they were uncomfortable with the game's title. So Parker Brothers ordered their R&D department to come up with a less warlike name. No luck – nobody could think of a name until a salesperson happened to hand the Parker Brothers president a piece of paper with the letters R-I-S-K written on it. A divine inspiration? No. According to company lore, R-I-S-K were merely the first letters of the names of each of Parker Brothers president's four grandchildren.

Historical Footnote: Risk was banned in Germany for years...until the object of the German version was changed from 'conquering the world' to 'liberating the world'.

* * *

PING PONG INVENTED IN UK

Ping-pong was invented in Englad in the 1890s as a rainy-day alternative to lawn tennis; 'table tennis' quickly became more popular than tennis had ever been. Parker Brothers imported it to the United States in 1902.

MISTAKEN IDENTITY

Next time someone says, 'You know, you really remind me of so-and-so' don't just laugh it off – GET PARANOID! According to the BRI's extensive files, a case of mistaken identity can lead to...

HARRASSMENT

Background: Slobodan 'Dan' Milosovic (spelled with an 'o'), has lived in London, since 1980. Unfortunately for him, he has the same name – more or less – as Serbian ex-president Slobodan Milosevic (spelled with an 'e').

What Happened: During the Kosovo war, reporters assumed there was some connection between the two, and camped out on Milosovic's doorstep. They not only harangued him with questions, they even began quizzing his neighbours. Eventually, Milosovic had to lodge a complaint with the Press Complaints Commission in protest against all of the attention. 'Milosovic was fed up with being hounded by the media', said the media.

LAWSUITS

Background: Kevin Moore, a 45-year-old Florida resident, was contacted some years ago by a woman named Anne Victoria Moore, who assumed she had finally located her ex-husband, also named Kevin Moore. He assured her she had made a mistake.

What Happened: Ms. Moore refused to believe him. At last report, Ms. Moore had spent more than eight months filing legal actions against Kevin Moore. First, she placed a claim on his house...then on his bank account...and then charged him with failure to pay child support. She persists, although numerous government agencies have informed her that this Kevin Moore is '11 years older than, six inches shorter than, and facially dissimilar to, her ex-husband'.

UNEMPLOYMENT

Background: In 1990 Bronti Wayne Kelly, of Temecula, California, had his wallet stolen. The man who stole it was then caught for shoplifting, and 'pretended to be Kelly when he was arrested'.

What Happened: Kelly wound up with a criminal record. And according to news reports, after losing his wallet in the theft, he also 'lost his apartment, car and most of his belongings between 1991 and 1995 because no one would hire him....Every time potential employers did a background check, they found the shoplifting arrest...The same man apparently also pretended to be Kelly when he was arrested for arson, burglary, theft, and disturbing the peace'. Today Kelly carries a special document that distinguishes him from the impostor, but – amazingly – 'he cannot have the criminal record carrying his name erased unless the fake Kelly is found'.

IMPRISONMENT

Background: In 1993, a 'woman with long blonde hair' broke into the house of a Mississippi man named Darron Terry. He caught her in the act...but she escaped. Following the burglary, Terry looked through some photographs and identified Melissa Gammill, 'a carefree single woman working at a mall food court', as the culprit. Three months later, Gammill was arrested.

What Happened: Gammill could not provide an alibi, because she couldn't remember where she'd been on the night of the burglary. She was charged with the crime, convicted and sentenced to ten years in prison. Luckily for Gammill, her lawyer, Debra Allen, believed that her client was innocent and developed a hunch that a lookalike had actually committed the crime. She pursued her theory until she stumbled across a mugshot of Pauline Meshea Bailey, who looks so much like Gammill that their photographs are practically interchangeable. In April 1995, Terry admitted he'd mistakenly identified the wrong person, and Gammill was set free after serving 10 months in prison.

ASSASSINATION

Background: During World War II, England's prime minister, Winston Churchill, was targeted by Nazi agents for assassination. They were constantly on the alert, waiting for an opportunity to strike. In 1943, their moment came. At an airport in Lisbon, Portugal (a neutral country), they saw Churchill, famous as 'a portly, cigar-smoking Britisher', board a commercial flight to England.

What Happened: According to Churchill in his 1950 memoir, *The Hinge of Fate:*

> The daily commercial aircraft was about to start from the Lisbon airfield when a thickset man smoking a cigar walked up and was thought to be a passenger on it. The German agents therefore signalled that I was on board. Although these neutral passenger planes had plied unmolested for many months between Portugal and England and had carried only civilian traffic, a German war plane was instantly ordered out, and the defenceless aircraft was ruthlessly shot down. Fourteen civilian passengers perished, among them the well-known British film actor, Leslie Howard.

The 'portly, cigar smoking Britisher' was in reality one Alfred Chenhalls. 'The brutality of the Germans was only matched by the stupidity of their agents', Churchill wrote. 'It is difficult to understand how anyone could imagine that with all the resources of Great Britain at my disposal, I should have booked passage on a neutral plane from Lisbon and flown home in broad daylight'.

THE DESTRUCTION OF AN ENTIRE CIVILIZATION

Background: When Hernán Cortés landed in Mexico with his 600 soldiers in 1519, the Aztecs were in control of most of present-day Mexico. They had been since around the year 1200.

Religion was a major part of Aztec life...and according to legend, the god Quetzalcoatl, who had light skin, light eyes, and a beard (just like Cortés) was supposed to return to earth. So when Cortés and his men started to march toward the Aztec capital city of Tenochtitlán (now Mexico City), word passed that Quetzalcoatl had come back.

What Happened: In the capital city, the Aztec king, Montezuma, received the visitors 'in fulfillment of the ancient prophecy'. The Spaniards were greeted with food, gold and women. Montezuma is quoted as saying to Cortés, 'Our lord, you are weary. The journey has tired you, but now you have arrived on the earth. You have come to your city....You have come here to sit on your throne, to sit under its canopy'. Cortés, in reply, assured Montezuma he had come in peace. Actually, he had come to conquer and quickly took Montezuma hostage. The Spaniards then proceeded to wipe the Aztec civilization out.

Often when actors are filmed in a car through the windshield, there's no rearview mirror.

SALT OF THE EARTH

A few facts you can use to spice up your conversation at dinner tonight.

SALT BECOMES YOU

• **Salt is life itself:** We each have about eight ounces of salt inside us. It's vital for regulating muscle contraction, heartbeat, nerve impulse transmission, protein digestion and the exchange of water between cells, so as to bring food in and waste out. Deprived of salt, the body goes into convulsion, paralysis and death.

• **Hypertension and salt:** Baby food makers have learned they can sell more if they salt it. Why? Because mothers are the ones who buy it and they like the taste better. Critics say babies don't need the salt and that hooking them on it early in life predisposes them to high blood pressure.

• **Salt can be poison:** It's healthy to eat about a third of an ounce of salt a day. If you eat more than four ounces at once, you'll die.

SALT SCIENCE

• Strangely enough, salt is made of two elements – sodium and chlorine – which, if put in your mouth by themselves, will either blow up (sodium) or poison you (chlorine). But merged into a compound – sodium chloride – they change into an essential ingredient of life. The salt taste comes from the chlorine – which is also vital for making the hydrochloric acid which digests food in our stomach.

• Scientists once thought the oceans were salty because rivers constantly washed salt out of soil and carried it to sea. But then they found pools of seawater trapped in underground sediments millions of years ago that show the ocean has always been about as salty as it is now.

• We can never run out of salt. There's enough in the oceans to cover the world in a layer 35cm deep.

• Salt is the only mineral that can be mined by turning it into a liquid (by pumping water in). Then they pump out the brine and turn it back into a solid by evaporation.

• Salt is hygroscopic, which means it absorbs water. That's why you can't drink seawater; it will dehydrate you.
• Salt is one of the four things the tongue can taste (the others are sweet, sour and bitter). Only sweet and bitter are inborn; salt is an acquired taste.
• The hypothalamus at the base of the brain measures sodium and potassium in body fluids. When they get too high (from either not drinking enough water or eating too much salt), it triggers the sensation of thirst.

SALT MISCELLANY

• Only 5 per cent of the salt we mine goes into food. The rest goes into making chemicals.
• When salt is made by vigorous boiling, it forms cubic crystals, but when it's naturally dried, it makes pyramid-shaped crystals. The pyramid-shaped crystals are particularly sought after for kosher use and in cordon bleu cooking.
• It takes four gallons of seawater to make a pound of salt.
• Salt is often found with oil and is often used by oil companies as an indicator of where to drill.
• For centuries, salt was served in a bowl, not a shaker. It couldn't be shaken, since it absorbs water and sticks together. The Morton Salt Co. changed that in 1910 by covering every grain with chemicals that keep water out – thus its famous slogan, 'When it rains, it pours'.
• The water in our bodies (we're 70 per cent water) has the same saltiness as the seas from which we evolved. The amniotic fluid surrounding foetuses in the womb is essentially saltwater.

SALT SUPERSTITIONS

• In Scandinavia, knocking over salt is considered bad luck…*if* the salt gets wet.
• In some cultures people believe that since salt corrodes, it destroys evil. As protection, they wear a sachet of salt around their necks, and sprinkle it on brooms before sweeping their homes.
• Hebrews, Greeks and Romans all salted their sacrifices.
• Bedouins won't attack a man if they've eaten his salt.

Pearls are made of calcium carbonate, the active ingredient in antacids.

THE BARBADOS TOMBS

The island of Barbados is known for its tropical climate, its sandy beaches – and its restless dead. Here are two legendary, unexplained mysteries surrounding people who have been buried on the island.

THE CHASE FAMILY CRYPT

Background Col. Thomas Chase and his family were wealthy English settlers living on Barbados in the early 1800s. They owned a large burial crypt in the graveyard of Christ Church. In 1807, Thomisina Goddard, a relative of the Chases, died and was interred in the crypt. A year later, Mary Chase, Thomas Chase's infant daughter, died mysteriously. (It was widely believed that Thomas Chase beat her to death; he was known as a violent man who beat his children – a number of whom showed signs of mental illness.) She, too, was placed in the crypt. But unlike Thomisina, who was placed in a wooden coffin, Mary's body was placed in a heavy lead coffin. After her casket was interred, the vault was sealed shut with a massive marble slab.

A Mysterious Happening

A few months afterward, Dorcas Chase (Thomas Chase's teenage daughter) starved herself to death. Like her infant sister, Dorcas was placed in a heavy lead casket and brought to the crypt. But when the family unsealed and opened the vault, they saw that something peculiar had happened. Mary Chase's tiny coffin had moved to the opposite side of the crypt – and it was standing on one end. Thomisina Goddard's casket had not been moved.

The family was shocked, but assumed the crypt had been broken into by grave robbers. They returned Mary's casket to its proper place, laid Dorcas's coffin next to it, and sealed the crypt even tighter than before – this time pouring a layer of molten lead over the marble capstone.

A Moving Experience

Thomas Chase committed suicide a month later. As with Mary and Dorcas, his body was placed in a heavy lead casket. This time when the crypt was opened, all the coffins were still in place. The crypt was again tightly sealed; it would not be reopened again by the family for another eight years.

In 1816 another child related to the Chase family died. This time when the vault was unsealed, the hinges on the doors were so rusty, they would not open; it took two strong men to finally pry them open wide enough to get the coffin inside. But when the family peered into the dark vault, they saw that the caskets had again been strewn about the crypt…except for Thomasina Goddard's, which was left untouched a second time.

The mourners were dumbfounded: the adult-sized lead coffins weighed more than 230 kg each, and the child-sized ones weren't much lighter. It took four strong men to return each of the caskets to their proper places, and it seemed inconceivable that any natural forces could have tossed them around the tomb.

Keep on Moving

Less than a month after this latest interment, a woman visiting another grave heard groans and 'loud cracking' noises coming from the Chase family crypt. Her horse became so agitated by the noises that it began foaming at the mouth and had to be treated by a vet. And a week after that, something spooked several horses tied up outside Christ Church; they broke free, ran down the hill and jumped into the sea, where they drowned.

By now the goings-on in the vault were public knowledge and the source of wild speculation; when the next member of the Chase family died, more than 1,000 people came to the funeral – some from as far away as Cuba and Haiti. They weren't disappointed: when the crypt was unsealed, all of the coffins were out of place, each one standing on end against the walls of the crypt – except for Thomasina Goddard's.

You Move Me, Governor

After this funeral, the governor of the island decided to investigate. He attended the next funeral, and once again the coffins had been strewn about. This time, he tested the crypt's walls for secret passages (there were none), had the floor of the crypt covered with sand to detect footprints and other marks, had a new lock installed in the crypt's door, and had the crypt sealed with a layer of cement to be sure the door would not be opened. To top it off, he and other officials stamped the wet cement with their signet

Doctors, more than any other profession, are most likely to be late for a doctor's appointment.

rings, making sure that it couldn't be tampered with without being detected.

On 8 April, 1820, the vault was reopened to inter another member of the Chase family. The cement was still in place, but when the family removed it, something heavy leaning against the door of the crypt prevented it from being opened. Several strong men tried to force the door open...and when they finally succeeded, something crashed down inside the crypt. They opened the door all the way...and saw that it had been held shut because one of the coffins had been leaning against it. This time *all* the coffins had been disturbed – including Thomasina Goddard's.

The governor and several others examined the crypt closely to try and find an explanation. There was none; there were no footprints in the sand and none of the jewellery on any of the bodies had been stolen. Completely mystified, the governor ordered that the bodies be removed from the crypt and interred in another crypt on the island. They were never disturbed again; they rest in peace to this day.

THE McGREGOR CRYPT

Background The Chase crypt wasn't the only one on Barbados to have strange things happen to it. In August 1943, a group of Freemasons unsealed a crypt containing the body of Alexander Irvine, the founder of freemasonry on Barbados. (Irvine's remains were interred in the 1830s in the same crypt as Sir Even McGregor, the owner of the crypt, who was laid to rest in 1841.)

Strange Happenings

The McGregor crypt was even more tightly sealed than the Chase crypt: the inner door was locked tight and cemented with bricks and mortar, which itself was covered with a huge stone slab. When they unsealed the crypt, the inner door of the tomb would not open. Peeking in through a hole, they saw that a heavy lead coffin was standing on its head, leaning against the inner door. The masons carefully moved it and opened the door – only to discover that Irvine's coffin was missing; McGregor's was the one up against the door. The mystery was never solved; the island's burial records confirmed that both men had been interred in the crypt nearly 100 years before, but no evidence was ever found to explain the missing coffin.

British anatomist Richard Owen invented the word 'dinosaur' in 1841.

OFF YOUR ROCKER

We'll bet you didn't know your favorite rock singers could talk, too. Here are some of the profound things they have to say.

'I'm a mess and you're a mess, too. Everyone's a mess. Which means, actually, that no one's a mess'.

– *Fiona Apple*

'It's really hard to maintain a one-on-one relationship if the other person is not going to allow me to be with other people'.

– *Axl Rose*

'I only answer to two people – myself and God'.

– *Cher*

'I'm not a snob. Ask anybody. Well, anybody who matters'.

– *Simon LeBon, of Duran Duran*

'There's a basic rule which runs through all kinds of music, kind of an unwritten rule. I don't know what it is'.

– *Ron Wood*

'I want to go out at the top, but the secret is knowing when you're at the top. It's so difficult in this business – your career fluctuates all the time, up and down, like a pair of trousers'.

– *Rod Stewart*

'I can't think of a better way to spread the message of world peace than by working with the NFL and being part of Super Bowl XXVII'.

– *Michael Jackson*

'Damn, I look good with guns'.

– *Ted Nugent*

'We use volume to drive evil spirits out the back of your head, and by evil spirits I mean the job, the boss, the spouse, the probation officer'.

– *David Lee Roth*

'I should think that being my old lady would be all the satisfaction or career any woman needs'.

– *Mick Jagger*

'God had to create disco music so that I could be born and be successful'.

– *Donna Summer*

'I can do anything. One of these days I'll be so complete I won't be a human. I'll be a god'.

– *John Denver*

'Just because I have my standards, they think I'm a bitch'.

– *Diana Ross*

The world's first ski chair lift was modelled after a device that loaded bananas onto cargo ships.

LIFE AFTER DEATH

Plenty has been written about people who nearly die, get a glimpse of the 'other side', and then somehow make it back to the land of the living. Here are four examples of another kind of 'rebirth': people who were thought to be dead, but were actually quite alive.

DECEASED: 32-year-old Ali Abdel-Rahim Mohammad, of Alexandria, Egypt
NEWS OF HIS DEATH: In 1999 Mohammad blacked out while swimming off the coast of Alexandria. His body was recovered and taken to the morgue.
RESURRECTION: After about three hours in the morgue refrigerator, Mohammad was awakened by a loud banging sound – an attendant was trying to close the refrigerator drawer in which Mohammad had been placed. So the 'corpse' reached up and grabbed the attendant's hand. According to one news account, 'his firm grip sent the attendant and a family who had apparently come to identify the body of a loved one stampeding out of the morgue yelling, "Help us!"'.

DECEASED: Henry Lodge, a 63-year-old California man
NEWS OF HIS DEATH: In 1986 Lodge was fixing some fuses when he had a heart attack. He was pronounced dead and his remains were transported to the Los Angeles morgue.
RESURRECTION: Just as the morgue's Dr. Philip Campbell was preparing to make an incision in the remains, Lodge opened his eyes and screamed, 'HELP!' Lodge made a speedy recovery and was soon released from the hospital; Dr. Campbell took a leave of absence from work for 'nervous exhaustion'.

DECEASED: Xue Wangshi, an 81-year-old Chinese woman
NEWS OF HER DEATH: On 2 December, 1995, Ms. Wangshi collapsed and stopped breathing. She was pronounced dead and sent to a nearby crematorium.
RESURRECTION: Workers put Ms. Wangshi on a conveyor belt that fed the deceased into the furnace, but in classic cliffhanger fashion, moments later they saw her move her right

hand. So they stopped the conveyor belt just in time, 'and Mrs. Wangshi sat up'.

DECEASED: Musyoka Mutata, 60, who lived in the village of Kitui in Kenya
NEWS OF HIS DEATH: In 1985 Mututa contracted cholera and was thought to have died. Funeral arrangements were made, and at the appointed hour pallbearers arrived in his home to take the body away for burial.
RESURRECTION: When the pallbearers sprayed Mutata with insecticide to ward off flies, he suddenly sat up and asked for a drink of water. According to newspaper reports, this was Mutata's second near-death experience: in 1928 his parents mistook him for dead after an illness, and when 'his body, wrapped in sheets and blankets, was being lowered into its grave, the three-year-old let out a scream and was saved'.
Update: Four months after his 1985 near-death experience, Mutata died again, this time for real. Rather than bury him right away, however, his family waited two days to be sure that he was really, really dead.

DECEASED: The entire Naua tribe, which until the turn of the century had made its home in the Amazon rain forest in Brazil
NEWS OF THEIR DEATH: No word on precisely when the tribe is thought to have become extinct; the last known report on the tribe and its whereabouts was a 1906 newspaper article titled, 'Last Naua Woman Marries'.
RESURRECTION: The Naua weren't dead – as far as anyone can tell, they were just hiding. After avoiding contact with the rest of the world for nearly a century, in August 2000, more than 250 members of the tribe emerged from deep in the rain forest to protest the Brazilian government's plan to incorporate the Naua native lands into a national wildlife park. It's too early to tell what will happen, but as the law stands now, the Naua are considered trespassers on their own land. 'We thought there were no more Naua', one Brazilian government told reporters. 'Our job now is finding them land. No humans are allowed in the park, just the forest and the animals'.

240 of the world's 450 different types of cheese come from France.

UNDERWEAR IN THE NEWS

Here's a question you've probably never considered: When is underwear newsworthy? We've got the answer because we've been studying the news to find out. The answer is, when it's...

ROYAL UNDERWEAR

In February 2000 Captain Nick Carrell, once a member of the queen's highly elite bodyguard unit, 'admitted trying to steal Queen Elizabeth's underwear and being caught red-handed by the monarch'.

The incident occurred during the infamous 1992 fire at Windsor Castle, when Carrell was helping remove belongings from the queen's private apartments (which were threatened by the fire). 'I was planning to steal a pair of the queen's knickers', a shame-faced Carrell admitted to the *Sunday People*. 'I was helping to clear out her private apartment when I pulled open a chest of drawers. I was amazed to see it was filled with the queen's underwear and I put out my hand to take a pair. Suddenly, I realized she was standing right behind me, watching my every move. I don't know what she thought, but she didn't say a word. It was all very embarrassing'.

LIFE-SAVING UNDERWEAR

'In 1994, fisherman Renato Arganza spent several days at sea clinging to a buoy after his boat capsized off the Philippines. Once rescued, he remarked that he had survived by eating his underpants'.

DEADLY UNDERWEAR

In 1999, two women sheltering under a tree in London's Hyde Park during a thunderstorm were killed when lightning struck the tree. According to medical examiners, the two women died because the metal underwire in their bras acted as an electrical conductor. 'This is only the second time in my experience of 50,000 deaths where lightning has struck the metal in a bra causing death', Westminster coroner Paul Knapman told the media. 'I do not wish to overemphasize any significance'. *(In These Times)*

CELEBRITY UNDERWEAR

• 'At the 1998 auction of Kennedy memorabilia, Richard Wilson paid $3,450 for a pair of JFK's long johns. Mr. Wilson plans to exhibit the underwear next to a slip and a pair of panties formerly owned by Marilyn Monroe'. *(Presidential Indiscretions)*

• In the early 1990s, an upset young man paid a visit to Father Fambrini, pastor at Hollywood's Blessed Sacrament Church. The man confessed that he'd raided Frederick's of Hollywood's lingerie museum and stolen some celebrity undies. Now, consumed with guilt, he wanted to return them, but didn't have the courage…so he asked Father Fambrini to do it. Father Fambrini agreed and returned the two stolen items: a bra belonging to actress Katey Sagal, and 'the pantaloons of the late actress Ava Gardner'. ('The Edge', *Oregonian)*

LIFESTYLE-ENHANCING UNDERWEAR

• In 1998, Monash University's Institute of Reproduction and Development in Australia announced the invention of air conditioned mens' briefs, which the Institute says will prevent heat build-up in the nether regions that is believed to inhibit fertility. Why not just ask infertile males to switch from tight-fitting briefs to looser, cooler boxer shorts? 'Because', says the Institute's David de Kretser, 'some men don't like the freedom'.

• In 1998, Florida entrepreneur Victoria Morton announced that she'd invented a bra that she claims can increase a woman's breast size by repositioning body fat, and she doesn't mean just body fat on the chest. 'If a woman has extra tissue anywhere above her waist', Morton explained in a press release, 'even on her back, she can use this bra to create bigger, firmer breasts'. *(Universal Press Syndicate)*

ARTISTICALLY INSPIRED UNDERWEAR

American artist Laurie Long wasn't just offended when she learned that some vending machines in Japan dispense panties worn by schoolgirls, she was also inspired. She stocked a vending machine with her own used panties, 'which have labels describing what she did while she wore them'. (*Stuff* magazine)

NUDES & PRUDES

It's hard to shock anyone with nudity today. But stupidity is always a shock. These characters demonstrate that whether you're dressed or naked, you can still be pretty dim.

NUDE... 'Bernard Defrance, a high school teacher near Paris, told his students that each time they stumped him with a riddle, he'd shed a piece of clothing – starting with his trademark bow tie. As it turns out, the kids were too smart for him. During one round of the game in November, the 51-year-old Defrance was left standing naked before his class. He was later suspended'.

PRUDES... 'In 1934, eight men were fined $1 apiece for bathing "topless" at Coney Island. "All of you fellows may be Adonises", said the presiding magistrate, "but there are many people who object to seeing so much of the human body exposed". A year later, a mass arrest of 42 topless males in Atlantic City, New Jersey, fattened the municipal coffers by $84. The city fathers declared: "We'll have no gorillas on our beaches".'

NUDE... 'A 41-year-old Allentown man known to police as "The Naked Bandit" pleaded guilty to robbing a string of convenience stores while in the nude, authorities said on Thursday. "His logic was that the last time he did some robberies, he had clothes on and was identified by his clothes", said Lehigh County District Attorney James Anthony.' *(Reuters)*

PRUDES... 'Matt Zelen dived into the pool to start the 100-yard butterfly, then remembered something: He'd forgotten to tie his racing suit. When the St. John's University junior felt his suit sliding off, he decided to kick it off and finish the race. Zelen, a contender for the 2000 Olympics, would have won the race by more than two seconds but he was stripped of more than just his suit – he was disqualified for violating a uniform code.'
(*Parade* magazine)

There are 20 days in the Aztec week.

NUDE... 'Police in Vinton, Louisiana, were bemused when a Pontiac Grand Am hit a tree and disgorged 20 nude occupants. It turned out that they were the Rodriguez family, Pentecostalists from Floydada, Texas. Police Chief Douillard commented, "They were completely nude. All 20 of them. Didn't have a stitch of clothes on. I mean, no socks, no underwear, no nothin". Five of them were in the trunk. The Lord told them to get rid of all their belongings and go to Louisiana.'

PRUDE... 'The Mayor of North Platte, Nebraska, kept his promise to walk naked down the street. Mayor Jim Whitaker said he'd walk "naked" if the Paws-itive Partners Humane Society raised $5,000. When his plan drew national attention – and angry calls – Whitaker revealed that he actually planned to walk a dog named "Naked" instead of walking in the buff himself.'

NUDE... 'A bare-breasted mermaid perched on a rock is causing a stir along Lyse Fjord in Norway. "One man jumped off a boat and swam over to me", Line Oexnevad, 37, said of her job as a siren. "Most people just look and cheer". Ms. Oexnevad, naked except for a blonde wig and a fish-tail, was hired as a tourist attraction.'

PRUDES... 'At the turn of the century [1900, that is], Boston, Massachusetts, refused to accept shipments of navel oranges from Los Angeles, terming the fruit's name "indelicate and immodest".' ('Only in L.A.', the *Los Angeles Times)*

NUDE... 'Police arriving at the scene of a two-car collision in Los Angeles found a totally nude woman behind the wheel of one car. The 35-year-old L.A. resident reportedly told police that when she began her drive, she thought she was a camel in Morocco, and when she saw the palm trees lining the downtown streets, she was sure of it...'. *(Bizarre* magazine)

PRUDE... 'Animal control workers in California recently received a call from a woman who insisted she needed to get a marriage license for a male and a female cat "before they breed".' ('Only in L.A.', the *Los Angeles Times)*

Cats have two sets of vocal chords: one for purring, one for meowing.

A 'TOON IS BORN

Here are the stories of how three popular cartoons were created.

THE JETSONS

Background: In 1960, Hanna-Barbera studios broke new ground with America's first prime-time cartoon series, *The Flintstones*. Airing at 7:30 on Friday nights, it became one of the Top 20 programs of the 1960–61 season. It did so well, in fact, that ABC wanted a second prime-time cartoon the following year.
Inspiration: So Hanna-Barbera just reversed the formula. 'After *The Flintstones*, it was a pretty natural move', says Joseph Barbera. 'The space race was on everybody's mind in the early 1960s...so we went from the cave days to the future, the exact opposite direction....if *The Flintstones* featured the likes of Stony Curtis, Cary Granite, and Ann Margrock, the Jetson family could go see Dean Martian perform in a Las Venus hotel such as the Sonic Sahara, the Riviera Satellite, or the Flamoongo'.
On the Air: *The Jetsons* originally aired at 7:30 PM on Sunday night – traditionally a kids' time slot in the days before cable TV. But against *Walt Disney's Wonderful World of Color* (NBC) and *Dennis the Menace* (CBS), it flopped. *The Jetsons* was cancelled after one season; only 24 episodes were made.

The following year (1963), however, ABC scheduled *Jetsons* reruns as a regular Saturday morning cartoon show. And this is when it really began to take off. The show was so popular with kids that for the next 20 years, the same 24 episodes ran over and over again on Saturdays.

REN & STIMPY

Background: Fresh from his success animating *The New Adventures of Mighty Mouse* for television, in 1989 an animator named John Kricfalusi pitched the Nickelodeon channel an idea he had for a cartoon called *Your Gang*.

Nickelodeon was interested in the show, but it insisted on buying all the rights to the characters, as part of its plan to create a stable of 'evergreen' cartoons, like those at Walt Disney and Warner Brothers, that could be broadcast for decades to come.
Inspiration: Kricfalusi didn't want to sell the rights to his

favourite *Your Gang* characters. Instead, 'he sold Nickelodeon a show about two ancillary *Your Gang* characters with whom he was willing to part: a paranoid Chihuahua named Ren (inspired by a postcard of a chihuahua in a sweater), and an excretion-obsessed cat named Stimpy (which originated as a doodle and was named after a college friend)'.

On the Air: When *Ren & Stimpy* debuted in August 1991, Nickelodeon had only six completed episodes to broadcast. But the show was such a surprise hit – Nickelodeon's Sunday morning ratings doubled on the strength of *Ren & Stimpy* alone – that Nickelodeon aired the six episodes over and over again for about a year until new episodes were ready. *The Los Angeles Times* reported: '*Ren & Stimpy* (has) started a national craze that helped turn Nicktoons into a major force in children's animation'.

Meanwhile, however, Kricfalusi and Nickelodeon had a falling-out. The cable station said the cartoonist was too slow with new episodes; Kricfalusi said that Nick was meddling creatively. In 1992, Nick fired *Ren & Stimpy's* creator and replaced him with a former partner. The show lost its edge and faded away. However, it's still considered the breakthrough series for modern TV animation. 'All new shows that have any kind of style have to tip their hat to *Ren & Stimpy*', says animation historian Jerry Beck. *Beavis and Butt-head* actually owes its existence to the show. *Ren & Stimpy's* success was the reason the channel was willing to pay for its own animated show.

BEAVIS AND BUTT-HEAD

Background: In the early 1990s, a defence industry engineer named Mike Judge grew tired of his job working for a company that made components for the F-18 fighter jet. So he quit and became a musician. After a few months of playing guitar in a bar band, he bought a $200 animation kit and began making cartoons to amuse himself.

Inspiration: 'One day in the summer of 1990', *Newsweek* reported, 'Judge was trying to draw this kid he remembered from junior high. It didn't much look like the kid, but when he came back to it a week later, it made him laugh, and that was enough. This was the birth of Butt-Head, with his short upper lip and massive gums. "The guy I tried to draw, he had that laugh: 'Huh-huh, huh-huh-huh'," says Judge...."Actually, my hair is really unmanageable, so I

Genetically speaking, a guinea pig is more closely related to a cow than it is to a rat.

may have gotten Butt-head's hair from myself".

Judge adds, 'There were probably four or five guys who inspired Beavis, just a little Bic-flipping pyro kid. I've noticed that 13-year-old metal heads haven't changed much over the years'.

A few years later, Judge decided to make an antisocial cartoon called *Frog Baseball* featuring Beavis and Butt-Head playing baseball using a live frog for the ball. 'I was thinking of when I was a kid and bored', Judge said. 'There's nothing to do. That's when kids start blowing up lizards. You're this 14-year-old guy with no car, you just have a bike and testosterone. It's a dangerous situation'.

'My mom didn't like *Frog Baseball* at all. I showed it once at this guy's house. He was having this cartoon viewing party, and everything else was very cartoony, standard stuff. When *Frog Baseball* came on, this girl kept looking at the screen and then at me. She says, "He isn't actually going to hit the frog, is he?" And then Butt-head hits the frog, and she says, "God, you look so normal"'.

On the Air: Judge entered *Frog Baseball* in a 'Sick and Twisted' cartoon festival, and a week later a company called Colossal Pictures bought it for the MTV series *Liquid Television*. But before they put it on the air, the channel tested it on a focus group to gauge their reaction. 'The focus group was both riveted and hysterical from the moment they saw it', says Gwen Lipsky, MTV's vice president of research and planning. 'After the tape was over, they kept asking to see it again. Then, after they had seen it again, several people offered to buy it from me'.

MTV put Beavis and Butt-head on *Liquid Televison* for two weeks in March 1993. The reaction was so positive that in May it was back full-time. It quickly became MTV's most popular show, with ratings twice as high as any other show on the network.

* * *

AMAZING LUCK

'On 2 February, 1931, a horse named Brampton was driving for the wire in a race in Dargaville, New Zealand, comfortably in the lead. But 40 feet (12 metres) from the finish line, the horse stumbled and fell, rolled over several times with his jockey clinging frantically to his back, and crossed the line as the winner'.

More than 50 per cent of all the lakes in the world are in Canada.

STIFF UPPER LIPS

We didn't get to rule half the world by being soft...or by being entirely sane. Sometimes it seems as if the British Empire was founded entirely on the back of some heroically bonkers bravery in the face of overwhelming odds. Makes you proud to be British!

The Empire was built with the help of two formidable secret weapons. The first of these was a truly inhumane and ruthless device – bagpipes, which sent tribesmen around the world heading for the hills, driven nearly mad by its relentless screech. But the second secret weapon was even more decisive. It was that unique mark of breeding that made the English officer class impervious to shot, shell and fear: the stiff upper lip.

STEADY ON, HORATIO

While Japanese samurai invented a whole ritual celebrating suicide as a mark of honour, British officers were brought up to face death as a minor irritant, as no more of an inconvenience than stubbing one's toe. Nelson, our greatest war hero, lying close to death after the Battle of Trafalgar, said casually 'Take care of my dear Lady Hamilton, Hardy, take care of poor Lady Hamilton'. He almost blew it with the strangely emotional 'Kiss me, Hardy', but thankfully regained enough sang-froid to utter 'Now I am satisfied. Thank God I have done my duty', before expiring quietly and unobtrusively like a real gent.

TOO MUCH OF A GOOD THING

Defeating Napoleon at the Battle of Waterloo made the Duke of Wellington a national hero. But the real glory in the stiff upper lip stakes went to his second-in-command, the cavalry general Lord Uxbridge, who had an inconvenient bit of bad luck in the later stages of the battle. While standing next to the Iron Duke Uxbridge's right leg was shot off at the knee. 'By God, sir', he remarked in surprise. 'I have lost my leg'. 'By God,' agreed Wellington. 'I believe you have'. The leg was buried with full military honours, while Lord Uxbridge was made Marquess of Anglesey and carried on regardless.

SLAP HIM, HE'S FRENCH

But it wasn't just the officers who were able to keep their peckers up. One 18th-century memoir describes an occasion when a private in the 1st Royal Dragoons had his arm amputated at the elbow, while a French soldier in the next bed was having a musket ball removed from his shoulder. There was no anaesthetic, of course, and the Frenchman was screaming as the surgeon dug around with his knife. The Englishman concentrated on chewing his tobacco in silence, and showed no emotion the surgeon sawed away at his shattered arm. When the job was done, he took his severed arm by the wrist with his remaining hand and used it to wallop the the Frenchman with 'a smart blow on the breech', saying irritably 'Here, take that, and stuff it down your throat, and stop your damned bellowing!'

AN ACTOR'S LIFE FOR ME

But you really needed a posh accent to do this kind of thing properly, and World War I gave the upper classes the chance to show that it wasn't just the occasional lunatic who relished the thought of death or maiming with a wryly cocked eyebrow and a self-deprecating quip. 'Over the top, chaps' became the war cry of a generation of smart young men, who went straight from Eton and Harrow to the trenches of the Somme, leading their men into the machine-gun fire of the enemy, sometimes smoking a pipe or kicking a football to demonstrate that they really couldn't be expected to take this sort of thing seriously. A German machine gunner said afterwards 'I noticed one of them walking calmly carrying a walking stick. When we started firing, they went down in their hundreds. You didn't have to aim, we just fired into them'.

LORD OF THE DANCE

The young officers were trying to live up to the established military tradition. In the great days of the Empire, General Gordon, whose upper lip was surely stiffest ever, used to stand insouciantly on the battlefield during close-quarters engagements, ignoring the bullets and the carnage, and carrying a light cane, which he used to point at the places he thought the soldiers should be firing at. Unfortunately, by 1914, with the invention of machine-guns, this brilliant tactic no longer worked. The horrors of World War I almost wiped out an entire generation, with the upper classes in particular seeing their numbers drastically reduced. By World War II, officers reluctantly accepted that it might be a good idea to duck occasionally. War had become a serious business, with no place for enthusiastic amateurs or charming eccentrics.

PAYING LIP SERVICE

As time wore on, the idea of the stiff upper lip became a bit of a joke. In P. G. Wodehouse's *Stiff Upper Lip, Jeeves!* the hapless upper-class toff Bertie Wooster is portrayed stoically resisting not death of maiming but the awful prospect of marriage.

But the true stiff upper lip spirit does still surface from time to time. In 1991 the IRA launched a mortar attack on 10 Downing Street. The bomb landed in the garden, causing a huge crater and shattering the building's windows. The Prime Minister, John Major, was conducting a cabinet meeting in the building at the time, and he was determined not to let the side down with any display of surprise or emotion. 'We had better begin again somewhere else', he said, trying not to notice that some of his ministers were cowering on the floor. Within ten minutes they resumed the meeting in another room as if nothing had happened. Splendid.

* * *

'In defeat he was unbeatable; in victory, unbearable.'

– Edward Marsh on Field Marshal B. L. Montgomery

'Be an example to your men, in your duty and in private life. Never spare yourself, and let the troops see that you don't in your endurance of fatigue and privation. Always be tactful and well-mannered and teach your subordiantes to do the same. Avoid excessive sharpness or harshness of voice, which usually indicates the man who has shortcomings of his own to hide.'

– Field Marshal Erwin Rommel

The BBC started regular TV broadcasts on 2 November, 1936, from Alexandra Place in London.

THE ROCK AND POP SITES OF BRITAIN

Next time you're out and about, take a good look around – you may be standing next to a bit of rock and pop history.

It's not just Route 66 and Graceland that are the focus of pop pilgrimages. Take a magical mystery tour around the landmarks of Britain's rock and pop culture.

EYE 2I IN THE MARQUEE

When rock 'n' roll took America by storm in the mid-1950s, it spawned imitation musical craze in the UK – skiffle. Pioneered by Lonnie Donegan, skiffle was rock 'n' roll with all the sex and rebelliousness taken out. All the key UK bands of the 1960s had their roots in the skiffle movement, and its epicentre was the 2I's coffee bar, at 59 Old Compton Street, in London's Soho. It was where Tommy Steele and Cliff Richard got their big breaks. Today, it's a branch of the Dome bar and restaurant chain.

Close by, was the Marquee Club. It was originally a jazz venue, based in Oxford Street, and later moved to Wardour Street, where it became the archetypal rock venue of the 1960s and 1970s (it eventually moved round the corner to Charing Cross Road). In the early 1960s a group of blues and skiffle musicians, led by father-figure of the British blues scene Alexis Korner and his band Blues Incorporated, would meet at the Marquee. Korner's band had a regular slot at the Marquee, and at various times included Brian Jones, Mick Jagger and Charlie Watts in its line-up. When Blues Incorporated moved on to a residency at the Ealing Club, in West London, Keith Richards passed through its ranks, as did Jack Bruce and Ginger Baker, later of 1960s supergroup Cream.

ROLLING ON THE RIVER

In Richmond, the Crawdaddy Club, run by an energetic young promoter named Giorgio Gomelsky, featured first the Rolling Stones and then the Yardbirds as regulars. By 1963, there were

On average, people who have asthma hear better than people who don't. Nobody knows why.

r&b venues all over London. Even in the Thames: about a mile upstream from Richmond is Eel Pie Island, just a few hundred metres long, home to the Eel Pie Hotel, a rundown joint that filled with intrepid blues fans every weekend. Such was their enthusiastic bopping that the hotel largely fell down. In its hey-day, the island could only be reached by a small footbridge on which bands' equipment would regularly get stuck.

TUNE IN, TURN ON

With the rise of psychedelic rock, clubs incorporated light shows to entertain the groovy hippy set. Pink Floyd put on all-nighters at the UFO Club, first in Tottenham Court Road and then at the former train shed, the Roundhouse, in Chalk Farm. It was all far out and very trippy and when UFO finished, there was the Electric Garden (renamed Middle Earth) in a basement venue in Covent Garden. The most popular bands went to play at larger and less intimate venues, such as the Saville Theatre in Shaftesbury Avenue, which was run by Beatles manager Brian Epstein. Just up the road, near Tottenham Court Road tube station, is the Astoria theatre. It's still used for gigs and clubs today, but started life as a Crosse & Blackwell pickle-making factory.

Many bars, small clubs and pubs thought that hiring bands during the week would be a good way to drum up trade between weekends. One such place was the Tally Ho pub, in Kentish Town, North London. It booked a struggling U.S. band called Eggs Over Easy in the early 1970s. The group built up quite a following, so more pubs took up the trend – and pub rock was born. The Acklam Hall in Westbourne Park was one of the most famous pub rock venues, with legends of the genre such as the 101ers (Joe Strummer's pre-Clash band) playing there. It also hosted the first Bad Music Festival in 1979.

UNHAPPY ENDINGS

But not all of London's rock 'n' roll landmarks have happy associations. In late 1966, Guinness heir Tara Browne, friend of the Beatles, crashed his car in Redcliffe Gardens, West Brompton. His death inspired the song 'A Day In The Life'. A block of flats in exclusive Curzon Place, Mayfair, hosted not one but two rock deaths – Cass Elliott, of the Mamas and the Papas, died of a heart attack there in 1974, and Keith Moon checked out four years

The average cigar smoker can smoke an average cigar in about an hour and a half.

later, in a different flat. In nearby Marble Arch, Jimi Hendrix died of an overdose at the Cumberland Hotel in 1970.

OUT AND ABOUT

Music made its mark out on the streets of London, too. Both the Rolling Stones and Madness shot album cover images on Primrose Hill, near Hampstead Heath (*Between the Buttons* and *Rise and Fall* respectively). And Japanese tourists still love to be photographed on the zebra crossing used by the Beatles on *Abbey Road*. The crossing actually is on Abbey Road – and the recording studio there is under almost constant siege by Beatles fans, too.

Oasis shot the cover image for *(What's the Story) Morning Glory?* in Berwick Street market, Soho, while Pink Floyd famously flew a giant inflatable pig over the old Battersea Power Station to promote their 1977 *Animals* album. It was a great stunt – until the pig floated free and made a break for it.

At Wimbledon Greyhound Racing Stadium, the band Queen assembled almost a hundred nude women to ride bikes to promote their 'Bicycle Race/Fat Bottomed Girls' single in 1978. The local bicycle hire shop refused to take the saddles back after the shoot. It is not known what became of the saddles.

GOT MY MOJO WORKING

Outside the capital, the true musical pilgrim still has lots to see. Any trip must include a stop in Liverpool, where it all began for the Beatles. The Cavern club gave them their first taste of the big time, and they played there almost 300 times. It closed in 1973, but was reopened some years later, rebuilt using the same bricks. Like its London club counterparts, the Cavern started out in the 1950s as a skiffle venue.

Over in Sheffield, the Mojo Club was a key northern venue for rock in the mid-1960s. It was run by a brash young DJ named Peter Stringfellow, and we all know what became of him!

Other promoters took over unusual venues to publicize their charges. When Led Zeppelin decided to start their own Swan Song record label in the 1974, they held the launch party in Kent's atmospheric Chislehurst caves. The label was going to be called Slut Records, so you can guess what sort of party it was.

THE FUN FACTORY

In Manchester, the Haciena became perhaps the most famous club in the country during the 1980s. The brainchild of Factory Records supremo Tony Wilson, it was the epicentre of the city's amazing dance scene, playing host first to New Order and then Happy Mondays. It was also at the forefront of the rave and 'Madchester' dance scenes of the late 1980s. When the club was closed and demolished to make way for housing in the late 1990s, the original fittings were painstakingly removed and sold at auction to devoted fans. They even made a film about the place, 2002's *24-Hour Party People*, starring Steve Coogan as Wilson.

ROCK SHRINES OF THE RICH AND FAMOUS

Can't get over to Paris to visit the grave of Jim Morrison? Graceland a bit too far away? Here are some local rock pilgrimage sites.

* The 100 Club, at 100 Oxford Street in London. It's been going since 1942 and has pioneered jazz, blues, r&b, punk, indie and much else. Pretty much every UK rock band you can think of has played there.

* Queen's Ride bridge, in Barnes, south west London, was made into an official memorial for Marc Bolan, who died in a car crash in 1977. There's now an engraved stone there.

Mendips, the Liverpool childhood home of John Lennon which he shared with his beloved aunt Mimi, was opened to the public as a museum in 2003.

Elvis in the UK? Well, he never performed here, but he did change planes at Prestwick in Ayrshire when he was in the U.S. Armed Forces. That's good enough for the true rock traveller. It happened in March 1960 and a plaque marks the spot.

An English Heritage blue plaque marks the house of Jimi Hendrix, in Brook Street, London. It was granted after a long-running argument with classical music buffs, who objected to the fact that it would appear on the house next door to where Handel once lived!

69 per cent of cake eaters eat the cake first, then the icing.

THE DARK SIDE OF PETER PAN

'All children except one, grow up. They soon know that they will grow up...this is the beginning of the end'. The first paragraph of James Barrie's classic story, Peter Pan, *introduced its central theme. It sounds innocent, but a look at Barrie's life gives it a more sinister twist.*

I WON'T GROW UP

'All of James Barrie's life led up to the creation of *Peter Pan*', wrote one of his biographers.

A pivotal point came in 1866 when Barrie, the youngest in a Scottish family of 10 children, was six: his brother David, the pride of the family, died in a skating accident. Barrie's mother was devastated. To comfort her, little James began imitating David's mannerisms and mimicking his speech. This bizarre charade went on for years – and only got weirder: when James reached 13, the age at which David had died, he literally stopped growing. He never stood taller than 1.5 metres, and didn't shave until he was 24. He always had a thin, high-pitched voice.

SUCCESS AND FAILURE

From childhood, Barrie's main interest had been creating stories and plays. After graduating from university, he moved to London to be a writer, and soon his work was being published.

In the 1880s, his novels about a 'wandering little girl' – his mother – captured the public's imagination and put him on the road to fame and wealth. He soon became one of Britain's most famous writers.

Despite his professional success, the gawky Barrie was painfully shy with women and the thought of marriage terrified him. After a nightmare, he wrote in his journal: 'Greatest horror, dream I am married, wake up screaming'. But that didn't stop him from putting lovely actresses on a pedestal. Barrie became enamoured of leading lady Mary Ansell, who appeared in his early plays. Motherlike, she nursed him through a life-threatening bout of pneumonia. And when he recovered, they decided to marry.

Around 60 per cent of UK adults play the national lottery on a regular basis.

It was a disaster. Barrie wasn't capable of an intimate relationship and was probably impotent as well – stuck, physically and emotionally in a state of perpetual boyhood. Eventually, Mary fell in love with a young writer named Gilbert Cannan and demanded a divorce. Barrie refused, because his marriage had provided him with the appearance of being normal. But when Mary threatened to tell the world that he was impotent and had never consummated their marriage, Barrie gave in.

THE LOST BOYS

In 1899, while still unhappily married, Barrie befriended young George, John and Peter Davies and their mother, Sylvia, in London's Kensington Park. The boy's father, Arthur Davies, was too busy tending to his struggling career as a lawyer to spend much time with his family. So childless Barrie was only too happy to play with the Davies boys. He became a frequent caller at their home and even rented a cottage nearby when they went on holidays in Surrey.

Barrie idolized the children's beautiful mother. But it was with the children that he could truly be himself. He met with them daily in the park or at their home. They played Cowboys and Indians together, or pretended to be pirates, forcing each other to walk the plank. Barrie made up stories for the boys, featuring talking birds and fairies, and acted them out.

PETER IS BORN

In 1901 Barrie ordered a printing of only two copies of a photo-essay book of his adventures with the Davies boys. He entitled it *The Boy Castaways of Black Lake Island* and gave one copy to the boy's father (who promptly left it on a train). The next year, Barrie published these adventures in a novel called *The Little White Bird.* In a story-within-a-story, the narrator tells 'David' (George Davies) about Peter Pan, a seven-day-old boy who flies away from his parents to live with fairies. All children start out as birds, the story goes, but soon forget how to fly.

Peter eventually flies home, and tearfully sees through the nursery window that his mother is holding a new baby and has forgotten him. Now Peter Pan can never go home and will never grow up.

The Cambodian language has 72 letters in its alphabet, the most of any language.

The Little White Bird was popular, and readers begged Barrie to give them more of Peter Pan.

Barrie knew exactly how to bring Peter Pan back. He had often taken the Davies boys to pantomimes at Christmastime. The plays always featured a young hero and heroine (both played by actresses), a Good Fairy, a Demon King, fight scenes, characters flying (on invisible wires) and a 'transformation scene', in which the ordinary world became a fairyland. During the performances, Barrie carefully observed the boys' reactions. They seemed to love every moment.

So why not, Barrie thought, put Peter Pan in a similar children's play for the London stage?

THE DARLINGS

Barrie always acknowledged that the Davies boys' free-spirited youthfulness was his inspiration for Peter Pan. 'I made Peter by rubbing the five of you together, as savages with two sticks produce a flame', he wrote on the dedication page of the printed version of the play. More than that, however, the Davies family – loving mother, impatient father and adorable sons – served as Barrie's model for the Darlings in the play. He even used, or thinly disguised, their real names:

- Mr. Darling was named after the eldest boy, George Davies.
- Jack Davies became John Darling.
- Michael and Nicholas became Michael Nicholas Darling.
- Peter Davies's name went to Peter Pan.

As for the author, he appears as Captain James Hook, whose right hand is gone. Barrie suffered paralysis of his right hand from tendonitis. Hook is relentlessly pursued by a crocodile who has swallowed a ticking clock, which biographers say was 'a metaphor of Barrie stalked by cruel time'. Porthos, his St. Bernard, became nurse-dog Nana, who exasperated the stuffy father (in real life, he was exasperated not with the dog, but with Barrie).

Barrie added a sister, Wendy, modelled after Margaret Henley, the deceased daughter of Barrie's friend, M. E. Henley. The six-year-old girl had called Barrie her 'fwendy' (friend) and from that child-word, Barrie invented the name Wendy. It rapidly became one of England's most popular girls names.

Spain gets its name from 'Spania', the Carthaginian word that means 'land of rabbits'.

WILL PETER PAN FLY?

Peter Pan was a radical departure for adult theatre. Barrie had an agreement with producer Charles Frohman to deliver a play manuscript. He offered Frohman another play for free if he would only produce his 'dream child', *Peter Pan*. 'I'm sure it will not be a commercial success', Barrie said of *Peter Pan*.

But Frohman, a wealthy American who liked risky ventures, said he would produce both plays. After reading the manuscript of *Peter Pan*, Frohman was so excited, he would stop friends on the street and force them to listen to passages from it. With an American staging now secured, it was easier for Barrie to find backing for a London opening.

The play was first performed at the Duke of York's Theatre on 27 December, 1904, with an actress, Nina Boucicault, as Peter Pan. Having an actress play the boy – a tradition that continues to this day – began as a practical matter. The role was too demanding for a child; only an adult could handle all of the lines. And only an adult female could pass for a boy.

Peter Pan was an immediate hit, disproving Barrie's misgivings that an audience of adults wouldn't go for a play he'd originally written for children. One review compared Barrie's genius with that of George Bernard Shaw. Later, Barrie would cash in on the play's popularity by writing the novels *Peter Pan in Kensington Gardens* (1906) and *Peter and Wendy* (1911).

THE FATE OF THE LOST BOYS

But this story has no happy ending. Arthur Davies died of cancer, which left Barrie and Sylvia free to marry. Barrie went so far as to give her an engagement ring, but then she, too, died of cancer. Suddenly Barrie was the legal guardian of five boys, ages 7 to 17.

He devoted his life to them, imagining them as his own, but the boys felt he was overbearing in his possessiveness. Some biographers claim that the Davies brothers grew uncomfortable with their lives because they were always badgered about their relationship with the famous James Barrie. (On the other hand, Barrie had little affection to bestow on his real family. Barrie was also named guardian of his brother's grandchildren when their parents died – but although he paid for their education and upkeep, he refused to see them.)

60 per cent of pets in Britain have some form of health insurance.

George, the eldest Davies child and Barrie's favourite, died in World War I in 1915. Michael drowned in a pool at Oxford while being taught to swim by a close friend; there were rumours of a suicide pact. John married and distanced himself from Barrie. Peter Davies committed suicide as an adult in an attempt to escape, some say, from forever being called 'Peter Pan'.

Barrie ended up famous and rich, but a sad and lonely man. He was described as looking prematurely old and withered. Just before he died in 1937, he willed all proceeds from the copyright of *Peter Pan* to London's Great Ormond Street Hospital for Sick Children. Millions of pounds were raised as a result of Barrie's generous bequest. Under British law, copyrights may extend no longer than 50 years before becoming public property. In this special case, Parliament made an exception and allowed the hospital to continue offering the world's best paediatric care because of the boy who never grew up.

* * *

THE CLAPPING GAMBLE

The play's most original and magical moment comes when the fairy Tinkerbell, in an attempt to save Peter's life, drinks poison that Captain Hook had intended for the boy. Boldy, Peter addresses the audience and calls on them to save the fairy's life. 'Clap if you believe in fairies', he begs. Nina Boucicault, the first Peter, asked James Barrie, 'Suppose they don't clap? What do I do then'? Barrie had no answer. The director told the orchestra to start the clapping if the audience sat on their hands. But the ploy was not necessary: the audience suspended disbelief with a vengeance and Nina/Peter wept openly with Tinkerbell's return to life.

* * *

A 'lost boy' was a Victorian
euphemism for one who died young.

THE OTHER SIDE OF PETER PAN

Now that you know something about James Barrie and the origins of Peter Pan, how does it change the way you perceive the story? Here are some quotes from the original book.

ALL CHILDREN, EXCEPT ONE, grow up. They soon know that they will grow up, and the way Wendy knew was this. One day when she was two years old she was playing in a garden, and she plucked another flower and ran with it to her mother. I suppose she must have looked rather delightful, for Mrs. Darling put her hand to her heart and cried, 'Oh, why can't you remain like this for ever!' This was all that passed between them on the subject, but henceforth Wendy knew that she must grow up. You always know after you are two. Two is the beginning of the end.

MRS. DARLING FIRST HEARD of Peter when she was tidying up her children's minds. It is the nightly custom of every good mother after her children are asleep to rummage in their minds and put things straight for next morning, repacking into their proper places the many articles that have wandered during the day.

If you could keep awake (but of course you can't) you would see your own mother doing this, and you would find it very interesting to watch her. It is quite like tidying up drawers. You would see her on her knees, I expect, lingering humourously over some of your contents, wondering where on earth you had picked this thing up, making discoveries sweet and not so sweet, pressing this to her cheek as if it were as nice as a kitten, and hurriedly stowing that out of sight.

When you wake in the morning, the naughtiness and evil passions with which you went to bed have been folded up small and placed at the bottom of your mind; and on the top, beautifully aired, are spread out your prettier thoughts, ready for you to put on.

SUDDENLY HOOK FOUND HIMSELF face to face with Peter. The others drew back and formed a ring around them.

For a long duck the two enemies looked at one another; Hook shuddering slightly, and Peter with the strange smile upon his face.

'So, Pan', said Hook at last, 'this is your doing'.

'Ay, James Hook', came the stern answer, 'it is all my doing'.

'Proud and insolent youth', said Hook, 'prepare to meet thy doom'.

'Dark and sinister man', Peter answered, 'have at thee'.

Without more words they fell to and for a space there was no advantage to either blade. Peter was a superb swordsman, and parried with dazzling rapidity....Hook, scarcely his inferior, forced him back, hoping suddenly to end all with a favourite thrust...but to his astonishment he found his thrust turned aside again and again.

... 'Pan, who art thou'? he cried huskily.

'I'm youth, I'm joy', Peter answered... 'I'm a little bird that has broken out of the egg'.

This, of course, was nonsense; but it was proof to the unhappy Hook that Peter did not know in the least who or what he was, which is the very pinnacle of good form.

'To't again!' he cried despairingly.

He fought now like a human flail, and every sweep of that terrible sword would have severed in two any man or boy who obstructed it; but Peter fluttered around him as if the very wind it made blew him out of the danger zone.

'PETER', WENDY SAID, 'are you expecting me to fly away with you?

'Of course; that is why I have come'....

'I can't come', she said apologetically, 'I have forgotten how to fly'.

'I'll soon teach you again'.

'O Peter, don't waste the fairy dust on me'....

Then she turned up the light, and Peter saw. He gave a cry of pain; ... 'What is it'? he cried again.

She had to tell him. 'I am old, Peter....I grew up a long time ago...I couldn't help it'.

THE BIRTH OF THE COMPACT DISC

When CDs were introduced, we thought it was a conspiracy to make us replace our record collection with CDs. Well, maybe it was, but we have to admit that CD quality is pretty good. Here's the story of how they were invented.

AS SEEN ON TV

In 1974, the Philips Electronics company of the Netherlands started a revolution. They invented a laser video disc – the first product to make use of the 'general induction laser' that had been developed in the U.S. in the early 1960s.

But LaserVision, as it was called, was a brand-new technology and it had a problem: poor error detection and correction – which resulted in inconsistent sound and picture quality. Philips built a prototype to show to several Japanese manufacturers, but the LaserVison player performed so poorly that only one of the Japanese companies – Sony – was willing to work with Philips to fix their new product.

At the time, Sony was a leader in both magnetic tape and digital recording technology. They had already built the world's first digital sound recorder – which used magnetic tape, weighed several hundred pounds, and was as large as a refrigerator...but it worked. And it gave Sony a head start in working out how to correct the problems that Philips was now experiencing with LaserVision.

DISC JOCKEYS

Sony put its digital magnetic tape system on the back burner and began developing a system that would record audio directly to a laser disc. It wouldn't be easy – on top of all the technical problems that had to be worked out, there was also strong opposition within the company to spending money on risky new technology.

Norio Ohga, the company's earliest and most enthusiastic proponent of digital sound recording, faced resistance from company founder Masaru Ibuka, and all but three of Sony's audio engineers. Creatures of the analogue age, they had little faith in the basic concept of digital technology – converting sound into numbers and then converting the numbers back into sound – and doubted it would ever improve on conventional analogue recording. But Ohga, a former musician and aspiring symphony conductor, likened digital recording to 'removing a winter coat from the sound', and insisted that the project be given the highest priority no matter what the cost.

STEP BY STEP

By the spring of 1976, most of the audio compact disc's glitches had been worked out, and the compact disc development team proudly presented Ohga with an astonishing technical marvel: a compact disc the same size as an LP record; but instead of having the same recording capacity as its vinyl counterpart, the CD could hold 13 hours and 20 minutes of sound.

So why aren't today's compact discs as big as an LP and capable of holding 13 hours of music? Because they'd cost too much to produce – something Ohga realized after taking one look at the prototype.

THE SIZE OF THINGS

Ohga sent his engineers back to the drawing board to come up with something that made more financial sense – a smaller CD that approximated the capacity of a vinyl record instead of its physical size. But exactly what size? The decision was still a few years off.

Back in the Netherlands, Philips Electronics was at work on its own version of a compact disc that was 11.5 centimetres across and capable of holding exactly 60 minutes of sound. Sixty minutes was a nice round number, and the discs were small enough to fit easily into the tape deck on an average car stereo. But drawing from his background in classical music, Sony's Ohga pointed out a problem with the 11.5-centimetre standard that others had missed, as John Nathan writes in *Sony: The Private Life*:

> Ohga was adamantly opposed on grounds that a 60-minute limit was 'unmusical': at that length, he pointed out, a single disc could not accommodate all of Beethoven's *Ninth Symphony* and would require interrupting many of the major operas before the end

Top of the Pops is the UK's longest-running music show. It began 1 January, 1964.

> of the First Act. On the other hand, 75 minutes would accommodate most important pieces of music, at least to a place where it made musical sense to cut them....The disc would have to be 12 centimeters to accommodate 75 minutes. In the end, Philips agreed to Sony's specifications.

FINAL TOUCHES

In March 1980, Sony and Philips tested their competing error-correction systems on discs that had been deliberately scratched, marked with chalk and smeared with fingerprints. Sony's system worked better and was adopted by both companies.

Three months later, they jointly submitted their prototype to the Digital Audio Disc Conference, which had been formed in 1977 to select a single worldwide standard for recording digital audio sound.

Two other companies submitted competing technologies: Telefunken, which recorded digital information mechanically, and JVC, which recorded digital sound electrostatically, the same way that a standard cassette recorder puts analogue sound onto tape.

The Conference adopted both the Sony/Philips 'Compact Disc Digital Audio System' and the JVC system, leaving Telefunken out in the cold. But the compact disc system quickly surpassed JVC's system because, unlike the JVC system, the compact disc's laser read the information on the CD without actually touching it – which meant that discs would last almost forever.

JUST SAY NO

While both companies continued work on perfecting their players, Sony's Norio Ohga and a Philips executive named Hans Timmer began preparing the recording industry for the introduction of CD technology. In May 1981, they brought Sony's prototype CD player to the International Music Industry Conference in Athens, Greece.

While they expected to dazzle the record company executives with CD technology, Ohga and Timmer also realized that they would encounter some opposition. But they were astonished by just how much opposition they did run into. The record companies had millions upon millions of pounds invested in LP record technology – all of which could become worthless if CDs ever took off. And because every compact disc manufactured was, in essence, a perfect 'master' recording, counterfeiters could use them to make perfect bootleg recordings, something that had not been possible with LPs.

'Ohga must have been shaken, but he didn't show it', Timmer recalls. 'He was calm and kept explaining that CDs would never scratch and that the sound was superior. But they shouted him down'. Toward the end of Ohga's presentation, the executives stood up and began chanting, 'The truth is in the groove! The truth is in the groove!'

'We barely escaped physical violence', Timmer says.

KEEP ON TRUCKIN'

Ohga was determined to continue developing CD technology, even if the entire industry was against him. Not that he had any choice: Sony's fortunes were now inextricably linked to the success of compact discs. Sony had taken a financial drubbing on its Betamax video recorders, which had been driven out of the marketplace by VHS-format, and the company badly needed a hit product. Now they had invested tens of millions of pounds in CD technology. Compact discs had to succeed.

CD-DAY

On October 1, 1982, the world's first CD player – the Sony CDP 101 – went on sale in Japan...and with it, the world's first CD albums, courtesy of CBS/Sony records.

The CDP 101 sold for £600 and compact discs sold for around £10, twice the price of LPs. At those prices, the CDP 101 was a hit with audiophiles, but out of reach for most consumers. The *New York Times* wrote in March 1983:

> Some question whether the audio-disc will succeed. Even if prices come down – and industry experts expect they will – some analysts doubt whether consumers will be willing to sacrifice substantial investments in turntables and stacks of traditional recordings... The compact disc and player...is being likened in the music industry to the advent of stereophonic sound or the long-playing recording. Still, the CD's effect on record makers, manufacturers of audio equipment, and – most importantly – the music-lov-

ing consumer will probably be more gradual than the two previous revolutions, according to analysts.

SUCCESS AT LAST

The analysts were wrong. In November 1984, Sony introduced a new CD player, the D-50, that was half the size of the CDP-101 and cost only £140. 'The market came roaring back to life', John Nathan writes. By 1986, CDs players were selling at a rate of more than a million per year and consumers had purchased more than 45 million compact discs. And that was just the beginning: sales doubled to 100 million CDs by 1988, and quadrupled to 400 million CDs in 1992, compared to 2.3 million LPs sold that year, making them the fastest-growing consumer electronic product ever introduced.

* * *

REALLY BAD, AWFUL, TERRIBLE JOKES

Yes, we know these jokes are bad and you'll groan when you read them…and then you'll tell them to someone else.

A man walks into a psychiatrist's office with banana up his nose and says, 'What's the matter with me, Doc'? The psychiatrist says, 'You're not eating properly'.

Q: Why couldn't the sesame seed leave the gambling casino?
A: Because he was on a roll.

Upon seeing a flock of geese flying south for the winter, the bird watcher exclaimed, 'Migratious'.

Q: How many surrealists does it take to screw in a lightbulb?
A: To get to the other side.

Q: Did you hear about the dyslexic devil worshipper?
A: He sold his soul to Santa.

Q: What do you get if you don't pay your exorcist promptly?
A: Repossessed.

THE CAMBRIDGE SPY RING

I say, did you hear about those Cambridge toffs who joined the Foreign Office and wound up tipping the nod to the KGB? Not quite top drawer to betray one's country to the enemy. Rather a rum go, eh?

In the 1930s Britain was still recovering from the trauma of World War I and dealing with a worldwide depression. Even the ruling classes worried about the growing misery of the working poor. Five Cambridge students separately decided that only Communism – which would shift power and wealth to the masses – would bring justice and a decent life to ordinary Englishmen.

Recruited into the spy game by the Soviet Union, they infiltrated the British intelligence services so completely that Stalin knew every one of Britain's top secrets during World War II and the early Cold War years. The British secret service – even when faced with evidence – seemed incapable of admitting that these blue-blooded chaps could be traitors.

GUY BURGESS (1911–1963)

KGB Code Names: Paul, Hicks, Mädchen

Burgess was a witty and handsome gay man who had apparently never heard of 'the closet', a party animal with a well-known passion for fine claret. The idea of good-time Guy risking his life to help the grim, puritanical Soviet Union was like a transvestite flouncing forward to volunteer for road building in Siberia.

Moscow Is So Not Gay

In 1934 Burgess took a trip to Moscow, but found it utterly boring unless he was plastered. At one point, the Moscow police found Burgess passed out drunk in a park. All the same, he was a valuable spy to them; he had a brilliant mind for remembering data and was more serious about politics than any of his companions ever realized.

The BBC News

In 1936 Burgess began producing political interview programmes for the BBC so he could connect with high-powered politicians who would unknowingly drop information that would be useful to the KGB. At the same time, the Soviets were feeding Burgess interesting information so he could make friends with British espionage agents in MI6, the secret intelligence service responsible for gathering information overseas.

He's Clever, All Right

In 1939 Burgess joined MI6 and brought in his university chum, Kim Philby – the most infamous of the five spies and a master traitor who spied for the Soviets for nearly three decades. Burgess eventually moved on to the Foreign Office, where for six years he passed along briefcases full of secrets to the KGB. Not only did he remain undetected, but Winston Churchill called him a 'clever chap whose judgement can be relied on'.

A Guy in Washington

The pressure of being a double agent increased Burgess' wild ways. When, in the 1950s, the Foreign Office sent him to work in Washington D.C. (where he betrayed the U.S. as well as Britain), Burgess became a suspect of CIA counterintelligence because of his drunken mishaps and his vocal anti-Americanism. Finally, when a drunken Burgess cursed police who pulled him over for speeding and tore up their tickets shouting that he had diplomatic immunity, he was sent home to London in disgrace.

Surprise! Burgess had actually been looking for disgrace. He needed to get sent home because he'd been warned that his friend and fellow spy Donald Maclean was about to be arrested by the British. Burgess arrived in England just in time to save Maclean from interrogation.

Moscow or Bust

Burgess and Maclean made their escape to Moscow. The Soviets told Burgess he could drop Maclean off like a package and return home, but Burgess had blown his cover and was forced to live in the workers' paradise he'd spied for. Naturally he hated it. Even in Moscow, Burgess wore his Eton school tie. He found Russia dull and missed the social whirl of England so much that he drank himself to death.

DONALD MACLEAN (1913–1983)

KGB Code Names: Wise, Stuart, Lyric, Homer

The spy who was rescued by Burgess was the handsome, wealthy son of Sir Donald Maclean, a Scottish Member of Parliament. Once he'd discovered Communism, young Donald became a true believer. When the KGB asked him to stay in England to spy in the foreign office, he was disappointed. He'd hoped to go to the Soviet Union and work for the revolution there.

Wed to a Red

In 1940, Maclean married Melinda Marling, the beautiful daughter of an American executive (and an even more dedicated Communist than her husband). In 1944, Maclean was named first secretary to the British Embassy in Washington D.C. He also served on the committee that supervized the development of atomic energy, and his reports from America helped the Soviets work out how to build their own atom bomb.

Stalin, the Boss from Hell

Stalin pressed his secret agents hard. Maclean was expected to deliver secrets to the Soviet Embassy twice a week. The CIA began to notice how often Maclean was turning up at the Atomic Energy Commission offices and they cancelled his pass. Then CIA counterintelligence (which read communications from the Soviet Embassy to Moscow) decoded information that led them to Maclean.

There's No Quitting Now

Maclean knew he could be arrested at any time, but the Soviets wouldn't let him resign. Luckily, British 'intelligence' was unable to believe that Sir Donald's son could be a spy. Even when London called him home in 1951, instead of firing him, he was made head of the American desk at the Foreign Office. The day finally came when British intelligence could no longer ignore the facts, but on 25 May, 1951 – Maclean's birthday – Burgess arrived and spirited him off to Moscow, days before Maclean was to be arrested.

A Betrayer Betrayed

In Moscow, Maclean was given a flat, a dacha outside the city, and a well-paid job instructing KGB recruits in the art of spying. By Moscow standards he lived in luxury, but he wasn't happy. Things got worse after Melinda left him for fellow defector Kim Philby, then deserted the pair of them for America. Left alone and lonely, Maclean confided to friends that he was disillusioned with Communism and wanted to go home. He did, eventually. When he died in 1983, he was cremated and his ashes were buried in old England.

HAROLD 'KIM' PHILBY (1912–1988)

KGB Code Name: Söhnchen, Tom, Stanley

The man who ran off with Donald Maclean's wife was a master spy who began secretly working for the Soviets in 1934. It has been argued that of all the Cambridge spies, Philby was the most ruthless. He had an aristocratic charm and an ability to make friends easily. He was cool under pressure and could even make use of a boyhood stammer to gain time when being interrogated. He was selfish and remorseless, betraying his (four) wives and his friends, as well as his country.

It Runs in the Family

His father, diplomat St. John Philby, gave little Harold the nickname 'Kim' after the young Indian spy in Rudyard Kipling's novel. The elder Philby confounded oh-so-proper English society when, in his dotage, he converted to Islam and took a Saudi slave girl as his second wife. But Philby the younger would go on to astound his powerful associates far more than his father ever had.

Irony of Ironies

In 1944, Kim Philby was made Chief of Section IX of the British secret service. Section IX's whole purpose was – believe it or not – to combat Communist spies. Which put British intelligence in the unenviable spot of having a Soviet spy running their war against Soviet spies.

Death Count

During World War II, one of Philby's most important tasks for Stalin was to keep the British fighting the Germans long after many Germans were ready to surrender because they knew Hitler had lost the war. Stalin was afraid that Britain and America would make peace with Germany and that all three could turn on the Soviet Union. As Stalin's spy, Philby did everything he could to keep the fighting going, including blocking highly placed Germans from working for Britain and discouraging every plot to kill Hitler. Some historians estimate that as well as contributing to the deaths of many anti-Nazi Germans, Philby helped lengthen the war by more than six months, causing the deaths of thousands of soldiers as well as prisoners of war and prisoners in Germany's concentration camps.

During the Cold War, Philby sent British agents to spy on the Soviet Union and then reported their identities to the KGB so that those same agents could be 'liquidated'.

A Friend in Need

But when trouble came, it wasn't from an enemy. Old university chum Guy Burgess was staying with Philby in Washington D.C., in 1951, when the news came that Donald Maclean was suspected of working for the Soviets. If anyone would know what to do in Maclean's hour of need, it would be Burgess and Philby.

The Third Man

When Burgess defected to Moscow with Maclean, one hard-to-ignore question shook up British politics like an earthquake: who was the 'third man'? Who tipped Burgess and Maclean off about the imminent arrest? As Burgess' host in Washington, Philby immediately came under suspicion. Americans (including J. Edgar Hoover, head of the FBI) demanded Philby's head.

Many in MI6 thought the Americans were a bit dotty on the subject of Communists. They didn't believe that the charming Philby could be guilty. But the Soviet spies who were defecting to the West claimed that there was a Soviet informer in a powerful position in MI6. Suspicion kept returning to Philby.

In 1955 Philby was publicly accused of treason, publicly defended by powerful friends and colleagues, and publicly cleared for lack of evidence – but forced into resignation anyway. Still, that wasn't the end of Philby's double game. He kept on doing odd jobs for the British secret service – and he continued to send information to the KGB.

A Betrayer Betraying and Betrayed

In 1963, the British Secret Intelligence Service (MI6) again confronted Philby. This time he confessed and fled to Moscow. Even in exile he managed to continue his pattern of betrayal – this time by stealing the wife of his friend and fellow spy, Donald Maclean. Philby was never given as much power in the KGB as he wanted, and this seemed to him like a betrayal after all he'd done for the Soviets. Still, after his death in 1988, the Soviet Union gave their super spy a hero's burial and put his face on a postage stamp.

ANTHONY BLUNT (1907–1983)

KGB Code Names: Yan, Johnson, Tony

He was the only son of a parish priest in a provincial village, but Anthony Blunt knew the value of good connections; in his case, his mother's third cousin, a rather nice girl who became Queen Elizabeth II. At Cambridge Blunt was close to (and for a time possibly in love with) Guy Burgess.

The Artful Spy

A haughty, aesthetic type, Blunt became a professional art historian. During the war, he worked at MI5, Britain's domestic counterintelligence service. Blunt was only a junior officer but because he was related to royalty, he was socially tight with his superiors and picked up counterintelligence secrets that, as a junior officer, he should never have known.

Thanks to Blunt, Stalin's men knew where British government bugs were planted, which of their own agents wanted to defect to England, and the names of many of the British agents who were spying on them.

Sharing the King's Things

Blunt left MI5 after the war and became the Surveyor of the King's Pictures, maintaining the royal paintings and advising King George VI on new purchases. Yet even as he was visiting galleries with his royal boss and talking art, Blunt stayed in touch with the KGB, sometimes serving as a courier for Burgess, but also reporting any useful tidbits picked up at parties with former colleagues at MI5.

The Fourth Man

When Blunt discovered that Maclean was about to be interrogated, he tipped off Kim Philby in Washington. When Burgess came to London, Blunt helped his old chum arrange Maclean's escape. He even cleared away incriminating evidence from Burgess' apartment once Burgess was on his way to Moscow.

A: Blink.

Sir Anthony and the Imperials

Maclean's great escape in 1951 put suspicion on the elegant Mr Blunt, since the two had been so close. But suspicion didn't slow the art historian's rise in society. When George VI died in 1952 Blunt became friends with his widow, the Queen Mother, and in 1956 the young Queen Elizabeth II made him a knight.

Transatlantic Trouble

All was going swimmingly until 1963, when an American nominee for a presidential cabinet post told the FBI about a blot on his record. While attending Cambridge in the 1930s he had been a Communist – and Anthony Blunt had tried to recruit him as a Soviet spy. Confronted with these statements, Blunt made a secret immunity deal with the British government. In exchange for information the embarrassed MI5 kept mum about the Queen Mum's traitorous art collector.

You Said It, Maggie!

Blunt maintained his refined lifestyle until 1979, when the newly elected Prime Minister Margaret Thatcher ushered in a new era of anti-Communism and denounced Blunt as a traitor. She watched as he was stripped of his awards and knighthood and hounded by the press, and said with satisfaction: '... serves him right!' (And to think, he had voted for her just a few months earlier!)

JOHN CAIRNCROSS (1913–1995)

KGB Code Name: The Carelian

Cairncross was the only Cambridge spy who wasn't a blue blood. His father was a clerk in the civil service, so John arrived at Cambridge on a scholarship. He was a brilliant linguist, but he made few friends among the toffs who were his fellow students. He was spotted by Anthony Blunt at Cambridge and introduced to Guy Burgess. He was recruited to the Communist party in 1937 and worked in the Foreign Office alongside Donald Maclean.

Code-Breaker

Cairncross joined the Government Code and Cipher School at Bletchley Park in 1943, and drove – in a car provided by the Soviets – back and forth to the Soviet Embassy in London, where he handed over decoded German messages. His information enabled Soviet spies to change their codes every time British intelligence was about to crack them. The knowledge he passed on about British and American atomic weapons probably provided the basis of the entire Soviet nuclear weapons programme.

James Bond He's Not

After the war, he continued to pass secrets to a KGB contact who worried about his 'appalling memory'. While a master at stealing important secrets, he was never on time for a rendezvous. In fact, he was so disorganized that he often forgot them completely!

Nailed and Nailed Again

It was Anthony Blunt who ended Cairncross' spying career. In 1951 Blunt had hastily cleared incriminating evidence from Guy Burgess' apartment, but missed some notes written by Cairncross that were later found by MI5. Cairncross claimed he only passed some low-grade secrets to the Soviets to help them beat the Nazis, and he was allowed to resign without being prosecuted. But during Blunt's interrogation in the 1960s, Cairncross was implicated as an important Soviet spy. Once again Cairncross confessed and once again he was given immunity – so the embarrassed government could avoid yet another spy scandal. They even let him keep a government job; they sent him to live in Rome (some punishment!), where he lived most of the time until his death at 82.

NEVER TRUST A SPY

Together the spies stole hundreds, possibly thousands, of secrets for Stalin. They could never have been so successful had they not been so respectable – and so terribly British. It worked in their favour in the country they betrayed, although ironically they were so British that it prevented them being completely trusted abroad. Stalin never fully believed the Cambridge spies were giving him real information. The suspicious old Soviet leader thought that such nice English gents would never truly betray their country.

* * *

'What do you think spies are: priests, saints and martyrs? They're a squalid procession of vain fools, traitors too, yes; pansies, sadists and drunkards, people who play cowboys and Indians to brighten their rotten lives'.

– John le Carre's character Leamas, in *The Spy Who Came in From the Cold*

There's only one continent that has never seen a war: Antarctica.

DOWN OUR STREET

You can bet your life it would never get commissioned today: a soap opera about the daily lives of a bunch of poor folk in the grimmest part of it's-grim-up-north Manchester? But 40 years down the line, Coronation Street *is still going strong.*

It's got so many millions of fans that it doesn't even need a proper name any more. It's simply known as 'The Street' or 'Corrie'. It's the UK's most popular and longest-running soap, and has been doing it with style (well, a particularly northern brand of style, with pints, mushy peas and hairnets) since 1960.

LITTLE LIVES, BIG AUDIENCES

A masterpiece of mundanity, on the surface *Coronation Street* appears to be about the petty lives and loves of ordinary northern folk. But is it 'eck as like. *Coronation Street* is in reality a seething mass of jealousy, corruption, extra-marital passion and all manner of human folly. More people routinely tune into the marathon soap than any other UK television programme, and when it reaches a storyline climax, viewing figure records are regularly broken and iconic heroes, heroines and villains are created.

Remember the classic catfight between Hilda Ogden and Elsie Tanner? Remember evil Alan Bradley meeting a sticky end under the wheels of a Blackpool tram while in hot pursuit of a hyperventilating Rita? And then there's Richard Hillman, perhaps the finest UK television of our time, the *Street*'s very own mild-mannered serial killer. How the nation cheered when he tried to bump of his entire step-family, driving them into the local canal; how the nation sobbed when he succeeded only in drowning himself, whilst chipmunk-faced wife Gail, Grinch-like stepson David, and teen-mum stepdaughter Sarah-Louise (clutching baby Bethany Britney) all survived.

WHAT'S IN A NAME?

Coronation Street started out as an idea called *Our Street*, a comedy-drama about the residents of a working-class row of houses by a young scriptwriter called Tony Warren. This later transmuted

How can you tell when a kangaroo is nervous? It licks its forearms. Nobody knows why.

into *Florizel Street*. It only became *Coronation Street* just before going into production.

The first episode went out at 7:00 p.m. on 9 December, 1960. Since then, more than 4,000 episodes have been shown. Given such a long history, it's no surprise that many of the UK's best-known actors have stopped off on the *Street* at some point in their careers: Joanna Lumley enjoyed a stint in 1973, playing a receptionist called Yvonne who rejected a marriage proposal from Ken Barlow (who hasn't!). Oscar-winner Ben Kingsley popped into the Rovers for a pre-*Gandhi* pint in the late 1960s, and to celebrate the show's 40th anniversary in 2000 Prince Charles (playing himself) took part in a special live episode. At the other end of the social scale, so to speak, former Slade frontman Noddy Holder was a cast regular for a while in 2000 as well.

KEN BARLOW, LOVERMAN

He was in episode one and is the street's longest-standing resident, which is pretty amazing. At the last count he'd lived in eight different houses on the same small stretch of cobbles.

But that's not even half as impressive as Ken's roster of ladies; put at somewhere between 21 and 25, what is certain is that he married three of them, and proposed to many more. But marital bliss has always evaded poor Ken. Wife number one, Valerie Tatlock, was unfortunately electrocuted by a hairdryer as the couple were about to start an exciting new life in the Caribbean. The second Mrs Barlow, Janet Reid, got hitched to Ken on an impulse and eventually left him, returning only to take a fatal overdose in his bed.

And of course, his next marriage resulted in the stuff of *Street* legend – Ken's *ménage à trois* with third wife Deirdre and Cockney wide-boy and knicker manufacturer Mike Baldwin. Actually, make that a *ménage à quatre*, as Deirdre's enormous spectacles are so famous they probably have their own agent.

But don't feel too sorry for Ken. The articulate, broadsheet-reading ex-teacher and journalist has himself dallied with married and spoken-for ladies in the past, even resorting to that old classic, deliberately trashing his marriage to Deirdre by having an affair with his secretary.

EXPIRATION STREET

During its 40-plus years on air, 91 residents of the *Street* have died, which must make it one of the country's most dangerous post codes. It certainly attracts more than its fair share of murderers, criminals and lunatics.

Along with über-villains Alan Bradley and Richard Hillman, some of the soap's most fascinating baddies include Arnold Swain, a cuddly pet-shop owner who was revealed as a bigamist and then tried to get new wife Emily Bishop to say 'I do' to a suicide pact in 1981. And how did chirpy young childminder Carmel Finnan, with her shy crush on the hapless Martin Platt, morph into the nanny from hell in 1993?

Tragicomedy is also a *Street* speciality. Witness the end of poor sap Derek Wilton, struck down by a heart-attack and dying all alone in a company car bedecked with a giant paper-clip, while trying to get home to ever-nervous missus, Mavis.

STREET GIRLS

Coronation Street was promoting strong female characters long before feminism, post-feminism and girl power came along. Tony Warren, the show's creator, knew that while men may have earned the bread, in hard-up working class households it was usually the women who really looked after business.

And business was usually conducted in the Rover's Return, surely the grimmest pub in television history. Over a half pint of stout, *Street* legends such as Ena Sharples and her gaggle of gossiping cohorts would pronounce judgement on devil-may-care floozie Elsie Tanner, while toffee-nosed publican Annie Walker looked on disdainfully. It's a fine tradition that continues in a long line, from the monumental Bet Lynch, through to dippy-but-determined Raquel Wolstenhume, act-first-think-later Vera Duckworth and no-nonsense but loving mum Janice Battersby.

And, never afraid to put the cat among the racing pigeons, audiences looked very, very closely when the *Street* introduced its first transsexual character, Hayley (previously Harry) Patterson. And yes, the thespian who plays the caring Hayley really is all woman. Her romance and subsequent 'marriage' to café owner Roy Cropper (one of soap's great comic creations) gripped the nation in the late 1990s.

THE UNIVERSITY OF CORONATION STREET

Such is the pervasive influence of the *Street* on public consciousness, that it's been the subject of many serious academic studies. Reading them may be a bit of a struggle for most of us, unless you know what 'empirical reception' means, or what 'linguistic interactions' are (conversations, probably) .

But while the boffins scratch their heads and stroke their beards over the cultural significance of *Coronation Street*, its real fans know what it's all about: real life, plus a large of dollop of comedy, a side order of tragedy and a liberal sprinkling of high camp. For years, *Street* fans around the world have been sharing their love of the programme in get-togethers and conventions, known as 'ping fests'. Why 'ping', well, it started off as 'pint fest', as in 'let's have a pint down the Rovers', and somewhere along the line someone misheard 'pint' (probably after one too many) as 'ping'. The name stuck, and ever since that's what *Coronation Street* festivals have been called.

Pingfests have been held as far afield as Canada, Australia and the U.S. Attendees have even been known to dress up as their favourite character. It just goes to show how much people love this show. As Fred Elliot, the *Street*'s very own Foghorn Leghorn, would declare: 'there's nowt so queer as folk!'

* * *

SOME MEMORABLE QUOTES

'Drinking's a serious business. You gotta keep at it – like training for a football match.'

'Women want a bloke they can look up to and all they find are wimps.'

'Give him a chance? I wouldn't give him the steam off my tea.'

'We all need dreams. The trouble is I dreamt mine years ago, luvvie.'

'Me behind a bar. I'm in me element. I'm like Santa Claus in his grotto.'

'This place is like the village of the damned. No-one seems remotely normal.'

Quick fact: 20 per cent of drivers get 80 per cent of the traffic tickets.

PAUL IS DEAD!

The biggest, most widely discussed rumour about rock bands and performers ever was – appropriately – about the Beatles. In 1969, millions of fans were convinced that Paul McCartney was dead, and spent months trying to prove it. Here's the inside story.

HAVE YOU HEARD THE NEWS?

Although no one knows precisely when or how it started, sometime in 1969 a rumour began circulating that Paul McCartney of the Beatles was dead. The idea really took off one Sunday that September, when an Eastern Michigan University student identifying himself as 'Tom' called the 'Russ Gibb Show' on WKNR-FM.

The caller told Gibb he'd heard that McCartney had been dead for some time, that the rest of the Beatles knew about it, and that they had started inserting 'hints' of McCartney's death into their most recent record albums. Why were they keeping McCartney's death a secret? Maybe it was to let fans down easily – maybe it was to make as much money as they could before the death became public and the band had to dissolve.

But that was beside the point. The point was that Paul was dead, the caller told Gibb, and the proof was in the music.

GETTING IT BACKWARD

Gibb had been in the radio business for some time, and this wasn't the first dead-rock-star story he'd ever heard. Celebrity-death rumours were as common as they were unfounded, and Gibb initially dismissed this one as being just as ridiculous as the others – until Tom told him to play the Beatles' song 'Revolution 9' backward to hear one of the 'clues'.

When Gibb played back the part of the song where the voice says 'Number Nine' over and over, he thought he could hear the words, 'Turn me on, dead man'. He began to wonder if Paul McCartney really was dead, and he shared his suspicions with his listeners. Within minutes the switchboard was lit up with calls. Everybody wanted to know if McCartney was really dead.

PAPER TRAIL

The rumours might never have amounted to anything more, if someone named Fred LaBour hadn't been listening to the 'Russ Gibb Show' that Sunday afternoon.

LaBour, a University of Michigan second-year student who wrote for his college newspaper, *The Michigan Daily*, was supposed to write a review of the Beatles' new *Abbey Road* album for an upcoming issue. But he was still looking for some kind of angle that would make the article more interesting.

As LaBour listened to Tom and Russ Gibb discussing whether Paul McCartney was dead, he knew he had his angle – turn the rumour into a full-length article, a satire that pretended to take the whole idea seriously. LaBour thought it would make an interesting and amusing read. He had no idea how right he was.

The next day, LaBour wrote up his 'review' of *Abbey Road* and turned it in to John Gray, the arts editor for *The Michigan Daily*. Gray was so impressed that he decided to give it an entire page in the paper. 'Just how long did it take you to come up with this masterpiece'? he asked.

'It only took an hour and a half', LaBour said, 'and it's the best bull**** I ever wrote'.

HOT OFF THE PRESSES

LaBour's article ran on page 2 of *The Michigan Daily* with the headline 'McCartney Dead; New Evidence Brought to Light'.

The article claimed that Paul had been dead for nearly three years:

> Paul McCartney was killed in an automobile accident in early November, 1966, after leaving EMI recording studios tired, sad, and dejected. The Beatles had been preparing their forthcoming album, tentatively titled *Smile*, when progress bogged down in intragroup hassles and bickering. Paul climbed into his Aston-Martin, sped away into the rainy, chill night, and was found hours later pinned under his car in a culvert with the top of his head sheared off. He was deader than a doornail.

The article claimed that the surviving Beatles decided 'to make the best of a bad situation', because 'Paul always loved a good joke', LaBour quoted John Lennon as saying. The surviving Beatles decided to replace Paul with a body double and continue as if he hadn't died. To that end, the group held a 'Paul Look-Alike Contest' and found a living substitute in Scotland, a man named William Campbell.

Thanks to extensive voice training, lip-synching and a moustache (which John, George and Ringo also grew), Campbell had somehow managed to pass himself off as Paul McCartney for more than three years, despite the fact that the band had been inserting clues into their songs and onto their album covers all along. The *Abbey Road* album cover, for example, shows the four Beatles crossing the road: McCartney is the only one walking out of step, the only one who's barefoot ('the way corpses are buried in Italy', LaBour claimed), and is holding a cigarette in his right hand, when everybody knows he is left-handed. On top of that, the licence plate on one of the cars parked on the road reads '28IF' – which LaBour claimed was a coded way of saying that McCartney would be 28 if he were still alive.

CLUE ME IN

LaBour probably never intended for his joke to travel beyond the University of Michigan, but by the end of the day the story had spread to other nearby colleges, and from there to the rest of the country over the next several days. Wherever the rumour spread, people began studying the Beatles' recent album covers and listening to their albums backwards – and finding their own 'clues', which only added to the story's credibility and caused it to spread even further.

'In terms of media coverage', Andru J. Reeve writes in *Turn Me On, Dead Man*, 'the rumour reached an apex during the last two weeks of October. Major newspapers and network television had avoided comment up to this point, for they assumed that, like rumours of the past, the story would fade before the presses had a chance to warm up'.

SILENT PARTNER

So did Paul McCartney: recently married and burned out from the difficult *Abbey Road* recording session, McCartney was holed up with his wife and kids in Scotland and wasn't coming out for anything, not even to prove he wasn't dead. Like a lot of people, when he first heard the rumour, he thought it would soon pass.

But the rumour refused to die, and McCartney finally consented to giving Apple Records a written statement that he wasn't dead. But he still refused to make a public appearance. For many people, the fact that a written statement was all the Beatles' own record company could come up with was further proof that he really was dead.

PHEW!

It's probably fitting that *Life* magazine provided the most convincing evidence that death had not taken McCartney. *Life* sent a reporter and two staff photographers to McCartney's farm to 'bring back any visual evidence of Paul's existence, even if he refused to be interviewed'. McCartney not only refused, he heaved a bucket of water at them. Once he calmed down, however, McCartney let the photographers take some pictures of him with his family. *Life* ran one on the cover of the next issue.

Amazingly, some skeptics saw the *Life* magazine article as further proof that McCartney was dead – when you hold the magazine cover up to a bright light, the car in the Lincoln Continental ad on the reverse side appears to be impaling McCartney. For most fans, though, seeing the pictures of Paul with his family was enough, and the rumour receded as quickly as it had spread.

FOR THE RECORD

The only unresolved question was whether the rumours were orchestrated or fuelled by the Beatles themselves, perhaps to increase sales of *Abbey Road*.

'One undeniable fact became apparent', Andru Reeve writes: 'sales of Beatles albums did increase'. Priced £1 higher than earlier Beatles albums, *Abbey Road* sold slowly at first – until about the time that the rumours started circulating. Then, Reeve writes, it 'rocketed to number one and the other albums germane to the rumour (*Sgt. Pepper's*, *Magical Mystery Tour*, and the '*White Album*' resurfaced on the U.S. Billboard Top 200 LP chart after absences of up to a year and a half'.

THE GREAT PRETENDERS

Some people just can't help themselves – they'll always take the crooked path, even when the straight one seems easier. Just like this selection of some of the UK's choicest chancers.

We Brits are justly proud of our long and distinguished history. But we also have a pretty long and undistinguished history, too. Con-men, imposters, swindlers and shady characters who like to sail a bit too close to the wind, we've certainly had our fair share of them. Some have been more successful than others, but they all did it with true British style.

LAMBERT SIMNEL – KING FOR A DAY

On 24 May, 1487, Lambert Simnel, a ten-year-old carpenter's son from Oxford, achieved the peak of the impostor's art that is unlikely to be repeated or equalled. He was actually crowned King Edward VI of England, and went on to lead an army into the field on English soil. The ceremony took place at Christ Church Cathedral, Dublin, Ireland, which at the time was more or less under English control.

The Irish are coming!

England already had a king, of course, Henry VII, and he was naturally a little worried about this strange turn of events, particularly when Simnel and his supporters landed in Lancashire with a force of wild, half-naked Irish soldiers, augmented by German mercenaries. Henry himself had acquired the throne through battle (from Richard III), and this looked like a serious attempt to steal it back from him.

Too many Edwards

Simnel was impersonating a real person, Edward, Earl of Warwick, one of Henry's potential rivals for the crown. The word on the streets was that Henry had had Warwick killed. When Simnel appeared, pretending to be Warwick, Henry's enemies rallied to his cause. It turned out that Warwick was still alive – Henry was holding him prisoner in the Tower of London, and decided to parade him through the streets as proof of his existence.

Henry 1 – Lambert 0

But by now the issue wasn't about who was who – politics had taken over. Henry was a Lancastrian, and in the recently ended Wars of the Roses his side had defeated the Yorkists to seize the British crown. Now, the Yorkists saw their chance to steal it back. Matters came to a head near the village of East Stoke in Nottinghamshire, when on 16 June, 1487, Simnel's army joined battle with Henry's troops. The result was a crushing victory for Henry, which secured his place on the throne. This probably explains why he was so magnanimous in victory. Instead of having the hapless Simnel executed, Henry gave him a job in the Royal kitchens, where he worked happily until his death in the 1530s!

The lucky loser

The story behind Simnel's rise from obscurity is the stuff of legend – he was literally spotted walking down the street in Oxford by a Yorkist priest, Richard Symonds. Symonds was struck by Simnel's resemblance to the old king, Edward IV, and there and then decided to use him in a plot to bring down Henry VII. He drummed up support amongst his Yorkist friends, then spirited Simnel away to Ireland, where he was coached in the ways of royal etiquette and reinvented as Edward VI. All in all, Simnel was lucky to have lost the battle of East Stoke – if the Yorkists had won, they would have wasted no time in bumping him off and putting someone more appropriate in his place. A life spent scrubbing pots and pans probably wasn't such a bad fate, after all.

THE TICHBORNE CLAIMANT

Arthur Orton, son of a butcher from Wapping, didn't aim quite so high as to be king, but he made a pretty big splash anyway. He claimed to be a baronet, Sir Roger Charles Tichborne, who had been lost at sea in 1854 at the age of 25, when the ship he was on went down with all hands. Sir Roger's mother, Lady Tichborne, always refused to believe her boy was dead, and the story of Sir

The filaments for the first electric lamp were made of bamboo.

Roger's disappearance and his mother's desperate hope for him spread around the world. As far as Wagga Wagga in Australia, in fact, where Arthur Orton was operating a small butcher's business of his own, after a series of low-life adventures in South America.

Spitting image?

Through a series of misunderstandings and schemings far too lengthy and complicated to go into here, in 1866 Arthur decided to put himself forward as the missing aristocrat – despite the fact that he looked nothing like him, was taller, enormously fat (Sir Roger was slim) and had different coloured hair. Sir Roger was also well-educated and spoke fluent French; Arthur was poorly educated and couldn't speak a word of French. Arthur also had an illiterate wife, and a baby daughter.

That's my boy

Nevertheless, the news that her son had been found at last after 12 long years was irresistible. When Lady Tichborne received a letter from 'Roger' in Wagga Wagga ('I deeply regret the truble and anxsity I must have cause you by not writing before') she sent money for his passage to England. Although on the face of it Orton's claim seemed unpromising, he was taken seriously. He'd tracked down a few people in Australia with connections to the Tichbornes, learning what he could from them, as well as memorizing some of the personal information Lady Tichborne had included in her letters to him.

In 1866 Orton, accompanied by a negro servant called Bogle who had once worked for the Tichbornes, set off from Australia on long voyage to Britain. On his arrival, Lady Tichborne proclaimed that her son had indeed returned. She gave him a generous £1,000 a year income, and handed over all of Sir Roger's letters and diaries. Equipped with this extra information, Orton was able to strengthen his claim.

Caught out in court

However, the rest of the Tichborne family and Sir Roger's friends were not so easily fooled. The fact that Orton was plainly someone else was completely obvious to them. But Orton, armed with Lady Tichborne's cash, was able to drum up a number of former servants, old soldiers, shady lawyers and other miscreants prepared (for a price) to support his claim.

Then, in 1868, Lady Tichborne died. Her surviving relatives wasted no time in bringing Orton's claim to court. It was to become the longest case ever heard in an English court. As the case dragged on Orton's claim began to totter. Even with his new-found wealth, the expense of keeping his shady supporters in beer and lodging started to mount.

Some of Orton's friends and relatives even turned up, claiming he was indeed Orton and not Sir Roger. In desperation, Orton (as Sir Roger) claimed that the trauma of the shipwreck had affected his memory and in his delirium he may have assumed the identity of Orton for a while! Unsurprisingly, this attempt to muddy the waters didn't work. In the longest speech ever given to an English jury, Orton's prosecutor, Attorney-General Sir John Coleridge, spoke of 'the cunning and odious scheme of a conspirator, a perjurer, a forger, an impostor, a villain.' Orton's claim was thrown out of court and he was arrested for perjury.

Hero of the mob

And this is where the British love of the underdog kicked in. Orton's case was taken up by the public. The jury at his perjury trial had to be protected from the mob, and when Orton was convicted and sent to Dartmoor for 14 years public opinion went wild. There were mass meetings, and a newspaper, the *Tichborne Gazette*, was set up, devoted to exposing the plot against our hero. His defence lawyer, Edward Kenealy, became a national celebrity, and was elected to Parliament, where he carried on his campaign for justice (he later lost his seat, and was disbarred).

The controversy dragged on for years, but by the time Orton was released in 1884 it had died down. After some years of dwindling celebrity, he died in lodgings in Marylebone, London, in poverty and obscurity, in 1888. His coffin was marked with the name of Sir Roger Charles Doughty Tichborne.

GREY OWL – NON-NATIVE AMERICAN

In 1935, England was taken by storm by an exotic visitor: a tall, handsome Apache from Canada called Grey Owl, who gave lectures with moccasins on his feet and feathers in his hair and pro-

A: Antarctica, with an average elevation of 2,500 metres.

moted books he had written about his life in the wild. He spoke at more than two hundred lectures, addressing a quarter of a million people. The high point was a royal command performance at Buckingham Palace, where the young Princess Elizabeth was a particular fan. He gave a striking account of himself: he had been born in Mexico, the son of a Scottish acquaintance of Buffalo Bill and an Apache woman. He spoke the Ojibwa language, and his years of hunting and trapping had taught him to throw knives and axes and track the wolf, elk and bear. His English name, he said, was a translation of his Indian name, Wa-Sha-Quon-Asin, which meant 'He Who Flies By Night', the name of the Grey Owl.

Save the beaver!

The Canadian government had already adopted him as a kind of national symbol, making films about his work with animals, and through the films, books and personal appearances he became an international superstar – and a rich man. To be fair to Grey Owl, there is no suggestion that his love for nature was anything but real. He wrote extensively about the beaver, and gave up his life of hunting and trapping to become the world's first full-time conservationist. Indeed, he may have saved the Canadian beaver from extinction, establishing a managed beaver colony and doing whatever he could to save the animals from trappers and the destruction of their habitat by commercial logging.

Heap big pile of hogwash

It was only when Grey Owl died in April 1938 that the real story of this extraordinary man came out. He had no Indian blood at all. He was Archie Belaney, an Englishman from Hastings. As a boy he had been abandoned by his alcoholic father to the care of maiden aunts, and he had grown up with an obsession for Red Indians. He had always said that he was going to Canada one day to live in the forests. On 10 March, 1906, he did just that, setting sail for Toronto at the age of 18 in search of the wilderness he had always dreamed of.

Archie had a natural tendency to reinvent himself, and apart from the long braided hair and buckskin outfits, this showed itself in another unfortunate habit: he was a serial bigamist, marrying four women, including two American Indians. Archie's Grey Owl persona had always had its doubters in Canada: after all, there weren't that many Red Indians who could play classical music on the piano and recite Shakespeare.

But in England, where no-one knew what a 'real' Red Indian was, he was more successful. He delighted our future queen by greeting George VI, her father, with the impressive greeting 'How Kola!', which he explained was 'Peace, brother!' in his native language. His books, inspired by the romantic style of *The Last Of The Mohicans*, were full of highly questionable accounts of battles with wolves and other exciting adventures.

The Battle of Hastings

Even though Archie had gone native in Canada, he made sure he stopped off in Hastings whenever he did one of his UK speaking tours. On one memorable occasion, his maiden aunts, no doubt stifling a giggle or two, sat in the audience while Archie stood up on stage, speaking with forked tongue. Luckily for him, his aunts never let on who he really was.

Eventually, the furious pace that Archie was forced to keep as Grey Owl caught up with him. Washed out from constant overwork, he returned to Canada in 1938 after one particularly gruelling speaking tour severely weakened by exhaustion. He contracted pneumonia, from which he died on 13 April that year. Eventually, Grey Owl's deception came out. But it was seen as being OK somehow. After all, no-one was hurt and lots of beavers were saved! Today, he is remembered in Canada as one of the fathers of the conservation movement, and in Hastings as one of her most famous sons.

HORATIO BOTTOMLEY – THE PEOPLE'S FRIEND

A less idealistic story is that of Horatio Bottomley M.P., who's life swung from the peaks of fame and success to disgrace and imprisonment. Politicians, eh? Some things never change!

Bottomley on the up

Horatio Bottomley came from the bottom. Born in 1860, he was brought up in a series of orphanages. He grew up with no family, feeling that the only person he could rely on was himself. He used his energy and charm to establish himself as a celebrity politician

The last time hanging was used in the UK was in 1964, for Gwynne Evans and Peter Allen.

and dodgy businessmen, full of grand schemes which usually failed. He drank heavily, and always had another idea ready when one of his schemes collapsed. He was attracted to journalism, and founded several publications. Like his other business ventures, these usually ended badly, and before World War I he had already been made bankrupt twice. The second time, in 1911, he had to resign his seat in Parliament.

What a load of John Bull

The War, though, gave Bottomley a new lease of life. He used it to make one of his magazines, *John Bull*, into a patriotic and war-mongering success, full of stirring stuff about the glory of the trenches and the evils of the Hun. The public lapped it up and Bottomley toured the country promoting the magazine – and himself. He hit a nerve with the public by concentrating mainly on stirring up hatred of the Germans (whom he loathed), and it paid off. In December 1918, he was again returned as M.P. for South Hackney with a large majority.

His word is his bond

World War I had all but ruined the British Empire, and the government issued special Victory Bonds to raise money to pay off its huge debts. The bonds were too expensive for ordinary people, especially demobbed soldiers, so Bottomley came up with another Big Idea: the Victory Club. This was an organization that allowed members to purchase shares in Victory Bonds, which Bottomley said he would buy himself, sharing out the profits. Long queues formed outside his offices, and soon he was taking £100,000 a day from eager investors, many of them former soldiers.

He hired a team of old soldiers to run the operation, but they couldn't deal with the huge demand. Money and information got lost, and people discovered that they could get their money back from the club several times over just by writing in more than once and demanding it. Bottomley did buy some bonds, but also used some of the money to buy more newspapers – and when public confidence in his scheme suddenly collapsed, he had a new problem. Everywhere he went, he was followed by crowds of angry club members demanding their money back. He didn't have it.

The body of Jeremy Bentham (1748-1832) is preserved in University College, London.

Alas, poor Horatio

In May 1922 Bottomley was arrested for fraud and, at the age of 62, the 100 kilo bon viveur was sent down for seven years. One of his jobs in jail was working with the prison tailor: one visitor, seeing him holding a needle and thread asked: 'Sewing, Horatio?'. 'No' he replied, 'reaping'. Released in 1927 he was a broken man. He tried a new career as a music hall entertainer, telling stories about his colourful past, but never again rose to fame, wealth or power. He died in May 1933.

ROBERT MAXWELL – THE MIRROR MAN

Another high roller laid low was Robert Maxwell. He was born Jan Ludwik Hoch in 1923, to a poor Jewish family in a remote mountain area of Czechoslovakia. He came to Britain in 1940, where he joined the army and served as a captain during World War II. He was to spend the rest of his life in Britain, trying to get himself accepted by the establishment as a businessman, politician and publisher.

Springing into action

He was certainly a brilliant man. He spoke several languages, and was a dynamic businessman. Publishing was his main thing, and in 1951 he set up Pergamon Press, the first of his many publishing ventures. He also acquired the distribution rights of the distinguished German scientific publisher, Springer-Verlag. He used this as a springboard for a series of expansions, takeovers and new ventures that made him one of Britain's richest and most powerful men. In 1984 he made his biggest coup, when he acquired the Mirror Group, publishers of the *Daily Mirror*.

Friends in high places

But, despite his successes, there had always been doubts about Maxwell's character. In 1969, and again in 1973, he had been declared unfit to run a publicly quoted company. But he had so many powerful friends and acquaintances that he seemed untouchable: from 1964 to 1970 he even served as a Labour M.P.

By the 1980s he was at his peak. His empire expanded to include newspapers, magazines, scientific publishers, 50 per cent of MTV and a host of other ventures. He recruited his two sons, Ian

We still don't know what Silbury hill, Avebury, Europe's largest manmade hill, was for.

and Kevin, into the business, which helped to prevent too much snooping into his affairs. In 1990 he floated Mirror Group Newspapers as a public company and bought the New York *Daily News*.

Speculate and accumulate

But as this deal was being done an American investigative journalist began asking uncomfortable questions about the pension funds of the Maxwell Group companies. It was the oldest trick in the book: use your employees' pensions to fund your own speculations. Faced with total meltdown of his whole operation, Cap'n Bob, as he was known, fell to his death from his yacht while cruising near the Canary Islands in November 1991.

Open season

It was only after Maxwell's death that speculation about his life and his business activities came into the open. He had ruthlessly suppressed criticism, making liberal use of the newspapers he owned and the courts to silence those who wrote about him. But within days of his demise, news began to emerge about the hundreds of millions of pounds that were missing from Maxwell companies (over 400 of them), and the whole house of cards came tumbling down.

His sons were tried for fraud, and Robert Maxwell, former Labour M.P., owner of the *Daily Mirror*, and millionaire businessman, became the target of accusations and speculations varying from the petulant to the psychotic. They have never completely died down. Take your pick: he committed suicide; he had a heart attack while urinating off the side of his boat; he was assassinated; he was secretly selling surveillance technology to the KGB; he was trying to blackmail the Israelis by threatening to spill the beans (on what, no-one knows). One thing seems certain: there was more to Robert Maxwell than we thought. He was given a hero's funeral in Israel, and the man of many names and many languages, who knew U.S. presidents and Soviet leaders, took his many secrets with him to the grave.

Nelson's Column was completed in 1842.

THE ANSWER ZONE

ANSWERS TO 'THE RIDDLER' ON PAGE 159

1. An echo.
2. Holes.
3. Mount Everest.
4. Envelope.
5. A ton.
6. A priest.
7. Only one…the last one.
8. Zero…Noah took animals on the ark, not Moses.
9. Only once. After the first calculation, you will be subtracting 5 from 20, then 5 from 15, and so on.
10. A secret.
11. You can't take a picture with a wooden leg… You need a camera!
12. Darkness.
13. Footsteps.
14. A coffin.
15. An umbrella.
16. Suicide.
17. The year 1961. It reads the same upside down. Won't happen again until the year 6009.
18. The letter 'V'.
19. 'Are you asleep'?
20. A promise.

ANSWERS TO 'THE HISTORY OF ROCK: QUIZ #1' ON PAGE 233

1.b. 'Hound Dog' was written in 1952 by Jerry Lieber and Mike Stoller specifically for Willie Mae 'Big Mama' Thornton. Her record went to No.1 on the U.S. R & B charts in 1953. Then a lounge act named Freddie Bell and the Bellboys made a joke out of it in 1955. That's the version that Elvis copied.

How did he first hear it? In 1956, after 'Heartbreak Hotel' had hit U.S. No.1, Elvis was hired to do his first gig in Las Vegas. Later, he'd be king of the town. But the first time around, he was fired – a two-week engagement at the Frontier Hotel was cut to one week when audiences failed to respond to the hip wiggler. But Elvis still lucked out: he wandered into the lounge and watched Freddie Bell's group perform their humorous takeoff of 'Hound Dog'. He thought it was hilarious... and decided to do it himself.

Note: The Bellboys had already recorded the song, and Elvis may have picked up a copy of their record to refresh his memory before he recorded his own version.

2.c. Blackwell had just taken a job writing for a publisher called Shalimar Music when Moe Gayle, the head of the company, called him into his office with an unusual offer: Elvis Presley was interested in recording 'Don't Be Cruel', but the deal was contingent on Blackwell giving up half his writer's credit (and thus half the royalties) to Presley. 'Elvis Presley?' Blackwell answered. 'Who the hell is Elvis Presley?'

Blackwell recalls: 'I just felt that I was getting the shaft, man. It took them about two weeks to convince me. They pointed out that if Elvis did become big, I would make a good deal more money this way than not doing it at all. And if he didn't become big, I really wasn't losing anything...so I said okay'.

It may have been an unjust arrangement, but it wound up an extremely lucrative one for Blackwell. 'Don't Be Cruel' was released in July 1956 as the flip side of 'Hound Dog'. The double-sided hit reached U.S. No.1 in August and stayed there for over two months; it was on the charts for six months, becoming the year's No.1 record and Elvis' favourite early record. Blackwell was instantly established as a major songwriter. He went on to write 'All Shook Up', 'Great Balls of Fire', 'Return to Sender' and many more rock 'n' roll hits.

England is only two-thirds the size of New England.

3.a. Fats Domino wrote the song from real life: 'I was walkin' down the street and I saw a little lady spankin' a baby. And I heard somebody say "Ain't That a Shame"'. But Pat didn't relate to it – he objected to it because the grammar was bad.

'(When the record company asked me to record) "Ain't That a Shame", I balked', Boone says. 'I said, "Look, I just transferred to Columbia University, I'm an English major. I don't want to record a song called 'Ain't That a Shame'". I mean, "ain't" wasn't an accepted word. It is now in the dictionary, but I was majoring in English and I felt that this was going to be a terrible thing if it was a hit. I tried to record it "Isn't That a Shame", but it didn't work'.

He finally gave in and used the original lyrics. It hit No.1 on the U.S. charts. Domino's version was a hit, too – but with Boone taking the lion's share of sales away, it only reached No.10.

4.a. In the mid-1950s, 'respectable' people – including Mrs. Kern – thought doo-wop rock was a travesty. According to one account, she was so appalled and outraged by the Platters' treatment of the song that she explored ways of stopping it legally. Of course, when the Platters' record became a hit – and sold more copies of 'Smoke Gets in Your Eyes' than anyone had before – her opinion changed. And she never turned down a royalty payment.

5.c. Hard to believe, but although he may have been the most influential rock musician ever, Berry only had one No.1 song – a novelty tune full of childish sexual innuendo called 'My Ding-a-Ling'. He'd been using it to close his concerts and did it as 'My Tambourine' on a live album in the mid-1960s. Then in 1972 he recorded it live again, in London. For some reason his record company released it as a single. As Bob Shannon and John Javna wrote in *Behind the Hits*: 'It's kind of depressing for music fans that the biggest single Chuck Berry ever had was this...this...thing! But what the hell, at least Chuck got a hit out of it'.

6.a. Radio stations found all kinds of reasons not to play it: it was too suggestive, he cursed on it (the part where he goes 'We-ell-a' sounded like he was saying 'Weh-hell-a'), he sounded black (most stations didn't play songs by black artists). But when the record was banned by BMI (Broadcast Music Inc., which licences music for airplay) because it was 'obscene', the record died.

Sun Records knew it could be a hit – and Jerry Lee Lewis

Bees are born fully grown.

could be another Elvis – if it was handled right. So they took Lewis to New York to try to get him on *The Ed Sullivan Show*. They flew to New York, but Sullivan wouldn't listen – Lewis didn't have a hit, and Sullivan didn't like that kind of music, anyway. So they called NBC and got the talent coordinator there to set up a meeting with the producer of *The Steve Allen Show* (a variety programme that ran head to head with Sullivan's). Allen's biggest coup had been to introduce Elvis Presley as a guest after Sullivan had turned him down the first time. Now the Sun people hoped they could get Allen to do it again. They took Lewis with them to the meeting. When the TV execs asked to hear a record, Lewis stepped out and played in person. The NBC execs were blown away and scheduled him for that Sunday night.

What people at NBC never found out was that the song Jerry Lee was going to play – 'Whole Lotta Shakin' – had been banned. Why? Because after NBC agreed to have Lewis on, the head of promotion for Sun Records called BMI and convinced them that if NBC didn't mind about the lyrics, why should they? He neglected to add that no one at NBC had actually heard the lyrics. But BMI gave in, and the way was clear for Jerry Lee's appearance.

On 28 July, 1956, America was introduced to Jerry Lee Lewis and 'Whole Lotta Shakin' Goin' On' on *The Steve Allen Show*. Jerry went crazy, playing piano with his feet and inadvertently involving Allen himself. At one point he jumped off his piano stool to play standing up and sent the stool careering across the stage: Allen, who was stomping and clapping with the rest of the audience, tossed it back toward Jerry. Then Allen grabbed another piece of furniture and tossed it. Reportedly, he was about to throw a potted plant when Jerry finished playing. The exposure sent the record zooming up the charts. By the end of August it was a million-seller and Jerry Lee Lewis was firmly established as the hottest new rocker in America.

7. b. Little Richard was so incensed by Boone's cover version of 'Tutti Frutti' (which outdid Richard's on the charts), he purposely made the follow-up, 'Long Tall Sally', too fast for Boone to sing. Nonetheless, Boone worked out how to adapt 'Long Tall Sally' and gave Richard a run for his money. Little Richard's version did beat Boone's – but only just. Richard hit No.7 on the Billboard chart; Boone hit No.8.

ANSWERS TO 'THE HISTORY OF ROCK: QUIZ #2' ON PAGE 367

1. a. The story told in Grace Slick's biography is that members of the Great Society (Slick's first band) kept trying to get her to write music. Finally they practically locked her in a room and told her she couldn't come out until she'd written some songs. She emerged with several, including 'White Rabbit', which was loosely based on the classical piece *Bolero* by Ravel. However, Slick has said repeatedly that 'White Rabbit' isn't about, drugs. Her explanation: 'We were talking about opening up, looking around, checking out what's happening. We were also talking about the fifties mentality, which was really bottled up'. She added: 'Feeding your head is not necessarily pumping chemicals into it'.

Most of the imagery she used came directly from Lewis Carroll's two books, *Alice's Adventures in Wonderland*, and *Through the Looking Glass* (see page 79). Three examples from the book *Behind the Hits:*

> 1. 'One pill makes you larger'. Alice was about three inches tall and wandering around Wonderland when she spotted a caterpillar. It was about the same height as her, except that it was sitting on top of a mushroom, smoking a hookah. She asked it how she could get big again; as the caterpillar was walking away, it turned back and said, 'One side makes you larger, the other side makes you smaller'. Alice asked, 'One side of what'? The caterpillar replied, 'The mushroom'. There weren't any pills in the story, but maybe they were magic mushrooms.
>
> 2. 'When the men on the chessboard get up and tell you where to go'. The premise of *Through the Looking Glass*: Alice is trying to get her cat to play chess with her; she falls asleep and dreams that she's a pawn on the chessboard and has to get to the other side to become a queen. Each chapter of Through the Looking Glass takes place on a different square of the chessboard, and the characters in it are characters in a game of chess. Occasionally they do tell her where to go (of course, she's lost). At one point, the White Knight guides her across a brook that turns out to be the space between the squares on the board.
>
> 3. 'When logic and proportion have fallen softly dead'. Everything is out of whack in Wonderland (although Carroll wrote a book about symbolic logic). What could be more illogical than the dialogue at the Mad Hatter's tea party? About proportion – Alice goes from three inches to 15 feet high. Hard to keep a sense of proportion with that happening. She mentions that it's

rather uncomfortable to be so many different heights in one day.

By the way: The dormouse, who's sitting in a teacup at the Mad Tea Party, says, 'Twinkle twinkle little bat. How I wonder where you're at'. He doesn't say, 'Feed your head'.

2. b. In 1996 an amusing story emerged from Lawrenceville Academy, a New Jersey prep school. Some people who had studied there in the early 1960s said that a student named Mark Sebastian – John's 15-year-old brother – had submitted the poem that became 'Summer in the City' to his English teacher ...and had gotten an 'F'. It might well have been true – John Sebastian didn't particularly like the poem when he first saw it, either. But he did like the chorus – the part that went, 'But at night there's a different world'. Mark gave it to John and asked if he could do anything with it. John said he'd see. He put Mark's poem aside for a few months and in the interim came up with a little piano figure that he liked but didn't have a song for. Then one night as John was drifting off to sleep, Mark's chorus, his own piano riff, and a set of new lyrics popped into his head.

'(Bassist) Steve Boone contributed a middle section', Sebastian says, and the song was done. His first impression of the song: certain notes sounded like car horns. 'I said, "Gee, this sounds sort of like Gershwin – sort of like 'An American in Paris'. Maybe we could put traffic on it"'.

The band went into New York's Columbia Studios for two nights. On the first, they did the entire instrumental track. The second night was for vocals...and sound effects. Sebastian says, 'I remember this hilarious old sound man who'd never had a job with a rock 'n' roll band before looking at us quite puzzled as we auditioned pneumatic hammers to find the one that had the right intestinal tone to it'. For car sounds, the old man brought in tapes of traffic jams and horns that he'd used when he worked in radio. The band listened to them for hours, then chose their favourites. John wanted the automobiles to start off softly, so the sound-effects man threw in a Volkswagen horn at the beginning.

The song was released in the summer, of course, and within a few weeks was No.1 in America. It was the Spoonful's only No.1 hit in their phenomenal string of seven consecutive Top 10 records between September 1965 and December 1966.

3. a. It started with a shopping trip. Roy and Billy Dees, a songwriter Orbison had been collaborating with, were sitting in the Orbisons' house when Orbison's wife, Claudette, announced she was going into town to buy some groceries. 'Do you need any money?' Roy asked. Dees said, 'A pretty woman never needs any money'. Then he turned to Roy and said, 'Hey, how about that for a song title?' Orbison liked the idea of doing a song about a 'Pretty woman', but not the part about the money. After Claudette left, they began turning the phrase into a song. And when she returned, carrying bags of food, she was greeted by the debut performance of her husband's second No.1 tune.

4. b. The Four Seasons and some session musicians were in a recording studio in the Abbey Victoria Hotel on Seventh Avenue in New York City, recording 'Walk Like a Man'. After a few takes, it was obvious to everyone in the studio that something was wrong. But Bob Crewe, the producer, refused to pay attention. 'Another take', he kept saying. Here's the story of the unusual session, as told by a participant, guitarist Vinnie Bell:

> As we were recording, there was a sudden pounding on the door. And there was the smell of smoke. And plaster was starting to fall from the ceiling. And water was leaking in...while we're recording! And there's this pounding on the door of the studio, and Bob Crewe wouldn't unlock it – he kept saying, 'We'll open it in a second, there's one more take'. And the water's pouring onto us, and we've got electric guitars in our hands – we were afraid we were gonna be electrocuted. Finally, the (firemen) axed their way right through the door – and Crewe's trying to push them out! And then we could see the smoke pouring through. It seems that the floor above us in that hotel was on fire! It was barely audible from inside the studio, but you could hear fire engines and all that – the whole bit. And this guy was so intent on making the record – on getting another take – that he kept trying to push these guys out...until they knocked him on the floor.

And that was it for the recording session.

5. b. The story behind this record – which was certified gold in 1969 and still refuses to die – is almost unbelievable. Paul Leka was a producer at Mercury Records in 1969. He persuaded the label to sign a friend named Gary De Carlo, and they did a recording session together. They thought everything they recorded was good enough to be a hit, so they decided to record one really cheesy song for the B-side of De Carlo's first single release. That way they'd save the good stuff for later.

The day of the B-side session, Leka ran into a friend he once wrote songs with. They remembered a tune called 'Kiss Him Good-by' they'd written years earlier and decided to make that the stinker. The only problem: it was just two minutes long. They wanted to make it twice as long to make sure it never got on the air – no disc jockey would dare play a four-minute record – so they added a chorus...except they couldn't think of any words for it. So Leka just started singing 'Na-na-na..'. and someone else started singing 'Hey-hey'. And that was it. They didn't bother with lyrics because it was just a B-side.

To Leka's astonishment and embarrassment, when Mercury heard it, they decided to release it as an A-side. The musicians all agreed it should come out under an alias – and came up with Steam because at the end of the recording session, they'd walked out on to the street and seen an enormous cloud of steam coming out of a New York manhole cover.

6. c. Satchmo was making an album of show tunes, and David Merrick was trying to promote his new musical, so he encouraged performers to sing songs from it. Armstrong had never heard of 'Hello Dolly'. And though he liked the tune, he was appalled that after all the innovative work he'd done in his career, his biggest hit was this silly, simple song.

7. a. Percy Sledge worked as an orderly at Colbert County Hospital in Alabama during the day and sang with a band called the Esquires Combo at night. One evening, the Esquires Combo was playing at a club in Sheffield, Alabama, and Sledge just couldn't keep his mind on the songs he was supposed to be singing. He was upset about a woman. Overcome by emotion, he turned to bass player Cameron Lewis and organ player Andrew Wright and begged them to play something he could sing to. Anything – it didn't matter what. The musicians looked at each other, shrugged, and just started playing the first thing that came into their heads. And Percy made up 'When a Man Loves a Woman', one of the prettiest soul ballads ever written, on the spot.

The Vatican City pharmacy sells birth control pills...but only to non-Catholic married women.

THE LAST PAGE

I hope you've enjoyed our first Bathroom Reader for the United Kingdom and that you are looking forward to many more to come.

So we invite you to take the plunge, sit down, and be counted by joining the Bathroom Readers' Institute. It's all free. You'll receive your attractive free membership card and a copy of the BRI newsletter (sent out irregularly via e-mail), discounts when ordering directly through the BRI, and more. Visit our website at www.bathroomreader.com for further details.

While we are working on establishing a UK address for the Institute, we have not yet finalized one as of our first printing.

Well, we have to get back to work now. There are many, many more books to come, and when it's time to go, you've got to go. So never forget:

Go with the flow!

The stonemasons had dinner on top before erecting the statue.